ENERGY, UTILITY, TRANSPORTATION AND ENVIRONMENTAL LAW FOR THE 21ST CENTURY

A Collection

PETER V. LACOUTURE, EDITOR

AMERICAN BAR ASSOCIATION
Section of Public Utility Communications and Transportation Law

Cover design by Andrea Siegert/ABA Publishing.

17 16 15 14 13 5 4 3 2 1

Library of Congress Cataloging-in-Publication Data
Energy, utility, transportation and environment law for the 21st century : a collection / edited by Peter V. Lacouture, Section of Public Utility, Communications and Transportation Law, American Bar Association.
pages cm
1. Public utilities—Law and legislation—United States. 2. Environmental law—United States. 3. Telecommunication—Law and legislation—United States. 4. Power resources—Law and legislation—United States. 5. Transportation—Law and legislation—United States. I. Lacouture, Peter V., editor of compilation. II. American Bar Association. Section of Public Utility, Communications and Transportation Law.
KF2094.E54 2013
343.7309—dc23 2013001890

ISBN: 978-1-61438-939-2

http://www.ShopABA.org

Contents

Foreword and Acknowledgments

This volume is the result of the realization by several members of the Book Board of the ABA's Section of Public Utility, Communications and Transportation Law (PUCAT) that the many interesting and informative articles that are published in *Infrastructure* each quarter should be preserved in a more permanent format and made available to a wider audience. The idea for this collection was the result of a discussion I had with my Robinson & Cole LLP partner, Dwight Merriam, former chair of the Section of State and Local Government, who has edited a number of collections of articles from his section's publication, *The Urban Lawyer*. I thank Dwight for the inspiration, although it has not been as easy a task to assemble this volume as Dwight made it out to be.

We anticipate that this will be the first in a series of anthologies of articles from *Infrastructure*. This volume includes articles from mid-2008 through the first issue of 2012. Because of the time that has elapsed since the original publication of many of the articles in *Infrastructure*, we asked the author of each article to provide an update, addendum, or postscript. Each update is published immediately following the original article and, although some authors offered to revise their original articles, the articles are published here as they originally appeared in *Infrastructure*.

There are, as one might expect, a number of themes that emerge from a series of articles in a publication of the Section of Public Utility, Communications and Transportation Law, including energy, telecommunications, and transportation. I have organized the articles in five somewhat logical chapters. The sixth chapter, "Other Articles," includes four articles that do not easily fit into any of the other categories.

I wish to acknowledge the efforts of many people in producing this volume. First and foremost are the authors of and contributors to the articles and updates. Biographical information about each is included in the section titled "About the Authors and Contributors" at the beginning of this volume. The editors of *Infrastructure* during the period covered by this volume, Linda Randell, Dynda Thomas, and The Honorable Richard D. Cudahy, deserve our thanks for inspiring the authors.

A special note of thanks to Judge Richard Cudahy, the present editor of *Infrastructure*. Judge Cudahy is a prolific writer for *Infrastructure* and has an introduction and a number of articles in this volume. Linda Randell, former editor of *Infrastructure*, former chair of the Section, and chair of the PUCAT Book Board, offered the following commentary on Judge Cudahy's contributions to *Infrastructure*:

> Judge Cudahy has written frequently for *Infrastructure* on a wide range of topics over the years, including the development of central station generation, supply of natural resources, water infrastructure in China, and the development of high-speed passenger rail service in the United States. His articles often have a historical bent but also look forward into the future. Judge Cudahy is a gifted writer, able to inform and entertain in equal quantity on almost any

subject. We are fortunate that the judge has chosen to submit articles to *Infrastructure* rather than to *The New Yorker*.

The recent chairs of the Section, including Rob Brubaker and Patty Dondanville, have been very supportive of the Section's Book Board and the concept of this anthology. We have included Editor's Notes and Chair's Columns as appendices to this volume for historical reference.

Linda Randell, the first and current chair of the Book Board, has been supportive and encouraging. Rick Paszkiet, of ABA Publishing, has advised the Book Board since its founding in October 2011 and is responsible for the production of this volume. Wendy Smith, also of ABA Publishing and the driving force behind *Recent Developments in Public Utility, Communications and Transportation Industries* (formerly the *PUCAT Annual Report*) for the past seven years, has provided valuable counsel. My assistant, Brenda Vucci, has demonstrated a high degree of patience with my organizing and reorganizing, editing, and re-editing. Finally, I owe a huge debt of gratitude to Leticia Tavares, Class of 2014 at Roger Williams University Law School in Bristol, Rhode Island. Leticia was the National Grid–Robinson & Cole LLP Fellow during the Summer of 2012. She managed to corral most of the authors, persuade them to write updates, extract biographical information from them, and organize all of the submissions, with little input or guidance from me. I have included additional biographical information about Leticia in "About the Authors and Contributors."

I trust that you will find the articles and updates that make up this anthology of the best of *Infrastructure* interesting and informative.

Peter V. Lacouture
September, 2012

Introduction

The infrastructure is almost by definition the foundation of our economy and in many ways of our society. Our quarterly publication by that name seeks to cover its full breadth and to do so at a practical depth. We don't have quite as many footnotes as a full-blown law review, but we try to penetrate below the level of superficial description to a surprising depth.

Peter Lacouture, the editor of this volume, has helpfully classified our various articles into subject fields extending to a fair sample of the broad panorama, which is the infrastructure—man's and woman's appendages to and modifications of the planet for the support and enrichment of human life. A fair number of articles in this volume concern energy in a variety of forms and its cousin, the environment. Some of this material is fairly narrowly focused, as on water-located wind farms. Other material covers the waterfront, as in a book review of Daniel Yergin's *The Quest*, involving all aspects of the evolving story of energy.

Selection of subjects for treatment in *Infrastructure*, either for assignment or among articles spontaneously submitted to us, follows a number of criteria. Sometimes we have favored offerings containing novel and thoughtful treatment of subjects of continuing interest. Sometimes we have sought topical articles on matters of strong current interest, like the environmental complications of shale gas recovery. In some cases, we have focused on a small but challenging part of the big picture. Sometimes we have tried to provide a panoramic view. Everything has been measured by the level of interest and the presumed degree of usefulness, as best we can estimate it. Occasionally we have had unusual opportunities, such as to publish Alfred Kahn's personal remarks at a recent conference in his honor, not long before his death.

One aspect of the various topics that we have tried to emphasize is the need for balance. Since a large proportion of the membership of this section consists of lawyers whose principal representation is of companies engaged in furnishing infrastructure services, we have sought to avoid special pleading in our clients' economic interest. These articles are certainly not without expressions of opinion—it would be pretty dull stuff without them—but there has been a real effort to provide a balance of opinions, giving the reader a full picture of pros and cons. Not surprisingly, this aspect of things is almost second nature to experienced attorneys, who are constantly engaged in dealing with views contrary to those of their clients. And, as a judge, I don't have to be reminded that every dispute has at least two sides.

Selection of authors has been another concern. For the most part we have called on members of the section who have worked in these fields for years and know them both theoretically and, perhaps in a special way, practically. Our section is composed of people who have actually tried to deal with many of the problems that they discuss and analyze. But in a number of situations, we have reached outside the section to tap the resources of acknowledged experts in fields like nuclear power and to professional leaders whose views command attention. And in these efforts to recruit talent, we have also sought to avoid propagandists and pleaders for special causes.

In bringing the articles up to date, we have asked the authors to do just that: to report any notable developments since their piece was written. For example, the article on high-speed rail was written before this development became politically controversial and its federal financing was opposed and rejected in some states as a wasteful use of resources. Whatever the author (in this instance, myself) may have thought of this point of view, these changing perspectives have been faithfully reported.

The most arresting instance of changing attitudes toward infrastructure developments has been the growing skepticism toward belief in climate change traceable to the emission of greenhouse gases. This entire phenomenon is critical to the full picture of energy production and use, and its honest and thorough treatment has been a primary concern of the authors and editors.

Hopefully, this volume will prove of interest, since its contents have been largely dictated by their presumed interest to the membership of this section, most of whom draw their livelihood from these activities and developments. The authors, of course, include lawyers whose practice involves the very phenomena described in *Infrastructure*, as well as academic, business, and government leaders in these fields and many other experts, including critics of developing practices involving the infrastructure. As an editor and occasional author, I think that this is an honest effort to provide you with the best in *Infrastructure* and in the infrastructure, and we hope you will enjoy it.

The Honorable Richard D. Cudahy
October 2012

About the Editor

Peter V. Lacouture is a partner at Robinson & Cole LLP, resident in the firm's Providence, Rhode Island, office.

Pete has practiced law in Providence since 1972, concentrating his practice in the areas of public utility and other facility siting, and environmental and land use law. He practices before state and local agencies, including the Rhode Island Energy Facility Siting Board, the Public Utilities Commission, the Coastal Resources Management Council, the Department of Environmental Management, and municipal zoning and planning boards. He has argued numerous cases before the Rhode Island Supreme Court.

He has edited *Recent Developments in Public Utility, Communications and Transportation Industries* (formerly the *Annual Report* of the ABA Section of Public Utility, Communications and Transportation Law (PUCAT)) since 2005, is chair of the PUCAT Publications Committee, secretary of PUCAT, and a vice chair of its Electricity and Alternative Dispute Resolution Committees.

He was awarded the Ralph P. Semonoff Award for Professionalism by the Rhode Island Bar Association in June of 2012. He has been listed in the area of Energy Law in *The Best Lawyers in America®* since 2007.[1]

Pete is Exeter (Rhode Island) town moderator, president and deputy chief of the Exeter Volunteer Fire Company No. 2, and chair of the Exeter Fire District. He serves as a trustee of the Rhode Island chapter of The Nature Conservancy. Pete earned a B.A. from Yale University and an LL.B. from the University of Virginia School of Law in 1972.

1. Copyright 2010 by Woodward/White, Inc., Aiken, S.C.

About the Authors and Contributors*

Malcolm L. Benge is a partner with the Washington, D.C., law firm of Zuckert, Scoutt & Rasenberger, L.L.P. He advises foreign and domestic clients on a wide range of aviation-related matters, including traffic rights, operating licenses, and regulatory compliance. His practice involves frequent participation in proceedings before the Department of Transportation and the Federal Aviation Administration. Mr. Benge also has extensive experience in the negotiation and documentation of airline commercial agreements and aircraft transactions. His expertise extends to the area of international trade. Mr. Benge holds a J.D. degree from the University of Pennsylvania and a B.A. from Wesleyan University.

Christian (Chris) F. Binnig is a partner with Mayer Brown LLP in Chicago, Illinois. He began practicing law in 1985 and has represented communications service providers and other clients as lead trial and appellate counsel in a wide variety of commercial and administrative litigation matters in court and regulatory proceedings throughout the country. Mr. Binnig has practiced before numerous federal appellate courts and is a member of the Northern District of Illinois trial bar. He is a member of the ABA's Litigation and Public Utility, Communications, and Transportation Law Sections.

M. Stanford Blanton is a partner with Balch & Bingham, LLP, where he serves on the firm's Executive Committee. Mr. Blanton specializes in energy law, particularly nuclear development, regulation, and policy. He represents the owner and operator of the country's first new nuclear reactors in 30 years, handling licensing and contract concerns. He also represents nuclear power plant owners in claims against the United States arising out of the Nuclear Waste Policy Act. Mr. Blanton chairs the ABA Section of Public Utility, Communications and Transportation Law's Nuclear Energy Law Committee. He graduated from the University of Alabama School of Law.

Robert L. Brubaker is a partner in the Columbus, Ohio, office of Porter, Wright, Morris & Arthur. Mr. Brubaker has practiced in the field of environmental law since 1972. He was the 2011-2012 Chair of the American Bar Association Section of Public Utility, Communications, and Transportation Law; a Fellow of the American College of Environmental Lawyers; a member of the U.S. Department of Energy's National Coal Council; and a Fellow of the American Bar Foundation. Mr. Brubaker is an adjunct professor at Capital University Law School and a 1972 graduate of the University of Chicago Law School.

---

* This section contains biographical information about the authors of and contributors to the articles and updates in this volume. It also contains similar information about the *Infrastructure* editors and the PUCAT chairs during the years covered by this volume.

Stephen J. Burdick is an associate in the Energy Practice at Morgan, Lewis & Bockius LLP. Mr. Burdick represents electric utilities and other clients in the nuclear industry on a variety of regulatory and litigation matters before the Nuclear Regulatory Commission, other state and federal agencies, and the federal courts. Mr. Burdick is actively involved in the licensing of new nuclear plants in the United States, including activities related to early site permit, combined license, and design certification applications. Mr. Burdick also has been involved in advising international clients on developing new nuclear programs and licensing new nuclear plants abroad.

Candice Castaneda is an associate with Paul Hastings LLP and a member of the Global Projects practice. Her practice focuses on energy-related projects, transactions, and controversies. Ms. Castaneda represents clients before the Federal Energy Regulatory Commission as well as in transactions involving electric transmission and generation, mergers and acquisitions, financing, ratemaking, cogeneration, utility holding company, and gas and renewable energy projects.

Gerald A. Connell has been an antitrust lawyer for 51 years, 21 with the Antitrust Division of the U.S. Justice Department, 19 with Baker & Hostetler LLP, and the last 11 as a solo practitioner. He was lead counsel for the United States in the trial of the case against AT&T that led to the breakup of the Bell System in 1984. In 2005-2006 he was Chair of the Public Utility, Communications and Transportation Law Section. He lives in Alexandria, Virgnia, and his office is in Stamford, Connecticut.

Melody R. Cross (formerly Barron) is an associate in the finance practice group at Schiff Hardin LLP's Chicago office. Melody has complementary practices in corporate finance and securities and futures regulation. Melody attended Vanderbilt University Law School, where she was Special Projects Editor of the *Vanderbilt Law Review*, and is as a member of the Order of the Coif. She graduated from Northwestern University with a B.S. in communication studies (argumentation and advocacy) and a double major in history.

The Honorable Richard D. Cudahy is a senior circuit judge of the U.S. Court of Appeals for the Seventh Circuit. Prior to his appointment to the court, he was the resident partner in the Washington, D.C., office of the former Chicago firm of Isham, Lincoln and Beale.

Judge Cudahy received his B.S. from the United States Military Academy at West Point and his J.D. from Yale University Law School. He then served as law clerk to Charles E. Clark, Chief Judge of the U.S. Court of Appeals, Second Circuit, and in the Office of Legal Advisor, Department of State. He is a member of the Wisconsin, Illinois, District of Columbia, and Connecticut Bars.

Judge Cudahy was a member of the ABA's Special Committee on Energy Law and has served on the Councils of the Public Utility Law, Administrative Law, and Natural Resources Sections. He is a member of the American Law Institute. He was a visiting professor in law at the University of Wisconsin, a Lecturer in Law at Marquette University, a Professorial Lecturer at the George Washington University National Law Center, and is now a Lecturer in Law at the DePaul University College of Law. He is the author of numerous scholarly articles, including one on deregulation in the *Yale Journal on Regulation* and one in the *Journal of Air Law and Commerce*.

Judge Cudahy is currently a member of the Advisory Committee to the Center for International Human Rights at Northwestern University and a member of the Foundation Advisory Board of the International Aviation Law Institute at DePaul University. He serves on the Visiting Committee of the Divinity School of the University of Chicago and is a member of the Judicial Advisory Board for the American Society of International Law. In 2010 he received the President's Award from the Energy Bar Association for his lifetime work in the field of energy law.

Judge Cudahy was appointed by Chief Justice Rehnquist to the panel of the U.S. Court of Appeals for the District of Columbia Circuit for the purpose of appointing independent counsels and served four years from 1998 to 2002. He has received the honorary LL.D. degree from Ripon College, DePaul University, Wabash College, and Stetson University. He is also the recipient of the David Peck Award for 1989.

Mark C. Darrell is Senior Vice President, General Counsel, and Chief Compliance Officer of The Laclede Group, Inc., based in Saint Louis, Missouri. He holds a B.A. in political science from Syracuse University and a J.D. from Georgetown University Law Center. He is Vice Chair of the Gas and Corporate Governance Committees of the American Bar Association Section on Public Utility, Communications, and Transportation Law and is Vice Chair of the American Gas Association Legal Committee.

Patricia Dondanville is a partner with Reed Smith LLP. Patty concentrates her practice in corporate finance and transactional matters, often representing energy companies. Patty also represents energy companies with respect to legislative and regulatory policy at the increasingly important intersection between the energy industry and the financial markets. Patty has authored more than 25 substantive comment letters to the Commodity Futures Trading Commission and other financial regulators in connection with rulemakings under the Dodd-Frank Wall Street Reform and Consumer Protection Act.

Patty served as Co-chair for, and remains a member of, the Edison Electric Institute's Contract Drafting Committee, which developed and maintains the EEI Master Power Purchase and Sale Agreement. The EEI Master Agreement was used as the basis for the ISDA North American Power Annex and is used as a template for many nonfinancial commodity trading contracts and purchase agreements. Patty is the 2012-2013 Chair of the American Bar Association's Public Utility, Communications and Transportation Law Section.

Kenneth B. Driver is a partner at Jones Day in Washington, D.C. His practice focuses on the representation of electric and natural gas utilities before the Federal Energy Regulatory Commission, state utility commissions, the U.S. Department of Transportation, the appellate courts, and the federal antitrust enforcement agencies. Ken is actively involved in the American Bar Association's Section of Public Utility, Communications and Transportation Law and has been chair of the section's Electricity Committee. He also is a member of Energy Bar Association. Ken speaks before various groups on energy-related topics.

Chris Fortier served as the Young Lawyer Liaison to the Section's Council from 2006 to 2012. He also served as chair the Young Lawyers Division's Public Utility, Communications and Transportation Law Committee from 2006 to 2008 and the Air and Space Law Committee from 2010 to 2012.

Ed Fortunato is currently the Managing Director of Fundamental Analysis at Constellation Energy. Ed has been with Exelon for 10 years. He has managed the proprietary trading book and the short-term analytics group at Exelon. He is also actively engaged with the OTC trading desks and portfolio management groups working to procure fuels effectively and manage power price exposure. Prior to Exelon he was a vice president of natural gas trading at Merrill Lynch and a senior energy trader at Edison Mission Energy. He has an M.B.A. with high honors in finance from Boston University and a B.B.A. from Baruch College.

Dorothy Black Franzoni is a member of Sutherland's Energy and Environmental Practice Group and Chair of Sutherland's Renewable and Alternative Energy Team. She is Chair of the Electricity Committee of the ABA Section of Public Utility, Communications and Transportation Law. She focuses her practice on commercial transactions, project development, and finance transactions in the electric industry, including nuclear, coal, natural gas, and renewable energy projects. Her experience includes power purchase and sale arrangements, power plant joint-ownership arrangements, project development for electric generating plants, power scheduling and bulk system operations matters, federal loan and loan guarantee programs, secured and unsecured loan arrangements, tax-advantaged leasing transactions, and publicly issued and privately placed debt financings.

Scott Fulton is General Counsel for the U.S. Environmental Protection Agency (EPA). Fulton's extensive career in environmental policy and law began in 1982, when he served as an environmental prosecutor and Assistant Chief in the Department of Justice, Environment and Natural Resources Division, where he contributed to the development of many of the liability principles that underpin the United States' environmental protection program. From 1990 to 1995, Fulton held leadership positions in EPA's enforcement program, first as Director of Civil Enforcement and subsequently as Principal Deputy Assistant Administrator in OECA. From 1995 to 1999 he served as EPA's Principal Deputy General Counsel, and from 1999 to 2007 as a judge on EPA's Environmental Appeals Board. Before being nominated as General Counsel, Fulton served as Deputy Assistant and Acting Assistant Administrator in EPA's Office of International Affairs.

Thomas P. Gadsden is a partner in Morgan, Lewis & Bockius's Energy Practice, resident in the firm's Philadelphia office. Mr. Gadsden's work focuses on public utility regulation, administrative law, and energy litigation. Mr. Gadsden has represented electric, natural gas, water, wastewater, and steam heat clients in a wide array of regulatory, litigation, and transactional matters before federal and state commissions and courts. Mr. Gadsden is a past chair of the American Bar Association's Section of Public Utility, Communications and Transportation Law and of the Pennsylvania Bar

Association's Public Utility Law Section. He is a graduate of Yale University and the Georgetown University Law Center and, since 1991, has been recognized by *The Best Lawyers in America* as one of the country's leading energy lawyers.

Kathryn J. Gainey is of counsel in the Washington office of Steptoe & Johnson LLP, where she is a member of the firm's Transportation Group. Ms. Gainey's practice concentrates on transportation regulatory and litigation matters, as well as complex civil and appellate cases. In the transportation arena, Ms. Gainey provides regulatory and litigation advice to clients relating to surface transportation matters, including transportation of hazardous materials. Ms. Gainey has represented clients in railroad regulatory disputes before the Surface Transportation Board (STB), including unreasonable rule or practice cases, rate cases, rulemakings, and other proceedings. She represents clients in cases involving the interpretation of federal statutes and regulations, preemption, judicial review of administrative action, jurisdictional issues, and challenges to legislation in state and federal courts and before arbitration panels.

Eric B. Gallon is a senior attorney at Porter Wright whose practice encompasses public utility and environmental law as well as corporate litigation. He is a 1999 graduate of the University of Chicago Law School and, since 2007, a contributor to the annual and quarterly reports of the ABA Section of Public Utility, Communications and Transportation Law.

Caileen N. Gamache is an associate in the Washington, D.C., office of White & Case, LLP. As a member of her firm's Energy, Infrastructure and Project Finance Group, Ms. Gamache focuses on energy regulatory, compliance, and enforcement matters under the Federal Power Act, the Public Utility Regulatory Act, and the Natural Gas Act. Ms. Gamache routinely represents clients before such agencies as the Federal Energy Regulatory Commission, the North American Electric Reliability Corporation, and various state public utility commissions, and she also frequently advises clients with respect to transactional matters related to the development and operations of both renewable and conventional fossil-fuel facilities.

William A. Graham, Jr. is an associate with Balch & Bingham, LLP, and works in the firm's Energy Practice Group. Mr. Graham represents owners and operators of electric transmission and distribution facilities on regulatory compliance issues before the Federal Energy Regulatory Commission and the Federal Court of Appeals. He also represents and advises clients on federal and state electric utility issues, including open-access transmission tariff issues and transmission-to-generation interconnection arrangements. He graduated from the Vanderbilt University School of Law.

Jay M. Gutierrez is a partner in the Energy Practice at Morgan, Lewis & Bockius LLP. For more than 30 years, Mr. Gutierrez's practice has focused on representing companies and governments in a variety of matters involving the ownership, operation, and regulation of nuclear power plants. These representations have involved coordination of such diverse issues as developing nuclear regulatory programs; operating plant performance and related management issues; responding to government investigations; counseling on new plant initiatives in the United States, the United Kingdom, Europe, and the Middle East; and addressing corporate governance and co-owner considerations.

David R. Hardy is a tax partner in the New York office of Osler, Hoskin and Harcourt. In addition to having previously served as chair of the Taxation and Accounting Committee of the ABA PUCAT, Mr. Hardy has been the chair of the Tax Committee of the International Bar Association (2006 and 2007), the president of the International Tax Institute in New York (2009, 2010, and 2011), and a member of the New York State Bar Tax Section's Executive Committee (2002 to date). His practice includes the taxation of energy corporations in cross-border acquisitions and financings.

Carrie J. Hightman is Executive Vice President and Chief Legal Officer, NiSource Inc., a $7.2 billion *Fortune* 400 energy delivery holding company, and reports to the CEO. She is responsible for legal, compliance, environmental, safety, sustainability, and a real estate portfolio. At NiSource, Hightman led resolution of a $450 million class action and established an award-winning ethics program, a sustainability program, and a women's leadership program. She is chair of the Illinois State Universities Retirement System Board, a $14 billion pension system, and the Illinois Board of Higher Education, a state oversight board. She was President, AT&T Illinois, responsible for all regulatory and legislative matters, external affairs, and public relations; partner and Energy, Telecommunications and Public Utilities practice group leader at Schiff Hardin LLP, a national law firm; staff counsel, Florida Public Service Commission; and associate counsel, Florida Office of Public Counsel. She is a 1979 graduate of the University of Illinois (B.A.) and a 1982 graduate of Florida State University (J.D.).

Allen A. Kacenjar, Jr. is a principal at Squire Sanders in Cleveland. His practice encompasses all areas of environmental law, with a particular emphasis on Clean Air Act (CAA) regulatory advocacy. This includes efforts to advance industry interests on numerous rules, including National Ambient Air Quality Standards, Clean Air Interstate Rule, Clean Air Mercury Rule, Utility MACT, Boiler MACT, Integrated Iron and Steel MACT, and Regional Haze Rule standards. Those efforts include formal and informal rulemaking advocacy as well as appeals before the U.S. Court of Appeals for the D.C. Circuit. Mr. Kacenjar is also highly active on greenhouse gas (GHG) issues, including the development of comprehensive comments on all EPA rules, crafting and implementing numerous GHG monitoring plans, and the assessment of GHG BACT and related permitting implications.

Alexandra D. Konieczny is a member of Sutherland's Energy and Environmental Practice Group. Her practice is focused on energy- and commodity-related projects, transactions, and controversies, including issues related to compliance with rules and regulations. Alexandra primarily advises clients on Federal Energy Regulatory Commission, North American Electric Reliability Corporation, and California RPS compliance issues. Alexandra graduated from Emory University School of Law (J.D.) in 2008 and from Emory University (B.A.) in 2005.

D. Alan Lindsey is Assistant General Counsel for UniversalPegasus International, Inc. UniversalPegasus provides engineering, survey, inspection, and construction management services for onshore oil and gas production, midstream, and pipeline projects; offshore subsea and platform projects; and power transmission. Prior to joining UniversalPegasus, Mr. Lindsey was an associate in the Houston office of Squire, Sanders & Dempsey, LLP. His practice focused primarily on environmental matters, including the Clean Air Act and the regulation of greenhouse gases. Mr. Lindsey graduated from the University of Houston Law Center in 2005 and the University of Missouri at Columbia in 1999.

Theodore (Ted) A. Livingston joined Mayer Brown LLP in 1973 and became a partner in 1980. He is a trial and appellate lawyer working primarily on commercial and regulatory-related litigation involving the communications industry. He has served as lead trial counsel for AT&T before state regulatory commissions and federal and state trial courts throughout the country. He has argued numerous cases in the federal courts of appeal. Ted has litigated antitrust, audit malpractice, and securities fraud cases, contract disputes, business torts, and consumer class actions—trying to decision several dozen cases, including major federal court jury trials.

J. Bruce McDonald is a partner in Jones Day's antitrust practice in Washington, D.C., and Houston, Texas. He represents clients in antitrust government investigations and enforcement actions, merger reviews, and antitrust private litigation. From 2003 to 2007, he served as deputy assistant attorney general in the Department of Justice's Antitrust Division, where he was responsible for antitrust enforcement in energy, transportation, telecommunications, and other regulated industries. He was appointed to the Electric Energy Competition Task Force created by Congress and also was part of the U.S. delegation that negotiated the airline "open skies" agreement between the United States and the European Union.

Michael D. McNeely, Law Offices of Michael D. McNeely, has been an antitrust lawyer for 36 years. Before entering private practice, Mr. McNeely served for 12 years as an assistant director of the FTC's Bureau of Competition, where he led a division responsible for antitrust enforcement in various business sectors, including pharmaceuticals and health care. Prior to his time at the FTC, Mr. McNeely was a trial attorney in the Antitrust Division, where his responsibilities included a lead role in the litigation that led to the AT&T breakup, policy work in the Division's Evaluation Section, and merger litigation.

Richard A. Meserve is a senior of counsel at Covington & Burling LLP and is President of the Carnegie Institution for Science. He was Chairman of the U.S. Nuclear Regulatory Commission from 1999 to 2003.

Andrew Vahid Moshirnia received his J.D. from Harvard Law School and his Ph.D. in educational technology from the University of Kansas. His research interests include intellectual property, cyberlaw, communications, and generative technologies. He has published pieces in legal and instructional technology journals on a variety of topics, including the plain view doctrine in digital searches, user-modified video games, and academic wiki use. He occasionally blogs for Citizen Media Law Project and Just Enrichment.

Michael L. O'Neill (J.D. expected May 2013) is a student at The Catholic University of America Columbus School of Law. From 2007 to 2012, he served as an energy policy analyst for Sutherland's Energy & Environmental Group. Before joining Sutherland, he served as a research assistant for Mike Gapes, MP, in the British House of Commons and as an intern for Representative Stephanie Tubbs Jones in the U.S. House. He was awarded a B.A. by the University of Notre Dame in 2006.

Charles A, Patrizia is a partner at Paul Hastings, LLP. He has over 30 years of experience in regulatory and trial proceedings, with a concentration in complex matters and matters relating to project development and construction, energy and the environment, and regulation of chemicals and pharmaceuticals. He has an active counseling and litigation practice in project construction and energy and environment, as well as counseling corporations and boards on compliance matters and governance issues in relation to policies and requirements of regulatory agencies.

T. Michael Payne recently retired from AT&T Inc. During his tenure with AT&T, he served as senior vice president and general counsel for AT&T Corp., Ameritech, Pacific Telesis, Southwestern Bell Telephone, SBC International, and Southwestern Bell Mobile Systems. Payne received his J.D., M.A., and B.A. degrees from St. Louis University. Payne is a past chair (2008-2009) of the American Bar Association Section of Public Utility, Communications and Transportation Law. He currently serves as vice chair of the Nominating Committee, the Program and CLE Meetings Committee, and the Communications, Cable and Internet Committee in that same section. Payne is a member of the American, Arkansas, California, Illinois, Missouri, and Texas Bar Associations and a fellow of the American Bar Foundation.

John C. Peirce is a partner in the Washington, D.C., office of Bryan Cave, LLP. His practice encompasses antitrust, unfair trade practices, and complex commercial litigation and arbitration, with particular emphasis on regulated industries. He has been active in the Council Group of the Section of Public Utility, Communications and Transportation Law for over 10 years and currently serves as Chair of the Antitrust Committee and as a Vice-Chair of the ADR Committee.

Martha Groves Pugh is counsel in the law firm of McDermott Will & Emery LLP and is based in its Washington, D.C., office. Martha focuses her practice on federal income tax issues, with a particular emphasis on the nuclear and energy industries. Martha has had extensive experience with various tax credits, including renewable energy incentives, such as production tax credits for wind, biomass, and geothermal projects and investment tax credits related to solar projects. Martha has been heavily involved in developing opportunities for clients related to the American Recovery and Reinvestment Act of 2009, including the Section 1603 Grant Program.

Linda L. Randell is Senior Vice President, General Counsel, and Chief Compliance Officer of UIL Holdings Corporation, which owns an electric utility and three gas utilities. Prior to joining UIL, Ms. Randell was a senior partner at the law firm of Wiggin and Dana LLP, where she was chair of the Utilities and Regulated Industries Practice Group. Ms. Randell received an A.B. from the University of Michigan *magna* *cum laude* and with high distinction in economics. She is a member of Phi Beta Kappa. Ms. Randell received her J.D. from the Yale Law School, where she was an editor of *The Yale Law Journal*. Ms. Randell is a past chair of the American Bar Association Section of Public Utility, Communications and Transportation Law, for which she presently chairs the Book Board. She is a past chair of the Connecticut Bar Association Antitrust Section. Ms. Randell is a member of the American Bar Association Standing Committee on Publishing Oversight. She is a member of the Board of Directors of The Yale Law Journal Company, Inc.

John J. Reilly is a commercial trial lawyer and has served as lead counsel in federal trial and appellate litigation throughout the United States involving environmental claims, antitrust, price-fixing conspiracies, monopoly, commercial and real estate disputes, RICO actions, and class actions, as well as arbitrations in both U.S. and global forums. In addition, John has been an arbitrator and counsel in numerous arbitrations involving commercial disputes, international disputes, and New York Stock Exchange proceedings, including several FINRA arbitrations of claims relating to securities and other investments. He has also advised and counseled clients regarding joint venture arrangements in several industries, including airline and shipping, and with respect to resale price maintenance programs, as well as in grand jury antitrust investigations into the shipping industry. John served as a captain in the United States Marine Corps from 1967 to 1971, with a tour of duty in the Republic of Vietnam. He serves as co-chair of the Maritime Committee of the Public Utility, Communications and Transportation Law Section of the American Bar Association and as a director of The Ireland-U.S. Council for Commerce & Industry, Inc. John is a member of the American Bar Association Section of Litigation and former chair of the New York County Lawyers' Association Committee on Admiralty and Maritime Law.

Margaret E. Rice is senior counsel for NiSource Inc., a *Fortune* 400 energy company. Maggie's practice focuses on environmental law, including environmental litigation and policy. Before joining NiSource, Maggie served as Deputy Commissioner of the City of Chicago's Department of Environment. Her primary responsibility in that position was managing the city's environmental enforcement and permitting programs. Prior to this, Maggie practiced environmental law and litigation in private practice and worked for the Seventh Circuit Court of Appeals. Maggie earned her J.D. *cum laude* from Northwestern University School of Law and her B.A. with distinction from the University of Wisconsin-Madison.

Katrina Robson is counsel in the Washington, D.C., office of O'Melveny & Myers LLP, and a member of the firm's Class Action, Mass Torts, and Antitrust and Competition practice groups. Katrina has represented clients in litigation and before regulatory agencies in antitrust, merger, intellectual property, consumer protection, and general commercial matters. She has co-authored articles appearing in various antitrust publications, including *International Antitrust Law & Policy: Fordham Competition Law 2009*, and contributed to the 2012 update to *Consumer Protection Law Developments*.

Millicent W. Ronnlund is an associate with Balch & Bingham, LLP, and a member of the Firm's Nuclear Energy, Energy, and Energy Litigation sections. She has worked on Early Site Permit and Combined License proceedings before the Nuclear Regulatory Commission for nuclear power plant owners and operators. Mrs. Ronnlund also represents clients on nuclear regulatory compliance issues and on commercial matters related to the construction and operation of nuclear power plants. She graduated from the University of Alabama School of Law.

John W. Rowe is Chairman Emeritus of Chicago-based Exelon Corporation, an electric utility serving Chicago, Philadelphia, and Baltimore. He led Exelon from its formation in 2000 through the completion of its acquisition of Constellation Energy in 2012. Rowe previously held chief executive officer positions at the New England Electric System and Central Maine Power Company, served as general counsel of Consolidated Rail Corporation, and was a partner in the law firm of Isham, Lincoln & Beale. Rowe is the past chairman of the Nuclear Energy Institute and the Edison Electric Institute. He is the lead independent director of the Northern Trust Company and a member of the board of directors of The Allstate Corporation and SunCoke Energy. Rowe serves as chairman of the Illinois Institute of Technology, New Schools for Chicago, and the Field Museum, and as president of the Wisconsin Alumni Research Foundation.

Rowe holds undergraduate and law degrees from the University of Wisconsin, where he was elected to Phi Beta Kappa and the Order of the Coif. He has also received that university's Distinguished Alumni Award. Rowe holds honorary doctorates from the University of Wisconsin, DePaul University, Illinois Institute of Technology, Drexel University, University of Massachusetts-Dartmouth, Bryant College, Thomas College, and Dominican University.

Linda S. Stein is a partner in the Washington office of Steptoe & Johnson LLP, where she is a member of the firm's Transportation Group. Ms. Stein's practice has focused on civil litigation, primarily involving railroad contract disputes and oil regulatory disputes. These disputes have been brought in various forums, including state and federal trial courts, as well as arbitration proceedings. Ms. Stein has represented railroads in railroad regulatory proceedings before the Surface Transportation Board, including rail rate reasonableness proceedings, unreasonable rule or practice proceedings, merger proceedings, railroad line construction and crossing proceedings, and rulemaking proceedings. Some of this work has involved an analysis of environmental impacts under the National Environmental Policy Act (NEPA). Her practice has also included numerous appellate court proceedings involving the interpretation of statutory provisions and constitutional issues.

Lisa Wing Stone is an attorney with VLP Law Group LLP, a geographically distributed "virtual" law firm that was founded in 2008. Prior to joining VLP, Lisa was a counsel in O'Melveny & Myers's Washington, D.C., and Los Angeles offices. With no central office, VLP relies on its technology platform to collaborate and to operate with a small, highly specialized staff. At VLP Lisa continues to specialize in clean energy and environmental law. She regularly advises companies on DOE-related matters, including several federally funded projects.

Leticia Tavares is a second-year law student (class of 2014) at Roger Williams University School of Law in Bristol, Rhode Island. Prior to attending Roger Williams, Leticia obtained her bachelor's degree from the University of Massachusetts at Dartmouth. At Roger Williams, Leticia is a member of the *Roger Williams University Law Review*, the Moot Court Board, and the Honors Program. She is also the Vice President of the Multicultural Law Student Association and Director of Events for the Tax and Business Law Society. In the summer of 2012 Leticia was the National Grid–Robinson & Cole summer fellow. During this fellowship, Leticia drafted memoranda and motions to the Rhode Island Public Utilities Commission and Energy Facility Siting Board. She also gained legal experience in the areas of business, contract, subrogation, and affordable housing.

Dynda A. Thomas is a partner with Squire Sanders (US) LLP in Cleveland, Ohio. She is the deputy practice leader of Squire Sanders' Corporate Transactions, Finance & Governance Practice Group and has extensive experience in the areas of mergers and acquisitions and project finance. She focuses her practice primarily in the energy, mining, and metals industries. Dynda also leads the firm's Conflict Minerals team and works with clients as they develop and implement conflict minerals compliance and reporting programs. She is actively involved in the American Bar Association's Section of Public Utility, Communications and Transportation Law for which she has served as Co-Editor of *Infrastructure*, Program Chair, and is currently serving as Budget Officer. Dynda is listed in the 2011 and 2012 editions of *The Legal 500 US* for her mergers and acquisition practice and has been recognized as an Ohio Super Lawyer in *Law & Politics* magazine continuously since 2007.

Michael J. Thompson is a shareholder with the firm of Wright & Talisman, P.C., in Washington, D.C. In his 30 years of practice, he has advised and represented natural gas pipelines, distributors, energy marketers, electric utilities, RTOs, ISOs, municipalities, cooperatives, energy consumers, and landowners in an array of regulatory and commercial matters, including managing, litigating and settling all types of rate, tariff, rulemaking, and complaint proceedings before the FERC and state utility regulatory agencies, and related appellate proceedings. He has been recognized in *Chambers USA: America's Leading Lawyers for Business* since 2004.

Carine M. Williams is an associate in the New York office of Squire Sanders. Carine's practice focuses on representing parties and amici in federal and state appellate courts, in the U.S. Supreme Court, and in federal trial-level matters involving complex constitutional questions and commercial transactions. She is a member of the firm's Public Service Initiative, and a member of the firm's commercial litigation and appellate and Supreme Court litigation practice teams. Besides federal civil rights and habeas law, she advises clients on questions involving federal civil procedure and federal jurisdiction, as well as with regulatory schemes involving banking, intellectual property, and natural resources. Carine graduated from Yale Law School in 2006.

Jonathan B. Wilson is a partner in the Atlanta, Georgia, law firm of Taylor English Duma LLP and the founding chair of the Renewable Energy Committee of the ABA's

Public Utility Section. Wilson advises developers and investors on securities and financing transactions involving renewable energy, including biomass, wind, solar, and alternative fuels. Mr. Wilson was graduated Phi Beta Kappa from the College of William and Mary and earned his J.D. fron the George Washington University.

Casey Wren is a partner in the Austin, Texas, firm of Duggins Wren Mann & Romero, LLP. His practice, which has spanned over 30 years, has predominantly focused on infrastructure utilities with significant representations of major electric, natural gas, and telecom utilities in a wide variety of complex commercial, corporate, financial, and regulatory matters. Besides the American Bar Association and PUCAT, for which he has served as council representative and chair of the Electricity Committee, Mr. Wren's résumé includes a number of professional and legal affiliations. Additionally, he is a Fellow of the American Bar Foundation. Mr. Wren graduated with honors in 1979 from the University of Texas School of Law.

Part One
Renewable Energy in 2009/2010—Challenges and Opportunities

Introduction

In 2010, two issues of *Infrastructure* were devoted to renewable energy, based in part on presentations that had been made at the Section's October, 2009 Council meeting.

These issues included an article by the Section's Renewable Energy Committee chair, Jonathan Wilson, on federal tax credits and incentives for renewable energy investment, and three articles on the challenges of expanding the transmission grid to support renewable energy development, written by Michael Thompson, Ken Driver (former chair of the Section's Electricity Committee), and Casey Wren. Greenhouse gas (GHG) regulation and the Supreme Court's decision in *Massachusetts v. EPA*[1] are the subjects of contrasting articles, one by Allen Kacenjar and Alan Lindsey and another by EPA General Counsel Scott Fulton. Former Section chair Rob Brubaker addressed this case and other aspects of climate change regulation that will affect the development of renewable energy. Finally, Electricity Committee chair Dorothy Franzoni and her colleagues wrote about the future hope of the Smart Grid, and former Section Chair Tom Gadsden discussed renewable portfolio standards (RPS).

The tone of the articles, as originally published in *Infrastructure*, were, in general, positive and hopeful. The government's administrative and legislative actions and court decisions all suggested that renewable energy development would occur and be successful in addressing some of the environmental issues the country was confronting. However, by the summer of 2012, when the authors wrote the updates to their articles for this volume, much of the optimism had faded. This was due in large part to the paralysis that has gripped the American political system over the past year and a half. Other factors that have, for a while, dimmed the outlook for renewable energy include the continuing poor state of the national economy and the dramatic reduction in natural gas prices due to its increased domestic availability. In contrast, in his update, EPA General Counsel Scott Fulton provides a positive review of the progress EPA has made in regulating greenhouse gases.

Peter V. Lacouture
September, 2012

1. 549 U.S. 497 (2007).

Chapter 1

Federal Tax Credits and Incentives for Renewable Energy Investments*

*By Jonathan B. Wilson***

The Energy Policy Act of 2005[1] created a series of tax credits and other policy changes aimed at encouraging the development of renewable energy technologies and the formation of capital aimed at building new energy-producing infrastructure. Following the credit crisis and global recession of 2008, the public appetite for government intervention to promote job creation and new investment paved the way for the expansion and extension of many of the policy shifts begun in 2005 through the American Recovery and Reinvestment Act of 2009 (the ARRA or Act).[2]

The ARRA includes an estimated $787 billion in tax incentives and new federal spending, with more than $43 billion in funding devoted to energy. The Act's energy-related appropriations range from government loans and grants for developing technologies in the areas of carbon capture, alternative fuel vehicles, and transmission grid modernization, to funds allocated to public agencies and nonprofit organizations for facility retrofits that improve energy efficiency, to funding for renewable energy research, development, and deployment activities, and more. The Act also includes significant energy-related tax incentives, including a number of incentives that modify or expand incentives provided by the Energy Improvements and Extensions Act of 2008 (EIEA).

The ARRA appropriates $4.5 billion to the Department of Energy's (DOE) Office of Electricity Delivery and Energy Reliability (OEDER) to be used for "electric-

* Originally published in *Infrastructure*, vol. 49, no. 2 (Winter, 2010).

** *Jonathan B. Wilson, of Taylor English Duma LLP in Atlanta, GA, is a member of the firm's business transactions, corporate, and taxation group.*

1. Energy Policy Act of 2005, Pub. L. No. 109-58 (Aug. 8, 2005).

2. Discussion of the American Reinvestment and Recovery Act of 2009, Pub. L. No. 111-5, also includes discussion of the American Recovery and Reinvestment Tax Act of 2009 (ARRTA).

ity delivery and energy reliability activities to modernize the electric grid," including implementation of "Smart Grid" programs created in the Energy Independence and Security Act of 2007 (EISA). Accordingly, some of the $4.5 billion will be made available for the Smart Grid Investment Matching Grant Program to reimburse investors for the cost of certain qualifying Smart Grid investments. The ARRA increases the eligible percentage of federal matching funds for such investments from 20 to 50 percent. The Act also provides financial support for Smart Grid technology research, development, and demonstration projects, and requires the establishment of a Smart Grid information clearinghouse.

The ARRA allocates $16.8 billion to DOE's Office of Energy Efficiency and Renewable Energy (EERE) to distribute to a variety of programs, including $3.2 billion for energy efficiency and conservation block grants; $5 billion for the Weatherization Assistance Program; $3.1 billion for the State Energy Program; and $2 billion for grants to manufacturers of advanced batteries and components.

The Act allocates $6 billion in new funds to support DOE's Innovative Technology Loan Guarantee Program. The program originally was established under the Energy Policy Act of 2005 and was intended to support early-stage clean energy technologies. The ARRA expands the type of projects that are eligible for loan guarantees under the program to include investments in renewable energy systems that generate electricity or thermal energy, including technologies such as wind, solar, and incremental hydropower. Eligible projects must commence construction by September 30, 2011.

Extension & Modification of Production Tax Credits. The EIEA amended section 45 of the Internal Revenue Code to extend the in-service deadline for certain renewable energy projects to be eligible for the 30 percent production tax credit (PTC). The ARRA further extends the in-service deadline to January 1, 2013, for qualified wind facilities, and to January 1, 2014, for the majority of other qualified facilities, including open-loop and closed-loop biomass, geothermal, landfill gas, municipal solid waste, qualified hydropower projects, and qualified marine and hydrokinetic projects.[3] The PTC generally must be claimed during the 10-year period beginning with the date the qualified facility is placed in service.

Extension & Conversion of Investment Tax Credits. The EIEA amended section 48 of the IRS code to extend the 30 percent investment tax credit (ITC) for solar energy property and qualified fuel cell property to January 1, 2017, added small wind energy property as a category of qualified investment for the 30 percent ITC, and extended the 10 percent ITC for microturbines to December 31, 2016. It also provided a new 10 percent ITC for combined heat and power systems, as well as geothermal heat pumps.

The ARRA adds a new subsection to section 48 of the code allowing a wide range of PTC-eligible facilities to claim ITCs rather than PTCs.[4] Wind facility owners may elect ITCs in lieu of PTCs for facilities placed in service from January 1, 2009, through December 31, 2012. Owners of other renewable facilities placed in

3. ARRTA § 1101.

4. *Id.* § 1102.

service from January 1, 2009, through December 31, 2013, including biomass, geothermal, landfill gas, trash, qualified hydropower, and marine and hydrokinetic facilities, are eligible to elect ITCs instead of PTCs.

Converting Tax Credits to Grants. Beyond the PTC to ITC conversion, the ARRA also allows a taxpayer to exchange unclaimed ITCs or PTCs for a dollar-for-dollar grant from the U.S. Treasury.[5] Eligible facilities include both those that have always been eligible for energy credits—in particular, solar and fuel cell projects—as well as the new PTC-eligible facilities. Most facilities are eligible for a 30 percent grant, but some (qualified microturbine, combined heat and power, and geothermal heat pump facilities) qualify only for a smaller, 10 percent grant. The ARRA contains provisions to coordinate the grant and ITC/PTC provisions to ensure that there is no double dipping.[6]

The grant will not be considered taxable income for federal income tax purposes, but will reduce the depreciation basis of the project by an amount equal to one-half of the ITC that was allowable before the conversion. The grant is not available to federal, state, and local governments and section 501(c) tax-exempt entities.

New Clean Renewable Energy Bonds. While the EIEA authorized $800 million of new clean renewable energy bonds (CREBs) to finance facilities that generate electricity from wind, closed-loop biomass, open-loop biomass, geothermal, small irrigation, qualified hydropower, landfill gas, marine renewables, and trash combustion facilities, the ARRA authorizes an additional $1.6 billion of CREBs. The ARRA also authorizes local governments, public power providers, nonprofit utilities, cooperative electric companies, and certain lenders to issue CREBs. In addition, the Act authorizes $3.2 billion of qualified energy conservation bonds.[7]

Additional ARRA Tax Incentives. The ARRA removes the $4,000 cap on the energy investment credit previously in effect for qualified small wind energy property placed in service after December 31, 2008.[8] It also eliminates the caps on the 30 percent credit for many nonbusiness energy properties, including solar water heaters, small wind facilities, and geothermal heat pumps. The Act extends the placed-in-service date for many nonbusiness energy efficiency improvements to December 31, 2010; increases the credit rate for those expenditures from 10 percent to 30 percent; and sets a single overall (and lifetime) cap for these expenditures at $1,500.

Incentives for Qualified Advanced Energy Projects (QAEP). The ARRA also provided tax credits to encourage investment in technologies and manufacturing facilities intended to promote the adoption of renewable energy technologies by creating section 48C of the IRS code. This program provides a 30 percent federal income tax credit for investment in property which "re-equips, expands, or establishes a manufacturing facility" or that produces renewable energy property.[9] Applications

5. *Id.* §§ 1104, 1603.

6. *Id.* § 1104, adding new Code § 48(d).

7. *Id.* § 1111, 1112.

8. *Id.* § 1103(a), *amending* Code § 48(c).

9. Department of Energy Notice 2009-72, Qualifying Advanced Energy Project Credit Notice, *available at* http://www.energy.gov/recovery/documents/Federal_Notice_48C.pdf.

for tax credits under the first round of allocations were due October 16, 2009. Most analysts expect that the 2009-2010 round of allocations will consume all of the allocated $2.3 billion.

The QAEP credit is an investment-based credit. The credit equals 30 percent of the taxpayer's basis in the property certified as eligible for the credit. There is no maximum tax credit per project. The credit is *not* refundable and taxpayers may *not* elect to receive a cash grant in lieu of the credit.[10] The credit may be claimed in the tax year in which the qualified property is placed in service. In general, property is considered placed in service when it is placed in a condition or state of readiness and availability for a specifically assigned function. Taxpayers may also elect to take the credit early based on qualified progress expenditures paid or incurred during project construction pursuant to Treas. Reg. §1.46-5(o). If the taxpayer does not have sufficient tax liability to utilize the full amount of available credit in the year the project is placed in service, any remaining credit may be carried forward up to 20 years or back one year.

To qualify for QAEP credit, property must be used to re-equip, expand, or establish a manufacturing facility for the production of specified advanced energy property or property that, after further manufacture, will become specified advanced energy property. Components may be specified "advanced energy property," but the relative value of the components to the finished product will be taken into consideration in the DOE ranking process described below.

Specified energy property is:

- Property designed for use in the production of energy from the sun, wind, geothermal deposits, or other renewable resources;
- Fuel cells, microturbines, or an energy storage system for use with electric or hybrid-electric motor vehicles;
- Electric grids to support the transmission of intermittent sources of renewable energy, including property for the storage of such energy;
- Property designed to capture and sequester carbon dioxide and sequester carbon dioxide emissions;
- Property designed to refine or blend renewable fuels (but not fossil fuels) or to produce energy conservation technologies (including energy-conserving lighting technologies and Smart Grid technologies);
- New plug-in electric drive motor vehicles, qualified plug-in electric vehicles, or components designed specifically for use with such vehicles, including electric motors, generators, and power control units; or
- Other property designed to reduce greenhouse gas emissions as may be determined by the IRS.

10. If the applicant does not have taxable income that can be sheltered with the QAEP credit, there are monetization transaction strategies that can be utilized.

The property must be tangible property (other than a building or its structural components) subject to the allowance for depreciation or amortization, and must be an integral part of the qualifying project. A manufacturing facility is defined as a facility that makes or processes raw materials into finished products (or accomplishes any intermediate stage in that process).

~~~~~~~~~~
~~~~~~~~~~

2012 Update

By Jonathan B. Wilson

Much of the optimism that accompanied enactment of the American Recovery and Reinvestment Act (ARRA)[1] in 2009 has to a large measure evaporated more than three years later. Treasury Department grants under ARRA § 1603 amounted to nearly $9 billion between February 2009 and February 2012, but their impact has been hotly debated. Proponents claim that the grants supported the development of approximately 12,810 megawatts (MW) in renewable energy generation capacity, approximately 150,000 to 200,000 construction jobs, and between 5,100 and 5,500 operational jobs.[2] Critics argue that most of those jobs were temporary and ended after the completion of construction. The Energy Information Administration estimates that operating costs in 2016 will amount to $517 per MW/hour for wind and $625 to $764 per MW/hour for solar generation, costs that are roughly five times the cost of coal-fired or natural gas-fired plants.[3]

The alternative fuel credits in Internal Revenue Code (IRC) § 6426 that were extended by the ARRA expired on December 31, 2009.[4] The Tax Relief, Unemployment Insurance Reauthorization, and Job Creation Act of 2010 renewed those credits until December 31, 2011, but that legislation was not adopted until December 17, 2010, nearly a year after the alternate fuel credits' expiration date.[5] As a result, many of the plants that would have produced qualifying alternative fuels were shuttered at the end of 2009. They were not reopened when the credits were extended because of the delay in enacting the renewal and the short time remaining in the program after the extension was finally approved.[6]

---

1. Pub. L. No. 111-5, 123 Stat. 115 (2009).

2. Marshall Goldberg, Gian Poro & Daniel Steinberg, Nat'l Renewable Energy Lab., Preliminary Analysis of the Jobs and Economic Impacts of Renewable Energy Projects Supported by the § 1603 Treasury Grant Program (NREL TP 6A20-52739) at 12, 17–18 (Apr. 2012), *available at* http://www.nrel.gov/docs/fy12osti/52739.pdf.

3. Benjamin Zycher, *Wind and Solar Power, Part I: Uncooperative Utility*, Energy & Env't Outlook (Am. Enter. Inst. for Pub. Pol'y Research (Jan. 2012)), *citing* Energy Information Administration, *2016 Levelized Cost of New Generation from the Annual Energy Outlook 2010*, http://www.eia.gov/forecasts/aeo/pdf/0383(2012).pdf.

4. Tax Relief, Unemployment Insurance Reauthorization, and Job Creation Act of 2010, Pub. L. No. 111-312, § 704, 124 Stat. 3296 (2010).

5. *Id.*

6. John Funk, *Biodiesel Jobs Are Threatened as a Tax Credit for the Industry Expires*, Cleveland.com, Feb. 8, 2010, http://www.cleveland.com/business/index.ssf/2010/biodiesel_jobs_are_threatened.html.

Although the Department of Energy issued approximately $2.3 billion in tax credits for the manufacture of qualified advanced energy projects under IRC § 48C,[7] few of those credits have been utilized. In addition, several high-profile business failures involving recipients of § 48C credits and other federal grants gave fuel to the arguments of critics who sought to portray the programs as costly and ineffective.[8]

The Obama administration's push for increased renewable generating capacity was also frustrated by Congress's failure to enact legislation for the cap and trade of greenhouse gas (GHG) emissions. One of the purposes of cap and trade would have been to monetize the value of non-GHG renewable generating capacity by creating a market for the sale of renewable energy credits (RECs) to the producers of GHG-producing non-renewable power. A cap and trade program was included as a section of the American Clean Energy and Security Act of 2009 but that legislation failed,[9] in part as a result of the argument that it would have increased the cost of electricity and would decrease domestic income and employment.[10] Similarly, the administration had hoped to encourage renewable power generation through a nationwide renewable portfolio standard (RPS) that was included as part of the American Clean Energy Leadership Act of 2009, but the prospect of a national RPS collapsed with the bill's demise.[11]

---

7. Internal Revenue Service, *Section 48C Tax Credits Allocated January 7, 2010*, http://www.irs.gov/businesses/article/0,,id=242969,00.html (last visited July 3, 2012).

8. For example, subsidiaries of VESTAS North American received over $51 million in Section 48C credits for the construction of advanced energy factories that were billed as creating jobs. *See* http://www.irs.gov/businesses/article/0,,id=242969,00.html (list of Section 48C tax credit recipients) (last visited July 6, 2012). In January 2012, however, VESTAS announced 2,335 worker layoffs, with the potential for more. Howard Pankratz, *Vestas to Lay Off More Than 2,300; Could Lay Off Another 1,600 in the U.S. Later This Year*, Denver Post (Jan. 12, 2012), http://www.denverpost.com/breakingnews/ci_19727018. Similarly, Cardinal Fastener & Specialty Co. received $480,000 in Section 48C tax credits (see http://www.irs.gov/businesses/article/0,,id=242969,00.html (list of Section 48C tax credit recipients) (last visited Jul. 6, 2012)) but filed for bankruptcy protection in June 2011. John Funk, *Cardinal Fastener Files for Chapter 11 Bankruptcy Protection from Creditors*, Cleve. Plain-Dealer (June 30, 2011), *available at* http://www.cleveland.com/business/index.ssf/2011/06/cardinal_fastener_files_for_ch.html (last visited July 6, 2012).

9. H.R. 2454, 111th Cong. (2009).

10. Nicolas Loris, *The Costs of Cap and Trade*, Milw. J. Sentinel, Sept. 4, 2010, http://www.jsonline.com/news/opinion/102906484.html.

11. S. 1462, 111th Cong. (2009).

Chapter 2

The Conundrum of Multistate Electric Transmission Expansion: Who Will Pay?*

*By Michael J. Thompson***

Large-scale, nationwide development of renewable electric generation capacity will require huge investments not only in wind turbines and solar generators, but also in new high-voltage transmission facilities. The nation's existing transmission infrastructure was not built, and has limited available capacity, to move power to our major load centers from the remote areas that offer the best locations for wind and solar generation installations.

The need for new, long-distance transmission facilities obviously raises the question of how the billions of dollars they will cost will be allocated among the consumers who ultimately must pay for them. When an individual utility builds new transmission, recovery of the facility's cost is generally determined by the state regulatory commission that has jurisdiction over that utility. When an independent, "merchant" facility is built, the developer must assume the risk that its customers will pay sufficient rates for service on the line to make the venture economically viable.[1]

It is a different ballgame, however, when new, high-voltage lines are developed within an interstate grid operated by a FERC-ordained regional transmission organiza-

* Originally published in *Infrastructure*, vol. 49, no. 2 (Winter, 2010).

** *Michael J. Thompson is a shareholder in Wright & Talisman, P.C., in Washington, D.C., where he represents interstate natural gas pipelines, other natural gas industry clients and the firm's electric utility clients in an array of regulatory and commercial matters.*

1. *See, e.g., Green Power Express, LP*, 127 FERC ¶ 61,031 (2009); *ITC Great Plains, LLC*, 126 FERC ¶ 61,223 (2009). Under the Federal Power Act, as amended, FERC has jurisdiction over transmission and sales for resale of electric power in interstate commerce, and over the "public utilities" that own or operate facilities for such activities. *See* 16 U.S.C. § 792, *et seq.* (Federal Power Act, Title II, as amended).

tion (RTO) or independent system operator (ISO).[2] Indeed, an advisory committee of the U.S. Department of Energy deems cost allocation to be "the single largest impediment to any transmission development, especially across multiple RTOs or across RTO and non-RTO regions."[3] The U.S. Court of Appeals for the Seventh Circuit recently confronted this thorny question in *Illinois Commerce Commission v. FERC*.[4] In a 2-1 panel decision, *ICC* affirmed in part and remanded in part orders in which FERC directed certain changes to the rules under which PJM Interconnection, L.L.C., an RTO, establishes responsibility for the costs of regionally planned electric transmission facilities in the multistate grid that it operates.

This case is noteworthy for its outcome, and it has drawn additional attention because of the distinguished authors of the majority and dissenting opinions: Circuit Judges Richard A. Posner and Richard D. Cudahy, respectively. This article summarizes the controversy and the court's opinions, and briefly discusses the decision's potential consequences for FERC's efforts to promote new electric transmission infrastructure.

Roots of the Controversy

When PJM was established as an ISO, FERC accepted rates that assigned the costs of facilities built by each member utility primarily to the company's own customers. But FERC conditioned its approval on the then-participating utilities' agreement "to propose a uniform, system-wide rate methodology" at a later date.[5] When the utilities submitted the new proposed methodology in 2005, PJM (now an RTO) had a much larger footprint. The commission set the new proposal for an evidentiary hearing and directed an administrative law judge to determine "specifically how the costs of providing transmission service in the PJM region should be allocated."[6] The judge subse-

2. *See Promoting Wholesale Competition, etc.*, Order No. 888, 1991-1996 FERC Stats. & Regs., Regs. Preambles ¶ 31,036 (1996), *order on reh'g*, Order No. 888-A, 1996-2000 FERC Stats. & Regs., Regs. Preambles ¶ 31,048, *order on reh'g*, Order No. 888-B, 81 FERC ¶ 61,248 (1997), *reh'g denied*, Order No. 888-C, 82 FERC ¶ 61,046 (1998), *aff'd in part and remanded in part sub nom. Transmission Access Policy Study Group v. FERC*, 225 F.3d 667 (D.C. Cir. 2000), *aff'd sub nom. New York v. FERC*, 535 U.S. 1 (2002) (ISO criteria); *Regional Transmission Organizations*, Order No. 2000, 1996-2000 FERC Stats. & Regs., Regs. Preambles ¶ 31,089 (1999), *order on reh'g*, Order No. 2000-A, 1996-2000 FERC Stats. & Regs., Regs. Preambles ¶ 31,092 (2000), *petitions for review dismissed sub nom. Pub. Util. Dist. No. 1 v. FERC*, 272 F.3d 607 (D.C. Cir. 2001) (RTO standards).

3. Electricity Advisory Committee, *Keeping the Lights On in a New World*, at 50 (Jan. 2009) *available at* http://www.oe.energy.gov/DocumentsandMedia/adequacy_report_01-09-09.pdf.

4. 576 F.3d 470 (7th Cir. 2009) ("*ICC*").

5. *PJM Interconnection, L.L.C.*, Opinion No. 494, 119 FERC ¶ 61,063, at P 10 (2007), *reh'g denied*, Opinion No. 494-A, 122 FERC ¶ 61,082 (2008), *aff'd in part, remanded in part sub nom. ICC*, 576 F.3d.

6. *Id.* at P 1.

quently recommended that the commission impose a "postage-stamp" allocation of the costs of all existing and new facilities in the PJM region.[7]

FERC, however, concluded that the costs of existing facilities should remain assigned to each PJM utility's local customers. FERC reasoned that a postage-stamp allocation for existing facilities would cause large, unjustified shifts of costs among existing users of the PJM grid and would create an incentive for adversely affected utilities to leave the RTO.[8] FERC likewise retained, with conditions, PJM's allocation method for new facilities operating at less than 500,000 volts (500 kV), based on assessing each project's benefits to load in each zone.[9]

But FERC agreed that a postage-stamp allocation is best for the costs of new facilities that operate at 500 kV or higher (500+ kV) and that are planned through PJM's regional expansion planning protocol. The commission determined that, although no regional consensus emerged concerning allocation for such new "backbone" facilities, evidence demonstrating the greater transfer capability and better reliability of 500 kV facilities relative to lower-voltage lines justified regionwide allocation of the costs of high-voltage facilities. The same considerations supported 500 kV as the cut-off between local and regional allocations of costs. FERC observed that this finding does not "suggest that every 500 kV project will benefit every load in PJM in equal measure. . . . Rather, we need to find and we do find only that the benefits of [500+ kV] facilities are . . . sufficiently broad that they support a postage stamp allocation."[10] The commission also stated that employing 500 kV as the demarcation for regional cost-sharing was consistent with prior agreements among PJM transmission owners, and with a portion of PJM's tariff that, it said, provides that regionally planned, 500+ kV facilities in the western portions of PJM are to be "financed by all Western Zones" of the RTO.[11]

The Seventh Circuit's Opinions

In petitions for judicial review, western PJM utilities and the Public Utilities Commission of Ohio (PUCO) challenged FERC's ruling with respect to existing facilities, while the Illinois Commerce Commission and PUCO attacked the federal agency's decision concerning new, 500+ kV facilities. The Seventh Circuit panel unanimously affirmed FERC's decision regarding existing facilities. The court deemed sufficient the agency's reasoning that because each member utility built its existing transmission facilities to serve only its own customers, there is "no economic basis for shifting any part of [the existing facilities'] costs to other members" of PJM.[12]

---

7. *PJM Interconnection, L.L.C.*, 116 FERC ¶ 63,007 (2006). "Postage-stamp" refers to assigning costs *pro rata* to all loads in the region based on their consumption of the energy transmitted on the PJM grid.

8. Opinion No. 494 at P 48-60.

9. *Id.* at P 69-75.

10. *Id.* at P 81.

11. *Id.* at P 79.

12. *ICC*, 576 F.3d at 474. No party challenged FERC's retention of PJM's methodology respecting new, low-voltage facilities.

However, the court held that FERC did not adequately support its ruling changing PJM's cost assignments with respect to new, 500+ kV facilities. According to the court, FERC's reliance on the consistency of the postage-stamp allocation with prior agreements among eastern PJM utilities for sharing of high-voltage costs was unfounded, because the objecting utilities were not parties to these agreements.[13] Further, the court found insufficient the commission's contentions that assessing the benefits of high-voltage facilities to western PJM loads would be problematic and likely would foster repeated litigation. Acknowledging that feasibility is a valid consideration in evaluating FERC's rate-making decisions, the court said the commission nevertheless must explain why such considerations favor its chosen outcome. Here, FERC's orders lacked "any indication" that the cited problems exceeded the difficulty of measuring the benefits of lower-voltage facilities to a sufficient degree to justify the different rate-making treatment for high-voltage investments.[14]

Most importantly, the court held that FERC failed to find that the benefits of 500+ kV facilities to western PJM utilities justified the costs that the postage-stamp allocation would impose on them. "FERC," Judge Posner wrote, "is not authorized to approve a pricing scheme that requires a group of utilities to pay for facilities from which its members derive no benefits, or benefits that are trivial in relation to the costs sought to be shifted to its members."[15] The majority did not address FERC's argument that its obligation under the Federal Power Act to encourage new investment in transmission infrastructure supported the postage-stamp allocation.[16] Finally, the court declined simply to defer to FERC's expertise "because we are not authorized to uphold a regulatory decision that is not supported by substantial evidence on the record as a whole, or to supply reasons for the decision that did not occur to the regulators."[17]

Judge Cudahy dissented from the court's ruling regarding 500+ kV facilities. From a policy standpoint, he chided the majority for failing to see the "big picture." Specifically, the dissent asserted, FERC's restructuring of the electric industry and markets has significantly taxed the transmission grid's capacity for long-distance transmission of power, and the "urgency of the need to build transmission and . . . for incentives to that end" clearly supported FERC's postage-stamp allocation of the costs of new 500+ kV facilities.[18]

The dissent's departure from the majority's legal reasoning centered on application of the substantial evidence standard. Taking exception to the majority's "unusually narrow conception of cost-causation,"[19] the dissent argued that FERC could not reasonably be faulted for not quantifying the benefits of new high-voltage transmission to those who contested the postage-stamp allocation: "until today, no court has

---

13. *Id.* at 475-476. The court's opinion does not mention the PJM tariff provision regarding high-voltage facilities in western PJM to which the commission referred.

14. *Id.* at 475.

15. *Id.* at 476.

16. Opinion No. 494-A at P 54-55, *citing* Federal Power Act section 219, 16 U.S.C. § 824s.

17. *ICC*, 576 F.3d at 477 (citations omitted).

18. *Id.* at 482 (Cudahy, J., dissenting).

19. *Id.* at 481.

found that cost causation requires FERC to monetize the benefits of reliability improvements in order to share the costs."[20] Indeed, Judge Cudahy asserted, the decisions the majority cited actually support the view that improvements in the grid's reliability are *presumed* to benefit all participants in the system. Accordingly, the judge wrote, the challengers of the postage-stamp allocation had the burden "to show that [they] would *not* benefit from" regionally planned 500+ kV transmission upgrades.[21]

Where Does FERC Go From Here?

The *ICC* panel's dispute over the quantum of evidence required to justify a system-wide allocation of costs on an integrated transmission grid invites a more detailed analysis than the scope of this article permits. However, it seems fair to observe that what the majority expects of FERC on remand is, at best, unclear.

The ambiguity stems in substantial part from the Seventh Circuit's reliance on decisions such as *Midwest ISO Transmission Owners v. FERC*.[22] Quoting then-Circuit Judge (now Chief Justice) Roberts' reference to seeking proportionality of benefits and costs in allocation disputes, Judge Posner wrote that FERC must have "an articulable and plausible reason to believe that the benefits [of new 500+ kV facilities] are at least roughly commensurate with" member utilities' respective sales of energy on the PJM grid.[23] Perhaps alluding to *Midwest*'s admonition that the "intertwined nature" of capital costs justifies a presumption that all users of a network benefit from reliability improvements,[24] the court stated that FERC "cannot use [such a] presumption to avoid the duty" to compare costs imposed with benefits to be realized.[25] The majority also took care to explain that FERC need not estimate benefits "to the last penny, or for that matter to the last million or ten million or perhaps hundred million dollars."[26] Nevertheless, its acknowledgment that all improvements in reliability benefit all users of the interconnected PJM grid highlights the uncertainty about what degree of proportionality the Commission must demonstrate.

FERC is thus challenged to discern what evidence will suffice to justify system-wide allocation of the costs of high-voltage transmission upgrades. This, of course, begs the question of to what degree precision is feasible in assessing the benefits of specific upgrades to specific users of an integrated transmission network. There is no question that computer models can provide estimates of benefits. But FERC has correctly recognized that the myriad assumptions necessary to derive such estimates, and the myriad arguments litigants can raise to challenge those assumptions, raise serious questions about the value of the effort.[27]

20. *ICC*, 576 F.3d at 480 (Cudahy, J., dissenting).
21. *Id.* (italics in original).
22. 373 F.3d 1361 (D.C. Cir. 2004) ("*Midwest*").
23. *ICC*, 576 F.3d at 477.
24. *See Midwest*, 373 F.3d at 1369-71.
25. *Id., citing Midwest*, 373 F.3d at 1368.
26. *ICC*, 576 F.3d at 477.
27. Opinion No. 494 at P 82-83.

This conundrum has potentially important implications for the nation's electric transmission grid. FERC continues to confront issues of how to allocate the costs of expensive new transmission facilities within ISOs and RTOs. For example, it recently approved "interim" revisions to the Midwest ISO's cost allocation rules to avert the departure of two of the system's transmission owners, motivated by impending allocations of the costs of new transmission facilities that will interconnect large wind farms in remote areas.[28] The underlying issue remains unresolved, however, pending the outcome of a regional stakeholder process.[29] Separately, the commission recently solicited comments on "whether the Commission should pursue generic reform . . . of cost allocation,"[30] citing industry claims that "the lack of mechanisms to allocate and recover the costs of certain types of new transmission facilities and upgrades to existing facilities" is a critical obstacle to the development of such infrastructure.[31]

Further underscoring the importance of this issue, proposed climate change and energy policy legislation now before the Congress would expand FERC's jurisdiction to include licensing of new high-voltage transmission facilities.[32] Some legislators have indicated they will insist that such authority include requirements that FERC must find sufficient benefits to particular consumers to justify any assignment to them of cost responsibility for new facilities. It seems reasonable to suggest that the *ICC* ruling may strengthen the prospects for such terms and, if a bill is passed, might also influence how the new law is implemented. There clearly is a lot riding on the outcome of this important debate. Equally clearly, it is far from being resolved.

---

28. *Midwest Indep. Transmission Sys. Operator, Inc.*, 129 FERC ¶ 61,060 (2009).

29. *See id.* at P 48.

30. *Id.* at 7.

31. *Transmission Planning Processes Under Order No. 890*, Notice of Request for Comments, Docket No. AD09-8-000, at 5 (October 8, 2009).

32. American Clean Energy and Security Act of 2009, H.R. 2454, 111th Cong. (2009); American Clean Energy Leadership Act of 2009, S.1462, 111th Cong. (2009).

2012 Update

By Michael J. Thompson

The FERC responded to the Seventh Circuit's remand in an order issued on March 30, 2012.[1] It again ruled that PJM's previous allocation method based on power flows, or "DFAX," is an unjust and unreasonable method of allocating the costs of transmission upgrades that operate at 500 kV or higher (500+ kV), and that the costs of such facilities should be allocated on a postage-stamp basis proportional to load in each transmission rate zone.

FERC emphasized the Seventh Circuit's acknowledgments that some expansion projects may benefit the regional transmission grid as a whole, and benefits to each user or class of users of the grid need not be precisely quantified.[2] Therefore, FERC said, the Seventh Circuit's decision requires only a showing that some customers in zones other than those currently flowing power over facilities that need upgrading will use or benefit from the improved facilities.[3] The heart of its rationale, however, is that PJM's regional planning process creates an integrated transmission network that produces benefits for "all parties connected to the transmission system regardless of nominal power flows."[4] It is reasonable to conclude, FERC said, that all users of the integrated network share these benefits roughly in proportion to their use of the grid.[5]

Commissioner LaFleur dissented, contending that the proper approach is a hybrid allocation methodology that combines aspects of both a postage-stamp allocation and the DFAX methodology.[6]

The Illinois Commerce Commission's and other parties' requests for rehearing of the Remand Order remain pending at this writing. Their principal argument is that the Remand Order does not satisfy the Seventh Circuit's directive to demonstrate both a causal link and proportionality between the costs of 500+ kV upgrades that are imposed on utilities in western PJM and the benefits of the facilities to those utilities and their customers.

---

1. *PJM Interconnection, L.L.C.*, 138 FERC ¶ 61,230 (2012) (*Remand Order*).
2. *Id.* at ¶ 51.
3. *Id.* at ¶ 53.
4. *Id.* at ¶ 113.
5. *Id.* at ¶ 117.
6. *Id.*, Dissent at 2–3.

In the meantime, FERC has approved partial "socialization" of the costs of some transmission upgrades for other regions[7] and has left open the door to similar allocations in recent, new rules requiring jurisdictional utilities to participate in regional and interregional transmission-planning processes.[8] There appears still to be considerable remaining life in this controversy.

7. *See, e.g., Midwest Indep. Trans. Sys. Operator, Inc.*, 133 FERC ¶ 61,221 (2010), *order on reh'g*, 137 FERC ¶ 61,074 (2011) (conditionally accepting postage-stamp allocation across RTO region of portion of costs of high-voltage "multi-value projects"); *Southwest Power Pool, Inc.*, 131 FERC ¶ 61,252 (2010), *reh'g denied,* 137 FERC ¶ 61,075 (2011) (accepting "highway/byway" proposal, which allocates all costs of transmission upgrades or expansions operating at or above 300 kV on postage-stamp basis across RTO region).

8. *See* Transmission Planning and Cost Allocation by Transmission Owning and Operating Public Utilities, Order No. 1000, III FERC Stats. & Regs., Regs. Preambles ¶ 31,323 (2011), *order on reh'g*, Order No. 1000-A, 139 FERC ¶ 61,132 (2012).

Chapter 3

Environmental Regulatory Impacts on Renewable Energy*

*By Robert L. Brubaker***

Recent trends in environmental regulation are making renewable energy[1] more valuable. Over the past year, the renewable energy "carrots" in the ARRA have coincided with increasingly aggressive environmental regulatory "sticks" directed at nonrenewable energy.

Climate change litigation, regulation, and legislation are on the verge of imposing a cost on CO_2 emissions. As the law evolves in this area, the trajectory of the price of CO_2 emitted (its level and its volatility over time) will have a profound impact on the renewable energy sector, and on the economy as a whole.

All three branches of government are actively engaged in developing law and policy—particularly in the context of climate change—that will shape the market for renewable energy. The judicial branch has led the way in forcing action on greenhouse gas (GHG) regulation. The Supreme Court laid down a challenge to the executive and legislative branches in the landmark climate change case *Massachusetts v. EPA*, 549 U.S. 497 (2007). By holding that CO_2 and other GHGs fit within the Clean Air Act's definition of "air pollutant" based on global warming concerns, the Court put pressure on EPA to begin regulating GHGs under the current Clean Air Act, and put pressure on Congress to produce a more suitable statutory framework for addressing climate change. The Second Circuit's decision in *Connecticut v. American Electric Power, Inc.*, 582 F.3d 309 (2d Cir. 2009), that the federal common law of nuisance encompasses the tort of contributing to global warming unless and until EPA or Congress provides a comprehensive scheme for

---

* Originally published in *Infrastructure*, vol. 49, no. 2 (Winter, 2010).

** *Robert L. Brubaker, an attorney with Porter Wright Morris & Arthur in Columbus, OH, practices in the areas of environmental law, government and regulatory affairs, and green practices.*

1. While definitions of "renewable energy" differ and are still evolving, the most prominent examples (such as wind, solar, hydro, and some biomass) all have a common characteristic: they do not emit or add to the atmosphere carbon dioxide (CO_2), the main greenhouse gas (GHG) of concern for climate change policy.

regulating GHGs, adds more pressure on the executive and legislative branches to address climate change.[2]

The executive branch has responded to the challenge from the courts with a series of proposals to begin regulating GHGs under the current Clean Air Act in 2010. In response to the Supreme Court's remand in *Massachusetts v. EPA*, EPA issued a finding that GHGs from new cars and trucks "cause or contribute" to "endangerment" of public health and welfare (a precondition for promulgating Clean Air Act standards regulating GHGs).[3] In September, EPA and the Department of Transportation jointly proposed the first-ever national GHG limits, to apply to model year 2012 through 2016 cars and light-duty trucks.[4] DOT's National Highway Traffic Safety Administration proposed more stringent corporate average fuel efficiency (CAFE) standards under the Energy Policy Conservation Act at the same time that EPA proposed to require the same level of fleetwide performance in GHG tailpipe standards under Title II of the Clean Air Act.

When the proposed tailpipe GHG standards are finalized, CO_2 and other GHGs will in EPA's view be "subject to regulation" under the Clean Air Act, and consequently subject to the Act's prevention of significant deterioration (PSD) preconstruction permit and Title V operating permit requirements. The statutory thresholds for PSD and Title V applicability (100 to 250 tons per year) are such that when applied to CO_2, tens of thousands of additional sources would be pulled into these permitting programs, overwhelming state and federal regulators. Therefore, EPA has proposed a "tailoring rule" to phase in these permitting requirements and initially apply them only to the 14,000 or so sources emitting 25,000 tons per year of CO_2 or comparable GHGs.[5] It is expected that EPA's proposed tailpipe GHG emission standards and GHG "tailoring" rule will be finalized by April 2010.

In addition to its initiatives to directly regulate GHGs under the Clean Air Act, EPA is pursuing or considering multiple new regulatory requirements for coal-fired power plants. These include continued and expanded new source review enforcement, more stringent requirements for new plant construction permits (possibly including GHG limits), revisions to the Clean Air Interstate Rule vacated by the D.C. Circuit in 2008, new maximum achievable control technology (MACT) standards for mercury and other hazardous air pollutant emissions from power plants to replace the Clean Air Mercury Rule vacated by the D.C. Circuit in 2008, potential classification of coal ash as a hazardous waste under the Resource Conservation and Recovery Act, cooling tower retrofits under the Clean Water Act to mitigate intake structure impacts, and new Clean Water Act effluent guidelines for power plant wastewater discharges. The costs of these initiatives aimed at coal (which is used to produce half of the electricity generated in the United States), if implemented, likely would accelerate the economic obsolescence of some coal-fired power plants and improve the economics of alternative sources of electricity, including renewables.

2. A very comprehensive, up-to-date, and user-friendly compilation of U.S. climate change litigation is maintained by Columbia Law School professor Michael Gerrard and is available at www.climatecasechart.com.

3. *See* 74 Fed. Reg. 66496 (Dec. 15, 2009).

4. *See* 74 Fed. Reg. 49454 (Sept. 28, 2009).

5. *See* 74 Fed. Reg. 55292 (Oct. 27, 2009).

Despite their moves to regulate GHGs under existing statutory authority, EPA and the Obama administration have stated their preference for comprehensive new legislation to address climate change. Congress obliged in June 2009 with the first-ever legislation limiting GHGs passed by the House,[6] and a similar bill introduced in the Senate in October 2009.[7] The Waxman-Markey bill, 1,427 pages long, includes a declining cap on U.S. GHG emissions,[8] and creates tradable allowances[9] commensurate with the cap (hence the name "cap-and-trade"). The bill also would mandate a combined efficiency and renewable electricity standard (CERES).[10] The Kerry-Boxer bill is similar to the Waxman-Markey bill, but it requires greater GHG emission reductions to be achieved by 2020 (20 percent instead of 17 percent below 2005 levels). The Kerry-Boxer bill would preserve EPA's authority to regulate GHGs under certain provisions of the Clean Air Act, including the PSD permit program, but the Waxman-Markey bill would not. The economic value of CO_2 allowances would be used in part, under both bills, to subsidize renewable energy. The price of a CO_2 allowance has been projected by EPA to be $13 in 2015 and $16 in 2020 under both the Waxman-Markey and Kerry-Boxer bills.[11] If a GHG cap-and-trade program becomes law, the market will determine the real price of a CO_2 allowance.

The actions and reactions of the judicial, executive, and legislative branches in the development of climate change law and policy each depend in significant measure on the others. The three branches are triangulating the future of the nation's energy infrastructure, and the part renewable energy will play in it. The process is intensifying, and will continue for the foreseeable future, with or without climate change legislation and with or without an international climate change treaty.

---

6. H.R. 2454, the "American Clean Energy and Security Act," known as the Waxman-Markey bill.

7. S. 1733, the "Clean Energy, Jobs, and American Power Act," known as the Kerry-Boxer bill.

8. The cap is set at 3% below 2005 levels beginning in 2012, and drops to 83% below 2005 levels in 2050.

9. One allowance must be obtained and surrendered for each ton of CO_2 (or other GHG with equivalent heat trapping properties, known as "CO_2e) emitted by a "covered source" subject to the cap.

10. The CERES targets for Retail Electric Suppliers are 6% of MWhrs supplied in 2012, and 20% of MWhrs supplied in 2020. Up to 25% of the CERES obligation can be met by energy efficiency, and states can petition to increase that level to 40%.

11. *See* http://www.epa.gov/climatechange/economics/pdfs/EPA_S1733_Analysis.pdf.

2012 Update

*By Robert L. Brubaker, assisted by Eric B. Gallon**

The forces of politics and markets are increasing turbulence in the electricity sector more than usual. From 2008 to 2011, the share of the nation's electricity generated from coal fell from 48 percent to 42 percent, while the share generated from renewable resources increased from 9 percent to 13 percent.[1] During that same time, the share of electricity generated from natural gas increased from 20 percent to 25 percent. These are big changes to the generation mix in such a short period of time, and the biggest surprise is how fast natural gas has increased its share.

Since this article was published in early 2010, there still is no explicit price signal for CO_2 emissions; if anything, the timing and magnitude of a direct or indirect tax on carbon is even more uncertain than it seemed two years ago. EPA has moved full speed ahead on the environmental regulatory "sticks" directed at non-renewable energy described in the article. EPA's first nationwide regulatory requirements for greenhouse gas (GHG) emissions, issued in 2011, have withstood the vigorous challenges of over 80 petitioners in the D.C. Circuit. However, the most significant changes in the landscape for renewable energy since early 2010 have not been due as much to regulatory policies or developments expected by planners at the time as they have been due to the increased domestic production of natural gas.

Legislation to reduce GHG emissions faltered in Congress and has now all but disappeared from view. The Waxman-Markey and Kerry-Boxer bills died in the Senate in the summer of 2010. Congressional gridlock on climate change and other environmental policies seems to have intensified after the 2010 midterm elections and in the run-up to the 2012 elections.

While the House has recently focused on bills that would restrict EPA's authority to regulate GHG emissions under the current Clean Air Act, the Supreme Court has reaffirmed such EPA authority. In *American Electric Power*

* Eric B. Gallon is a senior attorney in the Columbus office of Porter, Wright, Morris & Arthur.

1. U.S. Energy Information Admin., *Electricity Explained, Electricity in the United States*, http://www.eia.gov/energyexplained/index.cfm?page=electricity_in_the_united_states; *id.*, *Net Generation by Energy Source: Total (All Sectors), 1998 through April 2012*, http://www.eia.gov/electricity/monthly/epm_table_grapher.cfm?t=epmt_1_1 (last visited July 11, 2012).

Co., Inc. v. Connecticut,[2] the Court relied upon its decision in *Massachusetts v. EPA*[3] that CO_2 is "air pollution subject to regulation under the [Clean Air] Act" to rule that "the Clean Air Act and the EPA actions it authorizes displace any federal common law right to seek abatement of carbon-dioxide emissions from fossil-fuel fired power plants."[4] The Court held that it is for EPA to decide when and how to regulate GHGs under the Clean Air Act, and if EPA fails to regulate, "[s]tates and private parties may petition for a rulemaking on the matter, and EPA's response will be reviewable in federal court."[5]

Subsequent to the *Massachusetts* decision, EPA has moved forward with GHG regulation in earnest. EPA finalized its GHG "Endangerment Finding" in December 2009, which concluded that GHG emissions from new motor vehicles and new motor vehicle engines contribute to the endangerment of public health and welfare.[6] In April 2010, EPA Administrator Lisa Jackson issued the Timing Rule, which stated that a given air pollutant becomes "subject to regulation" for PSD and Title V permitting purposes on the date a regulation limiting emissions of that air pollutant "takes effect."[7] Around the same time, EPA and the National Highway Traffic Safety Administration (NHTSA) issued their final GHG limits for model year 2012 to 2016 cars and light-duty trucks,[8] making GHGs "subject to regulation" as of January 1, 2011.[9] EPA also finalized its Tailoring Rule in June 2010[10] (to phase in GHG permitting requirements in a way that covers only the largest emitters initially).[11] In consolidated appeals of these four related GHG rulemakings, the D.C. Circuit issued an opinion in June 2012 rejecting all challenges to the rules, relying heavily on the Supreme Court's *Massachusetts* decision and the automatic operation of intertwined sections of the Clean Air Act.[12]

---

2. Am. Elec. Power Co., Inc. v. Connecticut, 131 S. Ct. 2527 (2011).
3. Massachusetts v. EPA, 549 U.S. 497, 127 S. Ct. 1438, 167 L. Ed. 2d 248 (2007).
4. Am. Elec. Power, 131 S. Ct. at 2537.
5. *Id.* at 2358.
6. *See* 74 Fed. Reg. 66,496 (Dec. 15, 2009).
7, *See* 75 Fed. Reg. 17,004 (Apr. 2, 2010).
8. *See generally* 75 Fed. Reg. 25,324 (May 7, 2010).
9. EPA and NHTSA have since finalized standards for medium- and heavy-duty engines and vehicles (76 Fed. Reg. 57,106 (Sept. 15, 2011)), and issued proposed limits for light-duty vehicles for model years 2017 to 2025 (76 Fed. Reg. 74,854 (Dec. 1, 2011)).
10. 75 Fed. Reg. 31,514 (June 3, 2010).
11. EPA issued a final rule maintaining the thresholds EPA imposed under Step 2 of that rule. *See* 77 Fed. Reg. 41,051 (July 12, 2012).
12. Coal. for Responsible Reg. v. EPA, Case No. 09-1322 (D.C. Cir. June 26, 2012).

EPA's four final GHG rulemakings, along with other recent proposed and final EPA rules, particularly the Mercury and Air Toxics Standards[13] finalized in February 2012, have accelerated planned retirements of coal-fired plants. As much as one-fourth of the existing U.S. coal-fired generating capacity, or up to 60 gigawatts, have been projected to be removed from service between now and 2020.[14]

In April 2012, EPA proposed GHG New Source Performance Standards for new fossil fuel–fired electric utility generating units.[15] EPA proposed a standard based on the performance of combined-cycle gas turbines with no add-on controls (1,000 pounds of CO_2 per MWhr) and proposed that same standard be applied to coal-fired units (which would require carbon capture and storage technology to comply). The rules are scheduled to be finalized by the end of 2012. Critics of the proposal claim it is tantamount to a ban on new coal-fired generating capacity and will discourage commercial development of carbon capture and storage technology.

The relatively precipitous increase in regulatory requirements for coal-fired generation might have been expected to create a surge in demand for renewable energy. Instead, increased domestic production of natural gas has resulted in significantly lower prices for natural gas,[16] at the same time the recession has depressed demand and wholesale electricity prices. *The Washington Post* reported that "cheap gas has reduced incentives for energy conservation and efficiency. And it has left solar and wind, despite their own falling costs, heavily dependent on government mandates" to be competitive.[17] If natural gas continues to be relatively cheap and abundant, ratepayers, taxpayers, and their elected representatives may be less enthusiastic about the above-market costs of subsidies and mandates for renewable energy. The federal production tax credit for wind power installations is set to expire at the end of 2012, which

13. 77 Fed. Reg. 9304 (Feb. 16, 2012).

14. Metin Celebi, Potential Coal Plant Retirements in U.S. and Impact on Gas Demand (The Brattle Group), at p.13 (Feb. 27, 2012), *available at* http://www.brattle.com/_documents/UploadLibrary/Upload1018.pdf.

15. 77 Fed. Reg. 22,392 (Apr. 13, 2012).

16. Natural gas prices have remained below $2.70 per MMBtu (monthly average) throughout the first half of 2012 and dipped below $2.00 in April 2012. *See* http://www.gasearch.com/ngnp.php.

17. Steven Mufson, *Cheap natural gas jumbles energy markets, stirs fears it could inhibit renewables*, Wash. Post (Feb. 1, 2012), *available at* http://www.washingtonpost.com/business/economy/cheap-natural-gas-jumbles-energy-markets-stirs-fears-it-could-inhibit-renewables/2012/01/08/gIQApLr5hQ_story.html.

could greatly reduce the number of new wind projects.[18] Thus, despite EPA's concerted efforts to regulate and reduce GHG emissions and conventional pollutants from coal-fired generation, the ultimate beneficiary of those efforts may be the natural gas industry—not the renewable energy industry.

18. *See* Richard Harris, "Could Cheap Gas Slow Growth of Renewable Energy?" NPR (Feb. 2, 2012), *available at* http://www.npr.org/2012/02/02/146297284/could-cheap-gas-slow-growth-of-renewable-energy.

Chapter 4

Building and Paying for New Transmission Needed to Get Renewable Energy to Market*

*By Kenneth B. Driver***

The growth in the amount of renewable energy resources in the United States poses a major challenge for the nation's transmission grid, which must be extended and expanded to transmit renewable energy from distant renewable resources to customers. Between 2004 and 2008, the total amount of renewable energy connected to the transmission grid (primarily in the form of wind energy) grew substantially, as did the relative contribution of renewable energy as a percentage of each year's total increase in generation capacity. Although the rate of growth of renewable energy slowed in 2009 due to the economic downturn, the pace is expected to increase again in 2010 and the next few years. Currently, more than half of the resources trying to connect to the transmission grid around the country are wind resources.[1] Potential wind resource sites are not spread evenly across the country—the best inland wind resource regions are located in a central region of the country extending from Texas north to the Dakotas.[2]

One way the government is trying to meet the need for new transmission investment is through direct subsidies. In a July 29, 2009, solicitation issued pursuant to

* Originally published in *Infrastructure*, vol. 49, no. 2 (Winter, 2010).

** *Kenneth B. Driver is a partner in the Washington, D.C., office of Jones Day where his practice focuses on representing gas and electric utilities before FERC, U.S. DOT, state commissions and antitrust enforcement agencies as well as in appellate proceedings.*

1. U.S. Department of Energy, National Renewable Energy Laboratory, *2008 Wind Technologies Market Report at* http://www.nrel.gov/docs/fy09osti/46026.pdf.

2. U.S. Department of Energy, National Renewable Energy Laboratory, *United States—50-Meter Wind Resource Map at* http://www.windpoweringamerica.gov/wind_maps.asp.

section 1705 of the 2005 Energy Policy Act, as amended by ARRA, the Department of Energy proposed to make available $750 million to pay the credit subsidy costs for large-scale transmission projects.[3] Likewise, on July 29, 2009, DOE issued a solicitation under section 1703 of the Energy Policy Act, to provide up to $8.5 billion in loan guarantee authority for projects in energy efficiency, renewable energy, and advanced transmission and distribution.[4] So far, the conditions imposed as part of these grants—such as wage requirements and the "Buy American" provisions—seem to be limiting interest in the program. In any event, the amounts being made available through such government subsidies will cover only a small percentage of the nation's transmission investment needs.

This means that the vast majority of the costs of new transmission needed to transmit renewable energy to customers will be recovered in the rates of transmission service providers. Fundamental to this ratemaking process is deciding which types of customers should bear the costs of the new investments.

The Seventh Circuit recently grappled with these cost allocation issues in *Illinois Commerce Commission v. FERC*.[5] There, the PJM Interconnection had proposed, and FERC had accepted, a settlement that would allocate the costs of extra high voltage (EHV) transmission lines (built at 500 kV or above) to each PJM load-serving utility based on its pro rata share of the power consumed in the region. Judge Posner, writing for the court, held that FERC had failed to explain, for each load serving utility, how the benefits of EHV facilities were roughly commensurate with the costs. According to Judge Posner, if a utility on the western edge of PJM derived only $1 million in benefit from a transmission project built in the east, but could be required to pay $480 million, then "the disparity between benefit and cost" would be unreasonable.

In dissent, Judge Cudahy argued that FERC should not necessarily be required to measure precisely the costs and benefits of EHV facilities because all users of the transmission system benefit from having a robust and capable high voltage transmission system. He explained that the current transmission system is inadequate, and that EHV facilities are uniquely efficient and capable as compared to lower voltage lines. As Judge Cudahy explained, in prior cases, the courts and the agency have applied a presumption that enhanced reliability benefits all of the system's members, and that presumption should have been applied here as well.

Deciding how to allocate the costs and benefits of new transmission projects will play an important role in the debate over how to get renewable energy to consumers. FERC already deals with these cost-benefit assessments in many contexts affecting transmission investment. These matters range from innovative merchant transmission

---

3. U.S. Department of Energy, *Federal Loan Guarantees for Electric Power Transmission Infrastructure Investment Projects at* http://www.lgprogram.energy.gov/2009-CPLX-TRANS-sol.pdf. *See also*, http://www.lgprogram.energy.gov/keydocs.html.

4. U.S. Department of Energy, *Federal Loan Guarantees for Projects that Employ Innovative Energy Efficiency, Renewable Energy, and Advanced Transmission and Distribution Technologies at* http://www.lgprogram.energy.gov/2009-ren-energy-sol.pdf. *See also*, http://www.lgprogram.energy.gov/keydocs.html.

5. 576 F.3d 470 (7th Cir. 2009).

proposals, such as Chinook and Zephyr,[6] to programs such as the Southwest Power Pool's balanced portfolio system for allocating transmission costs across the region[7] and the California ISO's Location Constrained Resource Interconnection program.[8]

In October 2009, FERC requested industry comments on whether FERC should (1) enhance the transmission planning process, and (2) change the way it allocates the cost of new transmission projects.[9] FERC noted that current methods allocate costs across a single transmission provider, such as a single utility or single utility Regional Transmission Organization. According to FERC, currently there are few mechanisms that would allow the allocation of costs across multiple systems. FERC asked the industry whether it should establish processes to address cost allocation across broader geographic regions.

~~~~~~~~~~

6. *Chinook Power Transmission, LLC*, 126 FERC ¶ 61,134 (2009), *reh'g*, 128 FERC ¶ 61,074 (2009).

7. *Southwest Power Pool, Inc.*, 125 FERC ¶ 61,054 (2008), *reh'g*, 127 FERC ¶ 61,271 (2009), *reh'g pending*.

8. *California Independent System Operator Corp.*, 121 FERC ¶ 61,286 (2007), *reh'g denied*, 127 FERC ¶ 61,178 (2009). *See also*, *California Independent System Operator Corp.*, 119 FERC ¶ 61,061 (2007), *reh'g*, 120 FERC ¶ 61,244 (2007).

9. "Notice of Request for Comments," *Transmission Planning Processes Under Order No. 890*, Docket No. AD09-8-00 (issued October 8, 2009).
~~~~~~~~~~

Chapter 5

Smart Grid: Will It Get Renewables to Market and Promote Energy Efficiency?*

*By Dorothy Black Franzoni and Caileen N. Gamache, assisted by Michael L. O'Neill***

The "smart grid" is a broad term designed to summarily describe the capabilities of an advanced electricity transmission and distribution grid. Anticipated smart grid features include improvements in reliability, two-way communication capabilities for electricity pricing, demand and remote diagnosis and control of components of the transmission and distribution system, and integration of renewable energy. Although all of the specific contours of the smart grid have yet to emerge, the reality of a more intelligent grid is on the horizon.

Smart grid proponents cite several reasons in support of its development. Smart grid technologies have been estimated to have the potential to reduce power disturbance costs to the U.S. economy by $49 billion per year and to eliminate the need for approximately $46 billion in infrastructure investments over the next 20 years.[1] New storage capabilities, initially achieved in large part through charging all-electric vehicles in off-peak hours, will increase utilization of renewable energy by mitigating variable output. Consumers will benefit through greater ability to control costs and conserve energy by obtaining detailed, contemporaneous usage data to inform their consumption choices. Similarly, utilities will benefit through improved ability to control and utilize load. Finally, proponents argue, the smart grid is not a question of

---

* Originally published in *Infrastructure*, vol. 49, no. 3 (Spring, 2010).

** *Dorothy Franzoni is a partner at Sutherland Asbill & Brennan LLP in Atlanta, GA, and Caileen N. Gamache is an associate in the Washington, DC office. Michael O'Neill is an energy policy analyst in the Washington, DC office. They can be reached at dorothy.franzoni@sutherland.com, caileen.gamache@sutherland.com, and michael.o.o'neill@sutherland.com. [Ms. Gamache is now an associate with White & Case in Washington, DC.]*

1. *See* Electric Advisory Committee, *Smart Grid: Enabler of the New Energy Economy*, (December 2008) (*available at* http://www.oe.energy.gov/DocumentsandMedia/final-smart-grid-report.pdf) (last visited Jan. 19, 2010).

preference; it is a necessity. For each of the past 28 years, peak demand for electricity has outpaced transmission growth by almost 25 percent. The electricity delivery system is overburdened and without improvements, will not keep up with the nation's needs.[2]

Whose Projects Are Qualifying for DOE Smart Grid Grants?

The Department of Energy has identified five critical technologies that are central to the development of the smart grid.[3] First, the smart grid will require integrated communications for real-time two-way information and control to enable the grid to both "talk" and "listen." Second, sensing and measurement technologies are necessary to support time-of-use pricing, allow demand-side management, and enhance the efficiency and reliability of the grid by anticipating overload conditions. Next, the smart grid requires advance components such as solid state transfer switches, which provide undisturbed power using independent feeders and can mitigate most power quality issues, as well as transmission lines with advanced conductivity to allow the transport of electric energy over longer distances. The smart grid will also require advanced control methods that allow rapid diagnoses and precise solutions for load management. Finally, improved interfaces and decision support will be necessary to allow operators to understand and respond to the additional information provided by these technologies in ways that facilitate improved responses to system anomalies.

In the Energy Independence and Security Act of 2007 (EISA 2007),[4] Congress expressed its support of the development of a smart grid. EISA 2007 established a grant program to be administered by the Department of Energy, and directed the Federal Energy Regulatory Commission to adopt standards and protocols related to smart grid functionality and interoperability. In the American Recovery and Reinvestment Act of 2009,[5] Congress dangled the carrot for which smart grid proponents had been waiting by funding the Smart Grid Demonstration Program (SGDP) and Smart Grid Investment Grant (SGIG) program originally established by EISA 2007. The SGDP projects are intended to benefit either regional demonstrations of advanced technologies for use in planning and operations of the electric power system or grid-scale energy storage demonstrations. An example of the winner of a SGDP is FortZED in Ft. Collins, Colorado.[6] FortZED encompasses more than 7,000 customers and is aiming to be the world's largest active zero-energy district.

---

2. U.S. Department of Energy, *The Smart Grid: An Introduction, available at* http://www.oe.energy.gov/DocumentsandMedia/DOE_SG_Book_Single_Pages(1).pdf (last visited Jan. 19, 2010).

3. *Id.*

4. 42 U.S.C.A. § 17001.

5. 42 U.S.C.A. § 17386. *See also* DOE.gov, *American Recovery and Reinvestment Act of 2009, available at* http://www.oe.energy.gov/american_recovery_reinvestment_act.htm (last visited Jan. 19, 2010).

6. *See* FortZED Home Page, *at* http://fortzed.com (last visited Jan. 19, 2010). Information on other SGDP projects can be found at http://www.oe.energy.gov/recovery/1255.htm (last visited Jan. 19, 2010).

The purpose of the SGIG program is to facilitate the development of a variety of smart grid technologies, tools, and techniques necessary to accelerate the modernization of the nation's electric transmission and distribution system. On October 27, 2009, President Obama announced $3.4 billion in SGIG awards. One hundred applicants in 49 states will benefit from the awards. The largest portion of funding ($3 billion) will support digitized grid components such as smart meters that facilitate two-way communication and give consumers information and control over their energy consumption. For example, Baltimore Gas and Electric Co. in Maryland received $200 million to deploy smart meters to all its 1.1 million customers. Other funded projects include the installation of over 200,000 smart transformers designed to alert utilities before they fail, sensors that allow operators greater visibility of the grid to prevent blackouts and better incorporate renewable energy sources, and automated substations that enhance response time to power outages.[7]

FERC also recently adopted a Smart Grid Policy, in which it identified six areas to which the National Institute of Standards and Technology should give the highest priority in the smart grid interoperability standards development process, and adopted an Interim Rate Policy designed to encourage early investment in smart grid technologies.[8] The priority areas for interoperability standards development are: cyber security and physical security for equipment that can provide access to grid operations, development of a common information framework, wide-area situational awareness, demand response, electric storage, and electric transportation.

FERC's Interim Rate Policy provides incentive rate treatments for smart grid investments made prior to FERC's adoption of final interoperability standards. These include allowing single-issue rate treatment, permitting recovery of stranded costs of legacy systems being replaced by new smart grid equipment, and contemplating the possibility of allowing accelerated depreciation for smart grid investments. The rate treatment also covers recovery of stranded costs of smart grid investments that are never fully deployed due to circumstances beyond the investor's control, including such factors as the adoption of final interoperability standards that the equipment invested in cannot be upgraded to meet.

The effect a fully implemented smart grid could have on how we produce, deliver, and use electric energy has been compared to the dramatic effect the Internet has had on the ways in which we communicate. Not surprisingly, the challenges to realizing all of the benefits of a smart grid are substantial, and there are varying viewpoints on the pros and cons of various aspects of the smart grid. One fundamental element of a smart grid is to facilitate the increased use of generating capacity to meet load, which will require improved communication between bulk generation and transmission systems and between distribution systems and load. This will require a coordinated strategy among FERC, which has authority over the bulk transmission system, and state regu-

---

7. *See* Evan Lehmann, *Electricity: Obama Admin Invests $3.4B in 'Smart Grid' projects*, E&E ClimateWire, Oct. 27, 2009, *at* http://www.eenews.net/climatewire/2009/10/27/1 (by subscription).

8. Smart Grid Policy, 128 FERC ¶ 61,060 (Jul. 16, 2009), *available at* http://www.ferc.gov/whats-new/comm-meet/2009/071609/E-3.pdf

lators that have authority over distribution systems. To date, the smart grid has been developing in large part on a piecemeal, state-by-state basis, in many cases through technologies deployed to implement load management and real-time pricing. While greater federal oversight and involvement over interoperability standards by FERC is needed to fully achieve the benefits of a smart grid, finding the appropriate line to draw between matters that are related to retail sales, and therefore under state jurisdiction, and matters that are related to wholesale sales subject to FERC jurisdiction will be increasingly difficult.

A major concern with transitioning to a smart grid is cyber security. Another fundamental goal of the smart grid is to reduce the existing physical vulnerabilities of the grid through better two-way communications and better systems to monitor and control grid operations. This may cause new cyber vulnerabilities to emerge. Creating cyber-security systems that are impervious to outside interference, and at the same time that facilitate widespread interoperability and communication among millions of access points on generation, transmission, and distributions systems and on industrial, commercial, and residential loads is an enormous challenge.

Fully implementing a smart grid will require billions of dollars of capital investment over many years. Much of the necessary technology has only been imagined, and much is only in the early stages of development. Federal and state legislators and regulators will be faced with difficult questions of allocating costs of developing the smart grid between shareholders and consumers, and transmission owners and generators. For example, in response to FERC's proposed Interim Rate Policy, commenters argued forcefully both for and against permitting any recovery of smart grid costs before final standards are adopted. In defense of its decision to allow rate recovery, FERC cited the need for early deployment so that new technologies could be tested in the real world of utility operations. In FERC's view, rate incentives are necessary to encourage such investments.

Finally, we are all going to need to get a lot smarter about how we use electric energy. That will require access to better information and to education on how benefit from new technologies. As with the transformation from a paper-filled to a paperless world made possible by the advancement of computing and the Internet, a complete transformation to a smart grid where consumer appliances are smart enough to communicate with the grid, and consumers are smart enough to take full advantage of that functionality, will happen at an evolutionary pace.

Given that our economy relies heavily on the availability of an abundance of reasonably priced electric energy, maximizing the use of generation, transmission, and distribution capacity, increasing the availability of renewable energy, improving power quality, and reducing outages will undoubtedly yield tremendous benefits. Everyone from inventors and producers of smart grid technologies, to those involved with power generation, transmission, and distribution, to the general consuming populace, will be affected. Exactly how we as a nation go about achieving the full smart grid vision has yet to be decided and will be the subject of legislation and regulatory proceedings for many years to come.

~~~~~~~~~~
~~~~~~~~~~

2012 Update

By Dorothy Black Franzoni and Caileen N. Gamache, assisted by Michael L. O'Neill

Postscript: Has the Grid Gotten any Smarter?

The "smart grid" has continued to evolve through various initiatives at the federal, local and consumer levels since the foregoing article was published in the spring of 2010. At the federal level, the administration has engaged in several initiatives, spurred on in part by the 2012 State of the Union Address in which the President called for an "all-out, all-of-the-above strategy that develops every available source of American energy."[1] One such initiative is the administration's "Green Button" program, which encourages utilities to implement programs whereby consumers can securely download their own detailed energy usage and use that information to control energy costs.[2]

Administrative agencies have also initiated certain policy developments that may shape the industry's actions to enhance the efficiency and reliability of the grid, thereby augmenting the grid's "intelligence." For example, on March 15, 2011, the Federal Energy Regulatory Commission (FERC) issued Order No. 745,[3] which requires Independent System Operators and Regional Transmission Organizations to ensure that demand response resources participating within their markets are compensated for the cost-effective services they supply, including the ability to quickly provide balancing support to the grid.[4] More recently, FERC issued Order No. 764, a Final Rule on the Integration of Variable Energy Resources, which directs transmission providers and variable resource generator operators to take measures to facilitate the integration of renewable resources into the nation's energy supply.[5]

1. President Obama's 2012 State of the Union Address, delivered Jan. 24, 2012 (see full transcript at http://www.usatoday.com/news/washington/story/2012-01-24/state-of-the-union-transcript/52780694/1 (last visited June 27, 2012)).

2. Press Release, Office of Science and Technology Policy at The White House (Jan. 18, 2012), Administration Announces New Tools to Help Consumers Manage Electricity Use and Shrink Bills (available at http://www.whitehouse.gov/administration/eop/ostp/pressroom/01182012) (last visited June 27, 2012).

3. Demand Response Compensation in Organized Wholesale Energy Markets, 134 FERC ¶ 61,187 (2011) (Final Rule).

4. *Id.*, at p.10.

5. Integration of Variable Energy Resources, 139 FERC ¶ 61,246 (June 22, 2012).

Several state and local initiatives are also under way throughout the nation. Many such projects are supported by DOE-funded Smart Grid Investment Grants (SGIGs) discussed in the foregoing article. For example, Glendale Power and Water, owned by the city of Glendale, California, used its award of $20 million in SGIG funds to replace all 85,000 electric meters within the city with smart meters, and has begun implementing measures to improve operational efficiency and help consumers manage their electric usage. In Pennsylvania, PPL Electric Utilities Corporation is using its $38 million SGIG funds to install a technologically advanced distribution management system, distribution automation devices, and supporting communication systems in a pilot program in the Harrisburg area. Numerous other programs are under way throughout the country.[6] As of May 31, 2012, DOE has paid $2.3 billion under the SGIG program.[7]

Despite these advancements, work still needs to be done to ensure the grid is "smart" enough to integrate the nation's renewable resources. The U.S. Department of Energy's National Renewable Energy Laboratory (NREL) recently released a study that found that renewable electricity generation from technologies that are commercially available today could supply 80 percent of the total U.S. electricity generation in 2050.[8] The caveat is that although we have sufficient renewable generation technologies available, the electric system must develop the flexibility to integrate increased levels of renewable generation. The NREL report notes that this flexibility can come from many sources, including flexible conventional generation, new transmission, more responsive loads, grid storage, and other changes in power system operations, and concludes that "[n]ew 'smart grid' infrastructure would potentially greatly expand flexibility."[9]

Consumer education remains a challenge for the effective implementation of "smart grid" technologies. As discussed in the original article, in order for consumers to control their energy use, they must understand the technology and "buy in" to the program. A recent survey conducted by Distributed

---

6. Case Studies of SGIG recipients can be found at http://www.smartgrid. gov/recovery_act/ program_impacts/case_studies (last visited June 27, 2012).

7. Energy.gov, *Cumulative Federal Payments to OE Recovery Act Recipients, Through May 31, 2012*, http://energy.gov/oe/downloads/cumulative-federal-payments-oe-recovery-act-recipients-through-may-31-2012 (last visited July 6, 2012).

8. Renewable Electricity Futures Study, M.M. Hand et al. eds., 4 vols., NREL/TP-6A20-52409, Nat'l Renewable Energy Lab. (2012), *available at* http://www.nrel.gov/analysis/re_futures/.

9. *Id.* at 1–13.

Energy Financial Group found that consumers rate utilities' smart grid communications efforts "below average," and 40 percent of respondents rated them "ineffective."[10] A lack of consumer understanding has, in turn, led to some consumer resistance. According to one analysis,[11] two of the chief concerns among consumers are a fear that wireless smart meters and other devices are harmful to human health, and concern for the privacy of personal information, which some think could be jeopardized by cyber threats. Some state and local agencies have responded by requiring utilities to offer "opt-out" options to smart-grid programs. Utilities have also enhanced consumer education.

Despite many obstacles, the smart grid has indeed gotten smarter over the past couple of years. If the attention that smart grid development has received over the past few years is any indication, this will likely remain a dynamic area of the industry to watch going forward.

10. SMARTGRID.GOV, IT'S THE PLANNING, STUPID! HOW UTILITIES ARE MESSING UP WITH SMART GRID COMMUNICATIONS (June 27, 2012), *available at* http://www.smartgridnews.com/artman/publish/ Business_Consumer_Engagement/It-s-the-planning-stupid-How-utilities-are-messing-up-their-smart-grid-communications-4912.html (last visited June 27, 2012).

11. Jeff Evans, *"The Opt Out Challenge": Electric Light and Power* (posted July 3, 2012) (http://www.elp.com/index/display/article-display/2266391833/articles/electric-light-power/volume—90/issue-02/sections/the-opt-out-challenge.html?cmpid=ELPWeeklyJune122012 (last visited July 6, 2012)).

Chapter 6

A Roadmap to the Greenhouse Gas Regulatory Revolution*

*By Allen A. Kacenjar, Jr. and D. Alan Lindsey***

In the past year, the Environmental Protection Agency (EPA) has proposed and finalized rules requiring nationwide reporting of greenhouse gas (GHG) emissions (the "Reporting Rule"),[1] concluded that GHG emissions endanger public health and welfare, and developed three key rules (the "Motor Vehicle Rule," "Reinterpretation Rule," and "Tailoring Rule") designed to bring GHG regulation to mobile and stationary sources under existing Clean Air Act (CAA) authority that remain pending. Two of these three rules were finalized in late March 2010 and will have broad permitting implications for both existing air emissions sources and GHG emitters that have not previously been subject to permitting requirements. The Tailoring Rule is now scheduled to be published in May 2010. Understanding the scope of these rules and preparing in advance for their implementation is key for adapting to this upcoming regulatory environment.

How Did We Get Here, and Where Are We Anyway?

Well before the Obama administration took office, EPA began assessing potential responses to the U.S. Supreme Court's finding in *Massachusetts v. EPA*[2] that GHGs were "air pollutants" under the CAA. However, immediately after the inauguration, EPA began moving far more quickly. In April 2009, EPA issued proposed findings that: (1) GHG emissions endanger public health and welfare, and (2) motor vehicle emissions

---

* Originally published in *Infrastructure*, vol. 49, no. 3 (Spring, 2010).

** *Allen A. Kacenjar, Jr., is a principal who works out of the Cleveland office and D. Alan Lindsey is an associate in the Houston office of Squire, Sanders & Dempsey L.L.P.*

1. 74 Fed. Reg. 56260 (Oct. 30, 2009).
2. Massachusetts v. EPA, 127 S. Ct. 1438 (2007).

contribute to that problem.[3] Those findings were finalized on December 7, 2009,[4] and became effective on January 14, 2010, triggering a cascade of additional regulatory actions by EPA.

Based upon its endangerment finding, EPA concluded that it has an obligation to regulate GHG emissions from new motor vehicles.[5] As a result, EPA joined with the National Highway Traffic Safety Administration to issue the proposed Motor Vehicle Rule on September 15, 2009.[6] That rule establishes the first-ever GHG emissions standards for carbon dioxide emitted per-mile-driven for passenger cars, light-duty trucks, and medium-duty passenger vehicles. The Motor Vehicle Rule takes effect starting with model year 2012 vehicles, and was released as a final rule on March 31, 2010.

While the Motor Vehicle Rule imposes unprecedented standards on automakers, its impact resonates far more broadly. EPA believes that imposing *any* CAA regulatory limit on GHGs, including the automotive standards proposed in the Motor Vehicle Rule, automatically triggers permitting obligations for GHGs as a "regulated pollutant" under the CAA. The CAA provides that facilities that emit 250 tons per year (tpy) (100 tpy for certain sources) or more of a "regulated pollutant" are "major sources" subject to permitting and emissions control requirements.[7] While relatively few facilities emit more than 250 tpy of most pollutants, more than *six million* facilities in the United States have the potential to emit 100 tpy or more of GHGs including hospitals, shopping malls, apartment buildings, and schools.[8]

Recognizing the administrative gridlock and extraordinary burdens that its statutory interpretation would create, EPA issued two additional proposed rulemakings. First, in the draft Tailoring Rule, EPA proposed to temporarily raise the CAA permitting trigger for GHGs 100-fold, from 250 tpy to 25,000 tpy.[9] EPA asserted this revision would exempt many smaller sources from GHG permitting requirements while still requiring the largest emitters to begin taking steps to curtail GHG emissions. In its rule package, EPA took the unusual step of conceding that its proposed changes contradict the plain statutory language of the CAA. Instead, in this case, EPA elected to rely on the relatively untested legal doctrines of "absurd results" and "administrative necessity" to justify its proposed deviation.

Second, EPA conducted an "interpretive" rulemaking to define exactly when these GHG permitting obligations accrue.[10] The Reinterpretation Rule, which was finalized on March 29, 2010, attempts to resolve years of permitting litigation by establishing precisely when a pollutant first becomes "regulated" for purposes of the CAA. EPA

3. 74 Fed. Reg. 18886 (April 24, 2009).
4. 74 Fed. Reg. 66496 (Dec. 15, 2009).
5. The core provision at issue in *Massachusetts*, CAA § 202(a)(1), requires EPA to "by regulation prescribe . . . standards applicable to the emission of any air pollutant from any class or classes of new motor vehicles . . . which in his judgment cause, or contribute to, air pollution which may reasonably be anticipated to endanger public health or welfare."
6. 74 Fed. Reg. 49454 (Sept. 28, 2009).
7. 42 U.S.C. § 7479.
8. 74 Fed. Reg. 55292, 55304 (Oct. 27, 2009).
9. 74 Fed. Reg. 55292 (Oct. 27, 2009).
10. 74 Fed. Reg. 51535 (Oct. 7, 2009).

now interprets a pollutant to become regulated when a regulation that imposes an "actual control" on emissions of the pollutant "takes effect." The Reinterpretation Rule establishes January 2, 2011, as the date when the Motor Vehicle Rule will "take effect" under this test. As a result, any source seeking a CAA permit that will be issued after Jan. 2, 2011, may be required to address GHG emissions in the permitting process.

In apparent response to the flood of comments filed and direct questioning from Congress, EPA recently took the unusual step of previewing its plans for the final rules. Specifically, on February 22, 2010, EPA Administrator Lisa Jackson responded to an inquiry by several senators with a letter stating that, in addition to the deferral described above, the final Tailoring Rule will: (1) phase in permitting requirements more gradually than first proposed, and (2) include an initial permitting threshold "substantially higher" than the 25,000 tpy proposed limit. While those changes would offer welcome additional flexibility and time to develop business and legal strategy, they do little to address the ultimate concerns posed by requiring GHG permit limits on stationary sources.

Where Are We Going?

Although many believe that EPA's fast-track regulatory approach was intended to spur the adoption of comprehensive climate legislation, it appears to have had the opposite effect. Indeed, the recent political battle surrounding health care reform and the ongoing economic problems have increased opposition to climate change legislation in the near term.[11] Additionally, the Senate's current reluctance to move a politically difficult climate bill forward could become more pronounced as the 2010 elections draw near. EPA's recent softening of its GHG permitting deadlines is an apparent acknowledgement that EPA regulations—and not climate legislation—will be the first substantive GHG obligations imposed.

While the prospect of congressional action seems remote, the courtroom battles over EPA's parallel regulatory track have just begun. Recognizing the implications of EPA's endangerment finding and suite of related rules, an industry coalition filed the first legal challenge to EPA's endangerment finding on December 24, 2009. In a related move, another group filed a Petition for Reconsideration alleging that the endangerment finding was tainted by "Climategate" because "the purportedly 'scientific' information on which the Agency relied was the subject of a number of systematic manipulations, including collusion to withhold scientific information, deletion of e-mails and raw data to

11. On Capitol Hill, climate change legislation stalled in the Senate after the Waxman-Markey cap-and-trade bill was passed by the House of Representatives in June 2009. In November, the Senate Environment and Public Works Committee voted to send the Boxer-Kerry climate change bill to the full Senate—without amendment—despite a Republican boycott of the committee vote. However, a separate climate change bill being developed by Sens. John Kerry (D-Mass.), Joe Lieberman (I-Conn.), and Lindsey Graham (R-S.C.) may be able to gain some measure of bipartisan support. While the likelihood of comprehensive climate change legislation in 2010 remains uncertain, Congress may attempt to pass a more modest climate and energy bill without a cap-and-trade provision. Additionally, at least two bills have been introduced in the Senate to undo or delay EPA's regulatory action.

prevent discovery of key facts, manipulation of data and computer code to create false impressions, and concerted efforts to boycott key journals and exclude disagreement." In all, more than 16 petitions have been filed by states, industry groups, and individual corporations challenging the endangerment finding. Similarly, another coalition has challenged EPA's authority to require GHG reporting pursuant to the Reporting Rule that was finalized on September 22, 2009.

This wave of litigation will swell during the next several months, as industry and environmental groups file competing challenges on issues including: (1) the core purpose and meaning of the underlying CAA provisions, (2) the validity of EPA's scientific climate change assumptions, (3) EPA's failure to assess the magnitude and nature of related costs, and (4) whether and when any GHG permitting obligations accrue. Rather than deterring litigation, EPA's recent statements that it will change key parts of the proposed GHG rules may well trigger additional challenges—particularly from environmental groups who feel EPA has strayed too far from the statutory language. At least one key juncture in that litigation will come fairly soon, when parties ask the D.C. Circuit to take the unusual step of staying one or more of EPA's rules. While such requests are a certainty, the court's response is far less so, particularly given the high standards that apply to issuance of a stay. Absent a stay (or congressional intervention), EPA's rules will remain in place while the lengthy appeal process proceeds.

EPA's regulatory actions to address climate change truly represent a revolution in both the interpretation of the CAA and its application to sources not traditionally regulated. Given this dynamic process, it is nearly impossible to know what the regulatory landscape will look like after the smoke clears. What is clear is that we are in the midst of a major shift in environmental policy, which will ultimately require input from not just EPA but also the courts, Congress, and the regulated community.

2012 Update

By Allen Kacenjar, Jr., and D. Alan Lindsey

In the past two years, the flurry of GHG rule-related activity has continued on all fronts, including the finalization of EPA's first wave of substantive rules, appellate litigation regarding their legitimacy, and initial application of those rules to industrial sources.

On May 13, 2010, EPA finalized the Tailoring Rule setting GHG emission thresholds to define when PSD and Title V permits would be required for new and existing industrial facilities.[1] Following an initial phase-in period ("Step 1"), the Tailoring Rule currently requires all new facilities emitting GHGs in excess of 100,000 tpy CO_2e and facilities making modifications that increase GHG emissions by at least 75,000 tpy CO_2e to obtain permits with GHG emissions limits. Meanwhile, the permitting process itself has proven difficult and controversial, with high-profile battles over what constitutes the Best Available Control Technology for limiting GHG emissions across several industries. Additionally, sources emitting at least 100,000 tpy CO_2e have begun efforts to obtain operating permits—many for the first time.[2]

EPA's entire suite of GHG rules were promptly appealed by a broad coalition of industry groups and states. After extensive briefing and oral argument, on June 26, 2012, the D.C. Circuit upheld EPA's GHG vehicle and permitting rules. Specifically, the court held that EPA's Endangerment Finding and Motor Vehicle Rule were required by the Supreme Court's interpretation of the governing Clean Air Act provisions and fell within EPA's scientific discretion. The Court then concluded that the petitioners lacked the standing to challenge the Tailoring and Reinterpretation Rules because they could not prove harm, as those rules actually scale back permitting obligations that would otherwise exist.[3]

EPA continues to charge ahead with additional GHG regulations. For example, the agency recently proposed New Source Performance Standards

1. 75 Fed. Reg. 31,514 (June 3, 2010).

2. EPA issued its proposed Step 3 rule on Feb. 24, 2012, intending to maintain the Tailoring Rule's applicability thresholds for GHG-emitting sources at the Step 2 levels; the final rule is expected by July 1, 2012. 77 Fed. Reg. 14,226 (Mar. 8, 2012). Sources emitting less than 50,000 tpy of GHGs on a CO_2e basis will not be required to obtain permits for GHGs under Step 3 or any other action before April 30, 2016. 75 Fed. Reg. 31,514.

3. Coalition for Responsible Regulation v. EPA, No. 09-1322, 2012 U.S. App. LEXIS 12980 (D.C. Cir. June 26, 2012).

for GHG emissions for new fossil fuel-fired EGUs,[4] with similar obligations for petroleum refineries and other industry sectors expected to follow. Also, EPA and the National Highway Traffic Safety Administration established a national program to reduce GHG emissions and fuel consumption for medium- and heavy-duty vehicles[5] and proposed to extend the current light-duty vehicle standards to cover model years 2017 through 2025.[6] In the wake of EPA's recent D.C. Circuit victory, these rules appear to be just the beginning of GHG regulation, with new regulations on numerous other fronts (e.g., aircraft, ships) also possible.

4. 77 Fed. Reg. 22,392 (Apr. 13, 2012).
5. 76 Fed. Reg. 57,106 (Sept. 15, 2011).
6. 76 Fed. Reg. 74,854 (Dec. 1, 2011).

Chapter 7

Comments of the EPA on Climate Change*

*By Scott Fulton***

The U.S. Environmental Protection Agency (EPA) was at a crossroads on climate issues when the Supreme Court issued the *Massachusetts v. EPA* decision in 2007. The Court's ruling gave the agency explicit direction on how to address the vehicle-related petition it received.

The Court made clear that EPA was to treat greenhouse gases as "air pollutants" under the Clean Air Act, and needed to address the citizen petition on that basis. The Court then held that the Act requires EPA to consider the science of climate change meaningfully in determining whether greenhouse gas pollution is reasonably anticipated to endanger public health or welfare. The Court's instruction to limit the decision making to the science and the statutory criteria fits well with EPA's core principles. After technical staff conducted a comprehensive survey of the soundest available science and carefully reviewed hundreds of thousands of public comments, in 2009, the administrator determined that indeed greenhouse gas pollution is anticipated to endanger both public health and welfare, and that greenhouse gas emissions from motor vehicles do contribute to that problem. In addition to litigation in the D.C. Circuit, the agency has now received a number of petitions for reconsideration that are under review.

These findings obligate EPA to issue greenhouse gas emissions standards for new motor vehicles or new motor vehicle engines. Consistent with the president's direction, the agency is working with the Department of Transportation (DOT) on a joint rulemaking in which EPA will establish GHG standards for new motor vehicles under the Clean Air Act and DOT will establish fuel economy standards under the Energy Policy and Conservation Act of 1975 (EPCA). These standards will achieve substantial greenhouse gas emissions reductions and fuel savings. Together, they will reduce the lifetime oil consumption of the affected vehicles by 1.8 billion barrels while elimi-

---

* Originally published in *Infrastructure*, vol. 49, no. 3 (Spring, 2010).

** *Scott Fulton is general counsel for the U.S. Environmental Agency in Washington, D.C.*

nating 950 million metric tons of greenhouse gas pollution. The federal standards will lead to a single, harmonized, national program.

Some have suggested that EPA use its discretion to put off issuing its emissions standards, to avoid triggering Clean Air Act permitting requirements for stationary sources until Congress enacts comprehensive climate legislation. However, the president called upon DOT and EPA to harmonize emissions and fuel economy standards as the most efficient way to address these issues. This approach will allow automobile manufacturers to build a single light-duty national fleet that satisfies all requirements under both federal programs and the standards of California and other states. It will simultaneously reduce greenhouse gas emissions, increase energy security, increase fuel savings, and offer clarity and predictability for manufacturers. All of the relevant requirements can move forward in a responsible, productive manner even as work continues to secure new legislation for the long term. The EPA will do its part to ensure economic recovery as greenhouse gases are addressed in sensible ways.

Toward that end, close attention is given to the stationary-source permitting requirements that will ultimately flow from issuing vehicle standards. Implementing those requirements in a commonsense, deliberate manner will achieve meaningful progress in greenhouse gas reductions without hamstringing our economy. EPA's effort in the "Tailoring Rule" focusing permitting requirements first on the very largest stationary sources reflects that philosophy.

In the course of taking comment from the regulated community and other interested parties, EPA is mindful of concerns about practical, cost-efficient application of permitting requirements, so that requirements are phased in carefully. The agency has indicated that sources would not be subject to greenhouse gas permitting requirements this year. Also, EPA will focus on the largest sources of greenhouse gas emissions for a substantial period.

Moreover, the agency very carefully considered and learned much from the public comments received in these rulemakings, helping to improve upon the proposals. There is also a need to be mindful of the concerns of state and local permitting authorities, which look to EPA to interpret the Act's permitting requirements to enable them to meet their obligations under state and federal law responsibly.

Finally, in parallel with the actions taken on vehicles and the permitting requirements, EPA has issued rules to require larger sources of greenhouse gas emissions to keep track of those emissions and file appropriate emissions reports. Those rules do not include emissions standards; rather, they are aimed at ensuring information about the greenhouse gas emissions from the respective source categories is solid. This, again, is consistent with the determination to use discretion, thoughtfully and methodically, under the existing statute while proceeding in parallel to obtain climate legislation for the long term.

The intersection of climate science, the existing Clean Air Act, and the Supreme Court's decision raises to the forefront challenges that have been dormant for years. EPA is aware that the regulated community, the states, environmental organizations, and concerned citizens are looking for responsible action. EPA is confident that we can apply means of implementing the law that fit the circumstances, while staying within the bounds set by the Court.

~~~~~~~~~~
~~~~~~~~~~

2012 Update

By Scott Fulton

Postscript: Unambiguous Progress on Climate Change

At the risk of having the postscript overwhelm the underlying article, I would be remiss if I failed to highlight for the reader the significant progress made in addressing greenhouse gas (GHG) emissions since this article was penned. While EPA has proceeded in its typical fashion—thoughtfully, deliberately, and with ample opportunity for input from all quarters—the progress made over the last two years is really quite remarkable.

The changes in the regulatory landscape began with the foundational "Endangerment Finding" that GHG pollution is anticipated to endanger public health and welfare. Then, as required by the Clean Air Act (CAA or the Act) after making the Endangerment Finding, EPA finalized a joint rulemaking with the Department of Transportation (DOT) setting GHG standards for new motor vehicles under the CAA and fuel economy standards under the Energy Policy and Conservation Act (EPCA). EPA then issued a memorandum clarifying that, by operation of law, upon the effective date of the vehicle rule, January 2, 2011, greenhouse gases became a regulated pollutant under the Clean Air Act requiring Prevention of Significant Deterioration (PSD) and Title V permitting. In June 2010, EPA issued the "Tailoring Rule" designed to implement the permitting requirements in a commonsense, deliberate manner in order to achieve meaningful emissions reductions from stationary sources while avoiding an overwhelming increase in required permits. This Tailoring Rule limited PSD and Title V permitting requirements to the largest sources of greenhouse gases.

The Endangerment Finding, the Vehicle Rule, and the Tailoring Rule, taken together and in conjunction with the Clean Air Act, established regulatory requirements for greenhouse gases emitted from new motor vehicles, determined that such regulations subjected GHG emissions from stationary sources to PSD requirements, and limited the applicability of PSD requirements to sources on a phased-in basis. As is sometimes the case, the significance of these actions can be illustrated by the complexity of the litigation they inspired.

The full suite of GHG regulations was challenged in the U.S. Court of Appeals for the D.C. Circuit through a number of different actions and by a variety of petitioners.[1] These actions were briefed in three phases last summer and fall, then argued on February 28 and 29, 2012. Over the course of those two days, the court heard roughly six hours of oral argument; the courtroom was

1. Coalition for Responsible Regulation, Inc. v. EPA, 684 F.3d 102 (D.C. Cir. 2012).

full, with two overflow rooms receiving the arguments by audio feed. Issues included the basis for Endangerment Finding, the triggering effect of the vehicle standards on the requirement for stationary sources to obtain GHG permits, and EPA's decisions on timing and applicability in the Tailoring Rule. Notably, no one challenged the substance of the vehicle rule in its own right; it was challenged only for its triggering effect.

The judicial outcome was decisive and unanimous: the D.C. Circuit upheld all of the rules and found that EPA's interpretation of the governing Clean Air Act provisions was "unambiguously correct."[2]

With respect to the endangerment finding, the court found that the body of scientific evidence supporting the finding was substantial. It held that the agency had properly exercised its judgment in relying on the Intergovernmental Panel on Climate Change, and noted that the agency is "not required to re-prove the existence of the atom every time it approaches a scientific question."[3] Further, the court recognized the precautionary nature of Section 202 of the Clean Air Act, stating that EPA's job was to "prevent reasonably anticipated endangerment from maturing into concrete harm."[4] The court then upheld the Vehicle Rule, agreeing with EPA that once there was an endangerment finding, there was a nondiscretionary duty to regulate motor vehicles.

The court also affirmed EPA's view that the PSD and Title V permitting requirements of the Act are automatically applicable to a pollutant once that pollutant is regulated under any part of the Act.

Turning to the Tailoring Rule, the court dismissed the claims for lack of standing. It found that the rule had alleviated the harm that might otherwise have occurred and thus had not caused any injury to the litigants that could be remedied by the court. In a colorful illustration of what it deemed "speculative," the court dismissed the litigants' argument that the rule should be vacated to compel Congress to amend the Act, by citing to "Schoolhouse Rock" for the proposition that "it is not easy to become a law."[5]

At EPA we were encouraged by the outcome of this case, and see it as a historic beginning in our country's serious effort to confront the challenge of climate change. Following guidance from both the 2007 Supreme Court decision in *Massachusetts v. EPA*[6] and this year's D.C. Circuit decision, EPA has continued to move forward with care and deliberation to address the GHG mitigation challenge through a thoughtful application of the tools provided by the Clean Air Act. Second phases in the regulation of mobile and stationary sources

2. *Id.* at 113.
3. *Id.* at 120.
4. *Id.* at 122.
5. *Id.* at 147.
6. Massachusetts v. EPA, 549 U.S. 497 (2007).

have been finalized, further implementing a commonsense approach to the GHG regulation. And, in April 2012, EPA proposed a historic GHG New Source Performance Standard—the first of its kind—addressing greenhouse gas emissions from fossil-fired electric generating units. If a journey of a thousand miles begins with a single step, we are now well on our way, with the judiciary having confirmed that we are moving in the right direction.

Chapter 8

Renewable Portfolio Standards: Progress and Challenges*

*By Thomas P. Gadsden***

Preceding articles have highlighted the positive impact on the renewable energy movement of recent legislative and judicial developments, such as the tax credits and funding made available by the American Recovery and Reinvestment Act of 2009 and the U.S. Supreme Court's 2007 decision in *Massachusetts v. EPA*, 549 U.S. 497 (2007), holding that CO_2 and other greenhouse gases constitute regulatable "air pollutants" under the Clean Air Act. However, to a very great extent, the market for renewable power traces its roots to the enactment, on a state-by-state basis, of so-called "renewable portfolio standards."

Proponents of greater use of wind and solar energy sources—and, correspondingly, decreased reliance on foreign oil—have aggressively pursued their case for well over 30 years. However, it took the imposition of state mandates in the form of minimum standards for the renewable industry to gain momentum. And, the results have been dramatic. Between 2000 and 2008, electricity produced from renewable sources (excluding hydropower) grew at a compounded annual average of 12 percent per year. Indeed, in 2008 alone, wind capacity installations increased by 51 percent and solar photovoltaic installations by 44 percent.

In broad terms, a renewable portfolio standard, or RPS, requires that a designated percentage of a retail electricity supplier's energy sales or installed capacity come from renewable sources. By the end of 2009, approximately 30 states and the District of Columbia had some form of RPS program in place.[1] In most states, compliance, which is frequently measured through the possession of renewable energy credits

* Originally published in *Infrastructure*, vol. 49, no. 3 (Spring, 2010).

** *Thomas P. Gadsden, an attorney with Morgan, Lewis & Bockius LLP in Philadelphia, PA, represents electric, natural gas, and water clients on a range of state regulatory and transactional matters.*

1. Five other states and the Tennessee Valley Authority had set renewable "goals" in lieu of enforceable standards.

(RECs), is the responsibility of the individual suppliers—vertically integrated utilities in nonregulated states and default service providers and alternative generation suppliers in deregulated states.[2] By contrast, two states, Illinois and New York, have centralized the renewables procurement function in state agencies.

RPS program design varies considerably from state to state. As a general rule, states have established RPSs in the 15-25 percent range and have targeted full compliance (following as gradual "ramp up") for the 2020–2025 period. Some states, however, have been more aggressive. For example, California, by executive order, recently raised its RPS to 33 percent. Texas, on the other hand, created a statewide renewable megawatt standard to be achieved by 2015.[3]

Most state programs, however, share some common features. For example, many assess alternative compliance payments (ACPs) in the event suppliers fail to generate or procure the necessary number of RECs. In addition, numerous jurisdictions have established set-asides (e.g., a separately stated minimum solar RPS requirement) or provide extra credit for favored forms of renewable power. By way of illustration, Michigan offers a 3x multiplier for solar installations; Washington State a 2x multiplier for distributed generation; and Maine a 1.5x multiplier for "community-based projects."

Not surprisingly, the implementation of RPS programs has not been without challenge. One issue that had to be resolved early on concerned the ownership of renewable energy credits. More specifically, certain independent power producers who sold the output of their facilities to utilities under the Public Utility Regulatory Policies Act of 1978 (PURPA) contended that they had disposed of energy and/or capacity but had retained other attributes, including the RECs. In most instances, state commissions and courts have rejected that argument and have concluded that the utility purchasers acquired both the power and the associated RECs.

Disputes have also arisen due to the imposition, by certain states, of stringent geographic eligibility or delivery requirements. Thus, a handful of states have declared that existing plants cannot be used to satisfy RPS obligations; others exclude out-of-state facilities in an effort to promote local development and job creation, but thereby raising potential Commerce Clause concerns. Similarly, some RPS programs mandate that the renewable electricity actually be physically delivered within the state, while others permit RPS requirements to be met through unbundled RECs.

Though often eager to promote the development of renewable resources, state legislators and regulators have not been oblivious to the impact such initiatives might have on retail customers' rates. Indeed, many utilities are still saddled with long-term PURPA purchased power contracts that they were forced to execute in the 1980s and 1990s at "avoided cost" rates that, for a variety of reasons, turned out to far exceed actual market prices. With this history fresh in mind, states have taken a number of steps to address similar cost concerns, including (1) limiting the duration of purchase

---

2. Some states have exempted electric cooperatives and municipally owned systems, while others have relieved smaller investor-owned utilities (*e.g.*, less than 25,000 customers) of RPS compliance obligations.

3. As reported in Casey Wren's companion piece that follows, Texas has experienced explosive growth in wind power and has already exceeded its 2015 target.

contracts; (2) imposing minimum bidder and stringent credit requirements; and (3) establishing cost caps and noncompliance penalties. Thus, the majority of states that have implemented RPS programs have also determined that the purchase of renewable energy (or credits) should cause customers' rates to increase by less than 6 percent.

Apart from these structural safeguards, many states have given their regulators considerable flexibility when it comes to enforcing RPS compliance. For example, the Michigan Public Service Commission may grant extensions of its 2015 renewable energy standard deadline for "good cause." In like fashion, the New Jersey Board of Public Utilities may limit solar requirements if the total cost of solar purchase obligations for a reporting year exceeds 2 percent of the total retail cost of electricity for that year. Given the substantial uncertainties surrounding the future availability and cost of renewable resources, it seems critically important that state regulatory commissions be granted the discretion needed to adapt to changing times.

The renewable energy market has made tremendous strides over the past decade due, in large part, to the implementation by the states of RPS programs. As RPS requirements "ramp up," enforcement flexibility and measures supporting project development will be tested. And, while a national renewable energy standard has been debated, it seems likely that the states will continue to play a critical role in fostering renewable energy.

Chapter 9

More Lessons from the State Level: Texas*

By Casey Wren**

The development of wind-produced renewable energy in Texas has been a story of remarkable growth that has created some interesting economic, policy, and regulatory dilemmas that are worth studying.

Texas leads the states in total operating wind capacity, at 9,410 megawatts, and, were it a nation, Texas would rank sixth in the world in operating wind capacity, behind only Germany, the rest of the United States, Spain, China, and India. Already, the installed capacity of wind resources alone exceeds the legislatively mandated Renewable Energy Portfolio amount of 5,880 MW for 2015.[1]

Most of the wind capacity developed (and to be developed) in Texas is located in the Electric Reliability Council of Texas (ERCOT), which is an intrastate electric grid that has evolved with its own set of economic and regulatory attributes. Market-based restructuring in Texas has created much entrepreneurial activity in both traditional and renewable power generation markets. In particular, the last 15 years in ERCOT have seen a large growth in efficient, low heat-rate gas-fired generation, which, due to new technology and comparatively stable natural gas prices that more or less continued from 1983 until 2001-2002, entrepreneurs found to be the low-cost, low-risk option for investors and consumers. As a result, and despite the concerted effort to diversify the generation fuel mix in ERCOT with nuclear and coal-fired facilities in the 1970s and 1980s, today the ERCOT market is heavily dependent on gas-fired generation. According to the most recent reports of ERCOT, about 60 percent of capacity and 40 percent of energy operated in ERCOT is fueled by natural gas.

* Originally published in *Infrastructure*, vol. 49, no. 3 (Spring, 2010).

** *Casey Wren is a shareholder at Clark Thomas & Winters, a Professional Corporation, in Austin, TX, where he represents investor-owned electric and gas utilities as well as major telecommunication, water, and power generation companies. [Mr. Wren is now a partner at Duggins Wren Mann & Romero, LLP in Austin.]*

1. If the 18,500 MW of renewable wind generation currently planned is developed, renewable resources will account for more than 20 percent of the installed capacity in the state.

As economists like to say, what is important in economic analysis is often what is happening on the margin. And so, with all the market action in Texas on the margin involving one fuel—natural gas—not surprisingly gas prices finally began to rise in 2001 and 2002, and when they did, entrepreneurs looked for investment opportunities. Meanwhile, as part of the effort to develop competitive generation markets and protect consumers from manipulation of the market by incumbent generators, regulators in Texas sought to establish policies that would support new entrants into the power generation market. This meant favorable and timely interconnection service arrangements for new generation, with costs of interconnection mostly uplifted to the grid, standard terms and conditions for transmission service providers, and, perhaps most importantly, postage-stamp (as opposed to distance-sensitive) rate making for transmission service for remote generation. At the same time, intermittent (*i.e.*, non-dispatchable) generation was relieved of many of the ancillary service obligations of traditional generation. Add to this mix a state Renewable Energy Portfolio mandate, first adopted in 1999, as well as federal tax subsidies (the Production Tax Credit), and the stage was set for an eruption of wind development.

The result was that, almost overnight, multiple entrepreneurs, independently eyeing the same commercial opportunities, entered the wind space in West Texas. The result was a "Tragedy of the Commons,"[2] in which each wind developer, separately and independently consulting its own commercial self-interest, calculated the attractive revenues available in the energy markets in ERCOT due to the expected high natural gas prices and Renewable Energy Credits, but ignored the costs of the "Commons," in this case the transmission grid, for which they were not responsible. The upshot was that the Commons was soon enough congested, with its carrying capacity depleted. Thus transmission congestion management costs kept the wind production isolated, far away from load centers, and the market-clearing price of electricity (MCPE) in the West Congestion management zone of ERCOT fell quickly from the highest in the state to the lowest. Indeed, in 2008, there were many intervals—the 15-minute metering period used to calculate the ERCOT MCPE—in which the MCPE was negative.[3] Stated differently, the federal taxpayer was paying the wind operator to pay ERCOT a fee for the privilege of producing unwanted power.

The surplus of wind generation and the scarcity of transmission capacity led to calls for regulatory intervention.[4] The result was the CREZ—Competitive Renew-

---

2. *See* Garrett Hardin, *The Tragedy of the Commons, Science*, Vol. 162, No. 3859 (December 13, 1968).

3. It is interesting to note that, in many such intervals, the MCPE was marginally less than the value of the Production Tax Credit benefit available to wind operators, but only if the operator generated power.

4. Not surprisingly, the value of renewable energy credits has fallen dramatically as capacity growth has climbed well beyond the level of the 2015 mandate. The surplus of wind-operated capacity has lead to calls for increasing the size of the Texas renewable energy portfolio mandate, so far to no avail. But the rapid development of wind and the related collapse in renewable energy credit prices, as well as the paucity in development of other renewables such as solar and biomass, has led the Public Utility Commission of Texas to grant bonus renewable energy credits (valued at 2 for 1) for capacity generated by renewable energy resources other than wind.

able Energy Zone—initiative, mandated by the Texas Legislature in 2005 to increase transmission capacity to designated wind generation areas. The CREZ proceedings have almost concluded and have resulted in a commitment to invest in 15,000 megawatts of new transmission capacity at an estimated completion cost of about $5 billion, subject to a showing of financial commitment by wind generators. The estimated transmission build-out costs do not include the cost of collection transmission facilities, which will carry the wind power to the CREZ lines. Nor do the costs include the incremental ancillary costs associated with the import of large quantities of intermittent wind resources to load centers or the indirect cost of incremental wear and tear on base-load generation in Texas, some of which will be required to modify operations to follow load.

However, the build-out of the CREZ transmission means that Texas will continue to be a leader in wind development well into the future. It also means that Texas will achieve some significant fuel diversification with less reliance on natural gas for energy production, as well as reductions in emissions and water usage. It remains to be seen whether the Tragedy of the Commons will be a repeat performance, given the great potential for wind generation and the socialized, scarce transmission grid even after the CREZ build out. But it seems unlikely, if for no other reason than the wind capacity that is facilitated by the CREZ build-out approaches the limits of ERCOT's current ability to reliably manage wind penetration levels in ERCOT. In the end, the environmental and national security benefits of wind production, which is, of course, the Commons that most concerns us all, and the pace and skill of entrepreneurial and technical achievement, should not be discounted, but rather offer hope for the future.

2012 Update

By Casey Wren

Texas Renewable Energy Update: If You Build It, Will They Come?

In the last half of the first decade of the 21st century, there seemed to be virtually no limit to the appetite for newly developed wind energy production facilities situated in West Texas and the Texas Panhandle. Federal tax breaks, postage-stamp transmission ratemaking, rising natural gas prices, cheap and available credit, a legacy of inefficient generation, and an energy market heavily dependent on natural gas led to development of production facilities of all kinds, and especially renewable wind energy facilities located in the areas of the state with the highest-quality winds. But too frequently the new wind production facilities were far removed from load centers and isolated by transmission constraints. Texas led the country in wind energy development, but because of transmission congestion, the energy was bottled up in remote locations. The result was sometimes weird price signals, such as negative wholesale prices for electricity in March 2008 for up to 30 percent of the time in certain areas of the state. To relieve the congestion, an ambitious transmission build-out, known as the CREZ (competitive renewable energy zone) initiative and described in the preceding version, was administered by Texas regulatory authorities to move the emerging wind power production from remote rural areas to urban load centers.

Some of the priority transmission lines now have been completed and others are being constructed. But the confluence of events that shaped the development of wind energy has been buffeted by basic changes in the market. Natural gas prices have fallen, and access to credit is not what it was. On top of these developments, political changes and risks, including budget concerns arising from fiscal challenges, have called into question the availability and scope of federal tax breaks for renewable wind energy. Thus, while the transmission build-out continues, development of wind has slowed so much that the once-scarce transmission capacity in the CREZ region may be more robust than anyone would have thought or expected only a few short years ago. In Texas, the sequel to the Tragedy of the Commons may be “If You Build It, Will They Come?”

Part Two

Nuclear Power

Introduction

Just as renewable energy has encountered a number of new challenges since the articles in Chapter 1 were written and published in *Infrastructure*, nuclear power has faced a number of major challenges, including the March 2011 earthquake and subsequent tsunami that disabled and partly destroyed the Fukushima Daiichi Nuclear Plant on the eastern coast of Japan.

However, while the challenges in the renewable energy field have slowed progress, the licensing process for new nuclear plants continues, albeit with greater levels of scrutiny. The first article in this chapter, by Jay Gutierrez and Stephen Burdick, was published in 2009 and examined the regulatory, financial, and environmental issues that faced the developers of nuclear power plants. In their Afterword, they comment on the additional opportunities and challenges facing the industry but are generally optimistic about the long-term prospects.

Stan Blanton, chair of the Section's Nuclear Power Committee, and his colleagues described the NRC's improved licensing process for nuclear power plants in their 2010 article. In their update, they describe recent developments in the regulatory process and report on the issuance of combined construction permits and operating licenses for two nuclear plants (two units each) at the Vogtle Electric Generating Plant and at the V.C. Summer Nuclear Plant.

In the final article in this chapter, Richard Meserve, president of the Carnegie Institution for Science and former chair of the NRC, describes in detail the events surrounding the Fukushima disaster. He also examines the impacts of the accident on Japan, on regulation generally, and on the future of nuclear power. He expects that the accident will enhance the safety of nuclear power plants worldwide.

Dynda Thomas, former editor of *Infrastructure*, noted in her Editor's Note in the Summer 2011 edition that, while some countries were turning away from nuclear power, the Secretary of Energy "has stated that nuclear power remains a cornerstone of the U.S. energy system." She also expressed the hope, consistent with Dr. Meserve's expectation, that the countries that continue to depend on nuclear power will learn from the accident.

Peter V. Lacouture
September, 2012

Chapter 10

New Nuclear Power: Opportunities and Challenges*

*By Jay M. Gutierrez and Stephen J. Burdick***

Companies now considering new nuclear generation will be faced with a complex combination of opportunities and challenges. Success may depend on whether the regulatory, financial, and legislative challenges of the past are sufficiently considered by those now planning new projects. Those who do not learn from these past obstacles may be doomed to once again fall prey to them. This article highlights the regulatory, financial, and legislative issues that are likely to impact consideration of any new nuclear projects in the United States.

The first nuclear power plants developed and built in the United States enjoyed broad support from a stable financial community and bipartisan congressional leadership. By the late 1970s, further commercial development of the nuclear option had been hampered by a perceived unpredictable and destabilizing regulatory system, mismanagement of some nuclear projects, significant cost overruns and associated disallowances by state regulators, higher cost of capital, and lower than projected power demand. Orders for new nuclear plants came to a halt with the accident at Three Mile Island in March 1979. Projects not yet completed were either cancelled or subjected to considerable reevaluation and upgrades, resulting in a significantly higher cost than originally projected.

Over the past 20 years, the existing 104 operating reactors have enjoyed an exemplary safety record, and their reliable performance has contributed to the economic success of the nuclear industry. That record, when coupled with a relatively predictable and stable regulatory environment at the Nuclear Regulatory Commission (NRC),

---

* Originally published in *Infrastructure*, vol. 48, no. 3 (Spring, 2009).

** *Jay M. Gutierrez is a partner and the Energy Practice Group leader at Morgan, Lewis & Bockius LLP in Washington, D.C. He is also vice-chair of the Nuclear Committee of the ABA's Public Utility, Communications and Transportation Law Section. Stephen J. Burdick is an associate in the Energy Practice Group at Morgan, Lewis & Bockius LLP, specializing in issues involving new nuclear projects.*

has set the stage for consideration of a second generation of nuclear plants. In contrast to the initial development of nuclear power, however, new nuclear power projects are set to take off amidst unprecedented volatility in the capital markets and a prevailing congressional preference focused more on promoting renewable alternatives and other "green" initiatives.

Regulatory Issues

NRC Licensing

Under the older, so-called "Part 50" licensing regime, NRC licensing decisions followed a two-stage process. First, the NRC authorized construction of a uniquely designed reactor in a construction permit proceeding, without making a final safety decision; then years later, when the plant was substantially complete, the NRC focused on the ultimate safety sufficiency of the constructed design in an operating license proceeding.

This two-stage process resulted in applicants committing vast amounts of capital resources early in a project to procure long lead-time systems and components and to begin construction. All of this capital outlay occurred prior to an applicant securing the NRC approval necessary to eventually operate the plant. In addition, during the protracted period between construction authorization and issuance of an operating license—as long as 10 years—rules often changed, causing further and unexpected capital investment and delay. Given this history, and the demonstrated inability of the nuclear industry to control costs under these circumstances, the old way of licensing reactors was largely seen as an impediment to the development of new reactors.

In 1989, the NRC promulgated the so-called "Part 52" licensing process. This new process was designed to allow key regulatory decisions to be made before an applicant must obtain substantial funding from the capital markets for the engineering, procurement, and construction efforts. While a company considering new nuclear generation must still seek construction approval from the NRC, it may request a single combined license (COL), which includes both the construction permit and the operating license.

A potential COL applicant may now await and reference an NRC certification of a standardized reactor design, which removes design issues from the COL licensing proceeding. Similarly, prospective developers can "bank" sites through an early site-permitting process prior to incurring any construction costs. The new Part 52 also eliminates the open-ended nature of the former two-stage process by requiring a COL applicant to identify at the outset a predetermined set of inspections, tests, analyses, and acceptance criteria (ITAAC) that, if satisfied during the construction phase, will be sufficient to support an NRC decision authorizing operation.

Cumulatively, these many changes are intended to allow the private sector to better manage resources and secure regulatory approvals far in advance of the need to secure capital and commence construction.

Notwithstanding these intentions, the nuclear industry largely did not take advantage of these revised regulatory processes during the 1990s, except for a few design certifications. Thus, when the industry began to consider new baseload nuclear projects between 2000 and 2005, a large selection of preapproved reactor designs and an inventory of banked sites were unavailable.

In an attempt to jump-start pursuit of new nuclear projects, the Energy Policy Act of 2005 created three financial incentives:

1. **Production Tax Credits (PTCs)**—The PTCs provide 1.8 cents per kwh for energy produced during the first eight years of operation of qualifying plants. The PTCs have a 6,000 MWe limit that will be allocated pro rata to qualified applicants. To qualify, companies must meet various milestones, including the submission of a COL application by the end of December 2008.
2. **Loan Guarantees**—This incentive allows the Department of Energy (DOE) to make government loan guarantees for 80 percent of a project's cost. Congress so far has authorized only $18.5 billion in loan guarantees for new reactors, while the DOE is currently reviewing applications seeking loan guarantees for projects estimated to cost more than $100 billion.
3. **Standby Support Program**—The Standby Support Program is an insurance program that provides compensation to applicants for certain delays in operation caused by the regulatory process. This program will only be available to the first few qualifying applicants, and there is currently considerable uncertainty over what delays are covered.

Given these federal incentives, coupled with the increasing need for baseload generation, as well as the increased environmental costs of coal and the volatility of the price of natural gas, utilities now appear to be ready to consider new nuclear generation in earnest.

By the end of 2007, five COL applications had been filed with the NRC to construct and operate a total of eight nuclear units. In 2008, an additional 12 COL applications were filed seeking to develop an additional 18 units. In 2009, the NRC is expecting three more COL applications to be filed for five more units, with a few more applications anticipated during 2010 and 2011.

In part due to the scheduling milestones in the Energy Policy Act of 2005, as well as other market considerations, Part 52 is not being tested under ideal circumstances. For example, COL applications have been filed referencing designs not yet certified, and early site issues are being considered as a component of a COL application rather than as part of an early site permit application. The orderly progression of regulatory approvals embedded in Part 52 has been compressed for lead plants. Nonetheless, although the NRC has identified issues in processing this large number of new applications under an essentially untested process, the Part 52 regime appears to be working.

The NRC has issued design certifications and early site permits, and more are pending. The NRC has found all 17 submitted COL applications to be complete and ready for docketing, and most of the projects have been noticed for hearing. The regulatory schedules for these projects ultimately appear to support commencing construction of the new nuclear power plants in the 2012–2014 time frame, while some work that does not require NRC approval (e.g., excavation) may begin as early as this year for some plants. In short, the federal licensing of new reactor projects by the NRC appears to be working in a reasonably predictable and stable manner, and individual projects are on schedule.

State Regulation

Apart from the initial success under the federal regime just outlined, states will continue to play a critical role in the process for the vast majority of nuclear projects. Under traditional state regulation, many projects will first need to obtain a state determination that there is a need for power within the state that would be supplied by the new project. Additionally, many states will retain jurisdiction to review the prudency of a utility's decision as to the choice of reactor technology and the cost of engineering, procurement, and construction activities. These decisions will be considered in the context of alternative energy portfolio standards and retirement of plants that cause more pollution.

Whether applicants are granted the authority to immediately pass through the costs of construction to ratepayers also is a significant factor in overall project costs. The issue is whether a state will allow a utility to begin to obtain a return on its investment from ratepayers as costs are being incurred during the construction effort (construction work in progress) or whether utilities must wait until the project begins operation. This one financing element alone could make a difference of a few billion dollars in the price tag for a new two-unit nuclear facility.

In some states, enabling legislation will need to be enacted. For example, 30 years ago many states passed legislation prohibiting development of new nuclear power plants for economic reasons. These same states are now considering the repeal of such prohibitions, to set the stage for new nuclear projects. Additionally, states that want to further encourage nuclear development are considering enacting construction work in progress allowances to further enhance the prospects of project development. Finally, states are increasingly asserting an independent role on environmental issues, particularly the availability and allocation of limited water rights among competing commercial, industrial, and public projects. For many projects, water is the key threshold issue in whether to further consider a project.

Financial Issues

Beyond state rate treatment for new projects, the two commercial components that could significantly impact the prospects for future plants are long-term engineering, procurement, and construction (EPC) contracts, such that developers have a stable and predictable cost to plan against over the life of the project, and associated financing of the costs under those contracts.

Negotiating EPC contracts for nuclear projects presents a number of special challenges. The time required to complete reactor design certification and obtain a COL means that the lead time between signing an EPC contract and commencement of construction is extraordinarily long—perhaps four or more years. Due to these long lead times, it is particularly difficult for an EPC contractor to accurately predict the costs of labor and commodities (e.g., steel and concrete) so as to offer a fixed price. In addition, the interplay of the design certification and the COL issuance processes and potentially resulting design changes mean that the contractor is dealing with a somewhat changeable design. For these reasons, EPC contractors are unwilling to accept the same degree of cost risk that they would accept in a conventional construction project. To the extent EPC contractors will not or cannot take substantial cost risk, this risk will fall to the owner and, in the case of regulated utilities, the ratepayer. Steps to mitigate risk include cost sharing among multiple project participants and evaluating and more precisely fixing costs at predetermined milestones.

One goal of an EPC contract, in addition to price certainty, is a fixed time schedule. In a conventional EPC contract, the contractor has sole control of the project site until completion and testing of the plant, and as a result does not have the risk that there will be a delay due to actions by the owner. In the nuclear context, such "turnkey" projects are disfavored, as the owner-licensee must exercise greater control throughout the process, and especially once fuel is delivered to the site. There is also the risk of a delay due to action or inaction by the NRC. This necessitates the creation of a mechanism for determining whether a delay is caused by the contractor or results from actions by the owner or the NRC.

Other challenges for nuclear plant EPC contracts include the scarcity of qualified engineering and skilled labor personnel and manufacturing capacity limits for heavy forgings for reactor vessels. These issues create additional project risk that may not be fully covered by the EPC contractor.

Assuming an EPC contract can be negotiated, financing remains a significant variable. The market capitalization of leading financial institutions has been dramatically reduced. From 2007 to the present, a number of leading financial institutions have disappeared, merged, or survived with only drastically reduced market capital to lend. Beyond this unprecedented instability in the market, the utility sector as a whole faces significant capital needs for the current fleet of generating facilities and infrastructure issues apart from considerations of new nuclear build. With the need for capital to not only construct new generating facilities but also provide for transmission, while retrofitting old plants and other infrastructure demands, the potential for an industry-wide funding gap presents increasing concern.

These competing demands on the market cause some financial analysts to see first movers as having an advantage. Other, more conservative analysts believe a "wait and see" approach better positions a company to take advantage of a potential second wave of nuclear projects after further clarification on the regulatory, legislative, and financial fronts.

Those who counsel holding back argue that there is still considerable variation in the estimates for new build. They further argue that, despite the NRC's efforts in standardization and industry consolidation, Part 52 remains largely untested and a utility's ability to construct a massive project on time and on budget remains suspect. Similarly, while some point to recent experiences in Japan as evidence of the ability to construct nuclear plants on schedule and on budget, others point to current experiences in Europe for delays and cost increases.

These competing arguments suggest that all but the bold first movers will ultimately wait to construct new nuclear projects. Although a handful of utilities have already negotiated and signed EPC contracts, press releases indicate that these contracts do not necessarily commit these companies to construction. Such decisions may await both additional stability in the financial markets and clarification by state regulators, as well as the nature and scope of possible federal energy legislation.

Legislative and Environmental Issues

Although some argue that further legislative incentives may not be necessary to pursue nuclear, the relative value proposition for nuclear will only increase as the real costs and practical constraints of renewable power and the environmental costs of fossil generation are better understood and taken into account. Should there be a comprehensive clean air bill enacted that includes a cap and trade regime for fossil plants, or if the Environmental Protection Agency (EPA) initiates rule-making in this area, then nuclear will become more attractive from both a financial and environmental perspective. Indeed, many believe the "greening of nuclear" is the task that remains to enable the public to see nuclear in the same way that it currently views wind and solar, but with the added value of being able to provide significant baseload generation for the future.

President Obama and congressional leaders have made clear that climate change legislation is a top priority. In his first budget, President Obama assumed that a cap and trade system for greenhouse gases would pass in 2009, effective in 2012. The cap and trade proposal outlined in the budget calls for a 14 percent reduction in emissions below 2005 levels by 2020, with an 83 percent reduction by 2050. In the House of Representatives, Congressman Waxman (D-CA), who chairs the most important committee for such legislation, has recently proposed comprehensive energy legislation and has indicated that he intends to vote a bill out of his committee by May 25, 2009. While passage of climate legislation is more uncertain in the Senate, Senate Majority Leader Reid (D-NV) has indicated that a climate change bill will be a priority, and the addition of new Democratic senators improves the chances for passage in that chamber.

Also gaining traction in Congress is a federal renewable portfolio standard requiring utilities to provide a certain percentage of their energy from renewable sources. Congressman Waxman's proposed legislation for example, would require electricity suppliers to meet 6 percent of their load from renewable energy by 2012, and 25 percent by 2025. Renewable energy is not defined to include nuclear power in Congressman Waxman's bill, although the ranking member of the Senate Energy and Natural Resources Committee, Senator Murkowski (R-AK), has called for including nuclear power in any renewable portfolio standard.

Further, the EPA is currently reconsidering whether the Clean Air Act is an appropriate mechanism to regulate greenhouse gases. Action by the EPA could put pressure on Congress to pass cap and trade legislation, or it could result in regulation of greenhouse gases under EPA's current authority, thereby increasing the costs for fossil fuel-based energy. Any of these developments would appear to provide additional benefits to any company considering nuclear.

Conclusion

Companies considering new nuclear generation face significant opportunities and challenges. Some of the opportunities are provided by the streamlined NRC regulatory regime for issuing new reactor licenses, the financial incentives in the Energy Policy Act of 2005, and beneficial construction cost recovery mechanisms. Challenges remain, including unprecedented instability in the capital markets, negotiations for EPC contracts, and potential heavy scrutiny from state regulators.

While some companies continue to move forward under these conditions, the merits of the nuclear option will become clearer only after improvements in the financial markets and realization of its environmental and financial benefits when compared to other energy options.

2012 Update

By Jay M. Gutierrez and Stephen J. Burdick

The more than three years that have passed since our article, *New Nuclear Power: Opportunities and Challenges*, was published in 2009 can be characterized as a turbulent period for new nuclear power projects in the United States, but with some significant successes.

Additional Opportunities

New nuclear power projects have achieved a number of important milestones and successes over the past few years, resulting in additional opportunities for these projects. For example, the U.S. Nuclear Regulatory Commission (NRC) has issued its first licenses in more than 30 years for construction of a new nuclear power plant. Specifically, in February 2012, the NRC issued combined licenses (COLs) to construct and operate two new nuclear units at the Vogtle Electric Generating Plant near Waynesboro, Georgia. Shortly thereafter, in March 2012, the NRC issued COLs to construct and operate two new nuclear units at the V.C. Summer site in Fairfield County, South Carolina. These plants are now under construction.

Additionally, the NRC continues to review other new reactor licensing applications, including early site permit, combined license, and design certification applications, and has recently issued amendments to other design certifications. During the past few years, the nuclear industry also has shown an increased interest in small modular reactors, and a number of companies are preparing applications for NRC approval of their designs.

Additional Challenges

New nuclear power projects likewise have faced increased challenges over the past few years. At the top of the list is the March 11, 2011, accident at the Fukushima Daiichi nuclear plant in Japan. This event resulted in increased regulation through orders and other regulatory mechanisms, which impose additional costs, delay, and litigation upon new nuclear power projects.

Additionally, some "merchant" nuclear power projects face new economic challenges and must overcome lower electricity demand and lower prices in the United States without any cost-recovery mechanisms that may exist in a regulated environment. One utility recently canceled its new nuclear project in a merchant generation market, citing an "unfavorable economic outlook." Other examples of recent challenges include evolving regulatory requirements; a longer new reactor licensing process than hoped; and the NRC's suspension of license issuance until it has addressed the D.C. Circuit's decision to vacate and remand the NRC's Waste Confidence Rule regarding long-term storage of high-level waste.

Conclusions

These developments over the past few years have only heightened the opportunities and challenges faced by new nuclear projects that we discussed in 2009. Some of these projects have been able to overcome the challenges and navigate the many regulatory and financial obstacles to begin construction of new reactors, while others have stalled in the regulatory process or succumbed to economic pressures. These years have reinforced the continued struggle between the opportunities and challenges for these projects, and have reaffirmed our 2009 conclusion that "the merits of the nuclear option will become clearer only after improvements in the financial markets and realization of its environmental and financial benefits when compared to other energy options."

Chapter 11

The NRC's Improved Licensing Process for Commercial Nuclear Power Plants—in Theory and Practice*

*By M. Stanford Blanton, William A. Graham, Jr., and Millicent W. Ronnlund***

> *By developing Part 52, the Commission created a more predictable application process that allowed utilities to go through those steps sequentially. . . . But almost no one is following that ideal process. Instead, we are once again doing everything in parallel. . . .*
>
> —Commissioner Gregory B. Jaczko,
> Nuclear Regulatory Commission[1]

> *In theory, theory and practice are the same. In practice, they aren't.*
>
> —Albert Einstein

In 1989, the Nuclear Regulatory Commission revised its regulations for licensing commercial nuclear power plants by promulgating Part 52 of the NRC's regulations in Title 10 of the Code of Federal Regulations (Part 52).[2] After legal challenges called into question the NRC's authority to issue the regulation under the Atomic Energy Act of 1982 (AEA),[3] Congress expressly authorized the centerpiece of Part 52, i.e., the Combined Construction Permit and Operating License (combined license), by amending the AEA

---

* Originally published in *Infrastructure*, vol. 49, no. 4 (Summer, 2010).

** *M. Stanford Blanton is a partner and William A. Graham, Jr., and Millicent W. Ronnlund are associates with Balch & Bingham LLP, in Birmingham, Alabama, where all three specialize in energy.*

1. "New Opportunities to Invest in Nuclear Safety," Prepared Remarks for Commissioner Gregory B. Jaczko (February 12, 2009), *at* http://www.nrc.gov/reading-rm/doc-collections/commission/speeches/2009/s-09-001.html.

2. 10 C.F.R. Part 52.

3. *See* Nuclear Information Resource Service, et al. v. NRC, 969 F.2d 1169 (D.C. Cir. 1992).

via the Energy Policy Act of 1992. The combined license was intended to avoid the inherent difficulty in the NRC's old two-step reactor licensing process in Part 50 to the NRC's regulations (Part 50),[4] which required massive investment by the license applicant in the construction of the facility prior to NRC approval of the site, reactor design, or programs for the operation and maintenance of the plant. In addition to the combined license, NRC created in Part 52 two additional licensing tools, the design certification rulemaking and the early site permit (ESP), to make plant licensing even more efficient.

Taken together, as the quotation from the NRC Chairman Jaczko indicates, the certified design, early site permit, and combined license promised to create an orderly and efficient process in which all licensing issues in each step of the process would be resolved before proceeding to the next step, and all licensing issues would be finalized before significant investment in the physical plant by the licensee. Alas, as the quotation from Einstein indicates, theory and practice are not always identical, and that has been the case for at least the first few applicants for combined licenses. This article will explore the reasons for applicants' decisions to deviate from the "norm" as envisioned by NRC when it promulgated Part 52, the NRC's practical response to the economic and technical realities that led to those deviations, and the probability that as subsequent applications based on current designs are submitted, the process will return to the one that NRC envisioned when it promulgated the regulation.

Old Process: The Problems of Part 50's Two-Step Licensing Process

Each nuclear power plant currently operating in the United States was licensed under Part 50's two-step licensing process. As noted above, the NRC originally adopted the Part 52 process in order to resolve the problems caused by the "old" Part 50 two-step process for licensing the construction and operation of nuclear reactors. As the first step under Part 50, an applicant must apply for a construction permit, which requires, inter alia, review by NRC staff of the applicant's plans for construction, a safety assessment of the applicant's proposed site and the preliminary design of the reactor, a review and analysis of the preliminary design criteria for the facility and the technical qualifications of the applicant, and an environmental report. The construction permit requires a hearing at the NRC on both contested issues brought forward by "interested parties" who intervene in the proceeding as well as a mandatory hearing on uncontested issues.

If a construction permit is granted, the applicant may commence construction of the reactor (but not operation). After—and only after—completion of construction, Part 50 allows an applicant to take the second step by amending the application construction permit to request a license to actually *operate* the new plant, which triggers the opportunity for another hearing on safety issues already addressed in the construction permit hearings, as well as issues on emergency planning and environmental issues. The lack of finality inherent in the two-step licensing process resulted in extensive design changes and retrofits to plants between the construction permit and operating license phases and in extensive delays in the commencement of operation of completed plants in which the

4. 10 C.F.R. Part 50.

owners had made substantial investments during litigation by opponents of the plants in post-construction operating license hearings. Massive delays and cost overruns plagued plants licensed under the two-step process and led to one plant, the Shoreham facility on Long Island, being dismantled before it ever commenced commercial operation because it failed to receive an operating license over issues with its emergency plan.[5]

New Process: The Theory of Part 52

The new Part 52 process was developed in order to eliminate the regulatory uncertainty inherent in the two-step construction permit/operating license process. The goal of the new process is to enable license applicants and the NRC to finally resolve applicable licensing and regulatory requirements in advance of the commencement of construction of the reactor in order to avoid the post-construction design changes, retrofits, and hearing delays that plagued the Part 50 process. As originally conceived, the Part 52 process would resolve all licensing issues (i.e., safety and environmental issues) prior to construction by providing an applicant with a combined license. The single most important element of the combined license process is that the technically complex process of resolving reactor design issues is managed in design certification rulemakings, which are public notice and comment proceedings that each address a single proposed standard design. During these rulemakings, vendors propose a design control document (DCD), which describes the essential features and functions of the nuclear plant. All design safety issues are resolved in the rulemaking process, and the resolutions of these issues are final (with a few limited exceptions) for the purpose of combined license applicants who reference the certified designs in their applications. Similarly, a combined license that is issued based on a certified design finally resolves all issues regarding the design as constructed on the applicant's site, provided the applicant demonstrates through inspections, tests and analyses, and acceptance criteria (ITAAC) specified in the license that the facility has been constructed as designed.

Part 52 provides an additional avenue for resolving licensing issues before construction by allowing applicants to propose a reactor site in order to give the NRC (and intervenors) a chance to evaluate the site's suitability in terms of its geology, seismology, hydrology, and particular environmental concerns. If the proposed site satisfies NRC's safety requirements and environmental review under the National Environmental Policy Act (NEPA), the NRC may issue the applicant an early site permit (ESP), which resolves all site suitability and environmental issues regarding the site. As with the certified design, a combined license applicant may rely on all site safety and environmental issues resolved in an ESP proceeding as resolved for the purpose of a combined license application referencing that ESP.

As noted above, the NRC structured Part 52 so that an applicant for a combined license need only reference a certified DCD and finalized ESP in order to avoid revisiting any issues in the combined license proceeding that were resolved in either the design certification rulemaking or the ESP proceedings. The vision of the NRC in promulgating Part 52 was premised on this sequence—i.e., finalizing design and site issues before

5. Robert W. Williams, *Intergovernmental Conflict over Emergency Planning: the Politics of the Shoreham Nuclear Power Plant*, 30 (No. 2) Polity 285-314 (Winter 1997).

applying for a combined license. If that order is followed, the combined license proceeding would then focus primarily on the compatibility of the certified design to the approved site, the applicant's proposed programs, any ITAAC not included in the DCD or the ESP, and any new or significant environmental issues that arose since the issuance of the ESP.

Part 52: Theory vs. Actual

The NRC's vision for Part 52 assumed that fully certified designs would be available to be referenced by combined license applicants in order for the applicants to complete the expected 44-month combined license review,[6] and then complete construction, which is estimated to require as long as 48 months from the commencement of safety-related activities until the completion of startup. Combining those durations illustrates that a certified design would need to be available as long as eight years prior to the applicant's need for the power from the new plant. Given that none of the designs referenced in the first wave of combined licenses are expected to be finally approved by NRC prior to mid- to late-2011, waiting on a finally certified design would delay commercial operation of the new units until the 2019-2020 time frame.

In addition, in order to have avoided any concurrent design review and combined license proceedings, one would have had to ensure that no changes to the certified design would be required or desirable during the review of the combined license. Although three standard designs had been certified during the 1990s and one in 2006,[7] none of the first wave of combined license applicants referenced those designs in their applications without proposing to change the design from that certified. Those design changes are either being processed in the context of an amendment to the certified design or as departures from the certified design in the combined license proceeding. Other combined license applicants referenced pending applications for certified designs that have not yet been approved.

The reasons for applicants' pursuit of combined licenses in parallel with the review of amended or uncertified designs are varied. They include issues as straightforward as applicants' preferences for particular standard designs, coupled with a need for generation that would not allow the applicants to wait for the final approval of the design before beginning the combined license process. Reasons also include the complexities inherent in finalizing a certified design to the point required for a combined license application and, ultimately, construction, with the attendant and inevitable alterations to the design that occur during the process.

Economic and Financial Pressures

Aging baseload electric capacity, high productivity, and excellent safety records achieved by the existing fleet; increased emphasis on the reduction of greenhouse gas emissions

6. *See* NRC's "Frequently Asked Questions about License Applications for New Nuclear Power Reactors," § 1.3.1.3, NUREG BR-0468 (December 2009).

7. *See* "Design Certification Applications for New Reactors," *at* http://www.nrc.gov/reactors/new-reactors/design-cert.html.

from power plants; natural gas price volatility and supply uncertainty; new advanced reactor designs and increased confidence in the NRC's new licensing process combined to bring about a revival of interest in a new fleet of nuclear power plants early in the first half of the last decade. Thus, many utilities not only planned significant amounts of new baseload generation to be installed in the last half of this decade, new nuclear plants were the option of choice for many of these companies. In addition, the Energy Policy Act of 2005 (EPAct 2005)[8] provided several incentives for the construction of new nuclear plants, most of which were designed to most directly benefit the first plants to be licensed and/or operated. As a result, sixteen combined license applications to build 24 new reactors were filed with the NRC during 2007 and 2008,[9] with six filed shortly before the December 31, 2008, deadline imposed by EPAct 2005—most with the expectation that the proposed units would be fully licensed and constructed by the end of 2017. These reactor need dates would be unobtainable if the applicants had delayed submission of their license applications until the designs were finally approved. In response, applicants acted to condense the schedule by submitting combined license applications that would be reviewed concurrently with the design certification rulemakings that they referenced. As illustrated in the hypothetical timeline diagram below, pursuing a combined license while the design it references is still being certified generally results in receiving the combined license years before it would have been obtained if the applicant had instead waited for final design approval.

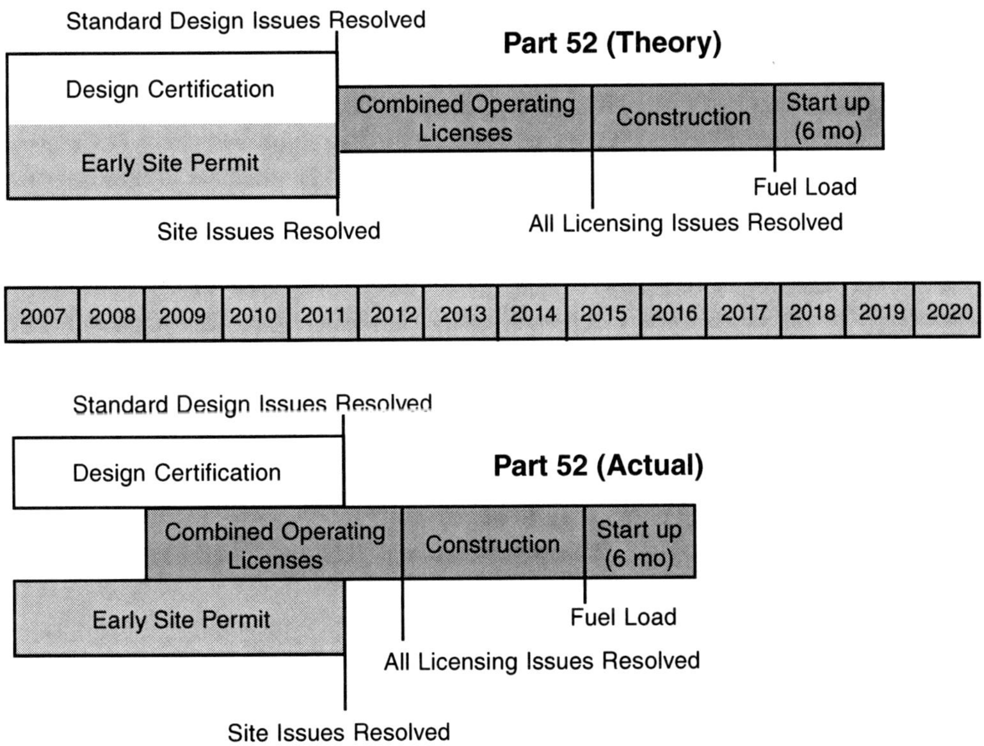

8. Energy Policy Act of 2005, Pub. L. No. 109-58.
9. *See* NRC website at http://www.nrc.gov/reactors/new-reactors/col.html.

Design Issues

NRC's regulations applicable to the certification of standard designs require applicants to provide in their DCD "a level of design information sufficient to enable the Commission to judge the applicant's proposed means of assuring that construction conforms to the design and to reach a final conclusion on all safety questions associated with the design. . . . The information . . . must include performance requirements and design information sufficiently detailed to permit the preparation of acceptance and inspection requirements by the NRC, and procurement specifications and construction and installation specifications by an applicant."[10] In translation, while all of the information necessary to enable the NRC to determine whether the fundamental design of the reactor is safe, much of the work involved in finalizing design details necessary for construction of the plant are not. As a result, an extensive amount of detailed engineering is necessary to advance a certified design to the stage where it can be constructed, or even referenced in a combined license. Although there is no requirement to do so, this work has typically not progressed in any substantial way until serious customers for the design appear.

As the finalization of certified designs progressed, the need to address issues in (or, in some cases, make improvements to) the design as reflected in the certified DCDs was revealed. For example, General Electric's Advanced Boiling Water Reactor DCD initially incorporated an ITAAC that was incompatible with the certified design and an element that was unable to be engineered as designed.[11] Another DCD (Revision 15 of the Westinghouse AP1000) assumed, for purposes of seismic analysis, that the reactor would be sited on solid rock. In order to certify the design for other than hard rock sites, Westinghouse submitted a revised version of the AP1000 DCD (i.e., Revision 16), which (among other things) changed the design to accommodate a soft soil site.[12] While many of the post-certification changes to the design are not major changes to how the plant operates or do not alter its physical appearance, if they are inconsistent with the certified DCD they must be approved by the NRC before a combined license referencing the amended design can be issued. Moreover, while many of these issues should not resurface after the designs are finalized and constructed, factors such as operational experience and advancements in technology make additional changes to the standard designs in the future more likely than not.

Customer Preference and NRC Resources

Another factor in applicants' decisions to pursue combined licenses in parallel with the design certification rulemaking for the standard design referenced in the application was

10. 10 C.F.R. § 52.47.

11. *See* STP Nuclear Operating Company (Combined License Application for South Texas Project Units 3 and 4), Departures Report (Rev. 3) - Chapter 02 - Departures Requiring Prior NRC Approval - Section 02.01 Tier 1 and Tier 2 Departures from the DCD (September 16, 2009) at pp. 2.1-3–2.1-4 and 2.1-13–2.1-14, *available at* Accession No. ML092931651.

12. Semiannual Update of the Status of New Reactor Licensing Activities, February 2007, at p. 2, *available at* http://www.nrc.gov/reading-rm/doc-collections/commission/secys/2007/secy2007-0039/enclosure1.pdf.

simple customer preference for the design in question. Applicants' preferences, combined with their need for plants to be constructed on schedules that were inconsistent with NRC's resources for reviewing the multiple design and license applications that were submitted, led applicants to reference pending DCD applications, notwithstanding that the NRC had not yet completed, or in some cases significantly begun, review of the referenced designs. Moreover, the number of pending designs has forced NRC to prioritize its review of standard designs, with emphasis on those designs referenced by developers whose projects have progressed the furthest commercially and in the other aspects of licensing. The result is that some applicants have suspended their projects or changed technologies because of the lack of progress in the certification of their referenced design. In any event, the review of these combined license applications will by necessity run in parallel with the certification proceedings for those designs.

NRC Response—Adaptability and Flexibility

As a result of the factors described above, only two of the five DCDs referenced in the combined license applications submitted in 2007-2008 had been certified (i.e., General Electric's Advanced Boiling Water Reactor and the Westinghouse AP1000). A total of seven combined license applications referenced one of these two designs. As noted above, however, even those certified designs were and are in the process of undergoing significant changes. In one case, those changes are a part of the combined license application itself. In the other, the changes are part of an amendment to the design certification rule that is referenced in the combined license applications and is being processed concurrently with those applications. The other nine combined license applicants referenced designs that have been submitted to NRC for certification, but not yet approved.

The concurrent design and combined license applications created procedural challenges for the NRC and applicants immediately, as they attempted to implement the new licensing process for the first time. As an initial matter, the NRC had to determine how to evaluate a combined license application when the reactor design has not yet been approved, and in fact is still changing. A related issue was how to retain the benefits of finality of issue resolution that are fundamental to the Part 52 process when parallel proceedings provided opportunities for intervention in the combined license proceeding before issues were finally resolved in the design certification rulemaking or ESP proceeding. Notwithstanding the deviation between the vision of Part 52 and the utilization of the regulation by the initial applicants, as expressed in the chairman's quotation, NRC anticipated a number of these issues when it promulgated Part 52 (and then amended it in 2007), and continues to effectively manage them in its implementation of the regulation.

First, as noted above, NRC regulations expressly allow a COL applicant to reference a pending (i.e., unapproved) application for a certified design. 10 C.F.R. §52.55(c) expressly authorizes a combined license applicant to reference "a design for which a certification application has been docketed but not granted." Such pending design certification applications are referenced at the risk of the applicant, which means that changes to the design that may be required in the design certification proceeding must be accounted for in the combined license application. A similar provision in Part 52 allows combined license applicants to reference pending applications for an ESP for the site proposed in the combined license application.

The NRC also recognized the validity of referencing pending design certifications and ESP applications in its Final Policy Statement on the Conduct of New Reactor Licensing Proceedings (policy statement).[13] The policy statement instituted the "Design-Centered Approach," through which the NRC requires that all design-related contentions raised in combined license proceedings be resolved in the design certification rulemaking proceeding. Those contentions are held in abeyance in the combined license proceeding if they are otherwise admissible in the combined license proceeding (i.e., even if the design-related aspect of the contention were resolved). The policy statement instituted a similar procedure for concurrent combined license and ESP proceedings; site suitability or environmental contentions in the combined license proceeding are referred to the ESP proceeding and are held in abeyance in the combined license proceeding if otherwise admissible. These considerations help to avoid the resolution of design or site suitability issues in the combined license proceeding with the attendant duplication of effort and risk of inconsistent results. Accordingly, the policy statement maintains the benefits of finality intended by Part 52 for the parallel proceedings.

Finally, the NRC's management of licensing proceedings involving concurrent combined license and design certification proceedings has given effect to its regulations and the policy statement in a way that allows both proceedings to progress without unwarranted delay or duplication of issues. In *Progress Energy (Shearon Harris 2 & 3)*,[14] the NRC interpreted the policy statement and 10 C.F.R. § 52.55(c) to reject a petitioner's contentions that a combined license application was incomplete simply because it referenced a pending amendment to a DCD. Accordingly, the commission expressly approved the processing of parallel certified design and combined license proceedings under the design-centered approach in a way that provides significant efficiencies, conserves NRC manpower, and maintains consistency of regulation.

Conclusion

While the initial wave of combined license applications has not fully met NRC's expectation for the orderly sequence of issue resolution it envisioned for Part 52, the agency and the participants in the licensing process have worked effectively to implement the process in a way that reconciles the fundamental principles of Part 52 with the practical technical and economic considerations that influence how power plants are ordered, designed, and constructed. While particularly challenging for the initial wave of applicants, the process should come closer to NRC's vision after those designs are finalized and constructed. Even then, however, the practical approach that the NRC has demonstrated in implementing its new regulation will be necessary in order to continue the momentum of the renewal of nuclear power.

~~~~~~~~~~

13. Conduct of New Reactor Licensing Proceedings; Final Policy Statement, 73 FR 20963 (April 17, 2008).

14. *Progress Energy Carolinas, Inc.* (Combined License Application for Shearon Harris Nuclear Power Plant, Units 2 and 3), CLI-08-15, 68 NRC 1, 4 (2008).
~~~~~~~~~~

2012 Update

M. Stanford Blanton, William A. Graham, Jr. and Millicent W. Ronnlund

Recognizing that revisions to pending design certifications impacted the schedule for both the designs and combined license applications referencing those designs, in November 2009 the National Regulatory Commission (NRC) issued Interim Staff Guidance DC/COL-ISG-011 permitting applicants to "freeze" a proposed design in order to facilitate scheduling for NRC review.[1] The freeze point establishes the basis upon which NRC may certify a design, and any changes submitted after that point are reviewed after the certification is issued.

In its licensing-basis information for the Amendment, Westinghouse Electric Co. designated Revision 17 (2008) as its "freeze point" for the licensing review of its AP1000 Design Amendment.[2]

The NRC implemented its updated rulemaking process for design certifications such as the AP1000 Design Amendment[3] and updated its internal procedures to anticipate combined license mandatory hearings in reliance on the Final Safety Evaluation Reports (FSER) issued for designs, rather than awaiting certification.[4] Under this new procedure, the Commission plans to affirm its adjudicatory decision on the combined license four months after the combined license's FSER and Final Environmental Impact Statement are completed, if the design has been certified. If the certification is still pending at the four-month mark, the Commission will affirm its adjudicatory decision on the combined license immediately after it affirms the final design certification rulemaking.

On December 30, 2011, the NRC certified the AP1000 Design Amendment, approving Revision 19 to Westinghouse's AP1000 DCD.[5] Additionally, the NRC approved an amendment to General Electric's Advanced Boiling Water Reactor design, effective January 17, 2012.

1. DC/COL-ISG-011, *"Finalizing Licensing-basis Information"* (ADAMS Accession No. ML092890623).
2. Rulemaking Issue Affirmation, http://www.nrc.gov/reading-rm/doc-collections/commission/secys/2011/2011-0145scy.pdf.
3. Streamlining Design Certification Rulemakings, SECY-09-0018 (Jan. 30, 2009).
4. Revisions to Internal Commission Procedures Section on Mandatory Hearings, SECY-11-0042 (Mar. 25, 2011).
5. *See* "Design Certification Application Review—AP1000 Amendment" *at* http://www.nrc.gov/reactors/new-reactors/design-cert/amended-ap1000.html.

Shortly after certifying the AP1000 Design Amendment, the NRC issued combined licenses for the Vogtle Electric Generating Plant Units 3 and 4, which incorporated by reference Revision 19 of the AP1000 DCD, on February 10, 2012,[6] marking the first license approved since the adoption of the streamlined licensing process promulgated by Part 52 and the first nuclear power plant license approved by the NRC in more than 30 years.[7] On March 30, 2012, the NRC also issued combined licenses to construct two reactors at the V.C. Summer Nuclear Plant.[8]

To avoid construction difficulties (for example, in incorporating design changes postponed by the "freeze point"), the NRC has established a Preliminary Amendment Request (PAR) process, permitting licensees to proceed with changes while awaiting approval of the corresponding license amendment request (LAR).[9] Work under an approved PAR is done "at risk," which means that a subsequent LAR denial requires the licensee to restore the site to its current licensing basis.

6. Vogtle Electric Generating Plant, Units 3 and 4; Issuance of Combined Licenses and Limited Work Authorizations and Record of Decision, 77 Fed. Reg. 12,332 (Feb. 29, 2012).

7. 10 C.F.R. Part 52.

8. V.C. Summer Nuclear Station, Units 2 and 3 Combined Licenses and Record of Decision, 77 Fed. Reg. 21,593 (April 10, 2012).

9. *See* COL-ISG-025, *Interim Staff Guide on Changes during Construction under 10 C.F.R. Part 52* (ADAMS Accession No. ML111530026).

Chapter 12

Nuclear Power After Fukushima*

*By Richard A. Meserve***

On March 11, 2011, the largest earthquake in modern Japan's history, coupled with the resulting tsunami, devastated the eastern Japanese coast. The aspect of the earthquake and tsunami that has attracted the widest public attention and ongoing concern is the continuing saga associated with the resulting accident at the Fukushima Daiichi nuclear plant. A complete assessment of the accident at that plant may require years, so the whole picture cannot yet be known. This article will seek to explore some of the ramifications of the accident based on the facts that are known today.

The Event

When the earthquake struck, units 1–3 at the Fukushima Daiichi site were operating. The other three reactors at the site were shut down for maintenance. There is some uncertainty as this is written as to the extent of the ground motion the earthquake produced above the design basis for the units, and what the impact was on the structures. In any event, the three operating reactors automatically shut down ("scrammed"). And because the earthquake resulted in the loss of offsite power, the emergency diesel generators started and provided backup power to run the plant's cooling systems. Then, approximately 55 minutes after the earthquake, a tsunami of about 14 meters struck the plant. The tsunami engulfed the diesel generators, their fuel supply, the backup batteries, and the electrical switchgear, resulting in an extended blackout of the entire station. The tsunami was well above the 5.7 meter design basis for the plant and apparently no thought had been given to the consequences of a tsunami exceeding the design basis.

When a reactor shuts down, the fuel in the reactor core still emits a substantial amount of radiation and heat—initially about 7 percent of the full power level, decaying rapidly thereafter. With the loss of backup power and with the diesels inoperative, the three reactors that were operating when the earthquake struck lost the ordinary

---

* Originally published in *Infrastructure*, vol. 50, no. 4 (Summer, 2011).

** *Richard A. Meserve is a senior of counsel at Covington & Burling LLP and is president of the Carnegie Institution for Science. He was chairman of the US Nuclear Regulatory Commission from 1999 to 2003.*

means to provide core cooling. Two of the reactors had reactor core isolation cooling (RCIC) systems, steam-driven pumps to provide cooling water to the core in an emergency, but these pumps eventually became inoperable or ineffective. (The third reactor had a passive cooling system that also failed, perhaps because it boiled dry.)

With the loss of cooling, the water in the reactors ultimately boiled off and uncovered the reactor cores. Once the fuel heated to about 1100 C., an exothermic reaction between steam and the zirconium cladding on the fuel produced hydrogen. The pressure inside the primary containments started to rise, requiring the operators to vent them. The vented gases contained hydrogen and radioactive gases and aerosols. These gases, which should have been vented outside the building through a stack, instead accumulated in the reactor buildings, presumably because the operators were unable to open the necessary valves or perhaps because they leaked from the over-pressurized primary containments. The resulting hydrogen explosions damaged the reactor buildings and likely the containments. (It is possible that the unit 2 containment was damaged by excess pressure rather than a hydrogen explosion.)

Unit 4 was shut down at the time of the tsunami and its entire core had been unloaded to the spent fuel pool. There were early reports that the pool had drained down, allowing that fuel to heat up and produce hydrogen, resulting in an explosion that severely damaged the unit 4 reactor building. More recent assessments suggest that the fuel in the unit 4 pool had not drained and that the fuel did not sustain significant damage. It is postulated that that the damage to unit 4 was instead from hydrogen produced in unit 3 that had escaped to unit 4.

Problems were also encountered with the spent fuel pools in units 1–3. Some water in the pools was lost, probably as a result of boiling or perhaps from leaks in the pools arising from damage to the structures. Water in the pools is necessary to provide both radiation screening and cooling. In the days after the accident, there was great concern that there might be a massive release of radioactivity from the pools.

Ultimately fire trucks and a concrete pumper were used to introduce sea water into the reactor vessels and the spent fuel pools in order to restore cooling. But the cores in the three operating reactors melted in the interval before cooling was restored. Over the following weeks, off-site power was restored, fresh water was reintroduced for cooling, and nitrogen was introduced into at least some of the containments to inert the atmosphere and prevent further hydrogen explosions. The site is slowly being stabilized, but the challenge in doing so is significant because equipment was extensively damaged and repairs must be made in the intensely radioactive environment inside the heavily damaged buildings. As this is written, no one can claim that the reactors are completely under control, although it is believed that the worst is over.

Massive amounts of cooling water (500 tons per day) are being introduced into the reactors and spent fuel pools to provide cooling and, until a recirculating cooling system is established, an equal volume of contaminated water is being captured and stored. Major efforts are underway to decontaminate and release or recirculate this water before all available storage is filled.

The radioactive releases to the environment from the accident were far greater than those arising from the Three Mile Island event, but are currently estimated as about 10–15 percent of the release from Chernobyl.

Impacts on Japan

Considerable public attention in Japan and around the world has focused on the possible health effects resulting from the accident. Current evidence suggests that these effects are likely to be minimal. Unlike Chernobyl, no workers have died as a result of acute radiation exposures. However, of the 2,300 workers that have undergone medical checkups, 102 are reported to have received radiation doses above 10 rem and 8 of those workers were reported to have received doses above 25 rem. The highest doses (about 68 rem) were to two workers who inhaled radionuclides. Doses at this level are calculated to increase the long-term risk of cancer by a small percentage.

So far as we know, no member of the public received a meaningful dose, in large part because of evacuations of people in the vicinity of the plant. Unlike Chernobyl, much of the release from the site was by way of contaminated water that escaped to the sea. The expected effects on humans from the contaminated water will be minimal so long as seafood is monitored to ensure that contaminated foodstuffs are not consumed. Nonetheless, the environmental and health impacts should and, no doubt, will be monitored carefully in the years ahead.

The attention to the Fukushima reactors is somewhat striking when one recognizes that no radiation-related deaths have occurred. By contrast, over 23,000 people are dead or missing as a result of the tsunami. This no doubt reflects the special attention that surrounds all things nuclear.

Some land areas were contaminated by radiation releases. Much of the heaviest contamination is to the northwest, in some cases outside the 20 km evacuation zone established by the Japanese government. Temporary restrictions on drinking water and food consumption in the prefectures surrounding the plant were imposed in the days and weeks after the accident. Extensive decontamination efforts will be required before some of the land can return to productive use.

Units 1–4 will never return to service. Although units 5 and 6, which were not operating at the time of the earthquake, are not believed to have suffered substantial damage, it seems doubtful that they will restart. The Hamaoka Plant, which is located about 200 km southwest of Tokyo, was also shut down in the aftermath of the accident until upgrades can be made because of concerns about its vulnerability to earthquakes and tsunamis. Other plants have not yet been allowed to restart. The unavailability of the nuclear plants means that Japan will have a very tight electricity supply for an extended period. The Japanese people are being called upon to reduce their use of electricity.

Japan is a country with limited energy resources. As a result, it sought before the Fukushima accident to increase its reliance on nuclear power from about 30 percent of supply to 50 percent in the coming years. As a result of the Fukushima event, the prime minister has announced that Japan will turn away from nuclear power and instead will rely on renewables. The future trajectory of Japan's energy policy remains uncertain as this is written.

Impact on Regulation

Nearly every regulator in the world is undertaking a review to assess the lessons to be learned from the Fukushima accident and the implications for its own reactors and regulatory systems. Because many of the details of the accident are not known and a complete understanding of why certain systems failed is not available, a thorough assessment of the lessons to be learned may require several years. Nonetheless, there is understandable pressure on regulators to provide assurance that any operating or future plants are safe.

The actions of the US Nuclear Regulatory Commission (NRC) are illustrative. The NRC has launched both short-term and a long-term efforts to assess the implications of the accident. The NRC has repeatedly offered reassurance that US reactors are safe and that, as yet, the evaluations triggered by the accident have not revealed any significant deficiencies in US plants, although some corrective measures have been taken. Moreover, the secretary of energy has stated that nuclear power remains a cornerstone of our energy system for the future. There is no doubt, however, the accident will eventually result in some regulatory changes. There are a few obvious areas that will be examined:

Spent Fuel Pools. There was considerable concern about the challenges that the Japanese confronted in maintaining water inventory in the spent fuel pools. The difficulties that the Japanese encountered has resulted in concerns about the vulnerability of pools at US reactors.

When nuclear power plants were first built in the United States, it was anticipated that the spent fuel would be removed for reprocessing to recover materials that could be recycled. Initially as a matter of federal policy and then as a result of economic considerations, recycling did not take place in the United States (with limited exceptions). As a result, the inventory of spent fuel at the plants has grown beyond the expectations of the plant designers. The NRC has accommodated this situation by granting license amendments to allow higher density storage in pools. The packing density of fuel in US spent fuel pools is understood to be larger than at the Fukushima plants, resulting in a larger heat load. There will no doubt be consideration of whether the NRC should require the removal of at least some fuel from spent fuel pools to dry cask storage.

Extreme Events. The Fukushima operators were confronted with a tsunami that far exceeded the design basis of the plant. One obvious response to the Fukushima accident is to assess and, as appropriate, to augment the capacity to survive extreme events. This would include not only vulnerability to extraordinary earthquakes and tsunamis, but also extreme weather, such as floods and tornadoes.

Mitigation Capacity. Perhaps the most shocking aspect of the Fukushima accident was the fact that various systems that were intended to provide defense in depth failed or proved to be unavailable, apparently as a result of the loss of all emergency AC power supplies. This has caused and will continue to cause continuing interest in the need for assured and reliable backups. In the aftermath of the terrorist attack of September 11, 2001, the NRC required that all operators put in place additional equipment (for example, portable electrical generation or supplementary water pumps) that would enable a response to extraordinary events, such as the large fire that might arise from an aircraft impact. There may be further aggressive efforts by operators and regulators to strengthen these backup measures.

Backup Power. Part of the challenge confronted by the Japanese operators was the failure of all backup power systems and the difficulty of restoring off-site power. It has customarily been assumed that reliance on battery backup systems would only be needed for a matter of hours before off-site could be restored or the diesels brought into service. The Fukushima accident certainly causes this assumption to be questioned. As a result, regulatory requirements may result for more extended backup power capability.

Fratricide. It was apparent that the Japanese had not fully prepared for the reality that a problem at one unit could affect the other units. This experience may result in more careful evaluation of the interactions among units at a multi-unit site. This is a more acute issue in Japan than in the United States because of the Japanese practice of putting six or seven reactors at a single site. In the United States, most plants have only one or two units, and only three plants have three units.

Emergency Planning. The failures in communication that were revealed in Japan have reinforced the need to have transparent and reliable communication channels between the operator, the regulator, emergency responders, the government more generally, and the public. The episode reinforces as well the importance of realistic drills so that all those involved in emergency response are prepared.

Explosive Gases. The Fukushima reactors, like similar reactors in the United States, were equipped with a system to vent gases in the primary containment through a stack to the outside atmosphere. The venting system evidently failed or could not be used in at least some of the units. There will no doubt be careful consideration of the adequacy of existing systems to limit the buildup of dangerous gases. Those systems include not only venting systems, but also recombiners or igniters that are intended to inert dangerous gases before the concentrations reach explosive levels.

In sum, as after the Chernobyl and Three Mile Island accidents, significant regulatory changes may result. It should be expected that the safety of nuclear power will be enhanced, perhaps significantly, as a result of the learning that arises from the Fukushima accident.

Impacts on the Future of Nuclear Power

The accident has understandably caused concerns about reliance on nuclear power. One of the impacts of the accident that will be understood only over time is how the accident will affect existing plants and plans for expanded reliance on nuclear power.

Even before Fukushima, the likelihood of a substantial surge in nuclear construction in the United States seemed implausible. The new designs, while far safer that the current generation of plants, are very expensive. Given the current and expected prices for natural gas, the apparent abundance of gas supply resulting from the development of techniques to recover gas from tight shales, and the absence on limits on greenhouse gas emissions, it is hard for many generating companies to justify new nuclear construction. While recent polls do not suggest that there has been a fundamental change in the generally favorable attitude toward nuclear power that is held by a majority of Americans, the Fukushima accident has no doubt heightened the resolve of those who are opposed to nuclear power. Perhaps one should expect more intense opposition at least in some parts of the country to life extension for the current generation of plants and for any licensing actions related to new plants.

The Fukushima accident is already having a demonstrated effect on nuclear policy in several countries. Although Germany had decided several years ago to eliminate its reliance on nuclear power, that policy had been subject to reexamination before the Fukushima event. Germany has now firmly decided to shut down its nuclear plants by 2022. Similarly, Italy had turned away from nuclear after the Chernobyl accident, but had recently contemplated new nuclear construction. In the aftermath of Fukushima, it has again rejected nuclear power. And Switzerland, which currently has five operating units, has announced that it will follow Germany's path and shut them down.

The nuclear renaissance was faring better elsewhere in the world. There are about 60 reactors currently under construction and many others are in the planning phase. Much of the new and planned construction is in Russia, China, India, Korea, and Japan. Although the future trajectory of reliance on nuclear power in Japan is uncertain, the other countries have not changed their policy, although they have expressed an intention to strengthen their attention to safety as a result of the accident.

One of the noteworthy developments in recent years has been the interest of many countries that do not currently have a nuclear power plant in acquiring one. The International Atomic Energy Agency has indicated that more than 60 countries have expressed some interest in nuclear power and it has estimated that perhaps 15 or so would proceed to build plants over the coming decade. The impact of Fukushima on these countries is unclear, although it appears that those countries that were most advanced in their efforts are proceeding. The factors that have caused their interest in nuclear power—security concerns over access to energy, environmental concerns, interest in advanced technology, comparative economics—persist. It is likely that the growth trajectory for nuclear power may be delayed as a result of Fukushima, but may not result in a radical change in direction in these countries.

* * *

The Fukushima accident has riveted the attention of the world on nuclear power and its potential dangers. The impact of the accident on future reliance on nuclear power will likely vary from country to country. Although the cost of accident was severe, one result is that safety of nuclear power plants around the world will be enhanced.

~~~~~~~~~~
~~~~~~~~~~

Part Three
TELECOMMUNICATIONS

Introduction

The first article in the Telecommunications chapter offers a historical perspective on the development of the telecommunications industry and the antitrust challenges that AT&T, its predecessors, and progeny have faced. This article appeared in the Fall, 2009 issue of *Infrastructure* and was written by Section members Gerry Connell (past chair of the Section), Mike McNeely and John Peirce.

In the summer of 2010, the FCC was considering the adoption of net neutrality rules. Council members Ted Livingston (chair of the Communications, Cable and Internet Committee) and his law partner, Chris Binnig, presented the two sides of the issue in a point-counterpoint debate. In their update to the article which was written for this volume, they bring the debate to date, summarizing the FCC's December, 2010 net neutrality order while noting that challenges to the order remain pending in court.

Andrew Moshirina describes potential treatment of telecommunication white spaces (unused radio wave spectrum) by the FCC in his article "Whither White Spaces?" In his update, he describes the transfer some of the spectrum to first responders and the FCC's Third Opinion and Order on white spaces (April, 2012).

The final article in Chapter 3, by Section members John Peirce and Mark Darrell, analyzes the Supreme Court's *AT&T Mobility, LLC v. Concepcion*[1] decision and attempts to predict how lower courts will interpret the case based, in part, on some early decisions. Their 2012 update summarizes recent decisions where courts have applied *Concepcion.*

Peter V. Lacouture
September, 2012

1. 131 S. Ct. 1740 (2011).

Chapter 13

Telecom: The Future Meets the Past*

*By Gerald A. Connell, Michael D. McNeely, and John C. Peirce***

In 1876 the Scotsman Alexander Graham Bell found a way to transmit the human voice using electric current: He invented the telephone. He could have, appropriately, said "What hath God wrought" as his first message, since his invention was to profoundly affect the world.

It didn't take long for the immense importance of this revolutionary method of communications to become obvious to many, Bell included. Bell held two important patents covering "the method of, and apparatus for, transmitting vocal or other sounds telegraphically. . . by causing electrical undulations," and the next year he and his investors formed the Bell Telephone Company to exploit those patents. In 1882 Western Electric was acquired to produce the equipment that would be needed by the Bell System.

In 1894 the Bell patents expired, and thousands of companies entered the telephone business in cities and towns across the country. Over the next 20 years Bell bought up many of the new independents, and also purchased Western Union, creating at least a near-monopoly in both voice and telegraph communications. Its motto was "One system, one policy, universal service" expressing its desire to manage the telephone system in the United States. In 1913, Bell resolved the antitrust concerns that its acquisitions and its policy had created by agreeing with the United States to divest Western Union, to permit interconnection of the independent phone companies to the Bell System, and to refrain from further acquisitions without the permission of the Interstate Commerce Commission. This agreement was set out in a document called the Kingsbury Commitment, a letter from a Bell vice president to the U.S. attorney general that blessed Bell's dominant position in the telephone industry, a position that continued to grow in the years to come.

---

* Originally published in *Infrastructure*, vol. 49, no. 1 (Fall, 2009).

** *Gerald A. Connell, past-chair of the Section and a former antitrust litigator with the U.S. DOJ and the law firm of Baker & Hostetler LLP, is now a sole practitioner in Connecticut. Michael D. McNeely is a solo antitrust practitioner in the Law Offices of Michael D. McNeely in Washington, D.C. John C. Peirce is a partner in Bryan Cave LLP in Washington, D.C.*

During the next 40 years AT&T introduced dial telephones, initiated trans-Atlantic and trans-Pacific service, established Bell Labs (whose scientists won seven Nobel Prizes), introduced coaxial cable, and customer-dialed long-distance calls. In 1934 the FCC was created to regulate interstate telephone service, blessing the AT&T monopoly.

AT&T was sued by the Antitrust Division in 1949 for monopolization, but that case was settled in 1956 with a consent decree in which AT&T agreed to confine its business to telephony.[1]

During the 1960s AT&T encountered many efforts of equipment makers to have their products attached to telephones. AT&T resisted all such efforts, even plainly harmless ones, on the grounds that any "foreign attachment" would impair the operation of the telephone network. It also resisted efforts of companies like MCI to engage in intercity telecommunications by refusing to allow connection to the local phone companies. All this led eventually to the filing of antitrust lawsuits by the United States, and by about a hundred private plaintiffs including, most significantly, MCI and the company that became Sprint.[2]

The United States case was the most important one for AT&T and it went to trial in 1981, seven years after its filing. The United States accused AT&T of monopolization. One of the key components of the government's theory of liability was the allegation that AT&T refused to interconnect its facilities (i.e., to share them) with the facilities of others in the market. The United States also relied heavily on the proposition that regulation by the FCC and the states was inherently ineffective in addressing AT&T's allegedly monopolistic conduct.

The case was in trial for most of the year, and a settlement was announced in early January 1982 when the case was in recess. The settlement required AT&T to divest its local operating companies, which continued to be regulated by state and federal commissions.[3] The surviving AT&T consisted of its long lines division, Western Electric, and Bell Labs. The decree also lifted the prohibitions of the 1956 decree that had frustrated AT&T as telephone switching and computer technologies rapidly converged. AT&T was now free to go into any business it desired—except for local phone service.

On January 1, 1984, the breakup of the Bell system occurred with the creation of the seven regional Bell operating companies, (RBOCs) that would now carry on the local telephone monopolies that had been part of the Bell system. The RBOCS got the right to the Bell name and logo, but they had to seek a waiver from the decree court to go into any business other than the local telephone business.

In time, the process of seeking waivers from the decree court grew in scope and importance, and came to be seen as a significant regulatory regime in its own right. An RBOC seeking to enter a new line of business would first seek the Antitrust Division's consent to the waiver, and often these matters were presented to the court as agreed-upon packages. Other waiver requests were contested, with the decree court as a prac-

1. United States v. Western Electric Co., 1956 U.S. Dist. LEXIS 4076, 1956 Trade Cas. (CCH) ¶ 68,246 (D.N.J. 1956).

2. *See, e.g.,* Litton Sys., Inc. v. AT&T Co., 700 F.2d 785 (2d Cir. 1983); MCI Communications Corp. v. AT&T Co., 708 F.2d 1081 (7th Cir. 1983).

3. United States v. AT&T Corp., 552 F. Supp. 131 (D.D.C. 1982), *aff'd sub nom.* Maryland v. United States, 460 U.S. 1001 (1983).

tical matter serving as the final arbiter of whether the RBOC could enter the line of business. In some instances, moreover, the court disapproved or significantly modified the terms of waivers the parties had agreed upon. The RBOCs, often prodded by the advent of new communications-related technologies, sought more waivers presenting more difficult legal and factual questions for the Antitrust Division and the court. The Antitrust Division, the decree court, and the RBOCs seemed destined to play out their roles in that singular arrangement indefinitely.

That arrangement ended, however, with the passage of the Telecommunications Act of 1996, which terminated the 1982 settlement, radically reshaped telephone regulation to create the possibility of new competition for the RBOCs in virtually every aspect of their telephone operations, essentially continued the AT&T decree's line-of-business restrictions, and specified that the telephone industry was to remain subject to the antitrust laws.[4] The keys to 1996 Act were requirements that the RBOCs share their facilities with would-be competitors, pricing regulation to make that sharing meaningful, and an opportunity for RBOCs to escape the line-of-business restrictions if they demonstrated that they had sufficiently opened their markets to competition. What ensued was a deluge of new entrants, a flood of regulatory proceedings before the FCC and state regulatory commissions throughout the country, and antitrust lawsuits by frustrated would-be entrants.

The new competitors saw early success in the regulatory sphere, but that success was eroded by appellate decisions that overturned key aspects of earlier FCC rulings favoring competitive entry. In addition, the RBOCs eventually succeeded in using the 1996 Act to free all their telephone operations from the Act's line-of-business restrictions.

At the same time, an explosion of new technology called into question whether old conceptions of telecommunications markets must give way to a far more expansive notion of the breadth of competition that telephone companies face. Two technologies directly affected the competitive landscape for traditional telephone companies. First came the introduction and rapid growth of mobile telephone service, which rapidly ate into the telecommunications demand that had once been the exclusive province of landline telephone companies. More recently, voice over Internet protocol, or VoIP, service, came on the scene. VoIP uses the Internet to complete voice calls, and presents a low-cost, ubiquitous service that is yet another threat to traditional telephone service providers.

In addition, traditional cable operators and direct broadcast satellite providers increasingly began offering telecommunications services, while traditional telecommunications companies began offering broadband Internet (DSL and, increasingly, fiber optic) as well as multichannel video programming.[5]

4. Pub. L. No. 104-104, 110 Stat. 56 (1996).

5. Substantial regulatory differences between the cable industry and the telecommunications industry continue to affect the competitive landscape. *See, e.g.*, National Cable & Telecommunications Ass'n v. Brand X Internet Services, 545 U.S. 967 (2005)(cable modem service is not a telecommunications offering).

Recognizing that traditional market definitions for "cable," "telephone." and "Internet" were obsolescent, the Justice Department in 2007-08 convened a symposium focusing on competition among providers of video programming delivery, local telephony, and broadband services. The broad consensus of the symposium was that "consumers face considerably more choice than they have had in the past: more providers, greater variety in video entertainment, and a wider selection of devices to access the Internet."[6]

The antitrust suits, however, went on, with varying degrees of success once they reached the federal courts of appeals. The typical allegation was that an RBOC had either refused to deal with a smaller competitor or else provided the competitor with inferior service, thus depriving the competitor of the means necessary to compete while preserving the "monopoly" power of the incumbent RBOC. Then came a trilogy of landmark Supreme Court decisions that appear substantially to limit plaintiffs' ability to pursue successful antitrust claims against telecommunications companies as well as other large incumbent regulated service providers. In *Trinko*,[7] the Court held that a monopolization class action could not proceed based on allegations that Verizon had improperly provided poor local phone service to competitors. The decision reiterates the principle that even a monopolist ordinarily has no duty to assist its competitors. The Court also relied heavily on the fact that Verizon was regulated to conclude that its conduct, while not immune from the antitrust laws, did not run afoul of those laws. These two aspects of *Trinko*—a position that a monopolist has no general duty to share facilities with others, and unquestioned reliance on the mere existence of regulation to excuse a monopolist's conduct—stand in stark contrast to the legal approach the Antitrust Division had taken in its 1974 action against AT&T.

In *Twombly*,[8] the Court rejected antitrust claims based on parallel conduct by RBOCs that each elected not to compete in one another's traditional service territories, holding that mere parallel conduct could be nothing more than "the natural, unilateral reaction of each [RBOC] intent on keeping its regional dominance."[9] In *linkLine*,[10] the Court extended its reasoning in *Trinko* to reject price squeeze monopolization claims. Even if, as alleged, AT&T reduced the price of its own DSL offering to the point where competitors could not purchase DSL transport service from AT&T and resell it profitably, AT&T even as a monopolist had no antitrust duty to make its competitors profitable: "If there is no duty to deal at the wholesale level and no predatory pricing at the retail level, then a firm is certainly not required to price both of these services in a manner that preserves its rivals' profit margins."[11]

Notwithstanding the *laissez-faire* trend in recent Supreme Court antitrust decisions, there are signs that the Obama administration may take a significantly more

6. U.S. Dep't of Justice, Voice, Video and Broadband: The Changing Competitive Landscape and Its Impact on Consumers (November 2008), *available at* http://www.usdoj.gov/atr/public/reports/239284.pdf).

7. Verizon Communications v. Law Offices of Curtis V. Trinko, LLP, 540 U.S. 398 (2004).

8. Bell Atlantic Corp. v. Twombly, 550 U.S. 544 (2007).

9. *Id.* at 566.

10. Pacific Bell Telephone Co. v. linkLine Communications, Inc., 129 S. Ct. 1109 (2009).

11. *Id.* at 1113.

activist approach both to antitrust enforcement against dominant firms and to regulation of the telecommunications and cable industries. Christine Varney, newly appointed assistant attorney general in charge of the Justice Department's Antitrust Division, staked out the administration's new approaches to monopolization and merger cases in a May 2009 speech to the U. S. Chamber of Commerce.[12] Entitled "Vigorous Antitrust Enforcement in This Challenging Era," the speech announced the immediate repudiation of the eight-month-old policy statement on monopolization law that had been jointly promulgated by the Justice Department and FTC at the end of the Bush administration.[13] Moreover, harking back to activist antitrust enforcement in the late 1930s, Varney discussed at length three decisions that, in her view, impose significant restrictions on the freedom of dominant firms to refuse to deal with competitors. Remarkably, these were the Supreme Court's 1951 *Lorain Journal*[14] decision (newspaper publisher enjoined from refusing to sell advertising to companies that also advertised with a local radio station), the Supreme Court's 1985 *Aspen Skiing*[15] decision (ski operator required to offer joint lift ticket with smaller competitor) and the D. C. Circuit's 2001 *Microsoft*[16] case (Microsoft required to unbundle Internet browser from operating system). Equally noteworthy is the fact that Varney relegated the last 25 years of Supreme Court antitrust jurisprudence to a one-sentence footnote that dismisses the Supreme Court's limits on monopolization theories in *LinkLine* and *Trinko*.[17]

More recently, Varney announced that the Justice Department and FTC are planning to hold workshops to revisit the 1992 Horizontal Merger Guidelines, with particular emphasis on unilateral effects, price discrimination, vulnerable customers, and other issues.[18] While it is too early to say whether the guidelines will be revised, or whether any revisions will involve stricter standards, the message is clear that the Justice Department and FTC in this administration are increasing their scrutiny of firms with large market shares.

This increased scrutiny encompasses the telecommunications industry. In a July 7, 2009, article entitled "Telecoms Face Antitrust Threat," the *Wall Street Journal* reported that "[t]he Department of Justice has begun looking into whether large U.S. telecommunications companies such as AT&T and Verizon Communications are abusing the market power they have amassed in recent years . . . ." While there is no formal investigation at this juncture, it seems likely the practices under study include exclusive deals between large wireless companies and manufacturers of cell phone hand-

12. Vigorous Antitrust Enforcement in This Challenging Era, Remarks of Christine A. Varney, May 12, 2009, *available at* http://www.usdoj.gov/atr/public/speeches/245711.pdf.

13. U.S. Dep't of Justice, Competition and Monopoly: Single Firm Conduct Under Section 2 of the Sherman Act, U. S. Department of Justice (2008) *available at* http://www.usdoj.gov/atr/public/reports/236681.pdf.

14. Lorain Journal v. United States, 342 U.S. 143 (1951).

15. Aspen Skiing Co. v. Aspen Highlands Skiing Corp., 472 U.S. 585 (1985).

16. United States v. Microsoft, 253 F.3d 34 (D.C. Cir. 2001) (en banc).

17. Vigorous Antitrust Enforcement, *supra*, at n.22.

18. Merger Guidelines Workshops. Speech by Christine A. Varney, Sept. 22, 2009, *available at* http://www.usdoj.gov/atr/public/speeches/250238.htm.

sets, restrictions by broadband and wireless carriers on competitors' applications and services.

The antitrust agencies are not the only ones scrutinizing the behavior of large telecommunications firms. The administration's newly appointed chair of the Federal Communications Commission has recently announced several initiatives that target the freedom of large telecommunications providers to determine unilaterally whether and how to transact with competitors. As example, the FCC is investigating exclusive cell phone handset contracts between manufacturers and wireless carriers, among other competitive issues in the wireless industry.[19] The FCC has also announced "net neutrality" proposals that would limit broadband carriers' ability to discriminate among the types of traffic carried on their networks.[20]

In sum, while several recent Supreme Court decisions tend to limit the scope of antitrust claims against large firms in the telecommunications industry, the Obama administration's antitrust and communications regulators have announced several searching inquiries into the conduct of such large firms towards competitors and consumers. The change in rhetoric from the executive branch is striking. But at this juncture, while there have been policy pronouncements, there are not yet any game-changing law enforcement proceedings. It remains to be seen to what extent the FCC will (re) regulate the unilateral conduct of large telecommunications companies, and how such regulation will interact with the antitrust agencies' apparent wish to roll back recent Supreme Court monopolization cases. In the end, it appears that it may be some time before the competition rules for large telecommunications companies are clear.

~~~~~~~~~~

19. *See, e.g.*, Notice of Inquiry, WT Docket No. 09-66, *available at* http://hraunfoss.fcc.gov/edocs_public/attachmatch/DOC-293568A1.pdf and GN Docket No. 09-157, *available at* http://hraunfoss.fcc.gov/edocs_public/attachmatch/FCC-09-66A1.pdf.

20. "Preserving a Free and Open Internet," remarks of FCC Chair Joseph Genakowski, September 21, 2009, *available at* http://hraunfoss.fcc.gov/edocs_public/attachmatch/DOC-293568A1.pdf.
~~~~~~~~~~

Chapter 14

Net Neutrality: Point and Counterpoint*

*By Theodore A. Livingston and Christian F. Binnig***

"Net neutrality" is a hot-button issue in the communications and Internet world. It features heated debate in Congress, at the Federal Communications Commission (FCC), on the blogosphere, and among academicians, economists, and media pundits. At the FCC, a battle is brewing over proposed "net neutrality" rules and a potential fundamental change in the way Internet access service is regulated.

In what follows, we attempt to strip away the rhetoric that has frequently burdened the net neutrality debate and present the opposing positions in point/counterpoint fashion.

* * *

Moderator: Could you begin by explaining what net neutrality is?

Proponent: "Net neutrality" is shorthand for both the historically open nature of the Internet and the principles necessary to preserve and promote that openness. By "open" we mean that the Internet is, literally, *neutral*—that is, it is equally accessible to anyone with a basic understanding of its protocols. That openness and neutrality has encouraged and empowered individuals and companies to innovate and develop a constantly expanding universe of different content, applications, and services that have improved the lives of Americans and contributed greatly to economic growth and development. The FCC in 2005 articulated the principles necessary to safeguard and promote this openness and neutrality.[1] These principles are that consumers (i.e., users

---

* Originally published in *Infrastructure*, vol. 50, no. 1 (Fall, 2010).

** *Theodore A. Livingston and Christian F. Binnig are partners with Mayer Brown LLP in Chicago, Illinois.*

1. Appropriate Framework for Broadband Access to the Internet Over Wireline Facilities; Review of Regulatory Requirements for Incumbent LEC Broadband Telecommunications Services; Computer III Further Remand Proceedings: Bell Operating Company Provision of Enhanced Services; 1998 Biennial Regulatory Review—Review of Computer III and ONA Safeguards and Requirements; Inquiry Concerning High-Speed Access to the Internet Over Cable and Other Facilities Internet Over Cable Declaratory Ruling; Appropriate Regulatory Treatment for Broadband Access to the Internet Over Cable Facilities, Policy Statement, 20 FCC Rcd 14986, 14987-88, para. 4 (2005) (Internet Policy Statement).

of broadband Internet access) of services are entitled to (1) access to any lawful Internet content of their choice; (2) run applications and use services of their choice; (3) connect their choice of legal devices that don't harm the network; and (4) competition among network providers, application and service providers, and content providers.

Opponent: A fundamental problem in discussing "net neutrality" is that the term often is defined in an open-ended way. My adversary's definition suffers from this and other maladies. It conflates one historical attribute of the Internet (its "openness") with "literal" neutrality (which the Internet has never encompassed); it presupposes (in a classic non sequitur) that regulation is "necessary to preserve and promote" this historical attribute; it fails to explain why the ends it espouses, in particular the concept of "literal" neutrality, are legitimate ends that promote consumer welfare and justify the type of regulation that it presumes (but never demonstrates) is necessary; and it largely ignores the facts.

Let's start with some historical facts. As Justice Thomas succinctly described in the Supreme Court's *Brand X* decision,[2] the Internet is nothing more than a network—albeit today a vast network—of interconnected computers. The Internet as we know it today had its beginnings more than 40 years ago, and initially involved *closed* packet-switching networks of interconnected computers with defined users and defined user rights. The historically "open" nature of the Internet to which my adversary refers didn't really begin until after 1979, with the private-sector development of the USENET computer network, and it didn't become widespread until the early 1990s, when the private-sector development of the World Wide Web and of browsers for navigating the Web popularized the Internet as a medium for information sharing and communication. Today, the Internet is best described as a privately-organized (as opposed to government-organized) collection of billions of interconnected computers and other software-driven devices that in this country is, and at all relevant times has been, free from the type of regulation my adversary espouses.

I agree with my adversary that this network, since the early 1990s, has been "open," in the sense that it is accessible by anyone with a basic understanding of its protocols *and with the economic means to obtain such access*. But that "openness" has been market-driven, not regulation-driven. The principles that the FCC espoused in its 2005 Internet Policy Statement have already developed on the Internet *without* any command-and-control-type regulations such as those my adversary proposes.

Moderator: I understand the FCC is proposing to codify those principles as rules and to add a rule prohibiting discrimination by network providers. Could you explain why you believe these rules, and in particular the nondiscrimination one, are necessary?

Proponent: First, the principles enunciated by the FCC in its Internet Policy Statement are necessary to ensure that we continue to promote the innovation and development at the edge of the network by application, service, and content providers that enrich lives and spur economic growth. If such a provider knows that its applications, services, and/or content may be blocked or degraded, it is naturally going to be reluctant to take the risks and make the investments necessary to develop new applications,

2. National Cable Telecomms. Ass'n. v. Brand X Internet Services, 545 U.S. 967 (2005).

services, and content. And while policy statements are fine, their enforceability is questionable. Rules on the other hand are unquestionably enforceable and will provide both edge innovators and consumers with greater certainty and therefore will better promote investment and innovation.

Second, in addition to codifying as rules the original four principles, the FCC has proposed adding a fifth—a rule prohibiting discrimination: "Subject to reasonable network management, a provider of Broadband Internet access service must treat lawful content, applications, and services in a nondiscriminatory manner." This means, among other things, that a network provider could not charge a content, application, or service provider a fee for priority or enhanced access to its access service customers.

This is critical. If a budding entrepreneur were forced to pay a fee for assured access to the network provider's access service subscribers, that could disincent the very investment and innovation that has made the Internet such a success. In place of a neutral and open Internet, we'd have one that distinguishes between those edge providers willing and able to pay and those who are not. More insidious, it would discourage investment and innovation even among those individuals and companies able to pay—because it would diminish or eliminate the potential profits they might otherwise expect to reap from new content, applications, and services.

On the other hand, the nondiscrimination rule won't, as some have insisted, force network providers to treat all data packets the same. As part of "reasonable network management" during times of high network use and to respond to congestion, network operators may give priority to the latency sensitive applications and services. Moreover, the nondiscrimination rule would not prevent a network provider from charging its subscribers different prices for different services, meaning that a consumer who wants faster download speeds because he/she wants to receive high-quality video can be charged more than a consumer who is satisfied with lower download speeds.

In addition, the nondiscrimination rule wouldn't relegate the Internet experience to a uniform best-efforts regime. First, content providers already employ private content delivery networks, or "CDNs," to transport their content to servers close to the access service customers likely to seek access to it. These CDNs eliminate much of the risk of delays and disruptions from congestion in the public backbone and aggregation networks.

Second, the FCC explicitly recognizes that a category of "specialized" or "managed" services should be exempt from the nondiscrimination rule. These are Internet-Protocol-based offerings provided over the same networks used for broadband Internet access service but available only to those that subscribe to them separately from the access service. These include subscription video services, certain business services subscribed to by enterprise customers, and telemedicine, smart grid, and eLearning applications—all of which require a prioritization or enhanced quality of service rather than best-efforts delivery.

The fact that network providers can charge their subscribers different prices for different services, the existence and proliferation of CDNs, and the fact that "managed" or "specialized" services will be excluded from the nondiscrimination rule all clearly operate to incent investment in and deployment of broadband networks.

Moderator: The response?

Opponent: The premise of my adversary's position—that codification of the principles enunciated by the FCC in its Internet Policy Statement is necessary to ensure continued development of the Internet—is unproven and belied by the historical facts. The hundreds of millions of Internet-based applications and services that have entered the market over the past 15 years vividly disprove this purported need for regulation. In response, my adversary offers only a hypothetical scenario—that providers of applications, services, and/or content over the Internet will be reluctant to take the risks and make the investments necessary to develop new applications, services, and content if the provider is faced with the prospect that its applications, services, and/or content may be blocked or degraded. This scenario is purely speculative, unsupported by the facts, and contrary to basic economic tenets. The economic risks that such providers face are ordinary economic risks that any entrepreneur engaged in a market-driven economic endeavor faces. It is the potential rewards associated with those risks that are responsible for the explosion of Internet-based applications, services, and content that has occurred over the last 15 years and continues to occur in an exponential fashion today.

Of course, the economic reality is that, like any network or any productive economic activity, the Internet and its component pieces are, at any given time, of finite capacity and can become constrained. But those constraints are temporary. The capacity of the Internet is constantly expanding and, while these capacity increases are not without cost, they regularly and reliably have occurred in response to market-driven demand. The salient point here is that our market-driven economy's vigorous investment in Internet-based applications, services, and content has occurred in the *absence* of regulation, and there is no empirical evidence that such investment has been dampened or chilled by market failures, such as the existence of monopoly bottlenecks or the existence and exercise in an anticompetitive way of market power by Internet network facility owners or operators.

Against this backdrop, my adversary's extolling of the FCC's proposed nondiscrimination rule is particularly difficult to understand. In a market-driven enterprise like the Internet, the market itself is a far better arbiter of the terms and conditions upon which content, applications, and services are made available to consumers. It is an economic axiom that any service or product should bear the costs of the resources required to provide that service or product. This is a bedrock principle of market-based economies, not a barrier to entry. If the economic value of a product or service does not exceed the costs of the resources required to provide that service or product, then the market will allocate those resources elsewhere. It is this market-based efficiency, and not regulation, that has driven the growth of the Internet and produced the concomitant consumer welfare benefits.

But even if this were not so, the FCC's proposed nondiscrimination rule makes no policy sense. Internet-based services, content, and applications vary widely in the amount of Internet capacity, or bandwidth, that they consume. Today, most of these services, applications, and content are made available to users on a "best efforts" basis without any guaranteed level of service quality, meaning that those services, applications, and content are subject to being degraded or blocked when capacity constraints occur. If a provider of bandwidth-intensive services, applications, or content wants to avoid such degradation or blockage, it should have the opportunity to purchase a higher level of service that guarantees that the amount of Internet capacity that its services, applications, or content require will be available—but it also should be required to pay for the additional costs (and the greater economic value) associated with such a guarantee. Economists and regulators in other network-based industries, including regulated industries such as the interstate natural gas transmission and interstate electric transmission industries, have long recognized this basic fact. In the interstate gas and electric transmission industries, differential pricing for "firm" transmission capacity and "interruptible" (or best efforts) transmission capacity is a long-established norm. Examples of this same type of differential pricing for different quality levels of service abound in unregulated industries as well. If I am an imported car dealer who wants to make sure that the cars I am offering for sale are delivered to my network of dealerships within, say, 10 days of those cars' manufacture, I am going to pay more for the car delivery service than I would if I chose to have those cars delivered on a less reliable basis, such as whenever the delivery service happened to have empty tractor-trailers available at the cars' port of entry.

My adversary's assertions that an Internet network provider's imposition of a fee for *assured* access to the provider's access subscribers would create an entry barrier that would transform a "neutral and open" Internet into an Internet "that distinguishes between those edge providers willing and able to pay and those who are not" ignores the cost and value difference between *assured* access and *unassured* (or best efforts) access and lacks any empirical support. There is no evidence that significant entry barriers exist for providers of Internet services, applications, and content. The rapid market success of such enterprises as Google, YouTube, Facebook, and countless other vibrant Internet-based businesses that started in someone's basement, garage, or dorm room, demonstrates the lack of such entry barriers. In any event, in a competitive market like the market for Internet access services, differential pricing of different quality levels of access service can exist only if there is a market demand for it.

My adversary's reference to the FCC's exceptions in its proposed nondiscrimination rule for "reasonable network management practices," for "specialized" or "managed" services, and for differential pricing of different quality of service levels provided to end-user subscribers, misses the primary policy point: Placing restrictions on, and thereby reducing the value of, a network owner's property rights necessarily discourages the network owner's incentive to make further investments and distorts the allocation of resources that would otherwise occur in an unregulated market.

A nondiscrimination rule along the lines proposed by the FCC also would be legally suspect. Eight years ago, in a lengthy decision that subsequently was affirmed by the U.S. Supreme Court,[3] the FCC held that broadband Internet access services are "information services" under the Communications Act of 1934, as amended, and pursuant to Congress's directive, are exempt from regulation under Title II of the Act, which governs the regulation of common carrier services.[4] The D.C. Circuit's recent decision

3. *Brand X, supra.*

4. In the Matter of Inquiry Concerning High-Speed Access to the Internet Over Cable and Other Facilities, GN Docket No. 00-185, 17 F.C.C.R. 4798, 202 WL 407567 (FCC 2002).

in *Comcast/BitTorrent*,[5] although tailored to the facts of that particular case (which involved an Internet network access provider's temporary degradation of a bandwidth-intensive Internet application as part of its network management practices), strongly suggests that the FCC's ancillary authority under Title I of the Act does not extend to the regulation of the terms and conditions upon which an Internet network access provider provides its access services. The decision effectively precludes the FCC from relying on either section 230(b) or section 706 of the Act as a basis for the FCC's exercise of its Title I ancillary authority over an Internet access provider's service terms and conditions. Neither the FCC nor my adversary has identified any other provision of the Act that would support the FCC's assertion of its ancillary jurisdiction under Title I. To the contrary, the FCC has initiated a proceeding to "reclassify" broadband Internet access services as "telecommunications services" subject to common carrier regulation under Title II—a proposal that is equally problematic from both a legal and policy standpoint.

Moderator: Do you agree that the FCC lacks authority to adopt and enforce the proposed rules?

Proponent: I agree that the D.C. Circuit's *Comcast/BitTorrent* decision casts serious doubt on the FCC's ability to use its Title I ancillary jurisdiction to promulgate and enforce net neutrality rules. While it might be possible, consistent with *Comcast/BitTorrent*, to cobble together a justification that may pass muster in the courts, relying solely on Title I, if the FCC were to attempt to do that, it would clearly lead to protracted litigation and uncertainty—which the industry and the country can ill afford.

The best way for the FCC to deal with the cloud cast by *Comcast/BitTorrent* is to render it irrelevant by simply classifying the pure transmission component of Internet access service as a telecommunications service. If that were done, it would remove any doubt that the FCC has the requisite authority. And that's precisely what the FCC has suggested it is planning to do in the Notice of Inquiry issued on June 10, 2010.

The opponents to such a reclassification assert that it would be unlawful for the FCC to in effect change its mind and decide now that Internet access is really two distinct services—a telecommunications service and a separate information service. I disagree. As the Supreme Court said in *Chevron*,[6] "[a]n initial agency interpretation is not instantly carved in stone" and an agency is free to "consider varying interpretations and the wisdom of its policy on a continuing basis," in response to changed circumstances—including even a change in administration.[7] The agency simply must adequately explain the reason for the change. Here, the FCC could justify reclassifying high-speed Internet access as a "telecommunications service" simply by reanalyzing the statute, agreeing with Justice Scalia's views expressed in his dissent in the *Brand X* case, and explaining how the policy landscape (or at least the FCC's perception of it) has changed.

5. Comcast Corp. v. FCC, 600 F. 3d 642 (D.C. Cir. 2010).

6. Chevron USA v. Natural Resources Defense Council, 467 U.S. 837 (1984).

7. See Chevron, 467 U.S. at 863-64; Motor Vehicle Manufacturers Association v. State Farm, 463 U.S. 29, 46-57, 59 (1983).

The FCC's original classification decision turned on its view of the word "offer." That is, because the Internet access service provider did not "offer" a separate stand-alone transmission service, the FCC concluded that the provider did not "offer" for sale a "telecommunications service to the public" and therefore that the only thing the provider did offer was an information service. Justice Scalia concluded that this was "an implausible reading of the statute."[8] Justice Scalia stated that it is flatly inconsistent with the common sense understanding of the term "offer" to construe it to apply only where the individual component is actually offered for sale on a stand-alone basis. To Justice Scalia, "[t]he relevant question is whether the individual components in a package being offered still possess sufficient identity to be described as separate objects of the offer, or whether they have been so changed by their combination with other components that it is no longer reasonable to describe them in that way."[9] He uses as an example a car dealer and a pizzeria. He agrees that the car dealer "offers" cars and does not "offer" their component parts—e.g., steel and carpet. On the other hand, he asserts that everyone would agree that the pizzeria "offers" delivery even if it only delivers pizzas that it makes—i.e., it does not "offer" delivery on a stand-alone basis.[10] Justice Scalia puts the transmission component of Internet access service, which he calls "high speed access to the Internet," in the same category as pizza delivery: It is a separate thing; and that is precisely how a consumer would view it. Accordingly, he concludes that "high speed access to the Internet" is a "telecommunications service" subject to Title II common carrier regulation and that the "applications and functions" to which the user gains access is a separate "information service."[11]

Opponent: My adversary suggests that the FCC can solve its current "authority" dilemma by "simply classifying the pure transmission component of Internet access service as a telecommunications service" subject to common carrier regulation under Title II of the Act. But to do so, the FCC would have to reverse the conclusions it reached in its prior orders classifying broadband Internet access service as a single, integrated information service subject only to Title I of the Act. While my adversary suggests the hurdle that the FCC must clear in order to reverse course is not very high, the hurdle may not be as low as my adversary posits. The legal test for determining whether an administrative agency has a reasoned basis for making such a change almost assuredly requires the agency to do more than decide it wants to rely post hoc on a Supreme Court justice's dissenting opinion. Of course, relying on such a dissenting opinion as the basis for revising one's legal analysis is a legally risky proposition in virtually any circumstance. It is all the more so in this case, because redefining Internet access service in the manner the FCC proposes is difficult to reconcile with Congress's intent in enacting the exemption from Title II regulation for "information services" as part of the Federal Telecommunications Act of 1996. The definition of "information services" that Congress enacted, which essentially adopted the same definition the FCC had used beginning in the late-1980s to identify "enhanced services," states that

8. *Brand X*, *supra* note 2, at 1005.
9. *Id.* at 1006-07.
10. *Id.* at 1007.
11. *Id.* at 1008.

all information services are provided "via telecommunications." In other words, all information services have a telecommunications component used for transmission. But that telecommunications component does not mean the service is classifiable as a telecommunications service or severable into separate telecommunications service and information service pieces. The purpose of Congress's enactment of an "information services" definition was to exempt from Title II regulation services used for information creation, gathering, and sharing (rather than for mere information transmission)—precisely the type of service that broadband Internet access service is.

In order for Congress's definitional distinctions to have meaning, some limiting test must be applied. The problem with Justice Scalia's dissent in the *Brand X* case is that the test it purports to apply is so fuzzy and subjective as to make it impossible to predict ex ante the outcome of its application to a particular service. In contrast, the FCC's prior orders classifying broadband Internet access services as information services applied an *objective* test that focused on the *functionality* of the Internet access services that were being bought and sold in the marketplace. This test is not appreciably different than the test that federal courts—including the U.S. Supreme Court—have used for years to define "product markets" in the antitrust context. Moreover, the relevant facts regarding the functionality of broadband Internet access services being bought and sold in the marketplace today haven't changed since the FCC conducted its prior analyses. The FCC's proposed reclassification of these services as telecommunications services therefore would be hard to describe as anything other than arbitrary and capricious.

Finally, even if the FCC's proposed reclassification of broadband Internet access services as telecommunications services could survive legal challenge, the consequences of such reclassification would be antithetic to consumer welfare. The FCC's "Third Way" proposal to classify these services as telecommunications services subject to Title II common carrier regulation, but then to "forbear" from applying most of the provisions of Title II to those services, is far different from declaring those services to be free from any regulation under Title II—which is the regulatory status those services have enjoyed since the Internet's inception. At a minimum, the FCC's proposed reclassification is sure to inject greater uncertainty and greater investment risk into the marketplace, especially if the FCC can change its mind about the regulatory status of those services as blithely as my adversary contends.

2012 Update

By Theodore A. Livingston and Christian F. Binnig

At the time we wrote this article in the summer of 2010, the FCC had not yet adopted any "net neutrality" rules. The Federal Communications Commission (FCC) finally did so in December 2010, when it issued its much anticipated order in *In the Matter of Preserving the Open Internet, Broadband Industry Practices*, GN Docket No. 09-191, WC Docket No. 07-52, colloquially known as the FCC's "Open Internet Order" or "Net Neutrality Order." The FCC commissioners' vote was far from unanimous. FCC Chairman Julius Genachowski voted for the order; Commissioner Michael Copps concurred; Commissioner Mignon Clyburn joined in part and concurred in part; and Commissioners Robert McDonnell and Meredith Atwell Baker dissented.

In the order, the FCC promulgated three new rules intended to preserve the open nature of the Internet. The first of these is the Transparency Rule (47 C.F.R. § 8.3), which requires a provider of broadband Internet access service to publicly disclose accurate information regarding its network management practices, service performance, and service terms and conditions sufficient to permit consumers to make informed service choices and to enable content, application, service, and device providers to develop, market, and maintain Internet offerings. The second rule, the No Blocking Rule (47 C.F.R. § 8.5), prohibits a provider of *fixed* broadband Internet access service from blocking lawful content, applications, services, or non-harmful devices, and prohibits a provider of *mobile* broadband Internet access service from blocking consumers from accessing lawful websites or applications that compete with the provider's voice or video telephony services, all subject to "reasonable network management" by the provider. The third rule, the No Unreasonable Discrimination Rule (47 C.F.R. § 8.7), prohibits a provider of *fixed* broadband Internet access service from unreasonably discriminating in the transmission of lawful network traffic over a consumer's broadband Internet access service.

In issuing these rules, the FCC largely excluded providers of mobile Internet broadband services from their scope (with the exception of the Transparency Rule and a portion of the No Blocking Rule). The FCC also excluded from its new rules certain specialized services, which the FCC loosely defined as services that share capacity with broadband Internet access service over a provider's "last mile" facilities that "differ" from broadband Internet access service. The FCC identified, as two examples of such specialized services, "existing facilities-based VoIP and Internet Protocol-video offerings."

The FCC's majority cited four statutory sources for its position that the FCC possessed the requisite legal authority to issue and enforce these "net neutrality" rules: Section 706 of the Telecommunications Act of 1996 (codified at 47 U.S.C. § 1302); Section 201 of the Communications Act of 1934, as amended (part of the Act's Title II provisions applicable to common carriers, codified at 47 U.S.C. § 201); and Titles III and VI of the 1934 Act, as amended, applicable, respectively, to radio and local television transmission (Title III) and to cable service and multichannel video programming distributors (Title VI). Whether the statutory arguments posited by the FCC's majority will pass muster with the courts remains to be seen. The FCC did not publish its net neutrality rules in the *Federal Register* until September 2011, and those rules did not become effective until November 2011. Numerous parties filed petitions for review of the FCC's Order, and those petitions were consolidated in the U.S. Court of Appeals for the D.C. Circuit. As of early July 2012, the date of this postscript, those consolidated appeal proceedings were pending.

Chapter 15

Whither White Spaces?*

*By Andrew Vahid Moshirnia***

Unused radio-wave bands are a little-known but valuable resource—not surprisingly the subject of a bruising battle. As Congress seeks to restructure the nation's use of airwaves, members of the House Energy and Commerce Committee continue to debate the future role of unused television bands of spectrum. There is a finite amount of usable radio-wave bands, making the unused bands a very important commodity. Outsiders to telecom are largely unaware that these unused "white spaces" exist, let alone how they should best be utilized. Those individuals in the know are divided on the issue of whether consumers would most benefit from a hands-off, open-development approach or a government-imposed licensing regime.

The electromagnetic spectrum is the range of all possible frequencies of electromagnetic radiation. Radio waves are a type of electromagnetic radiation in this spectrum and are used to communicate information. In general when considering radio waves and communication, the lower the frequency on the spectrum, the better. For example, lower frequency waves can more easily penetrate walls.

To prevent interference, bands of frequency are allocated for specific purposes. A large amount of the very desirable spectrum, bands located between 54 and 806 MHz, is devoted to television broadcasting. Broadcasters are assigned licenses to channels within the spectrum. In order to ensure that these channels do not bleed into each other, there are gaps of unused spectrum separating channels. Our transition to digital television has further enlarged the amount of fallow spectrum. Of course, not all channels on the dial are actually in use in all markets. Even before the transition, some broadcasters folded or simply choose not to service low density communities.[1] Allocated but unused spectrum is referred to as white spaces.

Though the FCC first issued a notice of proposed rulemaking to control the use of white spaces in May 2004, the process stalled, and no potential users have developed devices that are ready to make immediate use of white space. Progress has been slowed by two distinct questions: 1) Would white space devices interfere with existing users;

* Originally published in *Infrastructure*, vol. 51, no. 2 (Winter, 2012).

** *Andrew Vahid Moshirnia received his JD from Harvard and his PhD in educational technology from the University of Kansas.*

1. As a result, white space is most prevalent in rural areas.

and 2) should white space use remain open and unlicensed? While the first question has largely been settled, the second continues to provoke spirited argument. Proponents of unlicensed use of white spaces argue that it may serve as a platform for revolutionary and egalitarian innovation. Proponents of an incentive auction scheme see it as an opportunity for revenue generation and as a means to safeguard usage and ensure best use of the space.

This piece provides a brief overview of white spaces, the potential of "super Wi-Fi" white space devices that communicate over unused television bands, the apparent resolution of the debate over whether white space should be used at all, and the current battle over whether to require incentive auctions for white space use.

White Spaces and Super Wi-Fi

The United States has previously turned unused spectrum over to the public for unlicensed use. The 2.4 GHz "junk band" was released in 1985.[2] While the expected use for this band was for devices such as garage door openers and microwave ovens, this release saw the birth of revolutionary means of wirelessly connecting electronic devices, Wi-Fi. Currently, Wi-Fi is confined to two very high bands of the spectrum—2.4 GHz and 5 GHz. These waves reflect off of trees and buildings, making long-range transmission difficult without significant power application. Other devices also use the unlicensed 2.4 GHz band—microwaves, security cameras, and cordless phones—potentially interfering with Wi-Fi.

Eight large technology companies (Microsoft, Google, and others) want to utilize white space in order to deliver high-speed Internet access. They would like to manufacture "super Wi-Fi" white space devices that would use geographic databases to prevent interference with television transmissions or licensed users within a frequency band. If the frequency is fallow, the device would use that frequency to communicate. Due to the fact that white space frequencies are much lower than the current Wi-Fi frequency bands, white space devices would have a much larger range and more consistent signal. The use of white spaces could greatly increase high-speed Internet connectivity, providing access for rural communities and other users.[3]

Rural Rollout and the Digital Divide

It is no secret that millions of Americans in rural areas lack affordable broadband access. Approximately 28 percent of rural Americans lack access to Internet at 3 Mbps or faster.[4] This so-called "digital divide" has become more glaring as bandwidth-heavy applications have grown more popular. Increasing rural access is a priority of the FCC

---

2. The release comprised the industrial, scientific and medical (ISM) band of frequencies—900 MHz, 2.4 GHz, and 5 GHz.

3. It is for this reason that other countries, including the United Kingdom and South Africa, are currently looking into white space utilization to increase connectivity.

4. Michael J. Copps, *Bringing Broadband to Rural America: Report on a Rural Broadband Strategy* 12 (2009), *available at* http://ncbm.org/wp-content/uploads/2009/05/fcc-reportbringing-broadband-to-rural-america.pdf.

and the federal government has devoted considerable resources to addressing this problem.[5] However, there are significant logistical challenges to serving a diffuse population spanning rugged terrain. The difficulty and expense of laying fiber optic cables in these areas has focused attention on cost-effective wireless solutions.

A number of the nation's wireless Internet service providers (WISPs) utilize unlicensed spectrum (2.4 GHz and 5 GHz bands) to deliver Internet access to more than two million homes. However, the poor propagation characteristics of these bands and the noise introduced by other devices that also use those bands reduce the quality and cost effectiveness of rural wireless Internet service. At the same time, rural television markets have an abundance of white spaces, created by the absence of broadcasters looking to serve sparsely populated areas. By allowing WISPs to deploy on TV white space channels, Congress and the FCC are seeking to widen broadband penetration into underserved communities and improve the quality of rural broadband service.

The town of Claudville, Virginia, received an experimental license to utilize a white spaces network. For an equipment cost of less than $5,000,[6] the company Spectrum Bridge was able to bring broadband access to a community dependant on dial-up. Due to the propagation characteristics of white space spectrum, a single transmitter covered eight square miles, whereas hundreds of 2.4 GHz nodes would have been necessary to cover the same area. Other communities are employing white space devices to provide for video conferencing and distance training.[7] White space use offers the exciting possibility of improved national connectivity and solves some of the infrastructural challenges posed by fiber-based broadband deployment.

Emergency Personnel and Public Safety

White spaces may also provide a spectrum platform for public safety agencies that have been stressing their need for more spectrum since the World Trade Center attacks of 2001. Emergency services may saturate existing radio capacity while responding to a mass crisis. White space may provide a supplemental network during times of high load.

This approach may also lower costs and add significant value to existing emergency networks. Because public safety will be on a commercial band, emergency services providers can tap into the economies of scale in equipment production, which will bring down equipment costs. Assuming that the networks operating on this spectrum will be open platforms, the network development costs will be distributed, further lowering costs.

5. Michael Felberbaum, *Rural Broadband Plan Gets $103 Million Expansion*, Huffington Post, Aug. 22, 2011, http://www.huffingtonpost.com/2011/08/22/rural-broadband-plan_n_933383.html.

6. Donny Jackson, *TV White-Spaces Network Launched in Rural Virginia*, Urgent Communications, Oct. 22, 2009, http://urgentcomm.com/networks_and_systems/news/white-spaces-network-virginia-20091022/.

7. Educational benefits will not be confined to rural schools. White spaces may be used by local high schools to achieve a ubiquity of Internet access previously reserved for the campuses of major universities.

Though white space is well suited for a supplementary network for emergency services, there are significant barriers that would make unlicensed white spaces unsuitable for a primary emergency network. In an open environment, it will be difficult to ensure preemptive access, such that responders would be guaranteed a channel cleared of traffic. Network security might also pose a challenge, as network hardening—the reduction of vulnerabilities through the implementation of software patches, security systems, operation policies, and system configurations—may proceed more slowly in such an open environment.

However, it should be stressed that regardless of its role as a primary or supplementary emergency network, white space use may increase the value of emergency services by providing additional carrier capabilities. In areas where public safety networks are poor or crumbling, EMS personnel are likely to have access only to voice, not data transmission. If a long-range white space network is available, public safety can use that network to transmit information machine to machine, increasing information sharing and reducing response time.

White Space Fears and Regulatory Responses

Several groups oppose white space deployment entirely. Television broadcasters argue that the use of white spaces will interfere with TV signals.[8] Other groups use very low power devices on white space; church groups, theater troupes, and sports referees all use wireless microphones that operate in white space frequencies. These groups fear that white space devices will render their devices noisy or ineffective.

The FCC has sought to accommodate the broadcasters and smaller microphone groups, issuing power and channel restrictions for white space devices. However, the FCC appears to be satisfied that interference will be minimized by these precautions, so a total ban of white space use is unnecessary. In order to protect incumbent television broadcasters from interference, the FCC has used regulation to ensure the maintenance of databases containing the frequencies of all licensed TV band users for each relevant area. In order for a new device to tap into a purportedly unused white space band in a geographic area, the device must connect with these databases and receive confirmation that that band is truly vacant. This marks a change from the FCC's initial requirement that the devices, themselves, have the capability to detect vacant spectrum. Now the databases do the work that the on-device sensor would have done.[9]

To get the ball rolling, the FCC's Office of Engineering Technology has recently opened a testing window for white space, encouraging interested parties to use a set of white space tools to map the white space in their areas, with the information fed into and compared with existing databases. These databases should serve to protect full-power TV broadcasters if and when white space devices go online.

---

8. The National Association of Broadcasters (NAB) and the Association for Maximum Service Television filed suit in 2009, seeking review of the FCC's decision to permit the unlicensed use of white space.

9. However, the FCC recognizes that spectrum sensing may improve spectrum access and has left open the opportunity for the certification of sensor-only devices.

Auctions of Unlicensed Spectrum: Quasi-Licensure?

The FCC unanimously adopted a report and order in November 2008 stating that both fixed and mobile broadband white space devices could operate on an unlicensed basis. In September 2010, the commission again unanimously approved unlicensed use of unassigned TV channels. While these decisions were early victories for the open-use and development advocates, stakeholders continue to push back. While both sides agree that white space ought to be used, proregulation legislators proposed in July 2011 that the Spectrum Innovation Act of 2011 require that the allocation of spectrum for unlicensed use be subject to competitive bidding. A firestorm of debate ensued. Before the apparent failure of the budget supercommittee, numerous outlets reported that the body was considering curtailing white space in favor of TV band auctions. Proponents of incentives auctions argue that spectrum is a valuable resource and spectrum auctions may generate billions of dollars. In contrast, academics and white spaces supporters argue that innovation driven by unlicensed use will greatly outweigh the short-term revenue offered by incentive auctions.

Platform for Innovation

FCC Chairman Julius Genachowski has made clear his belief that opening white spaces to unlicensed use will spur innovation and the development of new technologies. The last major release of unlicensed spectrum, the so called "junk band" of 2.4 GHz, saw the advent of Wi-Fi and a revolution in mobile Internet access.[10] Supporters of unlicensed white space point to the tremendous economic value associated with Wi-Fi development and deployment. Richard Thanki, in a study commissioned by Microsoft, concluded that Wi-Fi usage in homes "may be generating anywhere between $4.3 and $12.6 billion in annual economic value for consumers in the United States." If two other unlicensed applications are also considered, Wi-Fi use in hospitals and radio-frequency identification (RFID) tags,[11] those figures climb to $16 and $37 billion.

The prevalence and utility of Wi-Fi also undercut the argument that exclusive licensure is required to boost overall network capacity and development. The current approach to smartphones and tablets is a model of network expansion through unlicensed use. Wireless carriers like AT&T, which do hold exclusive rights to spectrum, have struggled to provide enough broadband capacity to smartphone users. The solution to this network congestion has been to shift traffic to Wi-Fi. Approximately two-thirds of smartphone and tablet data is carried not over carrier networks but over Wi-Fi.

Supporters of Incentive Auctions and Quasi-Licensure

The current political climate creates additional pressures for the auction of white space spectrum. Before its apparent failure, the bipartisan supercommittee was tasked with

10. It bears repeating that during the last major release of unlicensed spectrum, regulators expected the band to be used for microwave ovens and industrial machinery.

11. Retailers use RFID to track merchandise. Other common uses include the E-Z Pass toll payment device and ID chips for pets.

hammering out a budget agreement that will reduce the deficit by at least $1.2 trillion over 10 years. Deficit reduction is a central political issue. However, a number of Republicans have pledged not to raise taxes. In this constrained posture, the sale of spectrum is one of the few palatable means to increase revenues. Communications and Technology Subcommittee Chairman Greg Walden (R-Ore.) stated that "there is more spectrum available today for unlicensed use than licensed spectrum available for all the commercial wireless providers combined. The question is whether we should give away billions of dollars' worth of this particular spectrum, especially if we are spending taxpayer money to relocate broadcasters and government users to clear it in the first place."[12] Indeed, FCC member Robert McDowell has noted the fiscal pressures, "Given today's unprecedented budget deficits, I question whether the U.S. can afford not to auction any and all spectrum recovered in this band."

Conclusion

White space devices are lumbering towards reality. The tantalizing prospect of greater broadband capacity brings the promise of wider access and lower costs. Extensive testing and reasoned regulating have diminished concerns that white space devices will interfere with broadcasters. However, the uncertainty caused by the continuing fight over whether to restrict and monetize white space access will only retard deployment. Whatever balance of licensed and unlicensed use is eventually struck, law makers would do well to recognize that previous releases of unlicensed spectrum have fostered revolutionary innovation; expecting a microwave, we gained a hotspot. There is no telling what uses for white space may prove to be "best" and so regulators must question the urge to define the "correct" path for white space deployment.

~~~~~~~~~~

12. Brendan Sasso, *Unlicensed spectrum a sticking point in House talks*, THE HILL, Oct. 26, 2011, http://thehill.com/blogs/hillicon-valley/technology/189923-congress-grapples-over-unlicensed-spectrum.
~~~~~~~~~~

2012 Update

By Andrew Moshirnia

In the short period of time since the publication of "Wither White Spaces," there have been several developments with regard to white spaces. In February, 2012, as part of a payroll tax cut bill,[1] Congress gave the D Block, a chunk of spectrum cleared during the digital TV transition, to first responders.[2] The First Responder Network Authority (FirstNet) will oversee the creation of the public-safety network.[3] The government also set aside roughly $1.75 billion to compensate television stations that voluntarily give up their spectrum.[4] The final bill did not contain provisions put forth by House Republicans that would have limited the FCC's ability to place conditions on future spectrum auctions and restricted the Commission's ability to manage white space broadband.[5]

In April, the Federal Communications Commission (FCC) issued its Third Opinion and Order on the use of white spaces.[6] In May, the National Association of Broadcasters dropped its court challenge of the FCC's earlier white spaces order.[7] One month later, professional sports organizations and theater groups similarly dropped their challenges.[8]

1. The Middle Class Tax Relief and Job Creation Act of 2012 (H.R. 3630).

2. *Id.*; Motorola, D Block Spectrum Act and the FirstNet Broadband Network: What Does It All Mean? 2 (2012).

3. Motorola, *supra* at 2.

4. Paul Barbagallo, *FCC Chairman Implores Broadcasters to Participate in 'Incentive Auctions'*, Bloomberg BNA (April 18, 2012), http://www.bna.com/fcc-chairman-implores-n12884908973/.

5. Harold Feld, *The Final Score on Spectrum Legislation: Bad Stuff Averted, Good Stuff Made Possible*, Public Knowledge, Feb. 17, 2012, http://www.publicknowledge.org/blog/final-score-spectrum-legislation-bad-stuff-av.

6. FCC, Third Report and Order and Memorandum Opinion and Order, In the Matter of Unlicensed Operation in the TV Broadcast Bands, ET Docket No. 04-186, Additional Spectrum for Unlicensed Devices Below 900 MHz and in the 3 GHz Band, ET Docket No. 02-380, FCC 12-36 (April 5, 2012).

7. Timothy B. Lee, *White Spaces and Happy Faces: TV Stations Drop Lawsuit against "Super WiFi,"* Ars Technica (May 3, 2012), http://arstechnica.com/tech-policy/2012/05/white-spaces-and-happy-faces-tv-stations-drop-lawsuit-against-super-wifi/.

8. Maisie Ramsay, *Last Lawsuit Dropped Against FCC White Space Order*, Wireless Week (June 5, 2012), http://www.wirelessweek.com/News/2012/06/policy-and-industry-Last-Lawsuit-Dropped-Against-FCC-White-Space-Order/.

Chapter 16

Can Arbitration Agreements Really Bar Class Actions? How Will Lower Courts Interpret *AT&T Mobility v. Concepcion*?*

*By John C. Peirce and Mark C. Darrell***

In *AT&T Mobility LLC v. Concepcion*[1] the US Supreme Court held that when private parties (even consumers with a claim worth $31) contract to arbitrate disputes individually, and not on a classwide basis, the Federal Arbitration Act (FAA) requires their contract to be enforced. Justice Scalia, writing for a 5–4 majority, explains that class actions are almost always incompatible with arbitration, so a state rule requiring class actions in consumer cases is, in effect, a rule prohibiting arbitration. Such a rule clearly is preempted by the FAA. Justice Breyer's dissenting opinion contends that if consumer products companies are allowed to contract out of class-action liability they will be able to cheat large numbers of consumers out of small sums, since lawyers will not take on small consumer claims unless they can represent a class. The majority opinion responds that in this case the district court found (and the Ninth Circuit agreed) that the Concepcions were more likely to recover their $31 claim quickly and fully under AT&T Mobility's arbitration process than as members of a plaintiff class. Denying the Concepcions a role as putative class representatives did not prevent them from effectively pursuing their individual claim, nor did the class-action waiver exculpate AT&T Mobility from small consumer claims.

---

* Originally published in *Infrastructure*, vol. 50, no. 3 (Spring, 2011).

** *John C. Peirce is a partner with Bryan Cave LLP, where his practice focuses on antitrust and trade regulation law and complex commercial litigation. Mark C. Darrell has been general counsel of Laclede Group Inc. and Laclede Gas Co. since May 2004 and has been senior vice president of Laclede Gas since 2007. He has over 27 years of experience in the energy business.*

1. ___ U.S. ___ (April 27, 2011).

The *Concepcion* decision has been vilified as a "devastating blow to consumer rights" and praised as a "victory for consumers over attorneys."[2] It inspired Sen. Al Franken, with 12 cosponsors, and Rep. Hank Johnson, with 62 cosponsors, to (re)introduce the "Arbitration Fairness Act," which would eliminate all predispute arbitration agreements from employment, consumer, and civil rights cases.[3] There is speculation that the new Consumer Financial Protection Bureau, ordered by section 1028 of the Dodd-Frank Act to seek out and destroy "anti-consumer" arbitration agreements in financial industry contracts, will intervene.[4]

Concepcion may eventually inspire a legislative or regulatory response; but long before Congress and Elizabeth Warren can act, the decision will be tested in the lower federal and state courts, several of which have been diluting the Supreme Court's arbitration rulings for more than a decade by playing the "unconscionability game."[5] *Concepcion* builds on two other recent decisions addressing arbitration agreements and class actions,[6] and this trio may indeed clarify the law of arbitration as well as that of class actions—to the extent that the lower courts go along.

The Broad (But Not Unlimited) Reach of the Federal Arbitration Act

Beginning with the decision in *Prima Paint Corp. v. Flood & Conklin Mfg. Co.*,[7] the Supreme Court has steadily mapped out the broad reach of the FAA's mandate that "[a] written provision in . . . a contract evidencing a transaction involving commerce to settle by arbitration a controversy thereafter arising out of such contract . . . shall be valid, irrevocable, and enforceable, save upon such grounds as exist at law or in equity for the revocation of any contract."[8]

In *Southland Corp. v. Keating*,[9] the court established that the FAA is substantive federal law that preempts inconsistent state statutes (in that case the California Franchise Investment Law) that limit the availability of arbitration. In *Allied-Bruce Terminix*

2. *Compare* Editorial, *Gutting Class Action*, N.Y. Times, May 13, 2011 at A-26, *available at* http://www.nytimes.com/2011/05/13/opinion/13fri1.html *with* John Tabin, *Consumers Win in Allegedly Anti-Consumer Supreme Court Ruling,* The American Spectator Blog (Apr. 28, 2011), http://spectator.org/blog/2011/04/28/consumers-win-in-allegedly-ant#.

3. S. 987 and H.R. 1873, 112th Cong., 1st Sess.

4. Daniel Fisher, *After Arbitration Ruling, Watch Warren's Consumer Bureau*, Apr. 27, 2011, http://blogs.forbes.com/danielfisher/2011/04/27/after-arbitration-ruling-watch-warrens-consumer-bureau/.

5. For a detailed analysis of this phenomenon, see Aaron-Andrew P. Bruhl, *The Unconscionability Game: Strategic Judging and the Evolution of Federal Arbitration Law*, 83 N.Y.U. L. Rev. 1420 (2008).

6. Rent-A-Center West, Inc. v. Jackson, 130 S. Ct. 2772 (2010); Stolt-Nielsen S.A. v. AnimalFeeds International Corp., 130 S. Ct. 1758 (2010).

7. 388 U.S. 395 (1967).

8. 9 U.S.C. § 2 (2006).

9. 465 U.S. 1 (1984). *See also* Moses H. Cone Mem'l Hosp. v. Mercury Constr. Corp., 460 U.S. 1 (1983).

Cos. v. Dobson,[10] the court held that the FAA's preemptive reach extends to the full reach of the commerce clause, thus preempting state laws restricting the arbitrability of even primarily local disputes, such as a dispute between an Alabama homeowner and an Alabama pest control franchisee. The Supreme Court has repeatedly held that the FAA preempts contrary state statutory and decisional law.[11] *Concepcion* falls squarely into this line of cases, as it holds that the FAA preempts contrary California common law.[12]

The FAA's preemptive force is limited by the proviso that arbitration agreements can be declared invalid "upon such grounds as exist at law or in equity for the revocation of any contract." The Supreme Court has not drawn any bright-line rules for applying this proviso, but has stated that it places arbitration agreements "on an equal footing with other contracts."[13] But holding that all kinds of claims can be arbitrated is not the same as holding that all arbitration agreements are enforceable. The court acknowledged this in *Green Tree Financial Corp-Alabama v. Randolph*,[14] holding that an arbitration agreement that was proven to be "prohibitively expensive" might be contrary to basic state contract law and thereby satisfy the FAA proviso; but the party seeking to invalidate an arbitration agreement bears the burden of proving the "prohibitive[e] expens[e]."

The "Unconscionability Game"

Some lower state and federal courts have resisted the Supreme Court's interpretation of the FAA's broad mandate, using creative interpretations of state law to invalidate arbitration agreements. Occasionally, this has involved open defiance. In Montana, following the *Casarotto* decision in which the US Supreme Court invalidated a Montana statute requiring conspicuous notice of arbitration agreements,[15] two of the state

10. 513 U.S. 265 (1995).

11. *See, e.g.*, Mastrobuono v. Shearson Lehman Hutton, Inc., 514 U.S. 52 (1995) (FAA preempted New York law barring arbitrators from awarding punitive damages); Doctor's Assocs., Inc. v. Casarotto, 517 U.S. 681 (1996) (FAA preempted Montana "conspicuous notice" requirement for arbitration agreements); Buckeye Check Cashing, Inc. v. Cardegna, 546 U.S. 440 (2006) (enforcing arbitration clause in a usurious payday loan contract that was allegedly void *ab initio* under Florida law); Preston v. Ferrer, 552 U.S. 346 (2008) (FAA preempts a California law vesting exclusive jurisdiction to resolve talent agency disputes in the state Labor Commissioner).

12. The Supreme Court also has held that federal statutory claims are arbitrable. *See, e.g.*, Mitsubishi Motors Corp. v. Soler Chrysler-Plymouth, Inc., 473 U.S. 614 (1985) (international antitrust claim arbitrable); Shearson/American Express, Inc. v. McMahon, 482 U.S. 220 (1987) (RICO claim arbitrable); Rodriguez de Quijas v. Shearson/American Express, Inc., 490 U.S. 477 (1989) (securities law claim arbitrable); Gilmer v. Interstate/Johnson Lane Corp., 500 U.S. 20 (1991) (age discrimination claim arbitrable).

13. *See, e.g.*, Rent-a-Center West, Inc. v. Jackson, 130 S.Ct. 2772, 2776 (2010); Gilmer v. Interstate-Johnson Lane Corp., 500 U.S. 20, 24 (1991).

14. 531 U.S. 79, 92 (2000).

15. *Supra* note 10.

supreme court justices refused to sign the arbitration order.[16] The Montana Supreme Court later held that an arbitration clause could be invalid under the "reasonable expectations" doctrine even if notice of the arbitration provision was printed in bolded all-caps above the signature line.[17] Thus, in Montana, the state courts have fashioned the "reasonable expectations" doctrine (a subspecies of unconscionability) into a judge-made rule *more hostile to arbitration* than the state "conspicuous notice" statute struck down in *Casarotto*.[18]

Montana is not (in this respect) unique. Several courts, state and federal, have invoked doctrines of common law unconscionability to invalidate arbitration agreements. For example, in *Circuit City Stores, Inc. v. Adams*,[19] the Supreme Court reversed a Ninth Circuit decision that had held California employment disputes were inarbitrable. On remand, the Ninth Circuit simply declared the arbitration agreement to be unconscionable.[20]

Unconscionability and similar common-law doctrines have been invoked to defeat arbitration clauses on grounds such as:

- The arbitration agreement is nonmutual or can be modified unilaterally.[21]
- The allocation of costs in the arbitration agreement is unfair.[22]
- The arbitration or its results must be kept confidential.[23]
- The arbitration clause unfairly limits a claimant's remedies.[24]

---

16. Richard C. Reuben, *Western Showdown: Two Montana Judges Buck the U.S. Supreme Court*, A.B.A J., Oct. 1996, at 16, *cited and discussed in* Susan Randall, *Judicial Attitudes Toward Arbitration and the Resurgence of Unconscionability*, 52 BUFFALO L. REV. 185, 220–221 (2004).

17. Zigrang v. U.S. Bancorp Piper Jaffray, Inc., 123 P.3d 237 (Mont. 2005); *see also* Kloss v. Edward D. Jones & Co., 54 P.3d 1 (Mont. 2002).

18. *See* Scott J. Burnham, *The War Against Arbitration in Montana*, 66 MONT. L. REV. 139 (2005); Susan Randall, *supra.*

19. 532 U.S. 105 (2001).

20. Circuit City Stores, Inc. v. Adams, 279 F.3d 889, 892, 896 (9th Cir. 2002).

21. *E.g.*, Pokorny v. Quixtar Inc., 601 F.3d 987 (9th Cir. 2010); Morrison v. Amway Corp., 517 F.3d 248 (5th Cir. 2008); Wisconsin Auto Title Loans, Inc. v. Jones, 714 N.W.2d 155, 172–76 (Wis. 2006); Iberia Credit Bureau, Inc. v. Cingular Wireless LLC, 379 F.3d 159, 169 (5th Cir. 2004); Dumais v. Am. Golf Corp., 299 F.3d 1216, 1219 (10th Cir. 2002); Armendariz v. Found. Health Psychcare Servs., 6 P.3d 669, 691–94 (Cal. 2000).

22. *E.g.*, Nino v. Jewelry Exch., Inc., 609 F.3d 191, 203 (3d Cir. 2010); McNulty v. H&R Block, Inc., 843 A.2d 1267, 1273–74 (Pa. Super. Ct.), *review denied*, 853 A.2d 362 (Pa. 2004); Ingle v. Circuit City Stores, Inc., 328 F.3d 1165, 1177–78 (9th Cir. 2003).

23. *E.g., Pokorny, supra*; Davis v. O'Melveny & Myers, 485 F.3d 1066, 1078–79 (9th Cir. 2007); Ting v. AT&T, 319 F.3d 1126, 1151–52 (9th Cir. 2003); Eagle v. Fred Martin Motor Co., 809 N.E.2d 1161, 1180–83 (Ohio Ct. App. 2004).

24. *E.g., Pokorny, supra; Ingle, supra;* Simpson v. MSA of Myrtle Beach, Inc., 644 S.E.2d 663, 670–71 (S.C. 2007); State ex rel. Dunlap v. Berger, 567 S.E.2d 265, 277–80 (W. Va. 2002).

- The arbitration agreement specifies an inconvenient forum.[25]
- The arbitration clause unfairly deprives the plaintiff of a class-action remedy.[26]

Most of these grounds are superficially neutral. But courts routinely enforce confidentiality agreements—unless they are contained in arbitration agreements. Courts enforce private agreements limiting damage remedies if they appear (for example) in warranties or invoices—but often not if they appear in arbitration agreements. Courts regularly approve cost-sharing agreements in court litigation—but often not in arbitration. Courts usually enforce contractual forum-selection clauses—but often not those in arbitration agreements. One commentator's statistical analysis showed that in 2002–2003 courts were twice as likely to find arbitration agreements unconscionable as other types of contracts.[27] Another described in detail the manner in which California courts have manipulated unconscionability standards to strike down arbitration agreements.[28]

The *Concepcion* Decision

Concepcion is the latest battle in the war over arbitration agreements. The Concepcions sought to bring a class action on behalf of customers who accepted AT&T Mobility's offer of a "free" cell phone and then were charged California state sales tax of about $31 for that "free" phone on their AT&T bill. Allegedly, AT&T Mobility's failure to disclose to customers its obligation (imposed by the State of California) to collect sales tax on such "free" sales exposed AT&T Mobility to fraud, deceptive trade practices, and other such claims.

The arbitration agreement and class-action waiver provisions at issue in *Concepcion* are remarkable. The principal features are:

- AT&T Mobility would pay all of the arbitration fees under AAA consumer arbitration rules.
- If the customer won in arbitration a sum larger than AT&T Mobility's last written settlement offer, AT&T Mobility would pay twice the customer's legal fees plus a $7,500 premium.

---

25. *E.g.*, Nagrampa v. MailCoups, Inc., 469 F.3d 1257, 1287–92 (9th Cir. 2006) (en banc); Keystone, Inc. v. Triad Sys. Corp., 971 P.2d 1240, 1243–46 (Mont. 1998).

26. *E.g.*, In re: American Express Merchants' Litigation, Italian Colors Restaurant v. American Express Travel Related Services Co., 634 F.3d 187 (2d Cir. 2011); Brewer v. Missouri Title Loans, Inc., 323 S.W. 3d 18 (Mo. 2010); Kristian v. Comcast Corp., 446 F.3d 25 (1st Cir. 2006); Kinkel v. Cingular Wireless LLC, 857 N.E.2d 250, 267–75 (Ill. 2006); Muhammad v. County Bank of Rehoboth Beach, 912 A.2d 88, 98–102 (N.J. 2006); *State ex rel. Dunlap v. Berger, supra*; Wong v. T-Mobile USA, Inc., 2006 U.S. Dist. LEXIS 49444 (E.D.MI 2006); Discover Bank v. Superior Court, 113 P.3d 1100, 1106–10 (Cal. 2005) (invalidated by the U. S. Supreme Court in *Concepcion*).

27. Susan Randall, *supra*.

28. Stephen A. Broome, *An Unconscionable Application of the Unconscionability Doctrine: How the California Courts Are Circumventing the Federal Arbitration Act*, 3 Hastings Bus. L.J. 39 (2006).

- AT&T Mobility agreed not to seek recovery of its attorneys' fees.
- Any hearing would be held in the county of the claimant's billing address. Arbitration hearings could be conducted by telephone and some cases could be handled as a "desk" arbitration decided on the parties' filings without a hearing.
- The arbitrator could award any remedy that would be available in a court.
- Class arbitrations were expressly prohibited.

Both the trial court and the Ninth Circuit rejected AT&T Mobility's program despite its consumer-friendly characteristics because it failed the special rule of unconscionability imposed by the California Supreme Court in *Discover Bank v. Super. Ct.*[29] Under *Discover Bank*, an agreement for nonclass arbitration in a consumer contract was invalid if the plaintiff merely *alleged* "that the party with the superior bargaining power has carried out a scheme to deliberately cheat large numbers of consumers out of individually small sums of money." Since just about every well-pled consumer class-action complaint contains such allegations, *Discover Bank* approximated a per se rule of invalidity for consumer class-action waivers in California.

Justice Scalia concluded that the FAA preempts the *Discover Bank* rule. While the rule purported to apply to court litigation as well as arbitration, it had a disproportionate effect on arbitration. In effect, it would destroy most of the advantages that cause parties to agree to arbitration: informal, streamlined procedures leading to swift and final results. Informality, confidentiality, efficiency, and finality are among the attributes of arbitration that are incompatible with classwide procedures. This part of the discussion in *Concepcion* rehearses and expands on Justice Alito's 5–3 opinion in *Stolt-Nielsen S.A. v. AnimalFeeds International Corp.*[30] that held that if an arbitration agreement is silent on the issue, the arbitrator cannot allow classwide procedures.

The decision stops well short of making every class-action waiver enforceable. The opinion dwells on the fact (as found by the lower courts) that the Concepcions clearly would fare *better* under AT&T Mobility's program than in a class action. Individual claimants are virtually guaranteed to receive a settlement offer of at least 100 percent of their claims, and may recover more than 100 percent of the claim either in settlement or after arbitration. In contrast, class members typically wait years for a settlement amounting to pennies on the dollar. The majority opinion does not disagree with the dissenters that an arbitration agreement or class-action waiver that shielded sellers from liability would be unenforceable.

The Situation After *Concepcion*

Concepcion will not be the last word on class-action waivers in arbitration agreements. While it struck down the *Discover Bank* rule, Justice Scalia's opinion does not foreclose other grounds for refusing to enforce class-action waivers in arbitration agree-

29. 113 P.3d 1100, 1110 (Cal. 2005).
30. 130 S. Ct. 1758 (2010).

ments.[31] Understanding what is likely to happen in the wake of *Concepcion* requires a closer look at how lower courts have responded to *Randolph*'s admonition that a plaintiff wishing to defeat an arbitration agreement bears the burden of presenting evidence that individual arbitration would be "prohibitively expensive."

Lower courts' analysis has often focused on whether plaintiff could afford legal counsel. Some courts have routinely enforced arbitration agreements containing class-action waivers when the plaintiffs' claims invoked statutes such as antitrust, civil RICO, and TILA, which provide for successful plaintiffs to recover their attorneys' fees and multiple or statutory damages.[32] Other courts have rejected nonclass arbitration agreements based on plaintiffs' evidence that their individual damages claims are too small to attract a contingent-fee lawyer. For example, *Brewer v. Missouri Title Loans, Inc.*[33] involved a car title loan that required disputes to be settled in nonclass arbitration. The state supreme court struck down the arbitration agreement and class-action waiver based on affidavits from "expert" lawyers averring that it would be "very hard, 'if not impossible,'" for the plaintiff to find a lawyer willing to take her case as an individual claim. The majority did not consider whether or not the plaintiff could have proceeded on her own, or with a less expensive lawyer. The dissent by Chief Justice Price pointed out that the amount in controversy exceeded $4,000, the statutes involved offered recovery of penalties and attorneys' fees, and "[t]he removal of [plaintiff's] right to arbitrate on a class basis may diminish her bargaining power and may diminish the amount of attorney's fees available, but it does not substantively or practically bar her from an adequate remedy for any harm she has suffered."

In re: American Express Merchants' Litigation, Italian Colors Restaurant v. American Express Travel Related Services Co.,[34] and *Kristian v. Comcast Corp.*,[35] both conclude that even though federal antitrust statutes provide for successful plaintiffs to recover treble damages and attorneys' fees, and also provide for civil and criminal enforcement by government agencies, class-action waivers in arbitration agreements nevertheless are unconscionable because the cost of expert witnesses and the amount of time that an individual plaintiff attorney would have to "invest" before recovering a fee would make any individual claim "prohibitively expensive" within the meaning of *Randolph*.

Does *Concepcion* repudiate these rulings? Perhaps. In *Concepcion* Justice Scalia enforced an agreement under which the plaintiffs obviously could not afford to pay a

31. Footnote 6 of the opinion, for example, explains that "States remain free to take steps addressing the concerns that attend contracts of adhesion—for example, requiring class-action-waiver provisions in adhesive [*sic*] arbitration agreements to be highlighted."

32. *See, e.g.*, Cappuccitti v. DirecTV, Inc., 623 F.3d 1118 (11th Cir. 2010); Cronin v. CitiFinancial Servs., Inc., 352 F. App'x 630, 636 (3d Cir. 2009) (unpublished opinion); Livingston v. Associates Fin., Inc., 339 F.3d 553, 559 (7th Cir. 2003); Snowden v. Checkpoint Check Cashing, 290 F.3d 631, 638 (4th Cir. 2002), Randolph v. Green Tree Financial Corp. – Alabama, 244 F.3d 814, 818 (11th Cir. 2001); Johnson v. West Suburban Bank, 225 F.3d 366, 374–75 (3d Cir. 2000).

33. 323 S.W. 3d 18 (Mo. 2010).

34. 634 F.3d 187 (2d Cir. 2011).

35. 446 F.3d 25 (1st Cir. 2006).

lawyer to represent them on their $31 individual claim. Justice Scalia's opinion dwells on the features of AT&T Mobility's arbitration agreement that enabled the Concepcions to pursue their claim pro se, at very little cost or risk. The Missouri Supreme Court in *Brewer*, the Second Circuit in *Amex Merchants*, and the First Circuit in *Kristian* all avoid discussing the dispositive issue in *Concepcion*—whether the plaintiffs could effectively resolve their disputes in individual arbitration—and focus instead on whether individual arbitration would be economically attractive for contingent-fee lawyers and economists. This type of analysis, based on self-serving affidavits from the lawyers and economists who profit most from class actions, should now be defunct.[36] The real question—whether the would-be class-action plaintiff has an adequate remedy in individual arbitration—is left for resolution by lower courts and arbitrators.[37]

~~~~~~~~~~

36. The legacy of *Concepcion* may depend in part on Justice Scalia's opinion for another 5–4 majority in Rent-A-Center West, Inc. v. Jackson, 130 S.Ct. 2772 (2010), holding that lower courts must enforce a contractual "delegation provision" specifying that the arbitrator and not a court must address any challenges to the validity of the arbitration agreement. This appears to offer parties an opportunity to contract out of the risk that their arbitration agreement will become a pawn in the "unconscionability game" as played in a court hostile to arbitration. Arbitrators, presumably, are neither biased against well-drafted arbitration agreements nor biased in favor of arbitration agreements that deter small meritorious claims.

37. Early signs are promising. In Arellano v. T-Mobile USA, Inc., 2011 U.S. Dist. LEXIS 52142 (N. D. Cal. May 16, 2011), the district court followed *Concepcion* in holding that citizen claims for public injunctive relief under the California Unfair Competition Law and the California Consumer Legal Remedies Act are subject to arbitration notwithstanding the state supreme court's holdings in Cruz v. PacifiCare Health Sys., Inc., 66 P.3d 1157 (Cal. 2003) and Broughton v. Cigna Healthplans of California, 988 P.2d 67 (Cal. 1999).
~~~~~~~~~~

2012 Update

By John C. Peirce and Mark C. Darrell

In the year following the *Concepcion* decision, the Supreme Court confirmed in *CompuCredit Corp. v. Greenwood*[1] that the Federal Arbitration Act (FAA) requires the enforcement of arbitration agreements "even when the claims at issue are federal statutory claims" unless the preference for arbitration is "overridden by a contrary congressional command." Even though the Federal Credit Repair Act[2] contains the words "right to sue," "class action," and "court," the Supreme Court found there was no "contrary congressional command" that would prevent enforcement of an arbitration agreement.[3] The Court also vacated decisions by the state Supreme Courts of California[4] and West Virginia,[5] striking down state policies against pre-dispute arbitration agreements in certain employment agreements and nursing home contracts.

Lower courts have split on some issues raised by *Concepcion.* In *In re American Express Merchants Litigation, Italian Colors Rest. v. American Express Travel Related Servs. Co.,*[6] the Second Circuit distinguished *Concepcion* and struck down an arbitration agreement in American Express's merchant charge card agreement on grounds that the merchant plaintiffs could afford to vindicate their federal antitrust claims only in a class action. The Second Circuit relied on *dicta* in *Green Tree Financial Corp.-Alabama v. Randolph*[7] that "the existence of large arbitration costs could preclude a litigant . . . from effectively vindicating her federal statutory rights in the arbitral forum." The Ninth Circuit[8] and the Eleventh Circuit[9] have rejected the Second Circuit's "vindication of statutory rights" argument, noting that it relies on "the very public policy arguments

1. __ U.S. __, 132 S. Ct. 665 (2012).
2. 15 U.S.C. § 1679 *et seq.*
3. *CompuCredit Corp.*, *supra*, 132 S. Ct. at 670–71.
4. Sonic-Calabasas A Inc. v. Moreno, __ U.S. __, 132 S. Ct. 496 (2011).
5. Marmet Health Care Center, Inc. v. Brown, ___ U.S. ___, 132 S. Ct. 1201 (2012).
6. 667 F.3d 204 (2d Cir. 2012).
7. Green Tree Financial Corp.-Alabama v. Randolph, 531 U.S. 79, 90 (2000).
8. Coneff v. AT&T Corp., 673 F.3d 1155 (9th Cir. 2012). *See also In re* Apple and ATTM Antitrust Litig., 2011 U.S. Dist. LEXIS 138539 (N.D. Cal. Dec. 1, 2011), rejecting a "deprivation of statutory rights" argument because "it is well established in the Ninth Circuit that claims involving federal statutory rights, and in particular federal antitrust claims, are subject to arbitration."
9. Cruz v. Cingular Wireless LLC, 648 F.3d 1205 (11th Cir. 2011).

that were rejected by the Supreme Court in Concepcion—namely, that the class action waiver will be exculpatory, because most of these small-value claims will go undetected and unprosecuted."[10] It seems likely that the Supreme Court will have to resolve this split in the circuits.

Another split seems to be developing on the question of when classwide arbitration is possible. The Supreme Court held in *Stolt-Nielsen, S.A. v. AnimalFeeds International Corp.*[11] that when an arbitration agreement is silent on the issue, parties cannot be compelled to submit to classwide arbitration. The First, Second, and Third Circuits have subsequently held that even when an arbitration agreement does not mention classwide arbitration, the court or the arbitrator may nevertheless find that the parties reached an implicit agreement to arbitrate on a classwide or collective basis.[12] Other courts have taken a more literal interpretation of *Stolt-Nielsen*, holding that arbitration agreements that do not mention classwide procedures are "silent" and cannot be interpreted to allow for a classwide arbitration.[13] It seems prudent for parties drafting arbitration agreements to state explicitly whether or not they wish to allow classwide arbitration.

On the whole, however, most lower state and federal courts have been following the Supreme Court's *Concepcion* decision by enforcing reasonable contractual arbitration agreements as written, and by recognizing that arbitration agreements are normally incompatible with class-action procedure. This trend seems likely to continue unless there is a change in the makeup of the Supreme Court (*Concepcion* was, after all, a 5-4 decision) or some future Congress amends the Federal Arbitration Act.

---

10. *Id.* at 1214.

11. 130 S. Ct. 1758 (2010).

12. Fantastic Sams Franchise Corp. v. FSRO Ass'n Ltd., ___ F.3d ___, 2012 U.S. App. LEXIS 13175 (1st Cir. June 27, 2012); Sutter v. Oxford Health Plans LLC, 675 F.3d 215 (3d Cir. 2012); Jock v. Sterling Jewelers, Inc., 646 F.3d 113 (2d Cir. 2011).

13. *See, e.g.,* Reed v. Fla. Metro. Univ. Inc, 681 F.3d 630 (5th Cir. 2012); Reed Elsevier, Inc. v. Crockett, 2012 U.S. Dist. LEXIS 23947 (S.D. Ohio Feb. 24, 2012); Bernal v. Burnett, 793 F. Supp. 2d 1280, 1283, 1287 (D. Colo. 2011); D'Antuono v. Service Road Corp., 789 F. Supp. 2d 308, 337, 344 (D. Conn. 2011).

Part Four
TRANSPORTATION

Introduction

The transportation articles from *Infrastructure* focus on railroads and antitrust issues facing the aviation industry.

The first article, written in 2009 by Section Railroad Committee co-chair Linda Stein, and her colleague, Kathryn Gainey, reviews actions by the Surface Transportation Board (STB) relating to a railroad's obligation to transport hazardous materials. In their update, they review the STB's decision terminating the proceeding that it had convened to examine policy solutions to the issue, deciding instead to make determinations on a case-by-case basis.

Judge Cudahy described the promise and challenges of high-speed passenger rail service in an article published in 2009. As he notes in his update, the development of high-speed rail was slowed by political posturing in 2009,[1] but by the summer of 2012 it appeared to be back on track, with federal funding having been redirected to states willing to make use of the funds. In addition, high-speed passenger rail service has, or shortly will, commence on several segments of rail lines in the Midwest.

Aviation Committee Chair Malcolm Benge described several antitrust developments in the aviation industry, with a focus on recent landing and takeoff slot transfers and exchanges at the metropolitan New York airports and Reagan National Airport in Washington, D.C. In his update, Mr. Benge summarizes the settlement of the Delta-US Airways slot exchange, which has been approved by the U.S. Department of Transportation. As part of the exchange, the airlines were required to divest slots at LaGuardia and Reagan National, which slots were subsequently sold by the FAA through an auction process.

Chris Fortier, former young lawyers division liaison to the Section, provides a description and critique of the market approach for dealing with airport congestion and other issues in an article from the Fall, 2008 issue of *Infrastructure*. In his update, Mr. Fortier summarizes the results of the airport slot divesture at LaGuardia and Reagan National.

The final article in Chapter 4 is Bruce McDonald's summary of merger review in transportation and energy industries. In addition to the U.S. Department of Justice

1. The editor's characterization, not the judge's.

(DOJ) and the Federal Trade Commission (FTC), these mergers are reviewed by the agencies having regulatory jurisdiction over their respective industries. In his update, Mr. McDonald reviews the FERC's decision not to adopt the DOJ's and FTC's revised 2010 merger guidelines.

Peter V. Lacouture
September, 2012

Chapter 17

Board Addresses Transportation of Hazardous Materials by Rail*

*By Linda S. Stein and Kathryn J. Gainey***

The Surface Transportation Board has examined the extent of a railroad's obligation as a common carrier to transport hazardous materials in two recent proceedings.[1] Rail transportation of hazardous materials involves several complex issues. As a common carrier, a railroad generally has an obligation to quote a common carrier rate and terms for service "on reasonable request."[2] In June 2009, the board decided a case raising the issue whether a railroad has an obligation to quote rates to transport hazardous materials when the shipper making the request arguably has a closer source of supply that would not involve transportation of those materials through highly populated cities. Specifically, Union Pacific Railroad Company (UP) asked the board whether it has an obligation to quote common carrier rates to transport chlorine, a toxic inhalation hazard (TIH), through multiple large cities when UP contended that an alternate supply of chlorine was available from sources closer to the destinations.[3] Based on the facts of the case, the board concluded that the shipper's request to transport chlorine was not unreasonable and that UP had an obligation to quote common carrier rates for the movements.[4]

* Originally published in *Infrastructure*, vol. 48, no. 4 (Summer, 2009).

** *Linda S. Stein is a partner and Kathryn J. Gainey is an associate in the transportation group of Steptoe & Johnson LLP in Washington, D.C.*

1. The board's jurisdiction over the transportation of hazardous materials by rail is not absolute. While the board has jurisdiction over the scope of a railroad's common carrier obligation, other agencies, including, the Department of Transportation (DOT) and the Transportation Security Administration (TSA), have jurisdiction over issues involving the safety and security of transportation of hazardous materials. *E.g.*, 6 U.S.C. § 1117 (2007 Supp. 2009); 49 U.S.C. § 5101 (2006).
2. 49 U.S.C. § 11101(a) (2006).
3. *Decision, Union Pac. R.R. Co—Pet. for Declaratory Order*, STB Fin. Docket No. 35219 at 1 (STB served June 11, 2009) (hereinafter "*Decision*"), *available at* 2009 WL 1630587. All filings in STB dockets are available from http://www.stb.dot.gov.
4. *Decision*, at 4-6.

A year earlier, in June 2008, the board held a public hearing to address possible policy solutions to the potentially catastrophic liability faced by railroads in transporting hazardous materials.[5] The hearing focused on indemnification, sharing of liability, and the availability of insurance to cover potential losses. The board has not issued any decision or proposed rules subsequent to the hearing.

Board Finds UP Has a Common Carrier Obligation to Transport TIH Materials

UP received a request from US Magnesium LLC (USM) to quote common carriage rates for the transportation of chlorine to 35 destinations.[6] UP quoted rates to 31 destinations but declined to quote rates to four destinations, contending that USM's request to quote rates to those four locations was unreasonable because it involved transporting TIH materials over a long haul of more than 1,000 miles through high-threat urban areas (HTUAs) when there are an "ample alternate chlorine supplies" within 300 miles of the destinations.[7] The four locations at issue involved rail transportation from Utah to various cities in Texas and Louisiana.[8]

In a petition filed with the board on February 18, 2009, UP asked the board to declare that it did not have a common carrier obligation to quote the rates requested by USM for the four movements at issue because the requested transportation "has not been used recently;" "would displace much closer sourcing options;" and "increases safety and security risks to employees and the public."[9] UP contended that USM's request conflicted with the policies of the Transportation Security Administration (TSA) and the Department of Transportation (DOT), including the suggestion of those agencies that railroads and shippers work together to "find ways to reduce TIH [materials'] transportation risks."[10]

USM opposed UP's petition and asked that the board compel the railroad to establish the requested common carrier rates.[11] USM claimed that UP's refusal to quote rates violated its "unqualified" common carrier obligation.[12] USM emphasized that it is North America's "sole producer of magnesium," that chlorine results from its pro-

---

5. *Notice of Public Hearing, Common Carrier Obligation of Railroads—Transp. of Hazardous Materials*, STB Ex Parte 677 (Sub-No. 1) (STB served June 4, 2008), *available at* 2008 WL 2271471 (hereinafter "*STB Notice*").

6. Union Pac. R.R. Co.'s Rebuttal & Reply to Comments, STB Fin. Docket No. 35219 at 2 (filed Apr. 30, 2009) (hereinafter "UP Rebuttal").

7. Union Pac. R.R. Co.'s Pet. for Declaratory Order, STB Fin. Docket No. 35219 at 2-3 (filed Feb. 18, 2009) (hereinafter "UP Pet."). HTUAs are designated by the TSA. U.S. Dep't of Transp. Comments, STB Fin. Docket No. 35219 at 1 (filed Apr. 10, 2009) (hereinafter "DOT Comments") (*See* 49 C.F.R. Part 1580 Appx. A).

8. *Decision*, at 1.

9. UP Pet. at 4.

10. *Id.* at 2, 4.

11. USM Opp'n Comments, STB Fin. Docket No. 35219 at 11 (filed Mar. 23, 2009).

12. *Id.* at 6-7 (citing 49 U.S.C. § 11101(b)).

duction process, and that UP previously shipped USM's chlorine to two of the four destinations at issue.[13]

In its rebuttal comments, UP responded that a rail carrier's common carrier obligation is not absolute.[14]

Several parties commented on UP's petition, including the DOT and TSA, which are federal agencies with jurisdiction over issues involving the safety and security of transportation of hazardous materials.[15] From the DOT's perspective, "the continued rail movement of hazardous materials, including [poisonous by inhalation or] TIH materials, is vital to the national economy and the Board itself noted that '[f]or many hazardous materials, including TIH [materials], rail is the safest and most efficient mode of transportation.'"[16]

In its decision, the board "clarif[ied]" that UP's common carrier obligation includes the obligation to quote rates and provide service to USM for the four chlorine movements at issue.[17] As a general matter, the board explained that a railroad should provide a common carrier rate to a shipper requesting one and should "provide rail service pursuant to those rates upon reasonable request."[18] The board noted that the phrase "reasonable request for service" is "not statutorily defined but depends on all the relevant facts and circumstances."[19] The board further explained that "a rail carrier may not avoid its common carrier obligation to provide service by evading the requirement to establish rates upon request."[20]

The board then addressed the specific question whether UP had provided a "sufficient explanation to relieve it of its common carrier obligation" to transport chlorine to all requested destinations.[21] The board concluded that UP had failed to do so—UP failed to establish that there are closer sources of chlorine to the relevant destinations and failed to establish that the transportation at issue was unsafe given that UP previously transported chlorine for USM to two of the four destinations at issue.[22]

Even if UP's request were construed as a request for "approval to impose additional safety and security measures on USM shipments" by eliminating long distance moves, the board decided that UP's request must be denied. A request for additional safety and security measures could only be granted if UP "prov[ed] that the safety and security regulations of DOT and TSA are unsatisfactory or inadequate."[23]

---

13. *Decision*, at 2.
14. UP Rebuttal at 3-5.
15. DOT Comments at 2-3; TSA Comments, STB Fin. Docket No. 35219 at 1-2 (filed Apr.10, 2009) (hereinafter "TSA Comments").
16. DOT Comments at 2-3.
17. *Decision*, at 1, 6 n.29, 7.
18. *Id.* at 3.
19. *Id.* at 3-4.
20. *Id.* at 4.
21. *Id.*
22. *Id.* at 5. The Chlorine Institute asserted that the supply of chlorine in the Gulf Coast region is inadequate. Chlorine Inst., Inc.'s Comments, STB Fin. Docket No. 35219 at 4 (filed Mar. 12, 2009).
23. *Decision*, at 6.

Relying on comments made by the DOT and TSA, the board found that UP did not satisfy this burden.[24]

The DOT and TSA commented that the safety and security of a TIH movement cannot be measured by the length of the route alone.[25] Specifically, the DOT took issue with UP's assumption that a shorter route is necessarily a safer route, stating that all 27 of the DOT's risk factors, not just the length of the route, need to be considered in assessing the adequacy of the route.[26] Other factors that must be considered include "the rail infrastructure characteristics along the route, proximity to iconic targets, environmentally sensitive or significant areas, population density and emergency response capabilities."[27] The DOT has required a railroad to "use routes with the fewest overall safety and security risks to transport security-sensitive hazardous materials."[28]

The DOT and TSA acknowledged that the safety and risk in transporting TIH "will never be zero," and that UP "is free to and encouraged to adopt" measures in addition to those adopted by the DOT and TSA to effect the safety and security of transporting TIH materials.[29] However, the federal agencies explained that they have developed a comprehensive set of regulations that effectively mitigate the safety risk associated with the transportation of hazardous materials and that a railroad could mitigate its risk in transporting hazardous materials by following the agencies' rules.[30]

The DOT and TSA further commented that although railroads "are the parties best suited to initially analyze safety and security risks along the[ir] routes," the security rules adopted by the agencies "were not intended to inhibit transportation."[31] According to the DOT, the security rules thus do not permit "railroads to decline to transport [TIH] materials between certain shippers and receivers."[32]

Board's Public Hearing Addresses Potential Policy Solutions to the Liability Risks Facing Railroads Transporting Hazardous Materials

In June 2008, the board held a public hearing designed to discuss potential industry-wide solutions to the liability risks railroads incur in transporting hazardous materials. Estimates of potential loss from an incident involving TIH materials range up to $423 billion for an incident in Des Moines and up to $778.1 billion for an incident in New York City.[33] The board's public hearing focused on potential solutions to cover the risk

24. *Id.* at 5-6.
25. DOT Comments at 10; TSA Comments at 4.
26. DOT Comments at 4-5, 10.
27. *Id.* at 10.
28. *Id.* at 5.
29. DOT Comments at 11-13; TSA Comments, at 4-5.
30. DOT Comments at 2, 7, 15; TSA Comments at 3.
31. DOT Comments at 3, 15; TSA Comments at 4.
32. DOT Comments at 5.
33. UP's Verified Statement of Warren B. Beach, Vice President for Fin. & Insurance, STB Ex Parte No. 677 (Sub-No. 1) at 5-6 (filed Aug. 21, 2008) (hereinafter "Beach V.S.") (citing 2006 estimate by the American Academy of Actuaries).

of TIH losses, and the participants examined proposals such as indemnity, shared liability, and private insurance.[34]

Proposals to Limit the Railroad's Liability. The board asked the participants to provide "specific potential policy solutions to the liability issue including solutions modeled on the Price-Anderson Act of 1957."[35] The Price-Anderson Act limits the liability of a nuclear power company from an incident involving the release of nuclear material, including transportation of those materials.[36] Under the Price-Anderson Act, nuclear power plant licensees contribute to a fund that covers damages in excess of required insurance levels.

The railroads supported a legislative proposal that would impose overall limitations on liability for rail transportation of TIH materials, including Price Anderson-type legislation.[37] Some shippers opposed this solution, citing factual distinctions between the Price-Anderson Act and a railroad's common carrier obligation.[38] DOT and some shippers emphasized that Congress alone may enact specific legislation concerning the risks of rail transportation of TIH materials.[39]

Proposals to Share Liability. The railroad associations proposed liability sharing models to the board. The Association of American Railroads (AAR) requested the board to issue a policy statement that would permit the railroads "to impose reasonable liability sharing requirements as a condition of TIH materials common carriage."[40] Under the AAR's proposal, railroads could include as a term for common carriage that the shipper would indemnify the railroad against liability for transportation of TIH materials in "excess of (1) the maximum amount of insurance that the railroad carries for TIH transport or (2) $500 million for Class I railroads, whichever is greater; and to provide reasonable assurances in the form of insurance or other means to support such indemnity."[41] The AAR reasoned that shippers should bear more liability because they "have the option whether to make and ship TIH materials."[42]

The American Short Line and Regional Railroad Association (ASLRRA) asked the board to make the small railroad's (Class II and Class III railroads) common carrier

34. STB Notice in STB Ex Parte No. 677 (Sub-No. 1), at 2.

35. *Id.* at 1-2.

36. Price-Anderson Act, 42 U.S.C. § 2210 (2000); Beach V.S. at 6 ("UP does not face 'bet the company' exposure whenever it transports a load of spent nuclear fuel.").

37. AAR's Supplemental Test., STB Ex Parte No. 677 (Sub-No. 1) at 2-4 (filed Aug. 21, 2008) (hereinafter "AAR's Supp. Test."); Am. Short Line & Reg'l R.R. Ass'n ("ASLRRA") Comments, STB Ex Parte No. 677 at 2-3 (Sub-No. 1) (filed Aug. 22, 2008) (hereinafter "ASLRRA Comments").

38. *E.g.*, The Fertilizer Inst. Test., STB Ex Parte No. 677 (Sub-No. 1) at 19-20 (filed July 10, 2008) (hereinafter "TFI Test."); Nat'l Grain & Feed Ass'n Statement, STB Ex Parte No. 677 (Sub-No. 1) at 8 (filed July 10, 2008).

39. DOT Statement, Presented by Clifford Eby, Deputy Federal Railroad Administrator, STB Ex Parte No. 677 (Sub-No. 1) at 15 (filed July 22, 2008); Chlorine Inst., Inc. Test., STB Ex Parte No. 677 (Sub-No. 1) at 12-13 (filed July 10, 2008) (hereinafter "Chlorine Inst. Test.").

40. AAR's Supp. Test. at 7.

41. AAR Test., STB Ex Parte No. 677 (Sub-No. 1) at 24 (filed July 10, 2008).

42. AAR's Supp. Test. at 3-4.

obligation to transport TIH materials "contingent on the willingness of all parties to a movement to share equitably the risk" of liability, including shippers and Class I railroads (the large railroads) interchanging the TIH materials.[43] The AAR opposed the ASLRRA's liability-sharing proposal, arguing that shippers should bear the primary risk and liability above the shortline's insurance coverage if an incident occurs on a shortline, and not a Class I railroad that was not involved in the incident.[44]

The shippers opposed liability-shifting policies, claiming that the railroads are responsible to ensure safe transportation of the cargo once the shippers have selected proper cars and complied with regulatory requirements.[45] They contended that liability-shifting proposals reduce "incentives [for railroads] to prevent accidents and improve their safety practices."[46] They feared the railroads would use a tariff publication to require a shipper to indemnify a railroad for the railroad's own negligence.[47] The shippers also maintained that the railroads' policy statement invades the jurisdiction of the Federal Railroad Administration (FRA) because the board has not been delegated authority to regulate either rail transportation safety or the transportation of hazardous materials.[48] The shippers assert that the ability of shippers to assume the costs of indemnification and damages is "irrelevant to the ... propriety of AAR's request."[49]

Availability of Private Insurance. The participants disagreed about the availability of insurance coverage for railroads. The shippers contended that concerns about "ruinous liability" for the railroads are unfounded because no such event has occurred.[50] The railroads disagreed.

The AAR indicated that available insurance for the Class I railroads is limited to approximately $1.1 billion with large self-insured retentions (typically $25 million) required.[51] The railroads consider $1 billion to be insufficient to cover their potential exposure for incidents involving TIH materials.[52] The railroads also expressed concern about insurance options, asserting that the reinsurance market will contract with additional large claims, liability insurance capacity has declined 30 percent in the last five years, and insurers are concerned with the "almost unquantifiable exposure related to a large release of TIH in a congested area."[53] Given the high cost of private insurance and its limited availability in the market, AAR posited that private insurance alone is

---

43. Letter from ASLRRA to STB, STB Ex Parte No. 677 at 2 (Sub-No. 1) (filed Dec. 22, 2008).
44. AAR's Supp. Test. at 13-14.
45. Agric. Retailers Ass'n et al. Supp. Comments, STB Ex Parte No. 677 (Sub-No. 1) at 23 (filed Aug. 21, 2008).
46. *Id.* at 24.
47. *Id.* at 7.
48. *Id.* at 8-9.
49. *Id.* at 30-31.
50. *Id.* at 24; Chlorine Inst. Test. at 10-12.
51. AAR's Supp. Test. at 14 & 15 n.8.
52. Beach V.S. at 4.
53. AAR's Supp. Test. at Ex. A at 2; Beach V.S. at 5.

unlikely to be the ultimate solution because the necessary levels of insurance coverage are not available in the insurance market.[54]

The ASLRRA emphasized that the risk of transporting TIH materials threatens the financial viability of the railroad. Shortline railroads cannot afford to insure the movement of hazardous TIH materials as few such railroads carry more than $25 million in insurance.[55]

The Fertilizer Institute (TFI), a trade association whose members produce and ship fertilizer that contains TIH materials, outlined a proposal to relieve part of the cost of railroads' liability insurance. Under the TFI's proposal, its members would agree with a Class I railroad that shippers would assume part of the cost of liability insurance in exchange for rate caps.[56] The shippers would maintain excess liability insurance coverage above the primary insurance level, but would not accept liability.

The board has not acted in Ex Parte 677 regarding potential policy solutions since holding the hearing in June 2008. The board has several options for its next move in Ex Parte 677. It could hold another hearing or could reopen the record for additional comments. Alternatively, the board could institute a rulemaking and propose new rules for comment or it could terminate the proceeding without proposing any rules.

54. AAR's Supp. Test. at 15.
55. ASLRRA Comments at 2-3.
56. TFI Test. at 15-17.

2012 Update

By Linda S. Stein and Kathryn J. Gainey

The Surface Transportation Board has continued to consider issues relating to a railroad's obligation as a common carrier to transport hazardous materials. In April 2011, almost three years after the public hearing in Ex Parte 677, the Board terminated the proceeding without deciding the issues discussed at the hearing.[1] Instead, the Board stated a preference for deciding disputes regarding the transportation of hazardous materials on a "case-by-case basis."[2]

In the same decision in which it terminated Ex Parte 677, the Board also terminated a process that it initiated in 2010 to create a TIH (Toxic by Inhalation Hazard) Common Carrier Transportation Advisory Committee (TIH Advisory Committee).[3] In April 2010, the Board had announced that it would create the TIH Advisory Committee to advise the Board regarding issues related to transportation of hazardous materials, such as the common carrier obligation to transport such materials and "a railroad's reasonable response to a shipper's request that it transport TIH cargo."[4] The Board had envisioned that the advisory committee would "seek industry consensus on the kinds of factors the Board could consider when parties raise issues of liability before this agency."[5] The liability issues would include AAR's proposed policy statement in Ex Parte 677 asking the Board to "approv[e] the right of a rail carrier to establish, as conditions of transport, reasonable liability-sharing arrangements with shippers and ask[ing] the Board to find that such conditions are reasonable service terms for rail common carrier transportation of TIH materials."[6]

In its decision declining to create the TIH Advisory Committee, the Board explained that parties had raised concerns regarding the Board's jurisdictional authority to address the risk of catastrophic liability and committee members'

---

1. Decision, *Establishment of the Toxic by Inhalation Hazard Common Carrier Transportation Advisory Committee*, STB Ex Parte No. 698, and *Common Carrier Obligation of Railroads—Transportation of Hazardous Materials*, STB Ex Parte No. 677 (Sub-No. 1) at 4 (STB served Apr. 15, 2011) (hereafter EP 677 (Sub-No. 1) & EP 698 Decision).
2. *Id.* at 4 n.8 (citing 49 U.S.C. § 11101).
3. *Id.* at 4.
4. *Id.* at 1.
5. *Id.* at 3, 4 n.8.
6. *Id.*

potential exposure to antitrust liability.[7] In that decision, the Board also declined to issue AAR's proposed "policy statement [described above] in the abstract."[8] In declining to issue AAR's policy statement, the Board opted to "resolv[e] disputes related to the reasonableness of both requests to transport TIH cargo and the carriers' responses on a case-by-case basis under 49 U.S.C. § 11101."[9]

Since the Board's decision to discontinue the proceeding in Ex Parte 677 and to decline to create the TIH Advisory Committee, several proceedings have been initiated at the Board seeking to clarify the conditions that a rail carrier may impose on the transportation of hazardous materials.[10] The Board has not yet resolved the issues raised in all of these proceedings.

---

7. *Id.* at 3–4.
8. *Id.* at 4 n.8.
9. *Id.*
10. *See, e.g., Am. Chem. Council, The Chlorine Inst., Inc., The Fertilizer Inst.*, and *PPG Indus., Inc. v. Ala. Gulf Coast Ry. and RailAmerica, Inc.*, STB NOR Docket No. 42129, and *CF Indus., Inc. v. Ind. & Ohio Ry., Point Comfort & N. Ry., and the Mich. Shore R.R.—Petition for Declaratory Order*, STB Fin. Docket No. 35517 at 6 (STB served Sept. 30, 2011) (dispute regarding "certain requirements for rail transportation of [TIH/PIH] materials promulgated by RailAmerica . . . and several of its railroad subsidiaries"); *Union Pacific R.R. Co.—Petition for Declaratory Order*, STB Fin. Docket 35504 at 4 (STB served Dec. 12, 2011) (proceeding regarding the reasonableness of Union Pacific's indemnification provisions in its tariff regarding transportation of TIH commodities); *Canexus Chems. Canada, L.P. v. BNSF Ry. Co.*, STB NOR Docket No. 42131, at 12–13 (STB served Feb. 8, 2012) (interchange dispute between two railroads for the transportation of chlorine from North Vancouver and Marshall, Wash.).

Chapter 18

High-Speed Rail on the "Fast Track"*

*By Hon. Richard D. Cudahy***

In the push for a renewed infrastructure, economic growth, energy efficiency, reduced pollution, and other benefits, high-speed railroad passenger service has gained a new lease on life. The appropriations committees of both the Senate and the House had provided $2 billion in stimulus spending for high-speed rail when White House Chief of Staff Rahm Emanuel appeared at the Conference Committee and, in the president's name, asked for $10 billion. The result: The stimulus legislation provided *$8 billion* for high-speed rail and administered a jump start that may plant this long-time dream deep in solid reality. And another billion a year is promised for each of the next five years. As further proof that high-speed rail has moved from long-term aspiration to current anticipation, President Obama personally instructed Transportation Secretary Ray LaHood, a former Peoria congressman, that high-speed rail was his top transportation priority and that LaHood should promptly get it done. This directive seemed on the way to realization when the strategic rail plan required by law emerged even before the congressional 60-day deadline set for its completion. Obama reportedly sees high-speed rail as his legacy like the interstate highway system was for President Eisenhower.

High-speed rail has, of course, been a long-held hope of transportation visionaries looking for, among other things, energy efficiency as well as broader goals in faster growth, reduced congestion, and environmental relief. For intercity travel, automobiles and airlines are the main alternative, and the current transportation system featuring these two modes consumes 70 percent of our oil demand and contributes 28 percent of our greenhouse gas emissions. High-speed rail for distances of 500 miles or less can compete effectively with airlines, which are part of the petroleum gluttony. And this leaves *long-distance* travel to the airlines, for which it is a priority. Although there has been some rivalry between Southwest Airlines and projected high-speed rail in Texas (state-sponsored and involving Dallas, Houston, and San Antonio), most air-

* Originally published in *Infrastructure*, vol. 48, no. 4 (Summer, 2009).

** *Richard D. Cudahy is a judge on the U.S. Court of Appeals, 7th Circuit, in Chicago and coeditor of* Infrastructure.

lines in Texas have come to terms with the prospect of high-speed trains, and there seems an appropriate place for all modes of transportation.

Passenger rail service in the United States dates from 1830, when the Baltimore and Ohio Railroad ran a horse-drawn passenger car a few miles out of Baltimore. A recent study by S.C. Stormount Corporation commissioned by Air Canada and CP Rail indicates that as many as half of the 1,500 air travelers surveyed would likely switch to high-speed rail given such an option. Outside the United States, rail ticket prices run slightly lower than the cost for air travel along the same routes. On another front, of course, even fast trains must contend with the storied affection of Americans for their automobiles, which may be the most potent factor potentially undermining the success of high-speed rail. But it would be a mistake to overrate the force of ingrained habits under radically new circumstances of cost and convenience.

It is well known that high-speed rail developments in foreign venues burgeoned at about the time that passenger rail service (except AMTRAK) ended in the United States. The French began to develop their Train a Grande Vitesse (TGV), which eventually provided regularly scheduled passenger service at speeds over 180 mph, and the TGV in 2007 set the world's speed record, reaching 357 mph.[1] The granddaddy of them all, the Japanese Shinkansen, or bullet train, has been in operation since 1964. As of 1994, the Shinkansen operated about 260 trains per day serving 400,000 passengers with an on-time record of 99 percent, traveling at speeds up to 180 mph with a system record of no injuries or fatalities. The German Federal Railway operates the Inter City Express (ICE). These trains are among the fastest in the world, achieving 186 mph on new lines. Great Britain, Belgium, Portugal, Switzerland, Austria, Spain, and the Netherlands are also participating in impressive electric powered system development. In addition to these steel wheel systems, Germany and Japan have separately developed a prototype magnetic levitation (maglev) technology, where speeding trains float in magnetic fields. Maglev technology was pioneered in the United States and will also be the recipient of stimulus subsidies.[2]

Earlier legislative support for high-speed and other surface transportation programs was provided in the Intermodal Surface Transportation Efficiency Act of 1991, signed by President George H. W. Bush, which provided funds for steel rail and maglev development. Such programs were already going forward in a number of states such as Florida. Florida created a High Speed Rail Authority consisting of voting members chosen by the governor and legislative leadership. The Florida Transportation Commission, the Department of Community Affairs, and the Department of Environmental Protection participate actively in providing technical and scientific information for the benefit of the governing body. Since Florida's population is expected to double over the next 25 years, marketing plans are needed to supplement feasibility studies. For example, the "Fluor-Bombardier" Marketing Plan, which deals with a scheme for a high-speed corridor between the international airports of Tampa and Orlando, furnishes

1. Brian Knowlton, *Obama Seeks High-Speed Rail System Across U.S.*, N.Y. Times, Apr. 17, 2009, at A16.

2. Ariane Bernard, *Research Model of French Train Beats a Speed Record, Hitting 357 Miles an Hour*, N.Y. Times, Apr. 4, 2009, at C4.

a management plan for the operations and maintenance of a high-speed train system. The Tampa-Orlando High Speed Rail Link will use Bombardier's FedTrain technology, which is a byproduct of a joint development arrangement with the Federal Railroad Administration.[3] As integral elements in building high-speed rail projects, the Florida High Speed Rail Authority carefully pursues environmental preservation and conservation principles. This Florida legislation employs very comprehensive public land use and environmental protection language. The Act also provides an opportunity for opponents of development of a high-speed rail system to voice their objections.

The scope of this sort of legislation and planning suggests the sort of problems requiring solution in the building of high-speed rail networks in the United States. Although high-speed rail solves many environmental problems, such as reduction of carbon dioxide emissions, it may create others, such as obnoxious noise and an increased need for grade crossing protection. In general, its undesirable aspects are intensification of difficulties associated with railroads since they first came on the scene. In some countries, wild animal track crossings have been provided as a conservation measure, raising memories of buffalo terrified by the Iron Horse crossing the Great Plains, accompanied by the chugging and hissing of steam locomotion. In addition, rights-of-way through populous areas will have to be carefully planned to allow for safe and convenient operation.[4] This intrusion of a new technology on the massed habitations of human beings should not present problems they have not dealt with for many years in other contexts. There is no reason to believe, for example, that the noisy approach of high-speed trains will be more problematic than the proximity of high-powered airplanes.

California and Texas have also engaged in planning and in designing governmental arrangements to accommodate high-speed rail. In California the California High-Speed Rail Authority is the principal state body responsible for planning, designing, and building a high-speed rail transit system. The most recent plan involves high-speed rail transit between San Francisco, Oakland, and Sacramento and another connection between Los Angeles and San Diego. With appropriate regard for the physical terrain, these high-speed networks are planned to include exclusive tracks that are fully grade-separated, either in open trench or tunnel, or on elevated guideways. These train lines are designed to be built within or adjacent to existing railways. Environmental reports suggest the following benefits for California: (1) costing two to three times less than expanding highways and airports to serve equivalent demands; (2) easing growing demand on highways and airports; (3) accommodating as many as 68 million passengers yearly by 2020; (4) energy efficiency; (5) quick travel times; (6) low passenger costs per mile; (7) being safer and more reliable than highway and air travel; (8) connecting existing airports and transit terminals along high-speed train corridors.

3. Brian Kingsley Krumm, *High Speed Ground Transportation Systems: A Future Component of America's Intermodal Network*, 22 Transp. L.J. 309, 312 (1994).

4. Kamaal R. Zaidi, *High Speed Rail Transit: Developing the Case for Alternative Transportation Schemes in the Context of Innovative and Sustainable Global Transportation Law and Policy*, 26 Temp. J. Sci. Tech. & Envtl. L. 301, 331 (2007).

In Texas, the high-speed rail study has focused on the Dallas-San Antonio-Houston triangle, and in 1992 the Texas Authority awarded a franchise agreement to Texas TGV Consortium to build a high-speed rail system. But, as earlier indicated, opposition from Southwest Airlines helped to derail the project. However, a unique partnership between the airline industry and high-speed transit companies has now developed.[5] These developments and others, primarily in populous states, have pointed the way for federally supported progress in this area. In addition, Chicago and appropriate destinations, within 500 miles, such as Milwaukee and Detroit, are a prime target for the location of high-speed service; and, since this area is home to the president of the United States, the secretary of transportation, and other key transportation decision makers, it is unlikely to be neglected in the development of high-speed services. Other high-speed rail transit projects projected by the Federal Rail Administration include corridors in the Pacific Northwest, California, the South Central area including Texas, the Gulf Coast, Florida, the Southeast, the Keystone area including Pennsylvania and Maryland, and the Northeast including northern New England.[6] Certain Canadian provinces have also engaged in high-speed planning activities, and the Bombardier company in Montreal is a developer of high-speed technology.

Other campaigns over the years have exploited the enthusiasm generated by high-speed rail. During the 1992 presidential campaign, candidates Clinton and Gore promised a high-speed rail network connecting major cities with trains running up to 300 miles per hour. The network would be financed partially from funds formerly committed to defense. The hope was that there would be a greater emphasis on high-speed ground transportation systems that would provide a new dimension for the nation's transportation infrastructure as well as providing an economic mechanism for the defense industry to make a transition from weapons manufacture to developing high-speed rail system components. The secretary of transportation in April of 1993 announced a proposal for a strategy in which the federal government would work in partnership with state and local communities to build high-speed rail corridors, which would create jobs and stimulate economic growth. The total proposed federal expenditure under the Clinton initiative during the ensuing five years would total $1.285 billion. Additionally, the Clinton administration hoped to leverage the federal funds invested in high-speed rail to generate at least $2 billion in investment in high-speed rail infrastructure from state, local, and private sources.

AMTRAK, established in 1970, was the remnant of passenger rail in the United States, and its high-speed efforts became focused on the Northeast Corridor running between Washington, D.C., and Boston.[7] Over the years, the Northeast Corridor became entirely electrified in time to accommodate higher speed Acela Express trains, which ran at average speeds of 87 mph and reached maximum speeds of 125 mph. It was a struggle to achieve successful operation of the Acela, and even today this service is hardly a match for TGV. However, achievements in the Northeast Corridor, which

5. *Id.* at 333 & n.241.
6. *E.g.*, *id.* at 331-36.
7. *Id.* at 326.

will continue to receive stimulus subsidies, point the way for high-speed service in the United States.

An interesting aspect of the Northeast Corridor development is the ownership of much of the track by AMTRAK.[8] Elsewhere, AMTRAK runs on trackage owned by freight railroads, and freight generally has priority over AMTRAK, although railroads are assessed a financial penalty for requiring AMTRAK trains to take to sidings. This arrangement has created difficulties for AMTRAK in making its schedules. In the Northeast Corridor, AMTRAK shares its tracks with freight. It is not clear how much additional right-of-way and track investment would be required to run higher speed service in the Northeast Corridor. However, for the time being, speeds there will be comparable to speeds projected for other regions in the country.

The near-term investment strategy for passenger rail during and after the stimulus phase contemplates development of: (1) new express high-speed corridor service (at operating speeds above 150 mph on primarily dedicated track) in select corridors of 200 to 600 miles; (2) development of emerging and regional high-speed corridor service (at operating speeds up to 90 to 110 mph and 110-150 mph, respectively, on shared and dedicated track) in corridors of 100 to 500 miles; (3) upgrade of reliability and service on conventional intercity rail service (at operating speeds up to 79-90 mph).[9]

There are a number of difficulties to be surmounted in bringing a functional high-speed rail system into existence. One of these is the loss of skilled personnel, including engineers trained in signal, track, and rolling stock design, and loss of expert rail planners and managers, because of the relatively low level of activity in the passenger rail field in the United States in recent years.[10] A variety of aggressive programs will have to be instituted to correct these deficiencies. Another constraint on development will, of course, be inadequate fiscal support. Although the states must participate in rail developments, in general they lack the fiscal capability to create high-speed rail systems where none currently exist, and federal support will be required. In addition, adequate cooperative arrangements with privately owned railroads will have to be achieved. In many cases, private railroads own the infrastructure and will necessarily become partners in whatever efforts are undertaken. This involves the imposition of a high-speed passenger capability on what is generally now a freight-carrying system. Also, multistate partnerships will be required to adequately plan, fund, build, and operate high-speed corridors. Leadership to create these partnerships must be forthcoming, and special emphasis must be placed on adequate safely standards.

The safety record of high-speed rail systems overseas is generally excellent, and it is certainly of great importance to duplicate it here. Safety requires not only the initial installation of an adequate signaling system but the training of personnel in all categories on the importance of safety and the means of its achievement. We already have in

8. Charles A. Spitulnik and Jamie Palter Rennert, *Use of Freight Rail Lines for Commuter Operations: Public Interest, Private Property*, 26 Transp. L.J. 319, 324 n.20 (1999).

9. William E. Thoms and Sonja Clapp, *Labor Protection in the Transportation Industry*, 64 N.D. L. Rev. 379, 391 & n.80 (1988).

10. U.S. Dep't of Transp., *Vision for High-Speed Rail in America* 7 (2009), *available at* http://www.fra.dot.gov/Downloads/RRdev/hsrstrategicplan.pdf (visited June 4, 2009).

this country a relatively safe airline operation, and there is no reason that high-speed rail cannot be even safer. And it would certainly not be a monumental achievement to make it safer than our highways. All this is of great importance not only on its own merits but because of its impact on the economics of the enterprise. Passenger usage should not be discouraged by fears of unsafe operation. This is one problem that can be decisively dealt with from the beginning, and the result can be an invaluable addition to America's transportation system, which seems to be a leader in every category but passenger rail.

~~~~~~~~~~
~~~~~~~~~~

2012 Update

By Hon. Richard D. Cudahy

High-speed rail was partially derailed in 2009, due to fiscal problems and partisan conflict, when the governors of three states rejected federal funds for the purpose. But it is now again gaining traction as 24 states seek to secure high-speed rail funds for themselves. And, notably, in February of 2012 the first 110 mph service outside the northeast was initiated on 80 miles of track between Porter, Indiana, and Kalamazoo, Michigan, en route from Chicago to Detroit. Michigan Governor Snyder has emerged as a champion of Chicago-Detroit high-speed service. Meanwhile, in Wisconsin, there is a controversy between the state and Talgo, a Spanish train manufacturer that built an assembly plant in Milwaukee, about whether the state will accept two state-of-the-art high-speed trains previously ordered.

In Illinois, crews have been at work for two years to upgrade track for 110 mph service between Chicago and St. Louis, and by the fall of 2012 that service will be initiated on a segment of the line. Normal, Illinois, where an intermodal station will be the focus of a downtown redevelopment, has become the "poster child" of community benefits from high-speed rail service. High-speed rail in the northeast United States corridor is planning upgrades from 110 mph to 200+ mph service. And in California the legislature has approved financing and secured $4.2 billion in federal grants for upgrading transit corridors in Los Angeles and San Francisco and for a new grade-separated 220 mph corridor in the Central Valley.

This update (and much of the original article) is based on developments supplied by the Environmental Law and Policy Center in Chicago.

Chapter 19

The Market Approach—The Best Approach?*

*By Chris Fortier***

The year 2008 brought changes to the commercial aviation industry, including capacity cutbacks and other cost-cutting measures. One debate continues amidst capacity cutbacks: How to reduce flight delays and cancellations. Major airports, such as those in the New York City area, have a reputation for departure delays. The airports, the Department of Transportation (DOT), and the Federal Aviation Administration (FAA) have long-term solutions by means of the construction of new runways and the use of NextGen—a series of proposed technology improvements and approach-pattern redesigns that will increase capacity, efficiency, safety, environmental impact, and user access to the skies. Meanwhile, the aviation community asks: How can DOT and FAA set up a short-term regulatory scheme that provides the best, most economical air service to the most passengers without compromising safety? Some advocate for a congestion pricing regime; others prefer that DOT make the decision after a detailed vetting process. Slot allocation for takeoffs and landings at airports continues to be a subject of controversy for federal regulators and the general and commercial aviation communities.

"Slots" are grants to use an airport's runways for landing or takeoff at particular times.[1] Although slots are used at airports nationwide, the busiest airports, such as JFK International and LaGuardia and Newark's Liberty International Airport, limit their slot allocations because demand exceeds airport capacity. In 2007, the FAA temporarily limited aircraft takeoffs and landings at JFK to 81 movements per hour from 6 a.m. to 10:59 p.m.[2] Currently, 90 percent of the slots are leased by airlines that were

---

* Originally published in *Infrastructure*, vol. 48, no. 1 (Fall, 2008).

** *Chris Fortier is an attorney based in Vienna, Virginia, (Washington, D.C. area) and the Young Lawyers Division liaison to the Section since 2006. You may reach him at crfortier@gmail.com.*

1. Tim Hepher, *Factbox: How Airlines Play the Slots Game*, Reuters, Oct. 22, 2008, *available at* http://money.ninemsn. com.au/article.aspx?id=637376.

2. *Operating Limitations at John F. Kennedy International Airport: Order Limiting Scheduled Operations at John F. Kennedy International Airport.* 73 Fed. Reg. 3516, No. 13, § (VI) (H)(4), at 3516.

grandfathered into the system when slots were first introduced to manage airport traffic congestion.[3] One-third of U.S. flights on any given day will fly New York-area airspace.[4] All three airports are known for delays that include lines to approach and land, many airplanes attempting to depart at the same time, and airplanes trying to pull into or back out of a cramped gate area. From January through August 2007, JFK, LaGuardia, and Newark airports had on-time performances that ranged from 57.48 to 59.1 percent. In 2008, there was only marginal improvement: JFK at 66.82 percent, LaGuardia at 58.63 percent, and Newark at 60.83 percent.[5] Compare these on-time performances to other major hubs such as Houston, Texas (averaging 77 percent in 2007 and 2008)[6] or Salt Lake City (79.74 percent in 2007 and 82.61 percent in 2008).[7]

Certain times of the day are worse than others. For example, on-time performance for flights into Newark between 8 and 9 p.m. is 33.9 percent; LaGuardia it's 36.8 percent between 9 and 10 p.m.; and JFK—the worst— was 23 percent between 7 and 9 p.m.[8] Late-day departures were only a little better. From 7 to 9 p.m. in July 2008, there was a 30 to 40 percent chance that your flight would take off on time from Newark; 27.5 to 45 percent chance at JFK; and 43 to 47 percent at LaGuardia.[9]

Dismal on-time performance not only inconviences travelers, it takes a toll on the economy: Individuals arrive late or miss meetings; airlines must accommodate passengers who miss connecting flights; and some passengers wait overnight to find an open seat on the next available flight. Additionally, individuals anticipate delays and schedule earlier flights in order to arrive on time. Such idle time between flights and meetings reduces productivity and constrains individuals' availability. In a January 2008 speech to the Aero Club of Washington, Transportation Secretary Mary Peters reported the cost of such productivity losses exceeds $15 billion.[10] Even Secretary Peters, anticipated delays that day and took an early flight to New York in order to ensure she would arrive in time for a meeting with the mayor. She ended up waiting an hour at Gracie Mansion for her scheduled meeting time.[11]

DOT Congestion Pricing Regime

In 2008, DOT issued two orders that infused a market-based element into the fee structure for operating aircraft in the New York City area: 1) airlines will pay more to fly into New York City during congested periods, and 2) new airlines will be able to bid to

3. Dorothy Robyn, Panel Remarks at ABA Forum on Air & Space Law, Washington, D.C., "Market-Based Remedies to Airport Congestion: Helpful or Harmful?" (Oct. 10, 2008).
4. Robin Shulman, *Contention Over Proposal for New York Airports*, WASH. POST. Sept. 1, 2008, at A4.
5. Bureau of Transportation Statistics, *Airline On-Time Data.* August 2008.
6. Shulman at A4.
7. Shulman at A4.
8. *Air Travel Consumer Report* at 10. U.S. Dep't of Transportation, Office of Aviation Enforcement and Proceedings, Aviation Consumer Protection Division.
9. *Id.* at 12.
10. Del Quentin Wilber, *DELAYED: The Soaring Toll*, WASH. POST, Jan. 28, 2008, at A1.
11. *Id.*

serve the area. DOT intends to create an economic climate where airlines operate flights in a manner that reduces congestion in New York City airspace.

DOT's July 14, 2008, order imposes a new fee structure at New York City area airports. The order, (73 Fed. Reg. 40430), asserts DOT's right to charge fees at airports based on the area's congestion. The order creates a two-part fee system that incorporates time of operation in addition to the current aircraft weight fee structure. An airport proprietor can impose the new fee system on users as long as fees are allocated to users on a "rational and economically justified basis," and total revenues "do not exceed the airfield's allowable costs,"[12] meaning "costs to the airport proprietor of providing airfield services and airfield assets currently in aeronautical use."[13] When the airport has construction or renovation projects, charges to users during congested periods may not exceed corresponding construction costs, which will be calculated to include reasonable amortization based on the term of the permanent project financing relating to the construction.[14] Flights that fall under the Essential Air Service Program[15] will continue to get charged under the weight-based fee system only.[16]

DOT's October 9, 2008, order allows an auction for slots at Newark Liberty International Airport. Slots surrendered by Continental Airlines were auctioned off to the highest bidder. Existing airlines will be able to keep 988 (of 1,101) slots at LaGuardia, 1,035 of 1,124 at JFK, and 1,154 of the 1,245 slots at Newark. Other airlines will have the opportunity to bid on the remaining slots at each airport. The winning airlines will have rights to individual slots for five years.[17] DOT intends to allow new entrants into the New York market while keeping congestion at manageable levels. As Secretary Peters stated:

> Without slot auctions, a small number of airlines will profit while travelers bear the brunt of higher fares, fewer choices and deteriorating service. Slot auctions, meanwhile, will keep flights to New York affordable, available and vibrant while giving all airlines an opportunity to compete in one of the world's most popular aviation markets."[18]

12. 73 Fed. Reg. 40,444, 2.1.4.
13. 73 Fed. Reg. 40,445, 3.
14. 73 Fed. Reg. 40,445, 5(b).
15. This program was formed after the airlines were deregulated in 1978 as a way to keep air service to rural and underserved communities. As airlines were no longer required by their operating certificates to keep serving these communities, this program was formed to make service to these underserved and rural communities economically feasible. DOT calculates a minimum number of seats as sufficient to serve that community from a DOT-specified hub and how many intermediate stops are acceptable. If necessary, DOT will subsidize such service, though it only provides subsidies for 104 out of the 746 communities in the program. *What Is Essential Air Service?* Prepared by the Office of Aviation Analysis, U.S. DOT, May 1, 1998, *at* http://ostpxweb.dot.gov/ aviation/rural/easwhat.pdf (Nov. 28, 2008).
16. 73 Fed. Reg. 40,445, 2.1.4(b).
17. Press Release, U.S. Department of Transportation, U.S. Transportation Secretary Mary E. Peters Announces $89 Million Commitment to Capacity Improvements at JFK International Airport, Releases Final Rules to Improve Service, Keep Fares Competitive at New York's 3 Capped Airports (Oct. 9, 2008), *at* http://www.dot.gov/affairs/dot15008.htm.
18. *Id.*

DOT and FAA see this two-part fee system (factoring in both departure and arrival time and weight) as the future of managing congestion and keeping the traffic flowing from the tarmac to the runway to the air. Infusing an economic element into the equation forces market players to change behavior on the basis of what they can afford and what they are willing to pay. Through these decisions, demand evens out over the course of a day creating less stress and congestion during the peak travel hours. Currently, landing fees are charged based on the departing or arriving airplane's weight. The weight system of fees creates greater incentives to use lighter airplanes, which in this instance are turboprops with fewer than 50 seats and 70- to 90-seat regional jets as opposed to 130-seat plus mainline jets. DOT's new two-part fee structure also takes into account peak usage times and how much other traffic uses that airport.

The market approach aims to make airlines realize true costs. In a world where players are bidding against one another for the right to use the airport at a particular time, they are forced to value the asset—in this case the slot—and figure out which price serves their purposes. DOT views market-based mechanisms as the best solution to manage traffic, as it allows passengers to make decisions that will ultimately reduce the strain on the air traffic system.

With congestion-pricing of landing slots, all airlines would be able to compete for peak service. They would pass these charges on to travelers, thus reflecting the true cost of a trip. Congestion-pricing would also allow airlines to adjust schedules immediately in response to ebbs and flows of traffic.[19]

In theory, such pricing would ease demand through natural behavior adjustments as people base decisions on what they can and cannot afford. In 1968, the New York Port Authority (the agency that manages Newark, LaGuardia, JFK, and Stewart airports) decided to manage congestion at Newark and LaGuardia airports by imposing a fee for aircraft with less than 25 passengers during peak usage hours. Landing fees for these aircraft were raised from $5 to $25 during peak hours. General aviation decreased 30 percent during peak periods and air traffic delays dropped by similar margins. A similar program was tried in Boston in 1988 and had similar reductions in numbers of flights, creating fewer delays.[20] Similarly, charging for slots using a market mechanism will allow airlines to tailor service that creates the most value for everyone in the marketplace. Airlines will then try to increase capacity of flights that fly during peak periods. For example, an airline scaling two regional jet departures previously scheduled for 5 and 5:30 p.m. will move the 5 p.m. flight to 8 p.m. and place a 737 in place of a regional jet, so as to fulfill the demand at 5 and 5:30 p.m.

In addition, airports are monopolies with respect to location, meaning airports do not deal with market pressures with respect to pricing and services. The airlines would

---

19. Evan Sparks, *How to Fix Airport Delays*, The American, Oct, 3, 2007, *at* http://www.american.com/archive/2007/ october-10-07/how-to-fix-airport-delays.

20. JayEtta Z. Hecker, Director Physical Infrastructure Issues, Statement for the record before the Joint Economic Committee, U.S. Congress, *Congestion Pricing Has Promise for Improving Use of Transportation Infrastructure*, U.S. General Accounting Office, at 12 (May 6, 2003). (These practices have since been dropped as a result of a successful lawsuit by commuter airlines).

be at the airports' mercy when it comes to usage and rights fees. "A monopolist airport may have an incentive to maintain congestion and reap the financial rewards of congestion pricing while avoiding the costs of expansion."[21] Airports, as new entrants, cannot emerge quickly and regulation covers the spectrum from ownership to heavy regulation of airports. Such circumstances would compel DOT to act in the public interest and charge the two-part fee as airports do not function in a normal market setting because of the regulatory scheme affecting them.

Criticisms of the Market Approach

How does the market approach to congestion management or slot allocation work with DOT's other air travel priorities? Any adjustment to compensate for one public interest problem will create a new working reality that may pose new challenges in fulfilling other public interest priorities. Some of these interests include providing essential air service to small communities, providing frequent service to midsized markets with proper equipment, and providing travelers the maximum number of service choices during their preferred travel times, amongst others.[22] These interests have been developed and fulfilled through a system of taxes and subsidies that have made it economical for airlines to provide such services. A new charge for congestion will change that system and those other taxes and subsidies will have to be rethought and recalculated to assure that important goals continue to be achieved.

Airports have been using congestion pricing to address air traffic problems. "The market is distorted by decisions about where to build airports, roadways, and railways. We should not price one element of that system at marginal cost and then expect the rest of the system to function properly."[23] Currently, LaGuardia charges $50 per scheduled flight for use of a runway during congested periods. The charge is $25 for off-peak usage.[24] For a jet with 50 passengers, the difference between peak and off-peak facility charges amounts to 50 cents per passenger. Such a structure does not achieve its goal because it does not have enough impact on users to alter their decisions and attach value to the runway use.

Many who doubt the effectiveness of market-based solutions believe that the government regulation, and not market pricing, can best divvy up slots between the airlines. For example, there is reluctance to rely on market pricing to determine that service to a new community should be established as opposed to expanding existing service to a community that the airport already serves. In 2008, when ATA Airlines pulled its service from Reagan Washington National Airport (National), the FAA and DOT held a traditional regulatory vetting process inviting airlines to propose how they

21. Neil J. King and Bruce Rabinovitz, *Congestion Pricing and Capacity-Related Delay at U.S. Airports*, 22 (No. 1) Air & Space Law., (2008) at 22.

22. *Id.* at 23-24.

23. Joshua L. Schank, *Solving Airside Airport Congestion: Why Peak Runway Pricing Is Not Working*, 11 J. Air Transport Management 417-425, 424 (2005).

24. *Id.* at 421.

would use ATA's four slots.[25] Five airlines submitted applications to DOT. Comair wanted to use two slots to serve Birmingham and two slots to serve Fort Walton Beach, Florida. Spirit Airlines wanted to use four slots to serve Fort Lauderdale. AirTran wanted to use two slots to serve Milwaukee and two to serve Jacksonville. Midwest Airlines wanted to use two slots to serve Kansas City and two to serve Milwaukee. US Airways wanted to use four slots to serve Pensacola, Florida. Similar to the situation in New York, DOT used a test to determine who would get available slots. The test is set out in 49 U.S.C. § 41718(b). At National, DOT can allocate 20 slot exemptions, preferably to new entrants and incumbent air carriers that have limited service into the airport. Communities without direct service to National and small communities also get priority in the process. Airlines providing competitive non-stop service to a current monopoly non-stop service at National or maximum competitive benefits also receive priority consideration for new slots.[26] DOT eventually awarded the slots to AirTran for service to Milwaukee and Spirit Airlines because it would provide the most competitive benefits to the Washington, D.C. area by adding service to two new destinations.[27]

Allowing DOT to maintain its regulatory scheme to authorize slot allocation means DOT is able to determine the best use of slots according to the public interest. DOT examined frequency of service, number of seats offered to a destination, how many slots an applicant already had, and if competition for an applicant's air service existed. The submissions for the former ATA slots in Washington, D.C., focused mostly on economic benefits to those destinations that the airlines were proposing to serve— and not to the Washington, D.C. area. DOT determined that Comair (Delta) and US Airways were entrenched carriers and had the capacity to provide service to their proposed destinations without the help of DOT. The other applicants did not have such luxury. Both AirTran and Midwest had applications for service to Milwaukee. As Midwest had the only service to Milwaukee, it had a monopoly on the route. Granting AirTran the slots to fly to Milwaukee created competition and the potential for lower fares between Washington, D.C., and Milwaukee. Spirit Airlines was also selected because it has a history of providing low fares and flying larger aircraft that have altered the markets it serves.[28] Disclosure of the airlines' plans allows for a dialogue in order to determine the best use for the slots. DOT can then analyze those plans and make the best decision on the public's behalf.

As we transition from the Bush to the Obama administration, we will likely see reduced emphasis on market-based proposals to solving the congestion problems in New York and other areas. Expect the Obama administration to end the market ap-

25. Flights serving Reagan Washington National Airport are limited to a distance of 1,250 miles. Order Granting Within-Perimeter Slot Exemptions at Ronald Reagan Washington National Airport. Docket DOT-OST-2000-7182. U.S. Department of Transportation. (Feb. 22, 2008).

26. Order Granting Within-Perimeter Slot Exemptions at Ronald Reagan Washington National Airport, Docket DOTOST- 2000-7182, U.S. Dep't of Transportation (Feb. 22, 2008).

27. Press Release, DOT 26-08. U.S. Department of Transportation, Spirit, AirTran Selected for New Daily Flights from Reagan Washington National Airport to Fort Lauderdale and Either Milwaukee or Jacksonville (Feb. 22, 2008) *at* http:// www.dot.gov/affairs/dot2608.htm.

28. National Airport Order at 10-11.

proach to congestion pricing and slot auctions while ramping up federal funding and accelerating implementation timelines for NextGen and other significant airport improvements.[29] A flying public will welcome these improvements to the system and appreciate the fewer delays and better service. This anticipated change of emphasis will also allow us to compare the results of the two approaches to solving the congestion problem as well as comparing how public policy priorities interact with one another. The debate over how to solve airport congestion will continue as long as passengers experience the chronic delays that plague the system in New York City, but the Obama administration's anticipated focus on accelerating NextGen's implementation is the right focus as it will increase the skies' capacity and restore the flying public's faith in the system.

29. WileyRein, LLP, *The Obama Agenda: Early Predictions on U.S. Aviation Policy, the Airlines, General Aviation, and the Airports*, Airworthy: Insights into Curre nt Aviation Legal Issues, Nov. 18, 2008, at 3; *available at* http://www.wileyrein. com/docs/newsletter_issues/ 626.pdf.

2012 Update

By Chris Fortier

The airline industry, the Federal Aviation Administration (FAA), and the U.S. Department of Transportation (USDOT) are now treating airline slots in New York (LGA) and Washington (DCA) as private property. Airlines have swapped slots and have participated in an auction to allocate slot pairs. While this behavior is normally illegal, the USDOT could grant waivers allowing airlines to trade slots, which it did in 2011.

Delta and US Airways had a nearly year-long drama with the USDOT when they initially attempted to seek a waiver to swap slot pairs at LGA and DCA airports. After nearly a year of negotiation, the USDOT agreed to grant the waiver only if both airlines dispose of one slot bundle (16 slots or eight daily flights) at DCA and two slot bundles at LGA (16 slots each) for an eligible new entrant and limited incumbent carriers. These terms are for airlines with extremely limited presences at either airport. The deal allowed Delta to fortify its New York presence with 132 slot pairs (allowing for an additional 132 daily flights) at LGA and for US Airways to strengthen its Washington, D.C. presence with 42 slot pairs (for a potential of 42 additional flights).

The process turned to allocating the divested slots at each airport. The USDOT and the FAA conducted an auction in November 2011, with the highest bidder winning the slot bundles. Frontier, Southwest, AirTran, JetBlue, Spirit, Allegiant, and Canadian carrier WestJet participated in the auctions. JetBlue was the big winner of the auctions, bidding $40,000,050.01 for the slots at DCA and $32,000,050.01 for the slots at LGA. WestJet won the other 16 slots for auction at $17,600,001.00. Travelers to either airport will notice the greater presence of US Airways and JetBlue at DCA and Delta, JetBlue, and WestJet at LGA.[1]

1. From the Chief Counsel's Office at FAA, http://www.faa.gov/about/office_org/headquarters_offices/agc/ReAllocation/.

Chapter 20

Antitrust Developments in the Aviation Industry*

*By Malcolm L. Benge***

Few industries can match aviation's current pace of consolidation. Over the last 18 months, Delta has absorbed Northwest, United has merged with Continental, and Southwest has sought government approval to acquire AirTran. Airline names long familiar to passengers already have vanished or will soon disappear from the skies. Two recent developments highlight the government's response to this wave of consolidation and the unique competition analysis that applies to the aviation industry.

United/Continental Merger

The United/Continental merger will create the largest airline by traffic, surpassing the combination of Delta and Northwest that was completed at the end of 2009. The merged entity will start out with a route network reaching 370-plus destinations, a flight schedule with over 5,800 daily departures, and a workforce of more than 86,000 employees.[1] Given the size of the combined enterprise and its presumed market power, one may wonder what persuaded the federal government to allow such a large merger to occur.

By agreement with the Federal Trade Commission, the review of airline mergers is conducted exclusively by the Department of Justice (DOJ).[2] The starting point for DOJ's analysis of a proposed airline combination is an examination of the "city-pairs" served by each carrier. A "city-pair" is the service operated by an airline between one city and another. Where the parties to a proposed airline merger have a large number of overlapping city-pairs, i.e., city-pairs where they both provide service, a combination

* Originally published in *Infrastructure*, vol. 50, no. 2 (Winter, 2011).

** *Malcolm L. Benge is a partner with the law firm of Zuckert, Scoutt & Rasenberger, L.L.P. in Washington, D.C.*

1. United Continental Holdings Corporate Fact Sheet, *at* http://www.unitedcontinentalholdings.com/index.php?section=media.

2. Memorandum of Agreement between the Federal Trade Commission and the Antitrust Division of the United States Department of Justice Concerning Clearance Procedures for Investigations, Appendix A (March 5, 2002).

of those carriers will reduce the number of competing airlines in that market diminishing the fare and service options available to passengers. Absent competition from other airlines in the same city-pair, DOJ will generally take a negative view of the merger's effect with respect to that market. An unfavorable assessment is particularly likely in city-pairs where DOJ perceives barriers to entry that make competition from new entrants unlikely. Too many overlapping city-pairs, and DOJ is likely to oppose a proposed airline merger or require it to be modified.

After reviewing the merger plans of United and Continental, DOJ determined that the networks of the two carriers were largely complementary but would still result in overlap on a limited number of routes where United and Continental offer competing nonstop service. Most problematic from DOJ's perspective was the overlapping service at Newark Liberty Airport, where Continental has a hub and operates a substantial share of all flights.[3] A merger with United meant an even greater share of the market would be controlled by a single airline. DOJ's competitive concerns were compounded by the restrictions placed on landing and takeoff operations—or "slots"—at Newark by the Federal Aviation Administration (FAA) in an effort to reduce airspace congestion in the New York metropolitan area. The limited availability of slots at Newark made new entry by other carriers particularly difficult.

Due to its concerns over the merger's competitive impact at Newark, DOJ was prepared to object to certain aspects of the United-Continental transaction. However, DOJ decided to terminate its investigation after United and Continental announced the transfer of 36 landing/takeoff slots at Newark to Southwest Airlines.[4] The slot transfer allowed Southwest to introduce service to Newark, addressing DOJ's concerns about new entry at Liberty Airport in the wake of the merger. With the only basis for objection to the United-Continental merger eliminated, DOJ had no choice than to allow the United-Continental deal to proceed.

The merger drew a rapid competitive response as its approval was quickly followed by Southwest's announcement that it would acquire AirTran. The United-Continental combination leaves just four legacy airlines with hub-and-spoke route networks: United/Continental, Delta Air Lines, American Airlines, and US Airways. Fearing domination of the aviation market by a small number of mega-carriers, some members of Congress criticized DOJ's decision not to oppose the United-Continental merger and even called for reregulation of the airline industry.[5]

---

3. Remarks of Carl Shapiro, Deputy Assistant General for Economics, Antitrust Division, U.S. Department of Justice, as prepared for the American Bar Association Section of Antitrust Law Fall Forum (November 18, 2010), p. 30.

4. Press Release, *United Airlines and Continental Airlines Transfer Assets to Southwest Airlines in Response to Department of Justice's Antitrust Concerns* (Aug. 27, 2010), *available at* http://www.justice .gov/atr/public/press_releases/2010/262002.htm.

5. Statement of Congressman James L. Oberstar, Chairman of the Committee on Transportation and Infrastructure (Aug. 28, 2010).

Delta-US Airways Slot Exchange

DOJ's hands-off approach to the United-Continental combination was in marked contrast to its forceful response to a recent airline industry transaction involving Delta and US Airways. Delta and US Airways proposed to swap landing and takeoff slots at LaGuardia and Washington Reagan National airports. As agreed by the parties, US Airways would transfer 280 slots at LaGuardia in exchange for 84 slots at Reagan National.[6] Because the transfer of slots at LaGuardia is currently restricted by the FAA, the parties to the New York-Washington slot exchange needed a waiver from the FAA's slot rules.

Airport Slot Restrictions and the Proposed Slot Exchange

Limited runway capacity at LaGuardia and Reagan National as well as congested airspace in the Northeast led the FAA over the years to impose a series of limitations on the number of landing and takeoff slots at both airports.[7] In addition, operations at LaGuardia and Reagan National are subject to "perimeter" rules that limit the number of nonstop flights to and from each airport longer than an established distance (1,500 miles at LaGuardia and 1,250 miles at Reagan National). Although Congress had ordered a phase-out of slot restrictions at LaGuardia,[8] the FAA retained its authority to regulate the "safety and movement of air traffic."[9]

Airspace congestion in the New York metropolitan area created such a severe impact on airline operations nationwide that in 2006 the FAA imposed restrictions on airline operations at all three major New York airports, including LaGuardia.[10] Exercising its authority to regulate the use of navigable airspace, the FAA assigned slots at LaGuardia to the carriers operating there and authorized them to lease or trade slot authorizations while the restrictions remained in effect. The FAA's order allocating slots at LaGuardia does not allow for the purchase or sale of slot interests to other carriers, and transfers can occur only through trades or leases. Consequently, the only way for a carrier to purchase or sell a slot is by obtaining a waiver from the FAA.

The slot exchange proposed by Delta and US Airways was deemed by the FAA to involve a sale of LaGuardia slots under the rules limiting airline operations at that airport.[11] The proposed transaction had the potential for enormous impact on competi-

---

6. Joint Request of Delta and US Airways for a Waiver, letter dated August 24, 2009 to J. David Grizzle, Esq., Chief Counsel, Federal Aviation Administration, from Ben Hirst, Senior Vice President and General Counsel, Delta Airlines, Inc. and Stephen L. Johnson, Executive Vice President, Corporate, US Airways, Inc.

7. *See, e.g.*, The High Density Rule codified at 14 C.F.R. Part 93, Subparts K and S.

8, 49 U.S.C. § 41715(a)(2).

9. 49 U.S.C. § 41715(b)(1).

10. Operating Limitations at New York LaGuardia Airport, 71 Fed. Reg. 77,854 (Dec. 27, 2006).

11. Petition for Waiver of the Terms of the Order Limiting Scheduled Operations at LaGuardia Airport, 75 Fed. Reg. 7306 (Feb. 18, 2010).

tion at both LaGuardia and Reagan National: it affected almost 10 percent of the total number of slots at Reagan National and more than 20 percent of all LaGuardia slots.[12] Approval of the transaction would make Delta's operations at LaGuardia two-and-a-half times larger than its nearest competitor and would allow US Airways to become three times the size of its closest rival at Reagan National.[13] The waiver request was therefore accompanied by competitive concerns not usually presented by the ordinary slot transfer.

The FAA's Tentative Decision and DOJ's Comments

The FAA maintained that it could grant the requested waiver only by finding that the proposed transfer "is in the public interest."[14] Its public interest inquiry is guided by several principles, including "avoiding unreasonable industry concentration, excessive market domination, monopoly powers and other conditions"[15] leading to an increase in fares, "encouraging . . . an air transportation system relying on actual and potential competition,"[16] and "encouraging entry into air transportation markets."[17] Based on these public interest considerations, the FAA was only willing to approve the slot exchange subject to certain conditions. Chief among these conditions was a requirement that US Airways and Delta divest slots at LaGuardia and Reagan National that the FAA would then reallocate through a bidding process to other airlines. The FAA's determination was set forth in a tentative decision, which it published in the *Federal Register* for public comment.[18]

DOJ weighed in with comments supporting the FAA's preliminary determination.[19] In DOJ's view, the Delta/US Airways slot deal was a thinly disguised attempt to buttress their respective competitive positions at LaGuardia and Reagan National in order to forestall inroads by low-cost carriers. According to DOJ's analysis, following the slot exchange Delta's share of slots at LaGuardia would increase from 24 percent to 49 percent, making it the dominant slot holder at that airport. US Airways also stood to benefit as its slots at Reagan National—where it already has the largest share of slots—would increase from 44 percent to 54 percent. Under the DOJ/FTC *Horizontal Merger Guidelines*, the increase in market concentration produced by the proposed slot exchange resulted in a presumption of enhanced market power.[20]

---

12. Notice on Petition for Waiver of the Terms of the Order Limiting Scheduled Operations at LaGuardia Airport, 75 Fed. Reg. 26322, 26323, n.8.
13. *Id.* at 26323.
14. *Id.* at 26323 (citing 49 U.S.C. § 40109).
15. 49 U.S.C. § 40101(a)(10).
16. 49 U.S.C. § 40101(a)(12).
17. 49 U.S.C. § 40101(a)(13).
18. 75 Fed. Reg. 7306.
19. Comments of the United States Department of Justice (Docket No. FAA-2010-0109) (March 24, 2010) ("DOJ Comments").
20. DOJ Comments, p. 5 (citing U.S. Department of Justice and Federal Trade Commission, Horizontal Merger Guidelines, § 1.51(1992).

DOJ was most concerned about the effect of the slot deal on market entry at LaGuardia and Reagan National by low-cost carriers (LCCs). Due to a long history of slot controls at both airports, the vast majority of slots were controlled by legacy carriers. At the time of the Delta/US Airways slot exchange announcement, LCCs held fewer than 7 percent of the slots at LaGuardia and only 3.3 percent of Reagan National slots.[21] According to DOJ's analysis, limited LCC presence and slot controls translated into higher fares and profits for incumbent carriers such as Delta and US Airways.

The proposed slot deal threatened to perpetuate in several respects what DOJ perceived as an anticompetitive environment at LaGuardia and Reagan National. Should the slot transfer proceed, DOJ was concerned that Delta and US Airways would engage in "slot hoarding" at LaGuardia and Reagan National, with little or no incentive to lease any of their large portion of slots to LCCs because of the threat to their revenues and profits. Conversely, because the slot exchange would result in reduced slot holdings for US Airways at LaGuardia, and for Delta at Reagan National, they would be likely to use their smaller slot portfolios to operate on routes with higher profit margins and less competition.

DOJ essentially concluded that Delta and US Airways were using the slot exchange to ensure that they would only face competition from other, higher-fare carriers at slot-controlled airports rather than from LCCs. By effectively locking up slots at LaGuardia and Reagan National, the slot deal appeared to DOJ as a way for each carrier to forestall entry by LCCs and create the conditions where they could maintain a fare premium.[22]

Under the FAA's tentative decision, the Delta-US Airways slot exchange would have been allowed to proceed but only on the condition that the parties to the deal dispose of 14 slot pairs at Reagan National and 20 slot pairs at LaGuardia by leasing them to "eligible new entrant and limited incumbent carriers."[23] DOJ supported the FAA's determination mandating the divestiture of slots and offered recommendations on the manner for distributing those slots to other carriers. DOJ examined three different options for reallocating slots suggested by the FAA in its request for public comments, each of which was intended to increase the number of slots available for new service at LaGuardia and Reagan National: (1) private sales with biweekly reports to the FAA on details of the sales efforts; (2) anonymous, cash-only sales in which the FAA awards slots to the highest bidder, and (3) a hybrid process where the FAA would manage the selling process but the terms and conditions of the slot sale would be negotiated by the buyer and the seller. DOJ strongly favored the second method as a way of avoiding any ability on the part of the seller to control the type of airline buying the slots.[24]

The FAA subsequently finalized its determination that it would grant the necessary waiver for the Delta/US Airways slot exchange only if the parties to the transac-

21. DOJ Comments, p. 7.

22. In reaching this conclusion, DOJ noted that the presence of an LLC on a nonstop route reduces fares by "roughly 25 percent." DOJ Comments, p. 7.

23. 75 Fed. Reg. 7306, 7310.

24. DOJ Comments, p. 21.

tion agreed to the proposed slot divestitures at LaGuardia and Reagan National.[25] The final decision adopted DOJ's recommendation that any ensuing slot sales be conducted on a cash-only, carrier-blind basis. Although Delta and US Airways had previously announced agreements with several carriers for the sale of 15 slot pairs at LaGuardia and 4.5 slot pairs at Reagan National in order to address concerns regarding entry by smaller airlines,[26] they were unwilling to agree to the number of slot divestitures mandated by the FAA and supported by DOJ.

Appeal of the FAA's Determination

Delta and US Airways have challenged the FAA's final decision by filing a petition for review of the agency's action with the US Court of Appeals for the District of Columbia Circuit.[27] The petitioners have raised multiple objections to the FAA's determination, including both its refusal to approve the transaction and the requirement for the divestiture of slots at LaGuardia and Reagan National.

The parties to the proposed slot exchange have challenged the FAA's decision on the basis that the applicable regulations governing slot restrictions at LaGuardia allow the FAA only to consider safety matters in deciding whether or not to grant a request for a waiver from those rules. In their view, Congress has not authorized the FAA to consider what effects a transaction may have on competition when examining a waiver request from the slot regulations. The slot exchange should have been approved under this interpretation of the applicable legal criteria, because the FAA found that the proposed transaction does promote safety and the efficient use of airspace, and no other factors are permitted to be taken into consideration by the FAA when ruling on a waiver request.

The petitioners also allege that Congress expressly considered and rejected granting any authority to the Department of Transportation and its component agencies (such as the FAA) that would allow for the review of asset transfers on the basis of their competitive effects. Under their interpretation, such authority was conferred exclusively on DOJ. The FAA's attempt to condition its approval of the slot exchange on divestitures is therefore beyond its regulatory powers. The parties get around the fact that DOJ also opposed the merger by arguing that they submitted their transaction to DOJ for approval and DOJ allowed the statutory period for review to pass without blocking the deal.

The appeal to the D.C. Circuit includes a constitutional challenge to the FAA's determination. Delta and US Airways argue that the forced divestiture of their slots at LaGuardia and Reagan National would result in the disposal of the slots at below-market rates, resulting in a "taking" of those slots without just compensation in viola-

25. 75 Fed. Reg. 26322. The decision was issued as a joint determination of the Department of Transportation and the FAA.

26. Comments of Delta Air Lines, Inc. and US Airways, Inc., p. 5, n.1 (Docket No. FAA-2010-0109) (March 22, 2010).

27. Delta Airlines, Inc. and US Airways, Inc. v. Federal Aviation Administration and U.S. Department of Transportation, (No. 10-1153).

tion of the Fifth Amendment. Essential to this claim is a determination that slot interests represent a property right subject to the takings clause, and not an operating privilege subject to absolute FAA control.

Other airlines have not been neutral in this dispute. Southwest Airlines has sought, and been granted, the right to intervene in the proceedings before the D.C. Circuit.[28] As the largest potential beneficiary of the FAA's determination, Southwest is seeking an outcome upholding the slot divestiture, thereby enhancing its prospects for access to LaGuardia and Reagan National.

With Southwest's intervention in the court challenge to the FAA's determination, what began as a relatively straightforward request for a waiver from the FAA's slot rules has become a full-fledged donnybrook. At stake is the competitive structure of two of the country's most lucrative aviation markets, where limits on operations in the form of slot restrictions create the circumstances allowing airlines to reap a fare premium. It remains to be seen whether DOJ's involvement in the dispute over the Delta/US Airways slot exchange portends a more activist stance with respect to airline competition. Given the current pace of consolidation among airlines, DOJ is almost certain to face additional developments requiring a decision as to how and to what degree it will need to shape competitive conditions in the aviation industry.

28. Motion for Leave to Intervene of Southwest Airlines Co. (Case No. 10-1153) (July 30, 2010).

2012 Update

By Malcolm L. Benge

Despite rumblings of additional mergers among the larger players in the aviation industry, there have been no recent combinations rivaling the United-Continental and Southwest-Air Tran deals. Nevertheless, competition among airlines is still receiving its share of attention from government regulators. The dispute over the Delta-US Airways slot deal, while ultimately resolved outside the courtroom, ended in a settlement involving a remarkable set of government-imposed conditions on the allocation of slots at both La Guardia and Reagan National airports. Notwithstanding the settlement, which was largely the work of the Department of Transportation (DOT), the Department of Justice (DOJ) warned airlines that it would continue to monitor the effects of the slot deal on competition and the traveling public.

Having initially appealed DOT's refusal to approve their slot deal, Delta and US Airways decided to end their court battle in favor of a negotiated resolution. Under the terms of the settlement with DOT, Delta and US Airways reapplied for a waiver of the ban on slot sales at La Guardia, but included a commitment to divest a slightly larger number of slots at La Guardia and Reagan National than they had originally proposed. After tentatively consenting to the amended waiver request and posting its terms for notice and comment,[1] DOT approved the modified Delta–US Airways slot deal on October 13, 2011.[2]

DOT's decision did not meet with universal acclaim. Reprising the role it had adopted in the aborted court proceeding, Southwest Airlines opposed the modified slot deal on the grounds that it would lead to an inefficient use of the limited takeoff and landing times available at La Guardia and Reagan National. According to Southwest, Delta and US Airways would be likely to use any expansion in the number of their respective slots for small aircraft operations, as opposed to the larger aircraft operated by Southwest. Southwest therefore argued that the transaction should be approved only if Delta and US Airways were required to divest a larger number of slots than proposed by the modified deal. Several smaller community interests expressed the concern that the transfer of slots from Delta to US Airways, and vice versa, would mean the loss of existing service if the transaction were allowed to proceed.

1. 76 Fed. Reg. 45,313 (July 28, 2011).
2. 76 Fed. Reg. 63,702 (October 13, 2011).

In deciding to approve the slot deal as modified, DOT explained that the circumstances that originally had led it to propose a higher number of slot divestitures had sufficiently changed to permit approval of the amended waiver request. In particular, DOT cited increased market penetration of low-cost carriers (LCCs) at both La Guardia and Reagan National as the principal reason it was now willing to let the deal proceed with only a slight increase in the number of slot divestitures over the carriers' original proposal. DOT cited statistics showing an increase in LCC operations at both airports since the slot deal was first proposed and a corresponding effect on the level of airfares.[3] Given the changes in the competitive environment at La Guardia and Reagan National, and the broader effect on airline competition resulting from the Southwest–Air Tran merger, DOT concluded that the amended slot deal was in the public interest.[4]

The most remarkable aspect of the approval was not the reversal of DOT's position but the unprecedented conditions that it imposed on its consent. DOT went to considerable lengths to increase the level of competition at La Guardia and Reagan National through the allocation and use of the airport slots that Delta and US Airways were required to divest. To mitigate the competitive harm that might result from the slot deal, the settlement resulting in DOT approval called for the parties to sell 32 slots at La Guardia and 16 slots at Reagan National. DOT specified that the sale would be conducted on a blind, cash-only basis through a website managed by the Federal Aviation Administration.[5] Only carriers having less than 5 percent of the airport slots at La Guardia and Reagan National, respectively, would be eligible to bid on the divested slots. As a further condition, DOT prohibited Delta or US Airways from operating any of their newly exchanged slots for 90 days after the date the divested slots were sold, in order to allow the slot purchasers to establish their own services at the affected airports. For the same reason, between the 91st and 210th day following the sale, Delta and US Airways would not be allowed to operate more than 50 percent of the total number of slots each carrier acquired through the slot deal.[6]

Of the 16 slots to be made available at Reagan National, DOT decided to offer them in one bundle of eight slot pairs (one takeoff and one landing per pair), while the 32 slots at La Guardia were offered in two bundles of eight slot pairs each. An eligible carrier could purchase only one slot pair at each airport. DOT bundled the slots, rather than permitting them to be sold as individual slot pairs, to ensure that the successful bidder would be able to introduce a "critical

3. 76 Fed. Reg. at 63,704–706.
4. 76 Fed. Reg. at 63,705.
5. 76 Fed. Reg. at 63,703.
6. *Id.*

mass of new services,"[7] i.e., sufficient daily flights to compete effectively with the incumbent carriers at La Guardia and Reagan National. If an airline should encounter difficulty obtaining gates and ground facilities for its operations with the newly acquired slots, Delta or US Airways, as the selling carrier, would be required under the terms of the settlement with DOT to make such facilities available to the purchaser upon reasonable terms and conditions.[8]

Various airlines offered multiple objections to the conditions imposed on the slot deal by DOT, most contending that they were not stringent enough. Of particular note was the argument that because Delta and US Airways received the slots at La Guardia and Reagan National free of charge, they should not be able to retain the proceeds from their divestment. DOT responded by restating its long-standing position that although airport slots represented an operating privilege and not a property right, it had the necessary authority to permit the buying and selling of slots as a matter of law and policy.[9]

Although DOT tried to strike a balance between the interests of large and small airlines by approving the Delta–US Airways slot deal subject to conditions, it demonstrated a striking willingness to tinker with the competitive structure of two of the most important aviation markets in the United States. While Delta and US Airways may have obtained DOT's blessing for their slot exchange, the arrangement is still not in the clear. Following DOT's announcement that it was approving the transaction, DOJ issued a press release stating that it would continue its investigation into US Airways' purchase of the Delta slots at Reagan National.[10]

7. 76 Fed. Reg. at 63,706.

8. 76 Fed. Reg. at 73,712.

9. 76 Fed. Reg. at 73,709.

10. DOJ Press Release (Oct. 11, 2011). DOJ stated in the same press release that it would not continue its investigation of Delta's purchase of US Airways slots at La Guardia because "that acquisition does not raise competitive concerns."

Chapter 21

Overlapping Jurisdiction: Merger Review in Energy and Transportation Industries*

*By J. Bruce McDonald***

Mergers and acquisitions in US industries that historically have been closely controlled by federal regulation today are subject to varying regulatory supervision and antitrust enforcement. Combinations in some industries remain governed solely by industry regulatory agencies, such as transactions involving railroads and passenger motor carriers. Combinations in other sectors face review by both the traditional regulators and the antitrust agencies, as in electricity. In yet other industries, there is only antitrust review of mergers and acquisitions, even where regulators have authority over prices and collaborations short of merger, as with airlines, natural gas, and ocean shipping.

This article summaries the overlapping jurisdiction of sectoral regulators in energy and transportation industries and the federal antitrust agencies, the Department of Justice (DOJ) Antitrust Division and the Federal Trade Commission (FTC). Regulatory agencies that have authority to review transactions involving companies or assets subject to their jurisdiction usually employ a "public interest" standard. The antitrust agencies review mergers and acquisitions to determine if they may "substantially lessen competition" in a relevant market.[1]

---

* Originally published in *Infrastructure*, vol. 50, no. 3 (Spring, 2011).

** *J. Bruce McDonald is a partner in Jones Day's antitrust practice in Washington and Houston. From 2003–2007, he served as deputy assistant attorney general in the DOJ Antitrust Division, where he was responsible for antitrust enforcement in energy, transportation, telecommunications, and other regulated industries.*

1. Clayton Act § 7 prohibits acquisitions the effect of which "may be substantially to lessen competition, or to tend to create a monopoly." 15 U.S.C. § 18. The antitrust agencies' investigative authority comes from the Hart-Scott-Rodino (HSR) Act, which requires that transactions that meet certain jurisdictional thresholds be reported to the antitrust agencies and that closing be delayed for a period of time to allow antitrust review. 15 U.S.C. § 18a.

Energy

Natural gas

The federal antitrust laws apply to transactions in the natural gas industry. The Federal Energy Regulatory Commission (FERC) does not have authority over acquisitions of natural gas or gas pipeline companies. Under the Natural Gas Act, FERC authority over natural gas mergers is limited to issuance of certificates of public convenience and necessity to operate interstate natural gas pipelines and approval of abandonments through transfer.[2] State public utility commissions also sometimes have jurisdiction to review natural gas deals.

In recent years, the FTC has taken federal responsibility for natural gas combinations, including those involving natural gas-gathering systems, transmission pipelines, and gas storage and distribution assets. In 2007, the FTC challenged Equitable Resources' proposed acquisition of Peoples Natural Gas Co., despite the prior approval of the Pennsylvania Public Utilities Commission.[3] The FTC alleged these firms were the sole competitors in the distribution of natural gas to a certain group of customers near Pittsburgh and that their combination would eliminate "gas-on-gas distribution competition." The FTC obtained an injunction from the Court of Appeals for the Third Circuit, and the parties abandoned the transaction.[4] In 2003, the FTC obtained a consent decree eliminating Southern Union Company's management control over the Central Pipeline, as a condition of Southern Union's acquiring Panhandle Eastern Pipeline Company, which competed with Central to supply natural gas to Kansas City.[5]

Electricity

Both FERC and the federal antitrust agencies have authority to review electric utility combinations, and the decision of one does not limit or supersede the decision of the other. State public utility commissions also may have jurisdiction over electricity transactions.

FERC has authority under the Federal Power Act (FPA) to review certain electric utility combinations under a public interest standard. Section 203 of the FPA requires FERC approval for an electric utility to sell or acquire utility assets or the securities of another public utility, if valued at more than $10 million, or to combine with another utility.[6]

FERC policy statements provide guidance to its analysis under section 203. In determining whether a proposed transaction is consistent with the public interest, FERC

---

2. 15 U.S.C. § 717f.

3. FTC v. Equitable Resources, Inc., 512 F. Supp.2d 361 (W.D. Pa. 2007).

4. *Equitable Resources*, Dkt. No. 9322 (FTC Jan. 31, 2008) (order dismissing complaint), http://www.ftc.gov/os/adjpro/d9322/080204complaint.pdf.

5. *S. Union Co. & CMS Energy Corp.*, Dkt. No. C-4087 (FTC July 16, 2003) (complaint), http://www.ftc.gov/os/2003/07/southernunioncomp.pdf; *S. Union Co.*, Dkt. No. C-4087 (FTC July 16, 2003) (decision and order), http://www.ftc.gov/os/2003/07/southernuniondo.pdf.

6. 16 U.S.C. § 824b(a).

will consider the effect of the transaction on competition, rates, and regulation, and the potential for cross-subsidization.[7] The policy statement uses the analytical framework used in the antitrust agencies' 1992 merger guidelines to assess the competitive effects of horizontal mergers.[8] FERC may condition its approval on "such terms and conditions as it finds necessary or appropriate to secure the maintenance of adequate service and the coordination in the public interest of facilities subject to the jurisdiction of the Commission."[9]

Electric utility mergers and asset acquisitions are subject also to the federal antitrust laws, and in recent years the DOJ has taken responsibility for most of these matters. In 2010, the DOJ reviewed but did not challenge the merger of Mirant Corp. and RRI Energy, Inc., which created a new company called GenOn Energy, one of the largest independent power producers in the United States.[10] In 2009, the DOJ expressed its concerns over Exelon's proposal to acquire NRG Energy Inc., which would have created the largest energy company in the country. The transaction was abandoned in July 2009.[11] In 2006, the DOJ challenged Exelon Corporation's proposed acquisition of Public Service Enterprise Group (PSEG), which would have combined the assets of two of the largest electricity generators in the mid-Atlantic region.[12] A proposed consent decree would have required divesture of six electric plants, but the transaction was abandoned when state regulatory approvals were not obtained.

Combinations involving both electricity and gas companies have sometimes been handled by the DOJ and sometimes by the FTC. In March 1998, DOJ challenged the combination of the parents of San Diego Gas & Electric Company and Southern California Gas Company, which DOJ believed would have given the postmerger business an incentive to raise gas prices to competing electricity generators, and required divestiture of two gas-fired power plants.[13] In March 2001, the FTC challenged the merger of the parents of electric utility Detroit Edison Company and natural gas distributor

7. *Inquiry Concerning the Commission's Merger Policy Under the Federal Power Act: Policy Statement*, Order No. 592, FERC Stats. & Regs. ¶ 31,044 (1996), http://www.ferc.gov/industries/electric/gen-info/mergers/rm96-6.pdf, *reconsideration denied*, Order No. 592-A, 79 FERC ¶ 61,321 (1997); *see also* FPA section 203 Supplemental Policy Statement, FERC Stats. & Regs. ¶ 31,253 (2007).

8. *Id.* See United States Dep't of Justice & Federal Trade Comm'n, *Horizontal Merger Guidelines* (1992), http://www.justice.gov/atr/public/merger-enforcement.html. FERC currently is evaluating to what extent it should adopt the antitrust agencies' 2010 Merger Guidelines. *Analysis of Horizontal Market Power Under the Federal Power Act, Notice of Inquiry*, 134 FERC ¶ 61,191 (2011) (NOI).

9. 16 U.S.C. § 824b(b).

10. Press Release, Mirant and RRI Energy Complete Merger (Dec. 3, 2010), http://www.genon.com/docs/GenOn%20Energy%20Day%20One%20PR_final.pdf.

11. Fed. Trade Comm. and Dep't of Just., Hart-Scott-Rodino Annual Report, Fiscal Year 2009, at 7 n.15, http://www.ftc.gov/os/2010/10/101001hsrreport.pdf.

12. Competitive Impact Statement, *United States v. Exelon Corporation and Public Service Enterprise Group Inc.*, No. 1:06CV01138 (D.D.C. filed Aug. 10, 2006), http://www.justice.gov/atr/cases/f217700/217717.pdf.

13. United States v. Enova Corp., 107 F. Supp. 2d 10 (D.D.C. 2000) (final judgment).

MichCon, alleging it would lessen competition for the distribution of gas and electricity, which were substitutes for some customers. The parties agreed to divest certain gas transportation, distribution, and storage assets.[14]

Nuclear

The Nuclear Regulatory Commission (NRC) has the authority to approve transactions involving nuclear power generating facilities under its license transfer authority under the Atomic Energy Act.[15] This statute requires that the NRC give notice to the DOJ and consider its advice on whether "activities under the license would create or maintain a situation inconsistent with the antitrust laws."[16]

Petroleum

Transactions in petroleum sectors are subject to the jurisdiction of the federal antitrust agencies, but not any industry-specific regulatory agency. Historically, the FTC has taken responsibility for transactions involving crude oil and refined products commodities,[17] which it has pursued aggressively, bringing merger cases at lower levels of concentration in the petroleum industry than in any other industry.[18]

Among recent petroleum market transactions handled by the FTC, in 2011 the agency concluded its investigation of Irving Oil's proposed acquisition of terminaling assets in Maine from ExxonMobil, with Irving Oil agreeing to a consent order to divest some of the assets. Had Irving Oil combined all of the ExxonMobil terminaling assets with its own, the FTC determined it would have reduced competition in gasoline and distillates terminaling in certain parts of Maine.[19] In 2010, the FTC issued a consent order allowing Pilot Travel Center to Acquire Flying J's travel center business. Divestiture of 26 travel centers resolved the agency's concerns that the acquisition would lessen competition in sale of diesel fuel to long-haul trucking fleets.[20] In 2007, the FTC

---

14. Decision and Order, *DTE Energy Co.*, Dkt. No. C-4008 (May 15, 2001), www.ftc.gov/os/2001/05/dtemcndo.pdf.

15. 42 U.S.C. § 2234.

16. 42 U.S.C. § 2135(c)(5).

17. *See* Bureau of Economics, Fed. Trade Comm'n, The Petroleum Industry: Mergers, Structural Change, and Antitrust Enforcement 13 (2004), http://www.ftc.gov/os/2004/08/040813mergersinpetrolberpt.pdf; FTC Merger Enforcement Actions in the Petroleum Industry since 1981, http://www.ftc.gov/ftc/oilgas/charts/merger_enforce_actions .pdf.

18. William E. Kovacic, Commissioner, Petroleum Industry Consolidation, Prepared Statement of the Federal Trade Commission for Hearing Before the S. Comm. on the Judiciary, 109th Cong. 1 (2006) ("no other industry is so carefully scrutinized"), http://www.ftc.gov/speeches/kovacic/testimonyrepetroleumindustryconsolidation.pdf.

19. Analysis of Proposed Agreement Containing Consent Order to Aid Public Comment, *In the Matter of Irving Oil Limited and Irving Oil Terminals Inc.* (Dkt. No. 101-0021), http://www.ftc.gov/os/caselist/1010021/110526irvingexxonanal.pdf.

20. Decision and Order, *In the Matter of Pilot Corporation, Propeller Corp., and Flying J Inc.* (Dkt. No. C-4293), http://www.ftc.gov/os/caselist/0910125/index.shtm.

reviewed Western Refining's acquisition of Giant Industries, which the agency unsuccessfully sought to enjoin to prevent perceived harm to competition in the supply of refined products to northern New Mexico.[21]

The DOJ has handled most matters relating to oilfield services. In 2010, the DOJ obtained a consent decree in Baker Hughes' acquisition of BJ Services, in which the parties agreed to divest to a new competitor two vessels used for stimulation services required for completing oil wells.[22] In 2007, the DOJ challenged CalDive International's acquisition of Stolt Offshore and obtained a consent decree that required divestiture of diving support vessels and saturation diving systems, and later brought a contempt action for the combined company's failure to comply with the divestiture order.[23]

Transportation

Air

The DOJ has the responsibility for reviewing airline mergers and acquisitions, that authority having been transferred from the Department of Transportation (DOT) under the Airline Deregulation Act of 1978.[24] The DOT no longer has a formal role in the antitrust review of airline combinations, but informally shares its views with the Antitrust Division. The FTC has no authority over airlines or other common carriers,[25] and state enforcement against airline transactions is preempted by the Airline Deregulation Act.[26]

The DOT does retain the authority to make certain regulatory decisions on questions that may arise because of an airline transaction. For example, where a proposed merger of major carriers would require the transfer of a carrier's fitness certificate, DOT must find that the proposed transfer is "consistent with the public interest," that is, that the transferee is fit to conduct the proposed operations. The DOT also must

---

21. FTC v. Foster, W. Ref'g, Inc., & Giant Indus., Inc., 2007 WL 1827098, No. 1:07-cv-00352-JB-ACT, (D.N.M., May 30, 2007) (denying motion for preliminary injunction). See J. Bruce McDonald, *The FTC's 2007 Oil Industry Merger Challenges: Another Year of "Special Vigilance,"* Texas Bus. Litig. J., Winter 2007, at 11–13 (State Bar of Texas), *available at* http://www.jonesday.com/files/Publication/02a77dfd-547e-46fe-a951-998b14e5657a/Presentation/PublicationAttachment/45933164-da3b-4c7f-bcee-a13416f9ca45/mcdonald2.pdf.

22. Competitive Impact Statement, United States v. Baker Hughes, Inc., No. 1:10-cv-00659 (D.D.C., filed Apr. 27, 2010), http://www.justice.gov/atr/cases/f258200/258203.pdf.

23. Competitive Impact Statement, United States v. Cal Dive International, Inc., No. 1:05CV02041 (D.D.C., filed Oct. 20, 2005), http://www.justice.gov/atr/cases/f212300/212319.pdf; Petition by the United States for an Order to Show Cause Why Respondents Cal Dive International, Inc. and Helix Energy Solutions Group, Inc. Should Not Be Found in Civil Contempt, United States v. Cal Dive International, Inc., No. 1:05CV02041 (D.D.C., filed Nov. 26, 2007), http://www.justice.gov/atr/cases/f227900/227960.pdf.

24. 49 U.S.C. app. § 1551 (1988) (terminating DOT authority held under §§ 408 and 409 of the Federal Aviation Act (49 U.S.C. app. §§ 1378, 1379 (1988))).

25. 15 U.S.C. § 45(a)(2) (excepting "common carriers subject to the Acts to regulate commerce, air carriers and foreign air carriers subject to part A of subtitle VII of title 49").

26. *See* Am. Airlines v. Wolens, 513 U.S. 219, 228–29 (1995) (holding state statutory obligations preempted, but not state law contract claims).

analyze and report to Congress on the effects of the transfer on "(1) the viability of each carrier involved in the transfer, (2) competition in the domestic airline industry, and (3) the trade position of the United States in the international air transportation market."[27] Nevertheless, DOT does not have the authority to make an independent competitive review in deciding whether to allow the transfer.[28]

Over the last three decades, the DOJ has reviewed every proposed airline combination of any size that could possibly affect US travelers. For example, in 2011, the DOJ reviewed but did not challenge Southwest Airlines' acquisition of AirTran Airways.[29] In 2010, the DOJ investigated the acquisition by United Airlines of Continental Airlines, which it did not challenge after the carriers committed to sell certain slot holdings at Newark Liberty Airport to Southwest Airlines.[30] In 2003, the DOJ reviewed but did not challenge KLM's acquisition of Air France, which created the world's largest airline by revenue, focusing on the significance of worldwide competition among international airline alliances.[31] In 1998, the DOJ filed a lawsuit to challenge Northwest Airlines' proposed acquisition of Continental Airlines.[32] That action was settled, permitting Northwest to retain its codesharing relationship and a 7 percent interest and certain voting rights in Continental.[33]

Rail

The antitrust agencies do not have authority over railroad combinations. The Surface Transportation Board (STB) has broad jurisdiction over all interstate transportation by rail within the United States. Its authority is "exclusive"[34] and preempts state economic regulation of railroads.[35] The STB statute expressly exempts from the antitrust

27. 49 U.S.C § 41105.

28. *See* Statement of Andrew B. Steinberg, Assistant Secretary for Aviation & International Affairs, U.S. Dep't of Transportation, before the Senate Committee on Commerce, Science, and Transportation, at 8–9 (Jan. 24, 2007) (describing primary role of DOJ Antitrust Division in airline merger review), http://ostpxweb.dot.gov/aviation/Speeches/Steinberg_testimony.pdf.

29. Press Release, Statement of the Department of Justice Antitrust Division on Its Decision to Close Its Investigation of Southwest's Acquisition of AirTran (Apr. 26, 2011), *available at* http://www.justice.gov/atr/public/press_releases/2011/270293.pdf.

30. Press Release, United Airlines and Continental Airlines Transfer Assets to Southwest Airlines in Response to Department of Justice's Antitrust Concerns (Aug. 27, 2010), http://www.justice.gov/atr/public/press_releases/2010/262002.pdf.

31. J. Bruce McDonald, *Transportation Update: Remarks to the ABA Section of Antitrust Law, Transportation Industry Committee,* at 2–3 (Mar. 31, 2004), http://www.justice.gov/atr/public/speeches/203369.pdf.

32. Complaint, United States v. Nw. Airlines Corp. and Cont. Airlines Inc., Civ. No. 98-74611 (E.D. Mich. filed Oct. 23, 1998), http://www.justice.gov/atr/cases/f2000/2023.pdf.

33. See DOJ Press Release, Department Announces Tentative Settlement in Northwest-Continental Lawsuit (Nov. 6, 2000), http://www.justice.gov/atr/public/press_releases/2000/6905.pdf.

34. 49 U.S.C. § 10501(b).

35. Friberg v. Kansas City S. Ry. Co., 267 F.3d 439, 443 (5th Cir. 2001).

laws rail mergers and acquisitions that have been "approved or exempted" by the STB.[36]

The STB reviews combinations of Class I rail carriers under a public interest standard,[37] which requires it to consider the effect of the transaction on rail transportation as well as whether the transaction would have "an adverse effect on competition among rail carriers in the affected region or in the national rail system."[38] For smaller rail carriers, the STB must approve the transaction unless (1) "there is likely to be substantial lessening of competition, creation of a monopoly, or restraint of trade in freight surface transportation . . . and (2) the anticompetitive effects of the transaction outweigh the public interest in meeting significant transportation needs."[39] In 2001, the STB issued new rules governing its review of Class I railroad mergers, imposing on the parties a higher burden to demonstrate that their proposed combination is in the public interest. The rules now require that a proposed merger "enhance, not merely preserve competition, in order to secure approval."[40]

The STB may condition its approval of a merger or consolidation on the applicant rail carriers' acceptance of certain conditions, such as the divestiture of parallel tracks or requiring the granting of trackage rights for other carriers, designed to alleviate potential adverse competitive effects of the transactions.[41]

The DOJ does have the statutory right to file comments in rail merger proceedings to address competition issues.[42] For example, in 2004 DOJ provided comments in the STB proceeding on Canadian National's acquisition of railroad assets from Great Lakes Transportation, recommending that the STB give competing railroads certain trackage rights and authorize connections to preserve competition.[43] In 1996, the DOJ filed comments in opposition to the merger of the two main western railroads, the Union Pacific and the Southern Pacific, which the STB nonetheless approved.[44]

---

36. 49 U.S.C. § 11321(a) (stating that any transaction approved by the STB "is exempt from the antitrust laws and from all other law").

37. 49 U.S.C. § 11324(c).

38. 49 U.S.C. § 11324(b).

39. 49 U.S.C. § 11324(d).

40. *Major Rail Consolidation Procedures*, STB Ex Parte No. 582, 2001 STB LEXIS 546, at *14 (STB June 7, 2001).

41. 49 U.S.C. § 11324(c).

42. 49 U.S.C. § 11325(b)(1), (c)(1), (d)(1).

43. Reply of the United States Department of Justice, *Canadian Nat'l Ry. Co., and Grand Trunk Corp.–Control–Duluth, Missabe and Iron Range Ry. Co., Bessemer and Lake Erie R.R. Co., and Pittsburgh & Conneaut Dock Co.*, STB Fin. Dkt. No. 34424 (filed Feb. 24, 2004), http://www.justice.gov/atr/public/comments/202651.pdf. The STB approved the acquisition with limited conditions. Decision, *Canadian Nat'l Ry.*, STB Fin. Dkt. No. 34424, 2004 STB LEXIS 230, at *1 (STB 2004).

44. See DOJ Press Release, Justice Department Urges Denial of Union Pacific/Southern Pacific Merger: Marks the Largest Railroad Merger Ever Reviewed (June 3, 1996), http://www.justice.gov/atr/public/press_releases/1996/0673.htm; *Union Pacific Corp.*, Decision No. 44, 1 S.T.B. 233, 1996 STB LEXIS 220 (1996).

Trucking

The STB must approve mergers, acquisitions, and leases between motor carriers of passengers, which if approved are exempted from the federal antitrust laws and from state review. The STB applies a public interest standard that does not include competition factors.[45] Nevertheless, the DOJ may participate in STB enforcement proceedings.[46]

In contrast to transactions involving motor carriers of passengers, mergers and acquisitions of motor carriers of property are subject to the federal antitrust laws.[47] The DOJ has responsibility for the antitrust review of trucking company combinations. In 2003, the DOJ reviewed but did not challenge the $1.1 billion acquisition by Yellow Corporation of Roadway Corporation, a competitor in the long-haul less-than-truckload business.[48]

Shipping

Although other agreements between ocean shippers that are filed with the Federal Maritime Commission under the Shipping Act are exempt from the antitrust laws, acquisitions involving ocean shippers are not exempt and remain fully subject to the antitrust laws.[49]

The DOJ takes responsibility for the antitrust review of ocean shipping combinations. For example, in 2005 the DOJ reviewed but did not challenge the acquisition by A.P. Moller-Maersk of Royal P&O Nedlloyd, a competitor in ocean shipping of containerized cargo.[50]

Conclusion

Multiple government agencies having authority to investigate and modify or challenge a transaction can present difficulties for merging parties. First and foremost, the antitrust and regulatory agencies bring to bear different standards, making it harder to

45. 49 U.S.C. §§ 14303(b), (f); 49 C.F.R. § 1182.

46. 15 U.S.C. § 21(b). The FTC does not have jurisdiction over motor "common carriers." 15 U.S.C. §§ 45(a)(2), 46(a)-(b).

47. 15 U.S.C. § 18a.

48. J. Bruce McDonald, Transportation Update: Remarks to the ABA Section of Antitrust Law, Transportation Industry Committee at 11–12 (Mar. 31, 2004), http://www.justice.gov/atr/public/speeches/203369.pdf.

49. 46 U.S.C. § 40307 (antitrust immunity for all activity permitted or prohibited by the Shipping Act); 46 U.S.C. § 40301(c) (not apply to acquisitions). Fed. Mar. Comm'n v. Seatrain Line, 411 U.S. 726, 729 (1973) ("Congress did not intend to invest the Maritime Commission with power to shield from antitrust liability merger or asset acquisition agreements which impose no ongoing responsibilities.").

50. Press Release, Acquisition of Royal P&O Nedlloyd N.V. cleared by the European Commission and the United States Department of Justice (Jul. 30, 2005), http://investor.maersk.com/releasedetail.cfm?releaseid=433978.

predict the ultimate outcome of government review. What conclusions the antitrust agency will reach under the "substantially lessening of competition" standard requires a careful evaluation of the facts, but how these are analyzed is well understood. Identifying what facts a regulatory agency actual will consider under a "public interest" standard presents a different challenge. Sometimes "public interest" requires an evaluation of competitive effect, as under the FERC statutes, but the regulators and antitrust agencies often reach different conclusions even on that issue. Further, other "public interest" factors may tip the balance. For example, industry regulatory authorities may be inclined to consider industry health, not just competition and consumer benefits, favoring merging parties. Industry regulators often are more closely tied to the legislature, especially at the state level, which can introduce more populist concerns.

The proposed Exelon/PSEG deal is a good example of how different agencies decided different outcomes were needed for the same transaction. The DOJ identified competitive problems with that electricity generator combination and required divestiture of specific generating plants. FERC also found competition problems, and it determined they could be resolved with a "virtual divestiture," requiring that the company take certain positions in financial forward markets. But the New Jersey PUC demanded that the merged company lower electricity rates, more than the company would agree, which led to the parties abandoning the transaction. Although the various remedies were not inconsistent, they were duplicative, burdening the deal.

Second, the presence of any government authority not bound by a strict deadline inevitably means the other authorities will take longer. For example, although the HSR Act gives the antitrust agencies a schedule that limits merger investigations, giving the parties some control over timing, where a regulatory agency also is investigating but has a later deadline or no deadline, most often the antitrust agency will take advantage of the extra time, delaying its decision.

Third, coordinating progress along various agency fronts can be a logistical challenge. Each authority has different requirements for filings, investigation timing, public comment, and decision making. It is important for the counsel representing parties before multiple agencies to work together and keep on the same schedule, not to mention take into account the needs of each other's substantive advocacy.

2012 Update

By J. Bruce McDonald

In the last 12 months, dual review of regulated industry mergers by antitrust enforcers and industry regulators has continued, presenting a few notable developments. The most significant of these is the decision by the Federal Energy Regulatory Commission (FERC) to retain its historical analysis of electric utility mergers under the Federal Power Act, which is based on the federal antitrust agencies' 1992 Merger Guidelines. FERC chose not to adopt the analysis of the antitrust agencies' revised Guidelines, which the Department of Justice and Federal Trade Commission issued in August 2010.

FERC has been using the basic framework of the 1992 Guidelines for more than 15 years to evaluate the competitive effects of mergers, focusing on the Guidelines' primary question: whether the merger would significantly increase concentration in the relevant market. FERC had developed a "competitive analysis screen" to allow a quick check on whether a proposed utility combination might create horizontal market power. In contrast, the antitrust agencies' 2010 revised Guidelines deemphasize market definition as the starting point for merger analysis and state that those agencies instead may begin with a more fact-specific inquiry using a variety of analytical tools, including direct evidence of competition between the merging parties and economic models designed to quantify the extent to which the merged company could raise prices postmerger.

FERC conducted an inquiry into whether it would adopt the 2010 Guidelines' analysis. Ultimately FERC declined to change its historical approach. FERC reasoned that using its competitive analysis screen allows FERC and others to quickly determine whether a proposed merger may present competitive problems, while also allowing a more extensive analysis of mergers that may be troublesome. FERC believes that this flexibility provides the dual benefits of a standard, conservative screen that can be used quickly and with certainty and the availability of a more complete analysis, which then could take advantage of the analytical tools described in the 2010 Guidelines. Wholesale adoption of the 2010 Guidelines would have brought significant change to FERC's merger analysis.

In other industry sectors, the federal antitrust agencies have been active in merger enforcement through 2011 and 2012. One continuing trend is the agencies' focus on possible vertical effects of mergers and the greater use of "conduct" remedies to address those effects.

Antitrust remains most concerned with mergers between direct competitors where the combination may lessen horizontal competition. Antitrust enforcers sometimes have given more attention to mergers of vertically related companies that may lead to restrictions on other market participants. For example, a manufacturer that acquires the supplier of a critical input may be able to undercut competition by other manufacturers by limiting their access to the input. The agencies sometimes are able to resolve concerns about these vertical effects by imposing a "conduct" remedy or ongoing conditions on the merged company, rather than blocking the transaction altogether.

A significant example, from the regulated telecommunications industry, is DOJ's challenge to the proposed joint venture between Comcast and NBC Universal, which DOJ alleged would give Comcast the ability to withhold NBC programming from other video-programming distributors. DOJ and the parties agreed to several conduct remedies designed to address these perceived concerns. The consent decree mandates that the joint venture license programming content to certain other distributors on "economically equivalent" terms and prohibits Comcast from discriminating against other distributors. The DOJ remedy also relies on the process to arbitrate distributor disputes established by the Federal Communications Commission, which also had jurisdiction to review this merger.

Mergers between companies in U.S.-regulated industries will continue to be subject to the overlapping jurisdiction of antitrust enforcers and industry regulators.

Part Five
ENERGY/ENVIRONMENT

Introduction

Chapter 5 contains an interesting range of articles from *Infrastructure* that address energy and environmental issues.

The first article is Judge Cudahy's description of huge, expensive dam, power, and water transfer projects in China. The judge notes that China is undertaking these major infrastructure projects while other countries have opted to seek solutions such as energy efficiency and conservation. In his update, the judge notes that drought has exacerbated China's water issues.

In their 2009 article, written a few months after the enactment of the American Recovery and Reinvestment Act (ARRA), Lisa Wing Stone and Katrina Robson examined the provisions of ARRA that were designed to benefit the electric power industry. They also examined the conditions that accompany ARRA funding and discussed the implications of such funding on traditional utility rate regulation. In their 2012 update, Ms. Stone and Ms. Robson review the impact of ARRA funding on energy projects and the economy three years into the six-year program. They acknowledge issues in some of the loan programs and note that the Department of Energy did not begin to disburse funds as quickly as was anticipated. However, the authors rate the program as a success in its impacts on energy development and the U.S. economy.

The fall 2009 edition of *Infrastructure* included an article titled "Climate Change Regulation: A Significant Challenge for NiSource and Other Energy Companies in the 21st Century" written by Carrie Hightman, executive vice president and chief legal officer of NiSource and Margaret Rice, senior counsel at NiSource. The article presents NiSource's view as to the impact of the American Clean Energy and Security Act of 2009 (ACES) which had been passed by the U.S. House of Representatives in June 2009. The authors characterized ACES as unfair and ill-timed and predicted that it could impact electric system reliability and greatly increase energy prices. In their 2012 update, the authors note that ACES was not passed by the Senate and died at the end of that congressional session. They comment that while comprehensive climate change legislation is "inconceivable" in the present political climate, the legislative pressures have been replaced by federal regulatory action.

In contrast, a recent development that has caused significant downward pressure on energy prices has been the rediscovery and exploitation of shale gas. In an article titled "The Emerging Impact of Shale Gas Resources," John Rowe, chairman emeritus of Exelon Corporation, and Ed Fortunato, managing director of fundamental analysis at Constellation Energy, traced the development and expansion of shale gas as a domestic energy resource. They acknowledged the environmental and social impacts that would accompany large-scale development and production of shale gas. In his update, Mr. Fortunato characterizes the impact of shale gas as "profound"—on energy prices, on competing energy sources, and on gas exports. He predicts that future impact may be even more significant.

Chapter 5 concludes with two articles on issues related to wind generation. In a 2010 article, Section member Chuck Patrizia and his associates, Candice Castaneda and Alexandra Konieczny, discussed four issues facing the developers and development of utility-scale wind farms. These include the intermittency of wind, transmission constraints, the retail cost of wind-generated electricity, and local opposition to specific projects. The authors used the Cape Wind Project as a case study to illustrate the final issue. In their 2012 update of this article, Mr. Patrizia and Ms. Castaneda address actions by FERC, RTOs, and others to address several of these issues. They also discuss the imminent loss of federal tax benefits to wind development, including the expiration of production tax credits and Section 1603 tax grants. They note that congressional action late in 2012 may extend these benefits.

In an article published in *Infrastructure* in 2011, Section member John Reilly and his associate, Carine Williams, outlined the regulatory framework for offshore wind development in the United States and analyzed the allocation of risks and liabilities under the lease, which has been signed by the developer of the Cape Wind Project and the U.S. Bureau of Ocean Energy Management, Regulation and Enforcement (BOEM) within the U.S. Department of Interior. In their update, they summarize three recent trends affecting offshore (outer continental shelf) wind projects. These trends are an expedited administrative process, continued public opposition to offshore wind projects, and the economic impact of greatly reduced natural gas prices on these projects.

Peter V. Lacouture
September, 2012

Chapter 22

China: A Mighty Thirst*

*By Hon. Richard D. Cudahy***

In China, enormous water projects seem to have carried the day in the face of substantial opposition. Most of us have read something about China's Three Gorges Dam Project, which is a huge impoundment of the Yangtze River to provide hydroelectric power and a measure of flood control. The estimated final cost of this installation is about $17 billion, but this is less than one-third the cost of the extraordinary effort to move water from the Yangtze north to Beijing and to the dry expanses of northern China. This South-North Water Transfer Project, originally proposed by Mao Zedong in 1953, arouses much of the same environmental and social concerns as the Three Gorges Dam. But it will go forward, because the extraordinary imbalance in China between a wet southern region and a dry northern region that is a center of population, agriculture, and industry, cries out for solutions.

The Three Gorges Dam, first suggested by Sun Yat Sen in 1919, will provide 18,000 megawatts of energy, will stand 600 feet tall, and create a reservoir 360 miles long and 175 meters deep. The project has aroused ferocious opposition, both in China and internationally, because (1) it will force the relocation of more than a million people, (2) will flood precious arable land and destroy ancient cultural relics and historic cities, and (3) the reservoir created by the dam will become filled with sediment and prevent the passage of some ships. But successful efforts to obstruct financing from international sources have not undermined Chinese commitment to the project.

Another concern about Three Gorges is the pollution traceable to the cities and towns surrounding its reservoir. According to one estimate, less than one-third of the industrial and one-tenth of the urban domestic waste water is treated before being dumped into the area to be occupied by the reservoir. More than 20 million tons of garbage are dumped every year in the areas around the reservoir. Apparently, the government will not have enough time to clean up the factories and coal mines along the river banks before the reservoir is formed, leading to heavy underwater pollution. In spite of these negative aspects, the Chinese have pressed on, in part out of satisfaction that the project will be a substitute for construction of numerous heavily polluting coal-fired electric generators.

---

* Originally published in *Infrastructure*, vol. 47, no. 3 (Spring, 2008).

** *Richard D. Cudahy is a judge on the U.S. Court of Appeals, 7th Circuit, in Chicago.*

The South-North Water Transfer Project, even more ambitious engineering-wise than Three Gorges, was triggered by perennial dry conditions in northern China, where demands for water based on rapidly developing population, industry, and agriculture put heavy pressure on the inadequate supplies. In some places, water shortages drove users to sink wells, and eventually the water table sank. Officials preached water conservation, and President Jiang Zemin said, "If a country can send satellites and missiles into space, it should be able to dry up its toilets."

Although China has average annual water resources of approximately 2,200 cubic meters of water per head of population, its water resources are unevenly distributed in geographic and seasonal terms. The heavily populated and polluted Hai, Huai, and Yellow River basins in the north have been faced with serious shortages of water in recent decades in meeting their domestic, industrial, and agricultural water demands. Approximately 80 per cent of the annual precipitation in these three river basins normally falls during the period from July to October, and dry years occur frequently. Historically, there was a dry period of 11 successive years from 1922 to 1932 in the Yellow River Basin. Southern China, with roughly 55 percent of the population and 35 percent of the cropland, has about 80 percent of the water resources. Northern China, with 45 percent of the population and nearly 60 percent of all cropland, has less than 15 percent of the water.The Yellow River, a prime water source in northern China, actually ran dry in its lower reaches for an average of 70 days a year for 10 years in the 1990s. Peasants along one stretch of the river, where water continued to flow, were ordered not to divert it for irrigation, so that it might flow on to provide water for an oil field further down the river. Guards were stationed along the river to prevent the opening of valves for irrigating the peasants' fields. And low water throughout the north exacerbated the pollution that is very widespread throughout that area.

To relieve these conditions, the Water Transfer Project was instituted in 2002 along the most easterly of three projected routes or schemes. These three routes will divert water from the lower, middle, and upper reaches of the Yangtze River Basin, respectively, to meet the increasing water requirements of the North China Plain. By 2050, the annual total water diversion will be about 45 billion cubic meters.

The eastern and middle routes will be built first, and their cost is estimated to be $19 billion (in U.S. dollars.) The total cost of all three routes may reach $56 billion. At full development, the eastern and middle routes are expected to divert 28 billion cubic meters of water from the Yangtze River, representing less than three percent of its average annual flow. The eastern route follows the Grand Canal—an ancient waterway designed for the shipment of goods—from near the mouth of the Yangtze River north to the Yellow and beyond for a total distance of 1,150 kilometers. Just recently, China began digging an 8.7 kilometer-long tunnel (8.3 meters in diameter) under the Yellow River to move water along the eastern route as far as the city of Tiamin about as far north as Beijing. Pumping will be used to move water to the Yellow River crossing. Poor water quality along that route will require major expenditures for treatment of pollution. Subsequent branch construction will take water eastward along the Shandong Peninsula.The middle route, now also under construction, will divert water from a reservoir on the Hanjiang River (a major tributary of the Yangtze) into a large canal that will deliver water as far as Beijing and Tianjin. The existing dam at the originating reservoir will have to be elevated from its present level and the normal reservoir level raised. The total length of the diversion canal will be 1,267 kilometers with a 142-kilometer branch to Tianjin, and another tunnel will be excavated under the Yellow River. Water from the Hanjiang River may not be sufficient, and it may be necessary in time to tap the Three Gorges Dam Reservoir and pump water from there to the outset of the middle route.

Construction of the middle route will be affected by several geological problems, mainly the slope stability of swelling clay and rock, and land subsidence in coal mining areas. Approximately 160 kilometers of the route have problems related to swelling soils and unstable rock formations. Some 51 kilometers of the diversion channel pass through seven coal mine areas, and land subsidence and ground fissures are expected along these parts of the route. Other problems include accumulation of flood water on the western side of the channel, and seismic activity. All these problems are reportedly being addressed in planning the construction and operation phases of the project.

The western route scheme is for the future, requiring dramatic engineering and involves diversion from three major headwater tributaries of the Yangtze to the upper Yellow River. Construction involves tunneling through mountain ranges of eastern Tibet and adjacent provinces with some pumping. Dams and tunnels will have to be built in mountainous areas with elevations ranging from 3,000 meters to 5,000 meters and prone to frequent earthquakes.

The western route will divert 17 billion cubic meters of water per annum. Compared with the eastern and middle routes, the western route is expected to provide the best quality water, and there is little need for displacement of people. However, the western route will face much greater engineering and construction challenges. Preliminary cost estimates exceed $37 billion (in U.S. dollars.) The difficult geological and other conditions of the route and its high cost mean that it is unlikely that construction of this route will begin before 2020, and there is a possibility it may not be constructed at all.

The financing of the Transfer Project will be in part through charges to provinces proportional to their take of water. It is planned that the system will have enough flexibility to transfer water from one sector to another if required. During the announced transitional period from a planned economy to a market economy in China, a quasi-market type of management will be adopted for the process of pricing and the transfer of water rights.

Although the central government is playing the key role in the planning, construction, and management of the Transfer Project, it will supply only 30 per cent of the capital cost for construction of the first phase of the eastern and the middle routes with a recently estimated total cost of $15 billion (U.S. dollars.)

The World Bank has approved the project, but the World Wildlife Fund has argued that investments in pollution control and water-saving measures such as reducing leakage and collection and treatment of waste water, together with improving irrigation practice and use of desalination equipment could save or extract a great deal of water. There are many environmental problems connected with the South-North Transfer Project, including some increase in salt water intrusion in the estuary of the Yangtze

River. The eastern route would require displacement of 50,000 people, and the middle route 275,000.In any event, the South-North Transfer is not a final solution to China's water problems. Even after its successful implementation, measures aimed at water conservation and the like will have to be continued and enhanced. This is at the heart of the current debate about the wisdom of huge investments such as that at the Three Gorges and in carrying out the South-North Transfer. At one time, there was virtually unanimous approval in the United States and around the world of these large-scale water projects. High dams were in vogue in the American West, in Egypt, and elsewhere. But times have changed, and now the environmental and social costs loom larger and purported alternatives are given more sympathetic consideration. The most obvious alternative to massive hydroelectric installations is energy efficiency and energy conservation, and to large-scale water transfer is conservation of water resources. A considerable amount can be accomplished through these relatively simple means, although the scale and scope of the big projects may satisfy plausible analysis and, more importantly, is bound to appeal to the imagination—especially of societies first undertaking development.

Principal Sources

- Fereidoun Ghassemi & Ian White, INTER-BASIN WATER TRANSFER: CASE STUDIES FROM AUSTRALIA, UNITED STATES, CANADA, CHINA, AND INDIA, 307-52 (2007)
- Elizabeth C. Economy, THE RIVER RUNS BLACK, 125-127, 205-209 (2004)
- Vaclav Smil, *China's Thirsty Future*, FAR EASTERN ECONOMIC REVIEW, Dec. 16, 2005, at 29.

~~~~~~~~~~
~~~~~~~~~~

2012 Update

By Hon. Richard D. Cudahy

Since 2011, a drought in Yunnan Province has exacerbated China's water problems. In another development, in November 2010, China began damming the mighty Brahmaputra River in Tibet. The entire expanse of Northeast India and Bangladesh depend on the flow of the Brahmaputra, leading to sharp controversy between China and India.

Chapter 23

The Stimulus Bill and the Electric Industry*

*By Lisa Wing Stone and Katrina Robson***

The American Recovery and Reinvestment Act (ARRA), signed into law on February 17, 2009, allocated upwards of $32 billion to energy programs. This significant investment—intended to provide seed money to fund a transformation to a clean and efficient energy infrastructure—represents both an enormous opportunity and an immense challenge to the electric power industry. Secretary of Energy Steven Chu promised to "carry out this economic recovery plan with the highest level of speed, transparency, and accountability." This emphasis on accountability combined with the regulatory oversight already exercised over public utilities means that the energy industry is likely to be subject to intense scrutiny by vocal critics. To the extent that there is inefficient use of funds or unexpected project delays, it will be readily visible and easily commented upon.

This article provides a four-part overview of the anticipated impact of the ARRA on the electric power industry. The first two parts summarize the provisions of the ARRA that are most likely to affect the industry, including all forms of electric utilities and other power producers. Part 1 covers funding programs for energy generation and transmission infrastructure research, development, and demonstration, and Part 2 discusses funding that will flow to utility customers to invest in energy efficiency improvements. The third part examines the unique "strings" and other considerations that come with ARRA funding, which in many ways is unlike any previous federal government funding program. Finally, the fourth part investigates the unique challenges electric utilities, as regulated entities, face in seeking ARRA funding, such as how it might impact their general rate cases and their participation in state PUC energy efficiency incentive programs.

---

* Originally published in *Infrastructure*, vol. 48, no. 3 (Spring, 2009).

** *Lisa Wing Stone and Katrina Robson are counsels in the Washington, D.C., office of O'Melveny & Myers. Both attorneys are members of the firm's Energy, Natural Resources, and Environmental practice group. [Ms. Stone is now an attorney with VLP Law Group, LLP.]*

Part 1: Energy Infrastructure Investment

The greatest portion of ARRA funding that is available to the electric power industry will support building and rebuilding of the energy infrastructure, including clean energy generation and transmission facilities.

Transmission/Smart Grid: $4.5 Billion

The ARRA provided $4.5 billion to the U.S. Department of Energy's (DOE) Office of Electricity Delivery and Energy Reliability to modernize the electric grid, enhance security of U.S. energy infrastructure and improve reliability. This money will fund implementation of the smart grid programs authorized by the Energy Independence and Security Act of 2007 (EISA), including smart grid technology research, development, and demonstration projects authorized in EISA section 1304, and the federal matching fund for smart grid technologies in EISA section 1306. Within this amount, funds have also been designated for workforce training ($100 million), resource assessment and analysis of future demand and transmission requirements ($80 million), and the development of interoperability standards for smart grid devices ($10 million).

Transportation Electrification: $400 million

The ARRA provided initial funding for transportation electrification demonstration and deployment projects through a program originally authorized under EISA section 131. The DOE's competitive grant funding announcement for this program (deadline May 13, 2009) identifies four program areas of interest: electric drive vehicle demonstration and evaluation; transportation sector electrification; combined proposals for the above two areas; and advanced electric drive vehicle education programs.

Clean Coal/Fossil Fuel initiatives: $3.4 billion

The Office of Fossil Energy received $3.4 billion for research, development, and deployment of technologies for using coal more cleanly and efficiently, such as integration of gasification combined cycle (IGCC) and carbon capture and storage (CCS) technology. The Joint Explanatory Statement of Conferees explains that Congress intended for this amount to be allocated as follows: $1 billion for fossil energy research and development programs; $800 million for the Clean Coal Power Initiative Round III Funding Opportunity Announcement (which had already closed on the date that the ARRA was signed); $1.52 billion for a competitive solicitation for a range of industrial carbon capture and energy efficiency improvement projects (CO_2); $50 million for a competitive solicitation for site characterization activities in geologic formations; $20 million for geologic CO_2 sequestration training and research grants; and $10 million for program direction funding.

Renewable Energy Generation

The ARRA provides multifaceted support for the development of renewable energy generation facilities. The DOE loan guarantee program received an additional $6 billion (which is anticipated to support $60 billion in loans) to support "commercial technology" projects involving "renewable energy systems, including incremental hydropower, that generate electricity," "electric power transmission systems, including upgrading and reconductoring projects," and "leading edge biofuel projects that will use technologies performing at the pilot or demonstration scale. . . ." Unlike the previous funding available through this program, there is no requirement that the project use a "new or significantly improved" technology.

The ARRA also provides a three-year extension on the production tax credit (PTC) for most renewable energy facilities and offers expansions on and alternatives for tax credits on renewable energy systems. The PTC allows a credit for each kilowatt-hour produced at new qualified facilities during the first 10 years of their operation, as long as the facilities are up and running before the tax credit's expiration date. Alternatively, owners of non-solar renewable energy facilities can elect to earn a 30 percent investment credit rather than the PTC or to receive a grant equal to 30 percent of the tax basis for depreciable or amortizable facilities. Additionally, grants are available for renewable energy facilities that qualify for a business energy credit of 10-20 percent. This includes facilities that use fuel cells, solar energy, small wind turbines, geothermal energy, microturbines, and combined heat and power technology. Grants are limited to facilities that go online in 2009 or 2010 or facilities where construction began in 2009 or 2010 and was completed before the termination of the PTC.

Part 2: Energy Efficiency Investments

The second large bucket of ARRA funding affecting the electric industry flows through a variety of energy efficiency programs. The majority of this funding will filter through states or through existing programs to utility customers, as opposed to electric utilities themselves. These funds present a more nuanced challenge to electric utilities: how best to support customers in maximizing efficiency gains in a way that is complementary to the utilities' own mandated energy efficiency programs.

State Energy Program: $3.1 Billion

The State Energy Program (SEP) provides grants and technical assistance to states and U.S. territories to develop cost-shared energy efficiency and renewable energy projects under state-developed strategic and annual energy plans. Although the ARRA funding does not require matching state funds, it does limit grants to states that intend to adopt strict building energy codes and provide utility incentives for energy efficiency measures. Funds are allocated to state energy offices according to a population-based formula.

Weatherization Assistance Program: $5 Billion

The DOE Weatherization Assistance Program (WAP) provides funds to weatherize the homes of low-income families, seeking to reduce energy costs through increased home energy efficiency. Funds are distributed to states based on a formula that considers low-income populations, residential energy expenditures, and climatic conditions. In addition to providing more than a twenty-fold increase in the average annual funding of the WAP, the ARRA increased the statewide average expenditure limit per home to $6,500.

Energy Efficiency Block Grant Program: $3.2 Billion

The Energy Efficiency and Conservation Block Grant Program (EEBGP) provides funding to states and local governments for a wide range of activities that reduce energy use and fossil fuel emissions, determined at the discretion of the state and local government. Under the block grant program, states, larger cities (defined as cities with a population greater than 35,000 or one of the top 10 populated cities in the state), and larger counties (defined as counties with a population greater than 200,000 or one of the top 10 most populated counties in the state), are set an amount of funding determined according to a formula set by DOE (and published by the DOE on March 26, 2009). States are required to pass along at least 60 percent of their funds to smaller cities and counties. The remaining 40 percent may be spent at the state's discretion.

In addition to the formula block grants, an additional $400 million is allocated for distribution by DOE through competitive grants. No program has been established by the DOE for distribution of these funds, and, therefore, eligibility for these funds is not yet known.

Other Federal Agency Efficiency Funds: Upwards of $10 Billion

The federal government itself, as a real estate owner, also has significant funds allocated to refurbishing its buildings and facilities, which could include energy efficiency improvements. This includes the following agencies: the General Services Administration (GSA), which has $4.5 billion to convert federal facilities to "high-performance green buildings"; the Department of Defense, which has a total of $4.9 billion to improve, repair, and modernize DOD facilities, including health care facilities, and to conduct research, development, test, and evaluation projects into energy generation and efficiency; the U.S. Forest Service, which has $650 million for capital improvement projects; and the National Park Service, which has $735 million for critical repair and rehabilitation projects.

Part 3: General Recovery Act Considerations

The ARRA is unlike previous federal government spending programs in its size and breadth. As noted above, the Obama administration is placing a high emphasis on transparency in the distribution of these funds. Although all federal funding traditionally comes with significant rules and conditions, the ARRA funding will likely be one of the most highly monitored federal funding programs to date. Below are some of the universal rules that will apply to all parties seeking ARRA funding, including the electric power industry.

Reporting Requirements

The administration is requiring detailed and extensive reporting by all federal agencies responsible for ARRA fund distribution, as well as by all direct recipients of those funds. To date, the Office of Management and Budget (OMB) has produced two lengthy memoranda that delineate the detailed reporting obligations of federal agencies.[1] In addition to preparing an agency-wide ARRA plan and program-specific ARRA plans, every federal agency must submit weekly reports on its ARRA activity and plans, which are posted on www.recovery.com. Reporting by ARRA award recipients will begin October 10, 2009, with quarterly reporting to follow thereafter. The requirements of these recipient reporting requirements are still being drafted, but they are likely to be robust and to include details such as how all monies have been spent or committed, any sub-awards, number of jobs created, and detail on how the award has furthered the goals of the ARRA.

Accounting Requirements

In support of the goal of transparency, the administration is also requiring heightened financial reporting requirements for recipients of ARRA monies. ARRA funds may not be comingled with other sources of funding. Applicants must provide detailed budget information in their grant applications and recipients will have to produce detailed expenditure information in their reports. Awardees may also be asked to specifically identify how many jobs their actual performance under the financial assistance award created or saved, as compared to the amounts spent.

Buy America Provision

According to section 1605 of the ARRA, any stimulus funding for the "construction, alteration, maintenance, or repair of a public building or public work" is restricted to using domestic iron, steel, and manufactured goods. Federal agencies can waive the ARRA Buy American provision under specified circumstances, but such waiver should be obtained prior to the award.

A draft regulation published by the OMB on April 23, 2009, explains how this provision will apply to ARRA grants, cooperative agreements, and loans. This draft regulation defines a "public building or public work" as "a public building or, and a public work of, a governmental entity," which includes any federal, state, or local governmental entity.[2] Although the draft regulation does not define a "public building" or a "public work," it gives a lengthy list of examples, which includes "bridges, dams, plants, highways, parkways, streets. . . ., *power lines*, pumping stations, *heavy generation*. . . ."[3] Accordingly, any recipients of ARRA funds should pay particular attention to the sourcing of materials used on any infrastructure that could be considered to be publicly owned.

1. *See* February 18, 2009 and April 3, 2009 Memos, available at www.whitehouse.gov/omb.

2. 74 Fed. Reg. 18,449 (Apr. 23, 2009). The definition of "public building or public works" that has been traditionally used in federal procurement laws, and applies to any federal contracts using ARRA funds, is very broad and essentially includes any projects funded with federal funds, whether on public or private land: "building or work, the construction, prosecution, completion, or repair of which...is carried on directly by authority of, or with funds of, a Federal agency to serve the interest of the general public regardless of whether title thereof is in a Federal agency." 74 Fed. Reg. 14,623, 14,624, referencing FAR 22.401.

3. *Id.* (emphasis added).

Each individual funding announcement by the agencies will identify the specific criteria for that award. The administration has instructed each federal agency to prepare "transparent, merit-based selection criteria" for each ARRA funding program. The criteria must be consistent with legal requirements, may be tailored to the specific funding activity, and must "be formulated to ensure that the funding furthers the job creation, economic recovery, and other purposes of the Recovery Act."

This is a tall order, since there have been many identified purposes of the ARRA. The White House has explained that merit-based selection criteria should be designed to ensure that applicants have a demonstrated or potential ability to: (i) deliver programmatic results; (ii) optimize economic activity and the number of jobs created or saved; (iii) achieve long-term public benefits; and (iv) meet the ARRA's transparency and accountability objectives. In addition, built into the statute is a requirement that programs awarding funds going to infrastructure investment give preference to projects that are "shovel ready" and can be implemented quickly. Finally, guidance from OMB encourages agencies to consider weighting their selection criteria for funding awards in favor of applicants who have previously received funding and have proven their ability to deliver the goals of the Recovery Act.

Part 4: Considerations Specific to Electric Utilities

In addition to the general considerations that all stakeholders for any ARRA funds should keep in mind, due to their existing status as regulated entities, electric utilities should consider possible ancillary impacts of the ARRA on their relationships with their existing regulators.

The ARRA and the General Rate Case

As described above, the ARRA offers billions in funding to upgrade and expand energy generation and transmission infrastructures. While this funding appears to be a valuable resource for energy companies, ratemaking constraints add a significant layer of complexity for energy utilities.

In general ratemaking cases (GRCs), the public utility collects and presents data via testimony and work papers to a public utility commission on the cost of providing utility service for various types of ratepayers. Typically, a GRC will include data regarding the size of the utility's rate base, the amount and treatment of expenses, sales levels and revenues, allowable return on investment, and the costs of capital improvements and operation and maintenance, and rate design. After reviewing the data, sponsoring extensive hearings, and allowing for public comment through interveners, the public utility determines the rates that the utility will be allowed to collect. Those rates can and usually do vary by type of customer. Generally, a state utility commission will exclude grant funds received from other sources (such as the federal government) from the utility's "costs." In simple terms, the utility cannot charge ratepayers for capital improvements that were funded by the federal government through the ARRA or otherwise.

To the extent that a utility's rates already include capital improvements or operation and maintenance costs, the utility should tread carefully in seeking ARRA funding for the same or related projects. Pending rate cases may have to be revised to reflect ARRA funding. Utilities and commissions will have to come up with ways to fairly reflect the positive impact on utility rates of ARRA grants while recognizing that those benefits may not be recurrent.

The reverse is also true: utilities should tread carefully if they choose not to seek ARRA funding. Activist commissioners and ratepayer advocates can also be expected to query utilities about the extent and results of their ARRA applications. Did the utility apply for all possible projects? If unsuccessful, was the rejection due to preventable deficiencies in the application process? Set against the backdrop of the current economic downturn, utilities should be prepared to explain their decision to "walk away" from available funding.

State PUC Energy Efficiency Programs

Many state PUCs have implemented energy efficiency programs that create an economic incentive for electric utilities to promote energy efficiency. State PUC energy efficiency and performance initiatives programs generally follow one of two models: decoupling utility revenues and profits by periodically adjusting actual and projected sales, and creating shareholder performance incentives for energy efficiency.

As discussed above, the ARRA commits significant funds to energy efficiency programs.

In an effort to ensure that this new funding does not cannibalize existing state energy efficiency programs, DOE is making the SEP funding contingent upon a commitment from the state that these funds "will not be used to supplant rate payer or other state funding for energy programs." Depending on the structure of the incentive program, regulators will want assurances that energy utilities do not "double dip" by receiving both ARRA funding and state PUC funding for the same amount of energy saved.

Electric utilities should carefully monitor the terms of their state's application funding for energy efficiency programs, for they could have a significant impact on the state-run incentive program. Furthermore, electric utilities in states with an existing or pending renewable energy standard (RES) that includes energy efficiency as renewable energy will want to pay particular attention to which efficiency gains (i.e., whether they are funded through the federal ARRA or through the state PUC) can be attributed to the utility for RES purposes.

Conclusion

The ARRA is approximately three months old and there remain many unanswered questions about its implementation. Whether or not this significant funding triggers major changes in energy generation and transmission infrastructure will not be known for years to come. We do know that there will be many stakeholders watching to see how these funding programs unfold, and how the electric industry responds.

~~~~~~~~~~
~~~~~~~~~~

2012 Update

By Lisa Wing Stone and Katrina Robson

June 2012 marked the midway point in the life of the American Recovery and Reinvestment Act (ARRA), which was signed into law on February 17, 2009, and is due to expire on September 30, 2015. Therefore, this is a fitting time to reflect on the progress of energy-related ARRA-funded projects.

Initial pressure to quickly deploy ARRA money in order to meet the economic stimulus goal of the ARRA was countered by administrative challenges faced by both the Department of Energy (DOE) and the private sector. The ARRA funding far exceeded previous annual budgets for DOE, and the agency faced resource constraints. In addition, many recipients of the funds had limited previous experience with federally funded projects and faced a steep learning curve on the nuts and bolts of the administration of such projects. Further complicating progress was the fact that elements of the ARRA statute, such as the Davis-Bacon Act and ARRA enhanced reporting, added another layer of complexity.

However, it is clear now that early growing pains have been overcome. The DOE has disbursed well over half of its funding. As of July 2012, the department reports that it has awarded $35.8 billion in ARRA funds (which includes $32.7 billion in contracts and grants and $2.5 billion in Section 1705 credit subsidies) and paid out a total of $26.7 billion to recipients. Due to the cost-sharing requirement in most energy-related programs (which requires the recipient to pay for at least 50 percent of the cost of the project from non-federal funds), this $35.2 billion in ARRA funding is reportedly supporting nearly $80 billion in clean energy projects. According to the DOE, this funding also has been maintaining 40,000–50,000 direct jobs each quarter since summer 2010.

Certainly, the DOE-administered ARRA programs have been the subject of some controversy. In particular, the loan guarantee program has been the focus of scrutiny in Congress and in the press. However, success stories also abound. Due to the emphasis on transparency by the Obama administration, there is a significant amount of data and information available at the federal government's ARRA site, www.recovery.gov, and the DOE's own ARRA web page, http://energy.gov/recovery-act. Many states also host web pages dedicated to ongoing ARRA projects in their own states. A few of the achievements being touted by the DOE include the following:

- As of January 2012, more than 10.3 million smart meters have been installed in homes and businesses nationwide through ARRA-funded projects, and the DOE is on track to meet its goal of deploying more than 15.5 million total smart meters.
- As of December 2011, the Weatherization grant program had funded energy-efficient energy retrofits in the homes of more than 650,000 low-income families, achieving average savings of $437 per year on their energy bills.
- Investments in renewable energy generation projects have produced enough capacity to power one million homes and are on target to meet the administration's goal of doubling U.S. renewable energy generation by 2012.

September 2015 is still three years away, and the second half of the ARRA story remains to be written. However, as of the midpoint, both the DOE and the project proponents look forward to many more success stories as more ARRA-funded projects achieve their milestones.

Chapter 24

Climate Change Regulation: A Significant Challenge for NiSource and Other Energy Companies in the 21st Century*

*By Carrie J. Hightman and Margaret E. Rice***

Editor's Note: Infrastructure presents the following commentary representing the reaction of NiSource Inc., a public utility holding company, to the American Clean Energy and Security Act of 2009, passed by the U.S. House of Representatives in June 2009. The views of NiSource are not the views of Infrastructure or of the American Bar Association but they represent the viewpoint of a significant company operating within the regulated industry. Infrastructure intends over time to present other commentary on this subject by other affected and knowledgeable parties—hopefully representing a range of views.

Legislative and administrative bodies throughout the country have proposed new laws designed to reduce greenhouse gas (GHG) and thereby minimize climate change. While most electric and natural gas utilities support reasonable GHG regulation, the legislative and regulatory proposals currently under consideration are unfair, ill timed, and cumulative. Proposals like the House of Representatives' American Clean Energy and Security Act of 2009 (ACES) could impact system reliability and would dramatically increase prices for electricity and natural gas. The price impacts will be felt most strongly in midwestern states like Indiana that have traditionally relied upon coal to provide baseload power.

---

* Originally published in *Infrastructure*, vol. 49, no. 1 (Fall, 2009).

** *Carrie J. Hightman is executive vice president and chief legal officer and Margaret E. Rice is senior counsel at NiSource Inc.*

The NiSource Companies

NiSource Inc. generates, transmits, and distributes electricity through its subsidiary Northern Indiana Public Service Company (NIPSCO) to approximately 457,000 customers in 20 counties in northern Indiana. NIPSCO operates a diverse fleet of generating units, including coal, natural gas, and hydroelectric facilities. On an average day, however, 95 percent of NIPSCO's electric generation is coal fired.

NiSource companies also transmit and distribute natural gas to a wide swath of the country from the Gulf Coast through the Midwest and into New England. NiSource's gas distribution subsidiaries (LDCs) serve 3.3 million customers in seven states and own 57,000 miles of distribution pipeline. NiSource's gas transmission and storage companies (NGT&S) own and operate about 16,000 miles of interstate natural gas pipelines, integrated with one of the largest underground storage systems in North America. More than one trillion cubic feet of natural gas flows through NGT&S pipelines and storage systems each year.

NiSource is a charter member of the U.S. Department of Energy's Climate Challenge. Through that program, NiSource has implemented various cost-effective methods for reducing CO_2 emissions. NiSource companies have reported CO_2 reductions of more than 34 million equivalent tons since 1990.

Impact on Electric Utilities

Of all this year's environmental proposals, the most widely discussed is ACES, also called the "Waxman-Markey" bill.[1] ACES, which was passed by the U.S. House of Representatives on June 26, 2009, would establish a cap-and-trade system to reduce GHG emissions and impose renewable energy requirements on electric utilities.

The impact of ACES, if enacted, on electric utilities would be profound. NIPSCO estimates that ACES would cost NIPSCO electric customers more than $100 million in 2012 alone, which amounts to about $200 per customer. NIPSO further estimates that the impact of ACES would increase dramatically by 2030.

The Senate also has its own proposals on both renewable energy and climate change. The Senate's renewable energy bill was reported out of the Senate's Energy and Natural Resources Committee in June. On September 30, 2009, the Senate Committee on Environment and Public Works released a discussion draft on climate change. At the same time, the EPA has proposed a number of regulations dealing with GHG emissions.

Electric Generation and ACES

ACES—GHG provisions. Discussions of ACES tend to focus on Title III, which addresses reducing GHG. The bill would regulate individual GHG emitters using a cap-and-trade system. Companies would buy or receive allowances equivalent to one ton

1. H.R. 2454, 111th Cong. (2009).

of CO_2.[2] The number of allowances available would diminish over time, thereby requiring commensurate reductions in GHG emissions.[3] The bill seeks to reduce 2012 CO_2 emissions in the United States by 3 percent from 2005 levels.[4] The targeted reduction in 2050 would be 83 percent.[5]

Coal-fired electric generators would, of course, not be the only entities impacted by Title III of ACES, though they would arguably be some of the most significantly impacted. This is, in part, because coal-fired generation tends to produce more CO_2 than other generating facilities. However, ACES also contains provisions that are unique to the electric generation industry. For example, section 722 phases in the cap-and-trade requirements industry by industry. The electric generation industry must comply with the cap-and-trade requirements by 2012, while most other industries need not comply until 2014 or 2016. In addition, section 116 imposes GHG performance standards on new coal-fired power plants but not on power plants burning other fuels. These performance standards impose limits on all coal plants that receive their initial permitting after January 1, 2009. Plants initially permitted after January 1, 2020 would have to reduce their CO_2 emissions by 65 percent.

ACES—renewable energy requirements. In addition to directly regulating GHG, Title I of ACES would also create new renewable energy requirements that apply only to "retail electric suppliers," or companies that sold more than four million MWh of electricity for purposes other than resale in a given year.[6] These companies would be required to meet a set percentage of their electricity demand through renewable sources. The required percentages start at 6 percent in 2012 and increase to 20 percent in 2020.[7]

Perhaps one of the most contentious issues in the debate about ACES has been the definition of "renewable energy." Power generated by wind, solar, and geothermal are, of course, included. But, in an effort to accommodate regional differences in the availability of certain types of renewable power, energy generated by certain waste-to-energy facilities would also be included as "renewable."[8] Nuclear energy is not considered "renewable" but is given favorable treatment in calculating the base quantity of electricity.[9] The same is true of fossil-fired units that capture and geologically sequester GHG emissions.

ACES—allowances for electric customers. The section of ACES addressing the disposition of allowances has received much attention.[10] Part H would allocate allowances without charge to electric consumers and companies. The number of allocations would decrease dramatically over time and phase out entirely by 2030—just 18 years

2. *Id.* at § 721.
3. *Id.*
4. *Id.* at § 702.
5. *Id.*
6. *Id.* at § 101(a)(19).
7. *Id.* at § 101(d).
8. *Id.* at §§ 101(12)(14) (17) & (18).
9. *Id.* at § 101(20).
10. *Id.* at § 782 *et seq.*

into the program.[11] This phase-out would create a significant gap between the number of allowances NIPSCO must obtain and its allocation.

Another problem with ACES is the emission allowance allocation formula for electric utilities that distributes 50 percent of emissions allowances based on electricity sales and 50 percent based on historic emissions.[12] The formula is unfair to utilities that rely heavily on coal for generation and is overly generous to utilities that own more nuclear, natural gas, and hydroelectric generation. NIPSCO is heavily dependant on coal for the generation of electricity and is allocated allowances covering only 60 percent of its emissions in 2012.

EPA Developments Related to GHG

ACES may be the most commonly discussed vehicle to address climate change, but it is not the only source of new GHG requirements. The U.S. Supreme Court's decision in *Massachusetts v. Environmental Protection Agency*, 549 U.S. 497 (2007), recognized the EPA's authority to regulate GHG under existing provisions of the Clean Air Act (CAA) to the extent that those GHG "may reasonably be anticipated to endanger public health or welfare." The EPA cleared the way for regulation on April 24, 2009, by proposing a finding that (a) atmospheric concentrations of GHG threaten public health and welfare and (b) that emissions (from motor vehicles at least) contribute to atmospheric concentrations of GHG.[13] Although this "endangerment finding" on its face applies only to motor vehicles, the finding will be expanded to other sources. The EPA has made clear that it intends to regulate GHG as a pollutant under the CAA if ACES or similar legislation does not become law.[14]

In a separate rulemaking, the EPA adopted new regulations that will require large sources to report GHG emissions.[15] The emission information will be used by the EPA to develop comprehensive data relevant to future climate policy decisions. The reporting rules will require reporting beginning in 2011 for emissions in 2010.

Making Coal Cleaner

As the discussion above makes clear, the electric industry may have to adapt to extensive regulatory changes in the 2010-2015 time frame. This timing is unfortunate because it outpaces the development of cutting-edge technology like integrated gasification and combined cycle (IGCC) and carbon capture and sequestration (CCS), which will reduce the environmental impact of coal-fired generation. It is expected that these new technologies will not be available on a commercial basis until 2025.[16]

---

11. *Id.* § 782(1).
12. *Id.*
13. 74 Fed. Reg. 18,886 (April 24, 2009).
14. *See* 74 Fed. Reg. 55,292 (October 27, 2009). ACES in its current form would probably preempt EPA regulation of GHG as a pollutant under the CAA. H.R. 2454 at §§ 831-35.
15. *See* 74 Fed. Reg. 56,259 (October 30, 2009).
16. Coal Utilization Research Council, *CURC-EPRI Clean Coal Tech. Roadmap* (September 2006).

With IGCC technology, coal is processed with oxygen and water under high pressure to form a syngas. The syngas is then cooled, stripped of sulfur compounds, and combusted in a gas turbine generator.[17] IGCC technology reduces the emission of SO_2, NO_x, and particulate matter from coal-fired generation.[18] CO_2 emissions would also be reduced by 10 percent and can be reduced even further if IGCC is used along with CCS.[19]

CCS separates CO_2 from flue gas using physical or chemical processes. The CO_2 is then compressed into liquid, transported to its ultimate disposal location, and injected into a suitable geologic formation.

IGCC and CCS could be widely available within the next 15 years.[20] One proposed plant that would combine IGCC and CCS technology is the FutureGen facility in Illinois. In the summer of 2009, the United States Department of Energy (DOE) and the owners of FutureGen entered into an agreement to fund design, financial analysis, and site investigation for FutureGen.[21] Support for CCS and IGCC can also be found in ACES, which would require EPA and other agencies to create a comprehensive strategy for promoting CCS.[22] ACES also would authorize energy companies to create a $10 billion fund to support the study and early deployment of commercial-scale CCS.[23] However, these innovative technologies will not be available quickly enough to blunt the impact of other provisions of ACES on electric consumers.

Impact on Natural Gas

Like electric customers, natural gas customers would be significantly impacted by ACES and the proposed GHG regulations.

Impact on LDCs

ACES would require gas distribution companies like the NiSource LDCs to purchase or otherwise obtain allowances for the emissions of their residential, commercial, and small industrial customers.[24] In other words, LDCs would be responsible for their customers' emissions even though the gas is combusted on property owned by the customer, and not the LDC. As is the case with electric customers, ACES initially allocates allowances to LDCs, but the allocations are not sufficient to compensate for the added costs of ACES in later years. The allocation amount would be 9 percent in 2016 and phase out completely by 2030.[25] In addition, LDCs would be required to spend an

17. Taylor Moore, *Coal Generation at the Crossroads*, EPRI Journ. (Summer 2005).
18. State Clean Energy-Environment Technical Forum, *Integrated Gasification Combined Cycle (IGCC) Background and Tech. Issues* (June 19, 2006).
19. *Id.*
20. Coal Utilization Research Council, *CURC-EPRI Clean Coal Tech. Roadmap.*
21. Ben Geman, *DOE Revives FutureGen, Reversing Bush Era Decision*, N.Y. Times (June 12, 2009); 74 Fed. Reg. 35,174 (July 20, 2009) (FutureGen ROD).
22. H.R. 2454 at §§ 111, 113.
23. *Id.* at § 114.
24. *Id.* at § 722(b)(8).
25. *Id.* at § 782(b), 784.

amount equivalent to one-third of their allowances on energy efficiency programs.[26] Thus, LDCs would have to buy a comparable number of allowances to cover customer emissions.

Overall, the impact on NiSource LDC customers would be approximately $200 million in 2016, increasing to over $1 billion in 2030. A large portion of this impact is caused by the phasing out of allocations between 2016 and 2030. The phase-out for natural gas does not appear to make good policy sense. It is unclear why the House chose to tax natural gas usage so heavily when the stated policy of many in Congress is to encourage natural gas as an alternative to more heavily emitting fossil fuels like coal.

Impact on Gas Transmission Providers

ACES would impact natural gas transmission systems in a number of ways. First, like other entities that emit GHG, gas transmission systems would be required to purchase allowances to cover their GHG emissions. However, unlike electric and gas utilities, no allowances would be allocated to gas transmission providers.[27] The obligation to purchase allowances for GHG emissions would become effective in 2014.[28] This requirement would have a substantial impact on NGT&S since it covers 70 percent of the CO_2 emissions from NGT&S compressor stations.

Second, ACES would impose performance standards for sources of fugitive and vented methane.[29] The exact nature of these performance standards is not entirely clear since the specifics of the program are left to the EPA. It is likely, however, that the standards would apply beginning in 2012 or 2013 and that they would cover approximately 90 percent of fugitive and vented emissions from NGT&S compressor stations. The standards would require equipment maintenance and modifications, the cost of which would most likely be front-end loaded. NGT&S estimates that ACES could cost $50 million in 2014 alone.

Added to this cost would be the expense of new reporting rules. Both ACES and the EPA propose GHG reporting rules that would require transmission companies to quantify and report GHG emissions.[30] Although electric utilities have been reporting their GHG emissions for years, gas transmission providers have not. The reporting regulations would require reporting of 2010 emissions beginning in 2011.[31] Only facilities that generate more than 25,000 metric tons of CO_2 equivalent would be required to report. However, at this point, transmission companies are uncertain which of their facilities would meet the reporting threshold. The determination will depend on the level of fugitive emissions at each facility, which is notoriously difficult to quantify.

26. *Id.* at § 784.
27. *Id.* at § 782.
28. *Id.* at § 722(c)(1).
29. *Id.* at § 811.
30. *See* 74 Fed. Reg. 56,259.
31. *Id.*

Conclusion

NiSource and its affiliates understand the need for reasonable climate change legislation. ACES and the EPA's proposed GHG regulations, however, were created with undue haste and, in their present forms, threaten to impact system reliability and dramatically increase energy costs for consumers. Before proceeding further, policymakers need to decide whether they want to encourage or discourage natural gas as an alternative to more emitting fossil fuels. Policymakers also need to better phase in requirements for existing electric generating facilities. Imposing significant new costs on coal-fired generation before alternatives are available could cause untenable cost increases for consumers. It is the electric industry's hope that IGCC and CCS technology ultimately will allow electric utilities to use coal more cleanly so that coal-fired generating facilities can continue to provide baseload power into the 21st century and beyond. In the interim, the nation needs reduction goals that are equitable, achievable and consistent with the timetables for development and deployment of new technology.

~~~~~~~~~~
~~~~~~~~~~

2012 Update

By Carrie J. Hightman and Margaret E. Rice

Much has changed since 2009, when *Infrastructure* published "Climate Change Regulation: A Significant Challenge for NiSource and Other Energy Companies in the 21st Century." Most of the article focused on the proposed American Clean Energy and Security Act (ACES),[1] a comprehensive climate-change bill that was passed by the U.S. House of Representatives in June 2009. ACES ultimately failed to garner enough support in the Senate and died at the end of the congressional session. Today, it seems inconceivable that a similar climate-change bill would be introduced, much less passed. The failure of comprehensive climate change legislation, however, did little to lessen the pressure exerted on the electric and natural gas industries by environmental regulators.

On the electric side, the Environmental Protection Agency (EPA) has taken over where Congress left off. Some of EPA's greenhouse gas initiatives were mentioned in the 2009 article, but these initiatives have since expanded to include proposed new source performance standards (NSPS) for future power plants.[2] The NSPS would require all new plants to match the greenhouse gas performance currently achieved by high-efficiency *natural gas* power plants, effectively prohibiting the construction of new coal plants without advanced (and still commercially unavailable) carbon controls. For existing coal power plants, however, the most significant issue in 2012 is not the EPA's regulation of greenhouse gases, but the agency's regulation of conventional air pollutants like sulfur dioxide, nitrogen oxides, mercury, and particulates. These pollutants are subject to strict new controls under EPA's 2011 Cross State Air Pollution Rule[3] (CSAPR) and 2012 Mercury and Air Toxic Standards[4] (MATS). Many are predicting that the emissions limits and deadlines in CSAPR and MATS will cause the nation's oldest coal plants to shut down, possibly threatening the stability of electric supplies. What is clear is that the new rules will almost certainly make energy more expensive for consumers.[5]

1. H.R. 2454, 111th Cong. (2009).
2. 77 Fed. Reg. 22,392.
3. 76 Fed. Reg. 48,208.
4. 76 Fed. Reg. 48,208.
5. Environmental Protection Agency, *Regulatory Impact Analysis for the Final Mercury and Air Toxics Standards* ES-14 (December 2011); Environmental Protection Agency, *Regulatory Impact Analysis for the Final Transport Rule* 14–15 (June 2011).

The natural gas industry similarly has come under the regulatory microscope. In the past few years, EPA has proposed new rules for polychlorinated biphenyls (PCBs)[6] and promulgated new air regulations for hydraulic fracturing.[7] In the near future, EPA is expected to issue air-quality standards for existing transmission sources. If any new regulations significantly increase the cost of natural gas, they could undermine natural gas's status as an alternative to coal.

Given all of the changes in the three years since 2009, it is difficult to predict where we will be in 2015, three years into the future. Some of the new rules mentioned above are currently being challenged in court, and we are in the middle of an election year that could change everything once again. It is possible, however, that we may find ourselves in 2015 moving toward a very different energy industry than the one we wrote about in 2009.

6. 75 Fed. Reg. 17,645.
7. http://www.epa.gov/airquality/oilandgas/pdfs/20120417finalrule.pdf.

Chapter 25

The Emerging Impact of Shale Gas Resources*

*By John W. Rowe and Ed Fortunato***

The first natural gas well in the United States was a shale gas well. In 1821, a 27-foot well was dug deep into a Devonian shale formation in Fredonia, New York, and the gas was piped through a wooden pipe to the town to illuminate its streets. In 1839, a geological survey team found gas in a shale formation outside the town of Marcellus, New York, and named it Marcellus Shale. The Marcellus Shale formation begins in central and western New York, and travels through central and western Pennsylvania into West Virginia. Originally, the formation was not considered viable due to the depth of the formation—almost twice as deep as others in the area.

Today, 170 years later, we have moved from 27-foot-deep wells shoveled straight into the ground to wells that are thousands of feet deep and drilled horizontally. Technological advances allowed for the rediscovery of Marcellus Shale in 2008, and have since provided the drilling capability to extract large amounts of natural gas at competitive prices. In fact, the Marcellus Shale "discovery" in 2008 marks the beginning of a paradigm shift in long-term gas production according to Terry Engelder, a professor of geosciences at Pennsylvania State University.[1] This shift represents a move away from importing natural gas into the eastern United States and towards domestic sources and international exports.

Shale is a fine grained sedimentary rock that may contain high concentrations of natural gas. Shale gas is a growing source of current and future natural gas supply in the United States and currently represents about 17 percent of total U.S. supply.[2] The

---

* Originally published in *Infrastructure*, vol. 50, no. 1 (Fall, 2010).

* *John W. Rowe is the chairman and chief executive officer, and Ed Fortunato is the manager of proprietary trading and fundamental analytics at Exelon Corp. in Chicago, Illinois.*

1. Terry Engelder, professor of Geosciences at the Pennsylvania State University, *Shale Gas: An industrial opportunity that can make a difference for America* (June 14, 2010).

2. *Marcellus Shale Safety Issues*, S. Envtl. Res. and Energy Comm., Session of 2010 (Pa. 2010) (testimony by John Hanger, Sec'y, Pa. Dep't of Envtl. Prot.), *available at* http://files.dep.state.pa.us/AboutDEP/AboutDEPPortalFiles/RemarksAndTestimonies/TestimonyEOGSafety_061610.pdf).

Pennsylvania Department of Environmental Protection (Pa DEP) stated that Marcellus Shale production could contribute up to 10 percent of the total U.S. natural gas supply by 2014.[3]

Deregulation of Natural Gas and Electric Industries

The natural gas and electric industries are very similar both in structure and operation. Prior to deregulation, local natural gas and electric utilities handled all three phases of the business (supply, transmission, and distribution) in a "vertically integrated" manner. Deregulation subsequently separated these three previously integrated phases and typically divested each function into separate companies.

Federal and state regulation of public utilities dates back to the 1930s. Over the years, there have been a number of regulations, including the Public Utilities Holding Company Act of 1935, Natural Gas Act of 1938, Public Utilities Regulatory Policy Act of 1978, and Energy Policy Act of 2005, which have shaped the relationship between utilities and their customers.[4] The 1985 Federal Energy Regulatory Commission (FERC) Order No. 436 (Open Access Blueprint) established the *voluntary* framework under which interstate pipelines were to offer transportation services to customers on a first-come-first-served basis.[5] Essentially, this order granted industrial customers the freedom to purchase gas directly from the producers and to use the pipelines as transporters rather than as merchants.[6] Order No. 436 resulted in immediate cost savings for end users, as spot gas prices were significantly lower than the contract prices traditionally offered by the pipelines. Subsequently, in 1992, FERC issued Order No. 636 (the Restructuring Rule), which *mandated* the unbundling of sales services from transportation services.[7] Mandatory unbundling increased competition among gas sellers and eliminated the market power of pipeline companies. Though each policy act addressed different aspects of the business, *interstate* commerce has always been under the authority of the Federal Energy Regulatory Commission (FERC), whereas *intrastate* affairs are regulated by the applicable state public utility commission.

Deregulation of the natural gas and electric industries opened the price of commodity supply to competition. However, the transmission and distribution of natural gas and electricity is still regulated, and not open to choice, as the prices for these services continue to be set by state- and federally-approved tariffs.

Natural Gas Market Evolution

The FERC orders stimulated natural gas trading activity on the New York Mercantile Exchange (NYMEX, currently CME) and resulted in market signaling to both consumers and producers. From 1996 to 2006, NYMEX prices indicated constraints in

3. *Id.*

4. A list of major legislative and regulatory actions is provided in the Appendix (Table 1).

5. *See Regulation of Natural Gas Pipelines After Partial Wellhead Decontrol*, Order No. 436, 18 C.F.R. §§ 2, 157, 250, 284, 375, 381(1985).

6. *See id.*

7. *See The Restructuring Rule*, Order No. 636, 18 C.F.R. § 284 (1992).

Table 1: Major Legislative and Regulatory Actions (1935-2008)

The Public Utility Holding Company Act of 1935

Natural Gas Act of 1938

"Phillips Case:" Supreme Court Decision Giving FPC Jurisdiction Over Wellhead Prices (1954)

Natural Gas Policy Act of 1978

Tax Credits for Unconventional Gas Recovery (1980)

FERC Order 380: Eliminated Minimum Bills for LDCs (1984)

FERC Order 436: Open Access Blueprint (1985)

Canadian Regulatory Reform Leads to Long-Term Increase in Sales to the United States (1985)

FERC Order 500: Take-or-Pay Cost Recovery (1987)

Repeal of the Power Plant and Industrial Fuel Use Act (1987)

Natural Gas Wellhead Decontrol Act of 1989

Clean Air Act Amendments of 1990

Moratorium on Offshore Drilling (1990)

NYMEX Issues First Natural Gas Futures Contract (1990)

FERC Pipeline Construction Rules Since 1991

FERC Order 636: The Restructuring Rule (1992)

Energy Policy Act of 1992

FERC Policy on Natural Gas Gathering System Ownership Since 1992

North American Free Trade Agreement (1994)

Outer Continental Shelf Deep Water Royalty Relief Act of 1995

FERC Order 637 (2000)

2002 Amendments to Deepwater Port Act of 1974

FERC's Hackberry Decision (2002)

The Maritime Transportation Security Act of 2002

The Pipeline Safety Improvement Act of 2002

The Alaska Natural Gas Pipeline Act (2004)

American Jobs Creation Act of 2004

The Energy Policy Act of 2005

The Gulf of Mexico Energy Security Act (2006)

The Pipeline Inspection, Protection, Enforcement, and Safety Act of 2006

The Energy Independence and Security Act of 2007

Lifting of the Moratorium on Offshore Drilling (2008)

Source: www.eia.doe.gov/oil_gas/natural_gas/analysis_publications/ngmajorleg/ngmajorleg.html

domestic natural gas production and a lack of opportunities to increase domestic natural gas production.[8] Highly volatile prices during that period were a clear manifestation of these supply constraints. Increasing the import of natural gas, primarily through liquefied natural gas (LNG), was the solution to meeting current supply deficiencies, with prices set by international gas pricing mechanisms. This view peaked in 2008, as the entire NYMEX natural gas curve shifted upward to reflect international pricing mechanisms.[9]

From 2006 to 2008, high price signals indicated to gas producers that they would be well paid to increase domestic production. This high premium for gas induced innovative production techniques. Unconventional extraction techniques such as horizontal drilling and fracturing, first developed in the oil industry, were applied to natural gas. These innovations enabled economically feasible shale gas extraction.

Conventional drilling involves a vertical insertion of a drill bit and pipe underground to pierce a reservoir of product and extract the product, similar to a straw in a glass. Although conventional gas requires fewer wells spaced further apart, careful seismic and exploratory drilling is often necessary and the most productive fields tend to require long lead times. Shale gas drilling involves initially drilling vertically in the ground up to 5,000 feet then moving horizontally across a field, up to 10,000 feet. Unlike conventional drilling, this method of drilling requires fewer unsuccessful exploratory wells and has shorter lead time requirements. Shale gas offers a lower cost, fewer barriers-to-entry and a more efficient drilling alternative to the conventional gas drilling technique. Drilling in shale requires a hydraulic fracturing process (the high pressure pumping of large volumes of liquids into the rock, often referred to as *fracking*), that allows trapped natural gas to migrate away from the rock and into pipelines.

Shale gas exploration has changed the U.S. supply outlook from "opportunity constrained" to "opportunity rich." Shale containing both oil and natural gas lies beneath millions of acres in a U-shaped formation extending from northeastern British Columbia and adjacent southern Alberta to Montana and North Dakota, continuing through Wyoming, Colorado, New Mexico, Texas, Louisiana, and then north into the Illinois and Appalachian Basins and into Quebec, New Brunswick, and Nova Scotia. In all, shale formations exist beneath six provinces of Canada and 23 U.S. states and are now recognized as promising sources of natural gas. This large area of opportunity, combined with the lower cost of extracting shale gas compared to conventional methods (millions versus. billions of dollars) offers fewer barriers to entry for potential natural gas producers. As a result, large numbers of small gas producers have begun to drill for shale gas, in contrast to the relatively small number of large players that have the capability of conventional drilling in the Gulf of Mexico.

The large Marcellus Shale formation is not the only shale formation in the United States. Nevertheless, only one other shale gas site, the Barnett formation in Fort Worth, Texas, has seen substantial development. Shale drilling techniques were first developed, over a period of 15 years, at the Barnett shale site. These techniques later enabled the economic feasibility of shale gas development. Other sites, including Marcellus

8. Pricing data courtesy of CQG.
9. Pricing data courtesy of CQG.

(PA), Bakken (ND), Eagle Ford (TX), Woodford (OK), and Fayetteville (LA) are in the initial stages of development with many more (Utica – N.Y., Antrim – MI, New Albany – IN) in the infancy stages.

Shale gas has the potential to revolutionize the domestic as well as international energy market. Other countries, including several in Eastern Europe as well as China and India, have begun to explore shale gas drilling, and their initial results seem encouraging. Increased amounts of domestic natural gas production, particularly from the Marcellus shale, could have significant geopolitical implications. Industry experts have begun to discuss the possibility of exporting Marcellus gas to Europe in the form of LNG. Europe, a large importer of LNG, currently receives most of its natural gas supply from Gazprom, a large Russian gas supplier.[10] U.S. natural gas exports could challenge Gazprom's market power over European gas supply. Increased competition in the European natural gas market could weaken the price link between oil and natural gas, a relationship Gazprom has aggressively attempted to preserve as recently seen through its winter natural gas shutoff to Europe in 2009.[11] Because natural gas prices are generally linked to the price of crude oil, a breakdown in the international oil to gas price relationship could reduce the cost of fuel in Europe, and across the globe. Ultimately, a decrease in natural gas revenue to Russia and the Ukraine could destabilize existing markets in Eastern Europe, and reduce prices for gas supply to Western Europe.

Shale Gas and Its Environmental Impact

Shale gas is by no means a panacea for energy supply. In fact, shale gas raises significant environmental and regulatory issues. For example, the Marcellus site is very close to population centers and their associated water reservoirs. Protecting these reservoirs and groundwater quality in general has been a focal point of legislative and regulatory policy debate.

Due to the depth of Marcellus gas wells, which can reach up to 7,000 feet, drilling activity often pierces fresh water aquifers on its way to the natural gas production zones. The fracturing process involves injecting the well with between two to four million gallons of fluid at rates of up to 4,200 gallons per minute and pressures up to 15,000 pounds per square inch, in order to break the reservoir rock.[12] During fracturing operations, the fluids are pumped into the well and then returned to the surface where they are reinjected, stored, and/or discarded.[13] This fluid injection process raises the risk of potentially contaminating underground fresh water aquifers, commonly used for drinking water. Although fracturing fluids are composed primarily of water, they also include numerous chemicals. For example, the Pennsylvania State Department of Environmental Conservation has identified the following chemicals used in fracturing

---

10. *See* Andrew E. Kramer, *Russia Cuts Off Gas Deliveries to Ukraine*, N.Y. Times, Jan. 2, 2009, at A6, *available at http://www.nytimes.com/2009/01/02/world/europe/02gazprom.html?ref=business.*

11. *See id.*

12. Engelder, *supra* note 1.

13. *Id.*

fluids: diesel fuel, benzene, ethyl benzene, hydrochloric acid, toluene, xylene, naphthalene, polycyclic aromatic hydrocarbons, methanol, formaldehyde, ethylene glycol, glycol ethers, hydrochloric acid, and sodium hydroxide.[14] These chemicals can be hazardous and will potentially infiltrate the drinking water reservoirs above the gas extraction site if not properly managed.

Additionally, natural gas development, production, gathering, and transportation activities release emissions, such as NO_x, volatile organic compounds, particulate matter, SO_2, and methane.[15] In February of 2008, deteriorating air quality in the Greater Green River Basin was attributed to emissions from oil and gas development activities, prompting the first ever ozone-related human health warning from Wyoming's Department of Environmental Quality in a region renowned for its clean air.[16] Further environmental concerns arose in Fort Worth and the surrounding areas as a result of suspected benzene emissions from Barnett Shale wells and gathering system compressor stations.[17] Currently, shale drilling is predominantly a state-regulated activity. Therefore, drilling companies are not required by federal law to report the chemical composition of fracturing fluid, an exemption under the Clean Water Act and Safe Drinking Water Act granted by the Energy Policy Act of 2005.

In June of 2009, U.S. Rep. Dianna DeGette of Colorado and U.S. Sen. Robert Casey of Pennsylvania jointly introduced in the House and Senate the Fracturing Responsibility and Awareness of Chemicals (FRAC) Act, H.R. 2766,[18] and S. 1215.[19] Currently under committee review, the FRAC Act seeks to amend the Safe Drinking Water Act by repealing the federal exemption of hydraulic fracturing under the Act and requiring public disclosure of the chemicals used in fracturing operations.[20] Additionally, state and local regulatory agencies are also proposing legislation to further regulate shale gas drilling. While the Pennsylvania and New York Departments of Environmental Protection and the Delaware River Basin Commission have focused considerable effort on identifying the chemicals used in the fracking process as well as mitigat-

---

14. Pa. Dep't of Envtl. Conservation, *Chemicals Used by Hydraulic Fracturing Companies in Pennsylvania* (June 30, 2010), *available at* http://www.dep.state.pa.us/dep/deputate/minres/oilgas/new_forms/marcellus/Reports/Frac%20list%206-30-2010.pdf.

15. *See* Chesapeake Energy, *Water Use in Deep Shale Gas Exploration* (Mar. 2010), *available at* http://www.chk.com/Media/CorpMediaKits/Water_Use_Fact_Sheet.pdf.

16. Wyo, Dep't of Envtl. Quality, *News Release: DEQ's Upper Green River Basin Winter Ozone Study to increase level of air monitoring this weekend* (Feb. 27, 2009), *available at* http://deq.state.wy.us/out/downloads/winterozonestudyfeb28.pdf.

17. *See* Al Armendariz, professor of environmental and civil engineering at Southern Methodist University, *Emissions from Natural Gas Production in the Barnett Shale Area and Opportunities for Cost-Effective Improvements* (Jan. 26, 2009), *available at* http://www.edf.org/documents/9235_Barnett_Shale_Report.pdf.

18. Fracturing Responsibility and Awareness of Chemicals Act of 2009, H.R. 2766, 111th Cong. (2009).

19. Fracturing Responsibility and Awareness of Chemicals Act of 2009, S. 1215, 111th Cong. (2009).

20. *See id.* (referred to Senate Environmental and Public Works Subcommittee); H.R. 2766 (referred to House Energy and Commerce Subcommittee).

ing the potentially hazardous effects on underground water tables, some state lawmakers and environmental lobbyists believe these regulations insufficient. State lawmakers continue to introduce legislation requiring stricter regulations, including a proposed moratorium prohibiting drilling near primary sources of water supply.[21]

Conclusion

According to Terry Engelder, there are 2.1 trillion barrels of oil in the world and we have already consumed about half.[22] Of the 200 billion barrels of oil initially available in the United States, only 30 billion barrels remain.[23] Engelder further estimates that global shale gas offers an alternative fuel source equivalent to approximately four trillion barrels of oil; one-third of that shale gas resides in the United States[24] The Marcellus site alone offers an estimated 450 Tcf of commercially viable extractable natural gas, which could satisfy approximately 20 years of *total* U.S. energy demand at current levels.[25] Engelder often refers to the United States as the Saudi Arabia of shale gas.[26] Simply put, Chairman of IHS Cambridge Energy Research Associates (IHS CERA) Daniel Yergin has described the "discovery" of shale gas as "the most significant energy innovation so far this century."[27]

Recent developments in shale production have caused dramatic changes in the energy industry. The most striking change has been in natural gas prices. In 2008, gas prices exceeded $10 throughout the forward gas market.[28] Currently, the average price of gas for the next 10 years is only about $7.[29] Naturally, this price decrease in natural gas has resulted in lower energy prices across the country. Lower energy prices have enabled consumers to spend less of their income on energy, but they have increased their disposable income. Lower natural gas prices, in particular, have improved the security of domestic supply while boosting industrial demand.

The emergence of shale gas and the resulting lower natural gas prices are expected to be game changers for the electricity generation business. The apparent abundance of domestic natural gas supply coupled with the continued slow economic recovery has translated into forecasts of low gas prices for a considerable period of time. Low cost and abundant natural gas is putting competitive pressure on other fuel sources. Given current and potential Clean Air Act regulation by the U.S. Environmental Protection

21. *See, e.g.*, H.R. 2608, Session of 2010 (Pa. 2010) (prohibiting fracking operations or horizontal drilling within 2,500 feet of a primary source of water); H.R. 2609, Session of 2010 (Pa. 2010) (proposing one-year moratorium on issuance of new natural gas drilling permits).

22. Engelder, *supra* note 1.

23, *Id.*

24. *Id.*

25. *Id.*

26. *Id.*

27. Daniel Yergin and Robert Ineson, *America's Natural Gas Revolution*, WALL ST. J., Nov. 2, 2009, *available at* http://online.wsj.com/article/SB10001424052748703399204574507440795971268.html.

28. Pricing data courtesy of CQG.

29. Pricing data courtesy of CQG.

Agency and the possibility of legislative or regulatory carbon constraints, dirtier and more inefficient coal-fired power plants will be pressured to retire, while the technical and economic feasibility of new gas-fired plants reduces the reliability threat those retirements might otherwise mean for the nation's electricity grid. Nevertheless, despite the promise of shale gas developments, the natural gas industry faces a number of new environmental and geopolitical challenges; protecting underground water reservoirs, higher taxes, royalties, and other regulatory issues remain to be addressed. The full impact of unconventional gas on the domestic as well as the global energy arena remains to be seen.

~~~~~~~~~~~
~~~~~~~~~~~

2012 Update

By Edward J. Fortunato

Since 2010, shale gas production in the United States has grown at least 2.5 times, from 10 billion cubic feet per day to 25 billion cubic feet per day, representing roughly 38 percent of total U.S. consumption.[1] Because of this increased supply, many changes discussed previously have become a reality.

During 2011, the United States became the world's largest natural gas producer. Natural gas prices have fallen, most severely in the spot market but also in the forward markets. During the fall of 2010, natural gas prices for the next 10 years were estimated to be in the $7 range, while today they are under $5.[2] The drop in prices has resulted in impressive changes: domestic gas consumption is at an all-time high, coal plants have been forced to retire, and we have seen decreased gas imports and increased natural gas exports. There have been no widespread environmental issues and there is no major legislation pending that would dramatically alter the cost or the way that shale gas is produced.

The future impact has the potential to be even more profound. Overland trucking is one of the areas that could change drastically. Converting the U.S. truck fleet from diesel to natural gas and manufacturing natural gas–fueled trucks have the potential to increase natural gas demand and change the dynamics of the entire trucking business. With the drop in gas prices, the price spread between natural gas and diesel fuel has never been as large, making natural gas a viable option for truck fleets. There are 3.2 million rigs and 7 million single-use trucks on the road in the United States, which consume about 32 billion gallons of fuel a year. The conversion of a portion of the fleet to natural gas would save significant money, reduce oil consumption, and reduce emissions.[3]

Shale gas and low prices have also had an impact on coal-fired power generation. The Energy Information Administration (EIA) forecast in its August (2012) Short-Term Energy Outlook noted that coal's market share of electric generation will drop to 37 percent this year, down from 42 percent in 2011 and 49 percent in 2007. Gas's share will climb to 31 percent from 25 percent in

1. http://www.eia.gov/naturalgas/monthly/pdf/table_01.pdf.
2. Pricing data courtesy CQG.
3. *Will Truckers Ditch Diesel?*, Wall St. J., May 23, 2012, or http://online.wsj.com/article/SB10001424052702304707604577422192910235090.html.

2011.[4] The weakening coal market share is reflective of the lower cost of gas generation and has resulted in the EIA estimate that coal plants generating 27,000 megawatts will retire in the next five years,[5] which is about 8.5 percent of total 2011 coal-fired generation. If those plants were running at full capacity, they could generate enough electric power for about 25 million homes.

Plentiful, inexpensive gas has resulted in chemical and steel plants running at higher capacity and several new ones being built as U.S. gas prices give energy-intense manufacturing an advantage against global competitors.[6] Methanex finalized plans in July to move an idle methanol plant from Chile to Louisiana to capture low gas prices. The plant is expected to start operations in late 2014.[7]

Even previously obscure businesses are being evaluated. Shell is discussing a gas-to-liquids facility in Louisiana that would convert natural gas to diesel fuel.[8] The export of natural gas in a liquefied state is also a real possibility. Cheniere is working on building a plant that would cool natural gas to liquefied form for export, one of roughly a dozen potential export projects in the works, primarily for the East and Gulf coasts. The first project, at Sabine Pass, Louisiana, has long-term contracts in place with four corporations around the globe to export liquefied natural gas.[9]

Four years ago gas and oil prices were at parity, and the United States and the rest of the world were planning for a high-priced, energy-constrained future. Shale gas in the U.S. has lowered the cost of heating and power generation, with the potential to have an even wider impact both domestically and globally. The impact of shale gas we discussed in 2010 was just the beginning; major initiatives are being put into place attempting to capture energy cost savings globally. The market signal to use gas and displace other fuels is being acknowledged, and we expect to see even more changes in the future.

4. http://www.eia.gov/forecasts/steo/report/natgas.cfm.
5. http://www.eia.gov/todayinenergy/detail.cfm?id=7290.
6. http://www.businessweek.com/news/2012-06-01/exxon-applies-for-permits-to-expand-plastics-production-in-texas.
7. http://texas.construction.com/texas_construction_news/2012/0831-idle-methanol-plant-moves-from-chile-to-louisiana.asp.
8. http://marcellusdrilling.com/2011/12/shells-major-shift-to-natural-gas-us-gas-to-liquids-plant/.
9. http://www.bizjournals.com/houston/print-edition/2012/08/10/billion-dollar-plans-to-ship-natural.html?page=all.

Chapter 26

Blowing in the Wind—Difficult Issues Facing Wind Generation

*By Charles A. Patrizia, Candice Castaneda, and Alexandra D. Konieczny**

Even as Congress considers proposed legislation to address climate change and the need to reduce U.S. use of carbon-based fuels, and in that context or separately as part of proposed "comprehensive clean energy legislation" considers extending or increasing tax and other incentives for renewable energy sources, wind energy is facing risks and opposition that could limit or delay its role in the U.S. energy mix. Wind-based energy is the fastest growing renewable segment,[1] benefiting from its relatively lower cost per kilowatt hour (kwh) produced and relative efficiency compared to solar (including photovoltaic), and the smaller installed base compared to hydroelectric facilities. Wind also offers more geographic opportunities than geothermal. Regardless of these benefits, wind projects are coming under increased scrutiny and delay.

Four types of issues constrain expansion of wind power and may limit or hinder the role of wind power, both overall and in particular areas. Several of these constraints are well-known and systemic in nature, and are elements that wind advocates have sought to address (and continue to address in proposed legislation at the state and federal level). The remaining constraints have only recently come into focus, and reflect the tension between the desirability of wind power based on its essentially zero emissions, and the other environmental impacts that wind power can produce.

---

* Originally published in *Infrastructure*, vol. 49, no. 4 (Summer, 2010).

* *Charles A. Patrizia is a partner at Paul, Hastings, LLP, and a member of the Section's council group. Candice Castaneda and Alexandra D. Konieczny are associates of the firm, working in the Global Projects Group. [Ms. Konieczny is now an associate at Sutherland in the Energy and Environmental Practice Group.]*

1. *See, e.g.*, RACHEL GELMAN & STEVE HOCKETTE, DEP'T OF ENERGY, 2008 RENEWABLE ENERGY DATABOOK 56-63, (Michelle Kubik, ed., July 2009) *available at* http://www1.eere.energy.gov/maps_data/pdfs/eere_databook.pdf (explaining that between 2000-2008 U.S. wind energy capacity increased almost 10 times, adding that by 2008, the United States surpassed Germany as the world leader in installed wind capacity) [hereinafter "DOE Renewable Energy Databook"]; WIND ENERGY ASS'N, AWEA WIND POWER VALUE CHAIN, AMERICAN 1 (2008) *available at* http://www.awea.org/pubs/ factsheets/value_chain.pdf (stating that in 2008 the nation's total wind power generating capacity expanded by 50% in a single year and injected over $17 billion into the economy) [hereinafter "AWEA Wind Power Value Chain"].

Resolution of these issues—both the systemic and those that arise from the tension between emissions concerns and other environmental concerns—requires political judgments to balance the societal benefits and costs. This article describes the issues and concerns.

Wind Power

Wind has successfully been harnessed for thousands of years—the advent of sails demonstrated that wind could itself be a prime mover, and many societies have used windmills to convert wind to rotary or pumping motion. Recent improvements in efficiency result from better designed and larger blades that convert more wind energy through rotary motion, improvements in control, and improvements in efficiency in generation.[2]

Of course, as even the earliest sailors knew, wind is variable—its speed, its direction, and even its timing and duration are uncertain. In electric generation, steadiness or at least predictability is more valuable than sheer speed.[3] Because of the overall characteristics, wind generators are individually small, and scaling to utility-size units requires enough area to locate multiple turbines.[4] Each of these inherent characteristics of wind and the turbines that are used to harness it poses constraints.

Constraints and Limitations

Intermittency

As already noted, from the time sailors first sought to capture the wind's power, the intermittency of wind has been a limitation. Wind is not fickle, and over a long enough period it is predictable at least within ranges on a seasonal or other basis, but on a moment-to-moment basis or over short durations, it is inherently variable—as to direction, speed, and duration. The effect of the variability is to limit the value of wind as a source of electricity, because the modern grid depends on the dispatchability of generation sources in order to match load and capacity. As a result of its inherent variabil-

2. *See e.g.* National Renewable Energy Laboratory, Technology Profiles—Wind Energy, Power Technologies Energy Data Book, (Jorn Aabakken, ed., 4th ed.), *available at* http://www.nrel.gov/analysis/power_databook/docs/pdf/db_chapter02_wind.pdf (providing a thorough analysis of wind technology developments) [hereinafter "NREL Data Book"].

3. *See* Dep't of Energy, Advantages and Disadvantages of Wind Energy (last updated Jan. 28, 2009) *available at* http://www1.eere.energy.gov/windandhydro/wind_ad. html (stating the "major challenge to using wind as a source of power is that the wind is intermittent and it does not always blow when electricity is needed. Wind energy cannot be stored (unless batteries are used); and not all winds can be harnessed to meet the timing of electricity demands") [hereinafter "DOE Advantages and Disadvantages of Wind Energy"].

4. *See, e.g.*, NREL Data Book (discussing small wind turbines); *see also* California Energy Commission, Wind Energy in California, (last updated May 15, 2009) *available at* http://www.energy.ca.gov/wind/overview.html (explaining that historically, turbines have been small to intermediate in size, although larger ones are now being built).

ity, wind must be treated on an "as available" basis, generating power when within the acceptable range of the turbines installed, and dropping off the system when it is not.[5] This creates the not-so-green solution of dependence on nonvariable power generation sources such as nuclear or fossil fuel to balance wind resources when the wind does not blow. While demand response, which enables electricity consumers to reduce or delay nonessential electricity use in response to price signals, can be used to provide some capacity and flexibility at a low cost, neither this nor any other solution to date has eliminated the need for baseload power sources.[6]

From a financial perspective—that is, the ability of a wind developer to find financing support—intermittency is addressed by use of probabilistic algorithms. Financial models can predict and lenders/investors can accept a projected revenue stream across an appropriate period, where the wind generator is expected to produce at a 90 percent or 70 percent or 50 percent probability. Thus, for example, a wind project with an overall rated capacity of 100 MW may have a P90 of 65 MW, a P70 of 75 MW and a P50 of 90 MW. That is, there is a 90 percent probability that it will, over a given period, generate 65MW, but only a 50 percent probability that it will generate 90MW over that same period.[7] Lenders may seek the certainty of the revenue stream at P90, limiting their risk to the debt service amount predicted at that level, while investors with greater appetite for risk take the remainder.

While financing mechanisms have adapted to account for wind's inherent variability, the day-to-day operation of the electric system has not so easily adapted. In order to accept the intermittency associated with wind energy, electric utilities must consider which other generation resources (which on an operating cost basis may be preferable to wind) will need to be turned down or limited, and what reserves must be maintained in what status in order to meet load when wind energy is not available.

These problems are being addressed, in part by seeking to broaden the geographic range over which wind energy is part of the capacity mix, in part by considering storage of wind energy (through compressed air pumped storage, conversion of wind energy to hydrogen or other fuels), and in part through better prediction models.[8] The

5. *Supra* note 4.

6. *See* Noelle Straub and Peter Behr, *Energy Regulatory Chief Says New Coal, Nuclear Plants May Be Unnecessary*, NY Times, April 22, 2009, *available at* http://www.nytimes.com/gwire/2009/04/22/22greenwire-no-need-to-build-new-us-coal-or-nuclear-plants-10630.html (including criticisms of Chairman Wellinghoff's assertion that renewable energy sources, particularly wind, may be enough. Quoting Jay Apt, a professor at Carnegie Mellon University's Electricity Industry Center, that "You need firm power to fill in when the wind doesn't blow. There is just no getting around that.").

7. *See* DEWI Wilhelmshaven, H. Klug, What Does Exceedance Probabilities P90-P75-P50 Mean?, *available* at http://www.dewi.de/dewi/fileadmin/pdf/publications/Magazin_28/07.pdf (discussing models in wind financing); *see also Modelling P50 versus P90 wind profiles*, Navigator Project Finance, *available at* http://www.navigatorpf.com/blog/ modelling-p50-versus-p90-wind-profiles; *Economics of Wind Energy*, American Wind Energy Ass'n, February 2005, *available at* http://www.awea.org/pubs/ factsheets/EconomicsOfWind-Feb2005.pdf.

8. *See* Michael T. Burr, *Beyond Intermittency*, Public Utilities Fortnightly, May 2010 (discussing advancements in forecasting).

Federal Energy Regulatory Commission recently issued a notice of inquiry to gather more information from the industry on how FERC can amend its rules and procedures to better integrate variable energy resources such as wind into the electric grid.[9] By taking this step, FERC shows that it is taking seriously the influx of wind resources into the nation's energy supply portfolio. However, at the time of publication of this article, the outcome of FERC's notice of inquiry—if any—is not known. Nonetheless, the intermittency of wind energy imposes additional costs beyond the capital and operating cost of the wind projects, and those operating issues still pose a constraint.

Transmission

Efficiently exploitable wind resources are not uniformly distributed geographically. Some locations, such as the Midwest, have steadier and more predictable wind, often for longer durations, than other locations. Unfortunately, those locations are often remote from existing load centers, and, therefore, remote from existing transmission lines.[10]

As a result, the development of wind projects must address not only the location and acquisition of a sufficient area for the turbines, but must also address the development and construction of new high-voltage transmission lines to bring the wind energy, once generated, to load centers where it can be used. The issue of who pays for those new lines continues to be a chronic constraint on the development of wind resources. For example, wind developers in the Midwest are currently embroiled in a FERC dispute involving the allocation of the costs of a proposed $725 million transmission line.[11] The current standard that FERC has adopted is whether the transmission line would have been built *but for* the particular wind projects, and only if the answer to this query is "yes" can the transmission provider allocate all costs of the network upgrade to the wind projects in development.[12]

---

9. Notice of Inquiry re Integration of Variable Energy Resources, 130 FERC ¶ 61,053 (Jan. 2010).

10. *See* DOE Advantages and Disadvantages of Wind Energy (citing remoteness of location as a disadvantage); NREL Data Book (stating that transmission infrastructure is required for expansion and upgrade of large onshore wind turbines); DEP'T OF ENERGY, CONNECTING TO THE GRID: A GUIDE TO DISTRIBUTED GENERATION INTERCONNECTION ISSUES (Interstate Renewable Energy Council, ed., Oct. 31, 2009) *available at* http://www.windpoweringamerica.gov/filter_detail.asp?itemid=2462 (discussing interconnection with the grid); *see also* Bill DeGrandis and Alexandra Konieczny, *It's Not Easy Transmitting Green*, LEGAL TIMES, March 16, 2009, *available at* http://paulhastings.com/assets/publications/1273.pdf?wt.mc_ID=1273.pdf.

11. *See, e.g.*, the Brookings Line proceeding in *Community Wind*, 131 FERC ¶ 61,165 (2010) (In this particular case, only 32 wind developers would have to shoulder the $725 million cost of the Brookings Line if the transmission provider succeeds in its desired allocation to developers).

12. Illinois Commerce Commission v. FERC, 2009 U.S. App. LEXIS 18311 at 13-14 (7th Cir. 2009) (finding that FERC is not authorized to approve a pricing scheme that requires a group of utilities to pay for facilities from which its members derive no benefits, or benefits that are trivial in relation to the costs sought to be shifted to its members). If costs are allocated to generators, they would then be reimbursed in transmission credits.

However, the application of this deceivingly simple standard by FERC and transmission providers has so far only caused delays and uncertainties. Because wind projects are relatively small (new installations are approximately 120 MW),[13] the cost of long transmission lines is a larger percentage of the project than would be case with the larger utility scale carbon-based or other projects. Developers therefore resist inclusion of the costs of transmission, and seek to have the interconnecting utility roll the cost of the lines into its overall system costs. Interconnecting utilities, however, are often not the purchasers of the power, and at least in some instances have no current need for the additional capacity. Nor do ultimate consumers wish to bear the cost of new transmission; the additional cost per megawatt hour (MWh)—once transmission is included—can make wind generation prohibitively expensive.

The problem of transmission is particularly acute for land-based wind generation. In those locations where wind generators can locate in coastal areas, transmission distances to load centers are shorter, and therefore costs lower, although these savings can to some degree be offset by the additional difficulties of locating on sea-based platforms.[14]

Resolution of the transmission issues requires adaptation or revision to FERC policies, and a willingness on the part of the different stakeholders to achieve some compromise on the sharing or spreading of the costs.

Tariff Cost

Partly as a result of the intermittency effects on value, partly as a result of the costs of transmission and delivery, and partly as a result of the capital cost of acquiring land and constructing the farms, wind energy is more expensive on a delivered kWh basis than alternative power sources. According to the *New York Times*, for example, wind energy is as much as 50 percent more expensive than coal.[15]

While Congress and state legislatures have sought to put a finger on the scales by providing tax benefits[16] and by imposing renewable portfolio standards, the higher relative cost of wind has deterred utilities from signing contracts to take power from

13. Dep't of Energy, Annual Report on U.S. Wind Power Installation, Cost, and Performance Trends: 2007, 12, (Energy Efficiency and Renewable Energy, ed., May 2008) *available at* http://www.nrel.gov/docs/fy08osti/43025.pdf (providing data as of 2007, stating that the average size of new wind projects that year was 120 MW in size).

14. *See, e.g.*, Mark Svenvold, *Wind Power Politics*, NY Times, Sept. 12, 2008, *available at* http://www.nytimes.com/2008/09/14/magazine/14wind-t.html?pagewanted=2&_r=1; *and* (providing the story of Bluewater Wind Park example in Delaware) [hereinafter "Bluewater Article"]; *and* Bluewater Wind, *available at* http://www.bluewaterwind.com/de_overview.htm.

15. Matthew L. Wald, *Cost Works Against Alternative Energy in Time of Recession*, NY Times, March 28, 2009, *available at* http://www.nytimes.com/2009/03/29/business/energy-environment/29renew.html.

16. For example, the New Jersey legislature recently adopted $100 million in tax credits for wind component manufacturers so as to encourage wind development off the New Jersey shore.

wind projects. This, in turn, hinders the development of wind projects, and in the absence of an offtaker contract, these projects are not financeable.[17]

At least so long as transmission and other issues remain a concern, tariff cost issues will also constrain development of wind projects. Those locations that have most increased wind power have done so on the basis of a societal choice to adopt wind power—Germany, Spain, and the United Kingdom—through feed-in tariffs or political imposition of wind power as a portion of portfolios. For example, in Spain the government passed the Electricity Act that established a renewable energy program, including wind, which guaranteed access to the grid and a premium for renewable generated power.[18] The Spanish government has set a target of 20,000 MW in capacity by 2010, which reports say Spain is on track to reach.[19] Another prominent international player in wind energy is Germany. Germany began its wind energy program in 1991, and passed the Renewable Energy Sources Act (Erneuerbare-Energien-Gesetz / EEG) which came into force in 2000. Similar to Spain, Germany has passed regulations giving renewable resources priority for grid connection, grid access, and power dispatch.[20]

NIMBY

As wind advocates work to address the transmission and cost issues associated with how *far* some wind projects are from their customer bases, another growing constraint involves how *close* other wind projects are getting. Opposition by local groups, in particular local environmental groups, has grown as a result of the tension between low-emitting renewable sources and their other impacts on the landscape and environment. In other words, wind projects are also subject to the NIMBY ("not in my back yard") syndrome.

The easiest example is the Cape Wind project—delayed for 10 years since its first proposal by opposition from residents of Cape Cod.[21] While political attention focused on the involvement of famous political figures with Cape Cod connections, opposition also came from other sources: the local Indian tribe, which regarded the area as part of its historic range, and local historic conservationists, who were troubled by the imposition of industrializing views. Resolution of the Cape Wind project ultimately required the personal intervention, attention, and decision of the secretary of the inte-

17. *See, e.g.*, *Financing,* American Wind Energy Ass'n, *available at* http://www.awea.org/resources/financing/financing.html (providing links to tax related sources of financing).

18. International Energy Agency, IEA Wind Energy Annual Report 2008, 239-251, (July 2009) *available at* http://www.ieawind.org/AnnualReports_PDF/2008/2008%20AR_small.pdf [hereinafter "IEA Wind Energy Annual Report 2008"].

19. Martin Roberts, *Spain wind power firms see steady growth in 2009*, Reuters, Feb. 2, 2009, *available at* http://www.reuters.com/article/idUSTRE51136D20090202.

20. German WindEnergy Ass'n, Wind Energy in Germany, *available at* http://www.wind-energie.de/en/wind-energy-in-germany/ (describing Germany's programs incentivizing wind energy and other renewables).

21. *See, e.g.*, Bluewater Article.

rior.[22] But this resolution may be temporary, as the Cape Wind project is now being peppered with federal lawsuits. As many as six groups filed suit in federal district court in Washington, D.C., on June 25, 2010, with arguments such as that the project will "exact a terrible toll" on federally protected migratory birds and whales, and that the federal agencies charged with reviewing the project consistently skimped on their review.

The Cape Wind saga, however, is neither isolated, nor singular in its focus. Other projects have also been affected and sometimes in cases that pit "green" against "green." For example, in West Virginia a court halted a $300 million wind farm project because the judge believed the massive turbines being built would kill endangered Indiana bats. As a result, the court held that the company must apply for special permit to build more turbines.[23] Another example involves a case where an Oregon wind farm was found in intermittent violation of state noise regulations. FERC gave the company six months to comply with regulations.[24]

Finally, many wind farms never even make it to the construction stage because of NIMBY conflicts. Offshore wind farms currently being proposed for Lake Michigan, for example, could offer hundreds of new jobs and virtually no noise or light pollution because of their offshore location, yet they face staunch opposition from the public over concerns that the wind farms would mar the view of the lake, thereby harming tourism and property prices. The overwhelming opposition to locating the wind farm two to four miles from the Lake Michigan shore resulted in a recent 9-1 vote of the Mason County board against the proposal of Scandia Wind Offshore, successfully frustrating Scandia's proposed plans.[25] Scandia now plans to scale down the wind farm and propose a new Lake Michigan location farther south, in Oceana County, where it is expected to face similar opposition. These examples illustrate the variety of NIMBY challenges wind projects face.

---

22. Beth Daley and Martin Finucane, *Interior secretary approves Cape Wind plan, nation's first offshore wind farm*, BOSTON GLOBE, April 28, 2010, *available at* http://www.boston.com/news/local/breaking_news/2010/04/cape_wind_annou.html; DEP'T OF INTERIOR, SECRETARY SALAZAR ANNOUNCES APPROVAL OF CAPE WIND ENERGY PROJECT ON OUTER CONTINENTAL SHELF OFF MASSACHUSETTS (April 28, 2010) *available at* http://www.doi.gov/news/doinews/Secretary-Salazar-Announces-Approval-of-Cape-Wind-Energy-Project-on-Outer-Continental-Shelf-off-Massachusetts.cfm.

23. Maria Glod, *Court halts West Virginia wind farm to protect bats*, WASH. POST, Dec. 10, 2009, *available at* http://www.washingtonpost.com/wpdyn/content/article/2009/12/09/AR2009120904106.html. *See also* Tiffany Trent, *Tilting at the Appalachian Windmills*, APPALACHIAN VOICE, August 2006, *available at* http://www.appvoices.org/index.php?/site/voice_stories/tilting_at_the_appalachian_windmills/issue/518 (discussing the impact on migratory birds that cross the mountains).

24. David Nogueras, *Oregon Wind Farm Violates State Noise Regulations*, OPB NEWS, (May 27, 2010) *available at* http://news.opb.org/article/7457-oregon-wind-farm-violates-state-noise-regulations/.

25. Dave Alexander, *Mason County Board Rejects Scandia Proposal for Offshore Wind Farm*, mlive.com (June 09, 2010) *available at* http://www.mlive.com/news/muskegon/index.ssf/2010/06/mason_county_board_rejects_sca.html.

Conclusion

Efforts to harness wind power are not new—and the constraints faced by wind projects are to a great degree inherent in wind itself and the locations most suitable for its use. Those constraints are now being reinforced, however, by the tension between increasing the amount of wind power and the concomitant requirement to build wind projects where the wind is most suited, and the other environmental risks and effects of large scale turbines in what have otherwise been remote areas.

Resolution of these constraints and tensions will require political determinations to balance the interests of society in reducing dependency on carbon-based fuels, and the effects of industrial operations on localities, wildlife, and other resources.

2012 Update

By Charles A. Patrizia and Candice Castaneda

Since this article was originally written, there have been additional developments in the energy industry affecting the interests of wind developers in the United States. This update seeks to briefly summarize some of the most significant developments.

1. Variable Energy Resource Order

The original publication referenced the notice of inquiry issued in 2010 by the Federal Energy Regulatory Commission (FERC or the Commission) to gather information on how the Commission can amend its rules and procedures to better integrate variable resources, like wind, into the electric grid.

Late in 2010, the Commission issued a notice of proposed rulemaking (NOPR) in follow-up to the comments it received on the notice of inquiry seeking to address certain issues associated with the intermittency of variable resources.[1]

On June 21, 2012, the Commission issued a final order on this NOPR. In the order, the Commission requires public utility transmission providers to offer customers the option of scheduling transmission service at 15-minute intervals and to revise the pro forma Large Generator Interconnection Agreement to require interconnection customers with variable energy resources to provide meteorological and forced outage data to the public utility transmission provider to support power production forecasting.[2] The Commission decided not to adopt a standard approach to generator regulation service originally proposed in the NOPR; however, the order provides guidance on how the Commission will evaluate proposed charges for generator regulation service. Commission Chairman Jon Wellinghoff stated that he believed that the "final rule eliminates undue burdens on these [variable] resources and will help transmission providers and their customers to effectively manage the costs of integration."[3]

1. Notice of Proposed Rulemaking re: Integration of Variable Energy Resources, 133 FERC ¶ 61,149 (November 2010).
2. Integration of Variable Energy Resources, Order No. 764, 139 FERC ¶ 61,24, at pp.1–5 (2012) (taking effect 12 months after publication in the Federal Register, sometime in summer of 2013).
3. *See* FERC Approves Final Rule to Integrate Variable Energy Resources, Docket No. RM10-11-000 (June 21, 2012).

This order does not address all of the issues associated with intermittency of wind generation. For example, as noted, the Commission did not yet adopt a standard for generator regulation service. The intermittency of wind energy imposes additional costs beyond the capital and operating costs of the wind projects, and those operating issues still pose a constraint.

2. Transmission Building and Cost-Allocation

Previously, this article discussed some of the difficulties associated with cost allocation for transmission development necessary for many wind projects. As explained previously, the issue of who pays for new transmission has not been resolved and was part of the impetus for the Commission's Order No. 1000. The standard that the Commission currently applies is whether the transmission line would have been built *but-for* the particular wind projects. If the answer is yes, transmission providers can then allocate costs of the network upgrade to the wind projects in development.[4]

Regional transmission organizations (RTOs), such as the Midwest Independent Transmission System Operator, Inc. (MISO), have filed revisions over the past year that attempt to reflect this cost allocation concept. MISO, for example, established a multi-value project (MVP) cost allocation category under which cost allocation for MVPs is applied to all load on a postage-stamp basis.[5] This cost allocation method, while somewhat controversial, addresses cost allocation for large projects, such as the Brookings Line. The Brookings Line had previously embroiled wind developers in the Midwest in a Commission dispute involving allocation of the costs of the proposed $725 million transmission line.[6] The Brookings Line has since been established as an MVP, and cost allocation will occur according to the postage-stamp methodology.[7]

---

4. Ill. Commerce Comm'n v. FERC, 2009 U.S. App. LEXIS 18311 at 13–14 (7th Cir. 2009) (finding that the Commission is not authorized to approve a pricing scheme that requires a group of utilities to pay for facilities from which its members derive no benefits, or benefits that are trivial in relation to the costs sought to be shifted to its members). If costs are allocated to generators as Network Upgrades, they would then be reimbursed in transmission credits.

5. Midwest Indep. Transmission Sys. Operator, Inc., 133 FERC ¶ 61,221 (2010), *order on reh'g,* 137 FERC ¶ 61,074 (2011) (MVP Rehearing Order). *See also* PJM Interconnection, L.L.C., 138 FERC ¶ 61,230 (2012) (accepting PJM's postage-stamp methodology).

6. *See, e.g.*, the Brookings Line proceeding in *Community Wind,* 131 FERC ¶ 61,165 (2010).

7. *See* Multi-Value Project Portfolio Results and Analyses, MISO (Jan. 10, 2012), *available at* https://www.misoenergy.org/Library/Repository/Study/Candidate%20MVP%20Analysis/MVP%20Portfolio%20Analysis%20Full %20Report.pdf.

As noted above, though, the Commission has directly taken action to address transmission concerns, through its Order No. 1000, as affirmed in Order No. 1000-A.[8] In that order, the Commission emphasized the critical need for additional transmission and cited the concern raised by the Department of Energy in 2008 that "[s]ignificant expansion of the transmission grid will be required under any future electric industry scenario."[9] The Commission also added that the North American Electric Reliability Corporation (NERC) "has identified approximately 131,000 megawatts of new generation planned for construction over the next ten years, with the largest fuel-type growth in gas-fired and wind generation resources."[10] As a result, FERC acknowledged that the existing transmission system is not built to accommodate these needs, and it therefore required public utility transmission providers to participate in certain regional and interregional transmission-planning and cost allocation procedures. Public utility transmission providers must submit their regional transmission coordination and cost allocation plan by October 11, 2012, and their interregional plan by April 11, 2013. After those filings have been submitted, the industry may have a better understanding of how additional transmission to support development of new generation resources, such as wind generation, may proceed. It is too soon to tell whether the requirements imposed by Order No. 1000 will result in the needed additional transmission.[11]

3. Expiring Tax Credits

As discussed in the original publication of this article, Congress and state legislatures have sought to counterbalance the often higher cost of wind development by providing tax benefits[12] and by imposing renewable portfolio standards. However, the higher relative cost of wind has still deterred utilities from signing contracts to take power from wind projects.

---

8. Transmission Planning and Cost Allocation by Transmission Owning and Operating Public Utilities, Order No. 1000-A, 136 FERC ¶ 61,051 (2011), *order on reh'g*, Order No. 1000-A, 139 FERC ¶ 61,132 (2012).

9. Order No. 1000, at ¶ 29 (citing Dep't of Energy, *20% Wind Energy by 2030*, at 93 (July 2008)).

10. *Id.*, at ¶ 45 (citing the NERC 2010 Long-Term Reliability Assessment, at p.12).

11. *See also* William D. DeGrandis & Candice Castaneda, Significant Federal Energy Regulatory Commission Activity in Transmission Incentives, Planning, and Cost Allocation (August 2011), *available at* http://www.paulhastings.com/assets/publications/1987.pdf?wt.mc_ID=1987.pdf.

12. For example, the New Jersey legislature recently adopted $100 million in tax credits for wind component manufacturers to encourage wind development off the New Jersey shore.

At this time, the tax benefits that the U.S. government has provided to wind development are in danger, further exacerbating the issue. Most critically, the federal production tax credit (PTC) and Section 1603 tax grants are expiring in the near future. The PTC was enacted as part of the Energy Policy Act of 1992[13] and provides a 2.2 cents per kWh income tax credit for the production of electricity from wind resources. The PTC is set to expire for property placed in service after December 31, 2012. The Section 1603 tax grant was enacted as part of the American Recovery and Reinvestment Act of 2009.[14] It allows wind developers eligible for PTCs or investment tax credits (ITCs) to elect to receive a grant in lieu of the tax credits. To be eligible, however, projects must have been under construction by December 31, 2011, and must be placed in service by either December 31, 2012 (for projects eligible for PTCs), or December 31, 2016 (for projects eligible for ITCs).[15] Entities such as the American Wind Energy Association (AWEA) have sought extension of the tax-related incentives.[16] Also, the FY 2013 Budget of the President would extend the renewable energy PTC, ITC, and Section 1603 grants. While Congress has considered such extensions, thus far those extensions have not passed.[17] It is still possible that these tax-related benefits will be extended, though. In a visit to Iowa in the spring of 2012, President Obama stated, "I'm calling on Congress to extend tax credits that are set to expire at the end of the year for clean-energy companies. . . ."[18] On June 8,

---

13. The Energy Policy Act of 1992, Pub. L. 102-486 (Oct. 24, 1992).

14. The American Recovery and Reinvestment Act of 2009, Pub. L. 115-5 (Feb. 17, 2009).

15. *See* Molly F. Sherlock & Margot L. Crandall-Hollick, CRS Report R41769, Energy Tax Policy Issues in the 112th Congress, at pp.16–20, and CRS-9 (March 28, 2012), *available at* http://www.fas.org/sgp/CRS/MISC/R41769.pdf (CRS Report); U.S. Congress, Joint Committee on Taxation, *Present Law and Analysis of Energy-Related Tax Expenditures*, Committee Print, 112th Cong. (March 23, 2012), JCX-28-12, at p.2, *available at* http://www.jct.gov/publications.html?func=startdown&id=4414, and Statement of Molly Sherlock Before the House Committee on Science, Space, and Technology (April 19, 2012), *available at* http://science.house.gov/sites/republicans.science.house.gov/files/documents/hearings/HHRG-112-SY21-WState-MSherlock-20120419.pdf (providing additional background regarding the tax incentives and Section 1603 grant).

16. *See, e.g.*, Production Tax Credit, AWEA (April 2011), *available at* http://awea.org/issues/federal_policy/upload/PTC_April-2011.pdf.

17. CRS Report, *supra* note 15, at pp.20 and 22.

18. *See* Michael Cohn, *Obama Calls for Extension of Wind Energy Tax Credits*, Accounting Today (May 25, 2012), *available at* http://www.accountingtoday.com/news/obama-calls-extension-wind-energy-tax-credits-62783-1.html.

2012, the House Ways and Means Select Revenue Measures Subcommittee held a hearing on extension of the tax incentives.[19] In August of 2012, President Obama's administration was also reported as stating that it was hopeful that the wind tax incentives would be renewed. Reuters reported that an anonymous senior White House official stated that the administration is hopeful that Congress will renew a $12 billion tax credit for wind power production, noting the number of jobs that a government report asserted might be lost if the incentive expires.[20] The future of these incentives will be an important factor as developers and lenders make investment decisions regarding wind projects.

---

19. *See* Michael Cohn, *Congress Considers Extending Expired Tax Breaks*, Accounting Today (June 8, 2012), *available at* http://www.accountingtoday.com/news/congress-tax-extenders-hearing-62901-1.html.

20. Timothy Gardner, *White House hopeful on renewal of wind tax credit*, Reuters (Aug. 14, 2012), *available at* http://www.reuters.com/article/2012/08/14/us-usa-obama-energy-idUSBRE87D0BI20120814.

Chapter 27

Liabilities Facing Developers of Wind Farms on the Outer Continental Shelf*

*By John J. Reilly and Carine M. Williams***

The focal point of offshore wind energy projects, debated and litigated for many years, now appears to be moving from court rooms to construction sites; and there are many lessons to be learned in this new phase. The Cape Wind Energy Project off the coast of Massachusetts demonstrates that wind farm projects on the outer continental shelf involve significant risks and liabilities.

Cape Wind will be on a site with some of the strongest sustained winds and shallowest waters in the United States.[1] With a $2–$3 billion construction budget,[2] it will produce 182 MW of electricity, enough power for 200,000 homes.[3] The project proposed in 2001, was finally approved in February 2011, and will start building by the end of this year, producing commercial electricity by 2013.[4]

* Originally published in *Infrastructure*, vol. 51, no. 1 (Fall, 2011).

** *John J. Reilly is a partner with Squire Sanders in its New York office where he is a commercial trial lawyer with a practice focused on maritime industries. Carine M. Williams is an associate with the firm, working in the Public Services Initiative, advocacy, and Supreme Court litigation groups.*

1. Mineral Management Services (MMS) record of decision at 3, *available at* http://www.nae.usace.army.mil/projects/ma/CapeWind/ROD.pdf.

2. *Id.*

3. Steve LeBlanc (AP), *John Kerry Urges Feds to OK Loans for Cape Wind Project*, BOSTON HERALD, Feb. 17, 2011, *at* http://www.bostonherald.com/business/general/view.bg?articleid=1317578; *see also* Dick McCarrick, *Cape Wind and Offshore Wind Power Generation*, ENVTL. LEADER, July 6, 2011, http://www.environmentalleader.com/2011/07/06/cape-wind-and-offshore-wind-power-generation/.

4. *Id.*

Background: The Evolution of a Renewable Energy Policy

A major barrier to the offshore wind farm industry in the United States was confusion over controlling law, the absence of strong policy support for renewable energy initiatives generally, and a lack of regulatory guidance until the Energy Policy Act of 2005 (Pub. L. No. 109-58) (EPAct), which encourages mass-scale development of renewable energy sources and includes a tax credit for the production of electricity from wind power.

Prior to the passage of the EPAct, considerable debate existed as to whether the Outer Continental Shelf Lands Act (OCSLA)—codified in 1953 to assert federal ownership and jurisdiction over minerals in and under the continental shelf— contemplated the lease of space for the development of wind energy *over* it. Section 388 of EPAct added section 8(p) to OCSLA. Under this new authority, the secretary of the Department of the Interior (DOI) was permitted to grant, in consultation with other federal agencies, leases, easements, or right-of-ways on the Outer Continental Shelf (OCS) for previously unauthorized activities that involved: (1) the production, transportation, and transmission of energy from sources other than oil and gas; and (2) the alternate use of energy-related or marine-related facilities for activities authorized under the OCSLA.

In 2006, the DOI delegated to the Minerals Management Service (MMS) exclusive authority to issue leases, easements, and right-of-ways for renewable energy projects on the OCS.

In 2009 MMS—now renamed the Bureau of Ocean Energy Management, Regulation, and Enforcement (BOEMRE)—issued regulatory guidance for the review and approval of offshore wind farm development proposals. The new authority, the Final Renewable Energy Framework, embraces five mandates: (1) safety; (2) protection of the environment; (3) coordination with federal agencies and affected state and local governments; (4) fair return for use of OCS lands; and (5) equitable revenue sharing with states.[5] Subsequently, the DOI signed a memorandum of understanding with 11 coastal states pledging to facilitate offshore wind power development.

In 2010, on the heels of these major regulatory changes, The National Ocean Council was established to implement a new national ocean policy. Working in coordination with the National Ocean Council, the DOI launched the "Smart From the Start" initiative, which aims to expedite wind farm development on the Atlantic OCS. DOI adopted a policy streamlining the proposal approval process and implemented an expedited leasing framework for wind farm projects. Under the Smart From the Start platform, the DOI also organized an interagency process to gather information regarding environmental and physical attributes of wind areas, to identify their other uses, as well as to make that information publicly available so that the feasibility and risks associated with wind farm development in identified areas can be readily assessed. Contemporaneously, the DOE launched the 2010 Offshore Wind Innovation and Demonstration (OSWInD) initiative.

5. Bureau of Ocean Energy Management, Regulation and Enforcement, Renewable Energy, http://www.boemre.gov/offshore/renewableenergy/index.htm.

In 2011, the DOE published: *A National Offshore Wind Strategy: Creating an Offshore Wind Energy Industry in the United States*. OSWind set a goal of 10 GW of offshore wind generating capacity by 2020, at a cost of $.10/kWh, and targets a production of 54 GW by 2030, at a cost of $.07/kWh.[6] The report states that the current projections of wind energy cost must be cut by more than 50 percent to reach the OSWInD targets. Reducing capital costs—including lowering financial risks and minimizing insurance and warranty premiums—will be vital to making this cut. The DOE plans to help reduce perceived project risks by: (1) developing validated turbine performance models that predict output; (2) helping to develop design codes and standards that protect turbine sustainability; and (3) partnering in demonstrations of offshore wind technology.[7] The DOE plans to support analysis of regulatory uncertainties, and to mitigate environmental and social science risks.[8] The DOE's Smart from the Start initiative also aims to reduce regulatory uncertainty by clarifying how its offshore regulatory framework will be implemented and by convening interagency data-gathering and data-sharing. Research will focus on environmental risks, including before-and-after control-impact studies of relevant marine ecology in key areas, and study impact on marine operations, looking at how the electromagnetic interference from offshore facilities might affect electronic navigation, detection, or communication equipment.[9]

Recent revisions to, or interpretations of, controlling rules also make leasing and construction of OCS wind farms less difficult. For example, BOEMRE recently finalized a rule that speeds up the lease permit process by allowing the bureau to skip a second notice request for interest if, after the first request, only one entity expressed interest.[10] Customs and Border Protection published a recent ruling that allowed foreign flag vessels—which would otherwise be barred from transporting passengers or merchandise between points in the United States under maritime cabotage laws[11]—to work on turbine installation, as well as the drilling and pile-driving activities precedent to the installation of wind towers.[12]

6. U.S. Department of Energy, A National Offshore Wind Strategy: Creating an Offshore Wind Energy Industry in the United States, February 2011 at 2, *available at* http://www1.eere.energy.gov/windandhydro/pdfs/national_offshore_wind_strategy.pdf.

7. *Id.* at 16.

8. *Id.* at 27.

9. *Id.* at 30.

10. Press Release, Dep't of the Interior, *Salazar, Bromwich Announce Elimination of Redundant Step for Offshore Renewable Energy Leasing*, June 13, 2011, *available at* http://www.doi.gov/news/pressreleases/Salazar-Bromwich-Announce-Elimination-of-Redundant-Step-for-Offshore-Renewable-Energy-Leasing.cfm.

11. Cabotage is the transportation of goods or passengers between two points in the same country by a vessel or an aircraft registered in another country. The United States, as well as other nations, protects its domestic transportation industries through cabotage laws. US maritime cabotage laws reserve to US-flagged vessels the right to transport cargo and passengers between US ports.

12. A copy of the May 27, 2010, ruling can be found by searching the US Customs and Border Protection database for CBP, HQ H105415 (May 27, 2010); *and see* The Jones Act (formerly 46 U.S.C. App. § 883, recodified as 46 U.S.C. § 55102, pursuant to Pub. L. No. 109-304 (October 6, 2006)).

Cape Wind Lease as a Road Map: Issues of Liability and Risk in Wind Farm Development

Horseshoe Shoal's shallow waters—depths range between 12 and 50 feet—and high winds are ideal.[13] The environmental and land-use profile of the area, however, has stoked many of the controversies. As detailed in the MMS's final environmental impact statement (FEIS) assessment, Horseshoe Shoal includes areas of important submerged aquatic vegetation, including eelgrass, considered to provide a "habitat area of particular concern" for certain fish.[14] Water birds fly through the sound year-round, and terrestrial birds migrate over the fall and spring. Bat species may likewise migrate through the area. Commercial and recreational fishing is popular; and seals, dolphins, whales, and sea turtles, including endangered species, can be found in these waters. As the FEIS observes, Nantucket Sound is a tourist draw, and tourism is vital to the economy in the area. Apart from the swimming, boating, and other water sports, charter fishing, whale watching tours, birding, kayaking, scuba diving, and canoeing can bring people into the project area. Two Native American tribal territories are located nearby—the Mashpee Wampanoag Tribe and the Wampanoag Tribe of Gay Head (Aquinnah); the Cape Wind project will apparently alter the view from at least one sacred site. Ninety-five shipwrecks are reportedly in the area. The Hyannis-Nantucket ferry regularly crosses the waterway, and planes to or from one of three airports in the area fly overhead.

The 130 turbines of Cape Wind will spread in a pattern across 25 square miles of Horseshoe Shoal. Proposals indicate that the 130 turbines will each reach 417 feet above sea level, be mounted on monopole foundations that are 16 to 21 feet in diameter, and be sunk approximately 80 feet into the seabed.[15] One-hundred-thirty 33 kilovolt submarine cables must be laid between each turbine generator and the offshore electrical service platform. In turn, the electrical service platform will transmit the energy generated by each turbine to landfall via another 115-kilovolt submarine cable.[16] This transmission cable, approximately 12.5 miles long and running through 7.6 miles of state waters before hitting land, will be buried six feet below the sea floor.

The Lease

The lease grants Cape Wind exclusive right to harvest wind energy in the project area and is subject to myriad terms and conditions, as well as the applicable laws and regu-

---

13. MMS record of decision at 16, *available at* http://www.boemre.gov/offshore/renewableenergy/CapeWind.htm.

14. US Dep't of the Interior, Minerals Management Service, Cape Wind Project, Final Environmental Impact Statement, June 2009. § 4.2.2, *et. seq.*, *available at* http://www.boemre.gov/offshore/AlternativeEnergy/PDFs/FEIS/Cape%20Wind%20Energy%20Project%20FEIS.pdf.

15. Plaintiff's brief in 02-117499 JLT, motion in support of summary judgment; Alliance to Protect Nantucket Sound v. U.S. Dep't of the Army, 288 F. Supp. 2d 64, 75 (D. Mass.2003).

16. MMS record of decision at 3, *available at* http://www.boemre.gov/offshore/renewableenergy/CapeWind.htm.

lations, as set forth by federal, state, and local authorities.[17] The lease explicitly provides that Cape Wind is not authorized to conduct activity on the OCS related to the exploration for, or development of, oil, gas, seabed minerals, or other renewable energy resources beside wind,[18] and it reserves to the federal government all rights not expressly granted to Cape Wind, including a right to suspend operations on the OCS in the interests of national security.[19]

The lease also provides that, where lease terms conflict with regulations, Cape Wind will be governed by the terms of the lease.[20] Thus BOEMRE can use contract terms to enforce a liability regime against Cape Wind that is more comprehensive than anything set forth in case law, statutes, or regulatory authority.

Indeed, the lease casts an expansive net of contractual liability over Cape Wind. In specific detail, the lease prohibits Cape Wind from conducting operations in the project area in a manner that could cause harm to the environment; create unsafe conditions; or adversely affect sites of historical, cultural, or archaeological significance without notice to and direction from BOEMRE.[21] Cape Wind must indemnify the federal government from any claim for "environmental injury of any kind" including the release of any petroleum, or other hazardous material, and for any "injury to persons" or costs incurred as a result of activities on the project area or because of conduct of Cape Wind employees, contractors, or subcontractors.[22] Under these broad categories of liability, the lease identifies risks Cape Wind has assumed in 14 subcategories and specifies how Cape Wind must mitigate risks and respond in the event that risk becomes reality.

Risks Relating to Environmental Injury

The bulk of the best practices that Cape Wind must adopt under the lease focus on mitigating specifically identified environmental risks associated with the construction and operation of the facility, as well as its eventual decommission.

Cape Wind must also follow an avian and bat monitoring plan pre- and postconstruction, install antiperching mechanisms, adjust lighting to minimize bird collisions, and report on avian mortality attributable to the project, including on the mortality of specified species.

To protect endangered species, Cape Wind must (1) follow conservation measures recommended by the National Marine Fisheries Service (NMFS), (2) hire endangered species monitors approved by the NMFS, and (3) monitor the area for any endangered

---

17. *Available at* http://www.boemre.gov/offshore/renewableenergy/PDFs/CapeWind_signed_lease.pdf.

18. *Available at* http://www.boemre.gov/offshore/renewableenergy/PDFs/CapeWind_signed_lease.pdf at 2.

19. *Id.* at 2.

20. *Id.* at 1.

21. *Id.* at 3. The lease also creates contractual liabilities for interference with or endangerment of activities carried out pursuant to any other lease issued under or governed by the Outer Continental Shelf Lands Act, whether that lease was granted prior to the Cape Wind lease, or subsequently.

22. *Id.*

species at least 60 minutes prior to certain activities—including pile driving relating to the installation of turbines and of the electrical service platform, and high-resolution geophysical surveying. Since the Marine Mammal Protection Act (MMPA) makes it illegal to "take" or "harass" any marine mammal, Cape Wind will apply for an MMPA incidental harassment authorization.

The lease also requires Cape Wind to mitigate impacts on essential fish habitat, as designated by the Magnuson-Stevens Fishery Conservation and Management Act, by following several MMS mandates developed in consultation with the NMFS. These requirements include a time of year restriction on work producing water silt to protect flounder spawning in winter; a soft-start for installations that gives fish a time to leave the area; periodic inspection of scour mats and cables to assess deterioration, and armoring if necessary; monitoring of the lowest water level, including sediments and some subsurface layers known as the benthic zone, and recovery of the benthic ecosystem; as well as monitoring and replanting eel grass. To mitigate the effects of electric and magnetic fields on fish, all of the offshore, high-voltage conductors for circuits will be shielded in cable, so that no external electric and magnetic field will be produced.[23]

Risks Relating to Injuries to People

Many of the competing land uses of Horseshoe Shoal are expected to continue after Cape Wind is erected. Although traffic of commercial and recreational vessels through the project area will be prohibited during construction of Cape Wind, after construction is completed this ban will be lifted.[24] Fishing in the area will not be prohibited. Cape Wind anticipates creating 391 full-time jobs during the manufacturing/assembly and construction stages of the project, and estimates that, ultimately, between 142 and 215 permanent employees will be required to run the wind farm.[25] People engaging in competing land uses in the project area and the employees (as well as contractors and subcontractors) who will make up Cape Wind's work force are all exposed to some degree of risk for which Cape Wind could be liable.

Maritime and Aviation Uses. After preliminarily issuing a presumed hazard determination in 2009, finding that the turbine structures would obstruct airspace and have adverse physical and electromagnetic impacts on air navigation, the FAA has since given clearance to Cape Wind.[26] The clearance was granted on condition that Cape Wind underwrite changes to the radar system at the Massachusetts Military Reservation.[27] Cape Wind plans to mitigate the impact of magnetic flux density by using

---

23. MMS record of decision at 18, *available at* http://www.boemre.gov/offshore/renewableenergy/CapeWind.htm.

24. Army Corps record of decision at 4, *available at* http://www.nae.usace.army.mil/projects/ma/CapeWind/ROD.pdf.

25. Global Insight, Economic Impact Analysis of the Cape Wind Off-Shore Renewable Energy Project at 3, *available at* http://www.capewind.org/downloads/Economic_Impact.pdf.

26. *See* MMS record of decision at 24; Patrick Cassidy, *FAA Gives Clearance to Cape Wind*, CapeCodOnline.Com, May 18, 2010.

27. Patrick Cassidy, *FAA Gives Clearance to Cape Wind*, CapeCodOnline.Com, May 18, 2010.

three conductor cables and by enclosing the interarray and off shore t voltage conductors with shielded cable.[28]

Cape Wind must use off-white paint on offshore structures to imp and night time lighting must be provided in accordance with the FAA and the United States Coast Guard. There will be helipad lighting, and all construction structures and equipment will be lit at night.[29] Lighting location, color, intensity and flash patterns will be designed to minimize impacts and address potential hazards.

During construction, monthly status reports will be submitted to BOEMRE and the US Coast Guard. In this time period, Cape Wind will be prohibited from using certain radio frequencies, and watercraft will be advised to keep a two wavelengths' distance from the construction cranes at the lowest frequency of interest.

Marine and port facility traffic management measures will be adopted with the Coast Guard and a control center will monitor traffic. Cape Wind will have to work with appropriate entities to make sure that mariners are educated on navigational safety issues related to the wind farm. And safety lines, mooring attachments, and access ladders will be placed on each turbine as approved by the Coast Guard.

Employee, Contractor, and Subcontractor Uses. To protect employees, the lease requires that Cape Wind: (1) operate in compliance with occupational safety and health standards, free from recognized hazards; (2) operate in compliance with regulations and orders intended to protect persons, property, and the environment; and (3). allow prompt access to any safety inspector authorized by any relevant federal agency and produce any relevant records.[30]

Risks Relating to Geological and Historical, Cultural or Archaeological Resources

Although geological risks have been assessed to be minimal, Cape Wind is required to conduct preconstruction surveys to record the baseline conditions of rock and sediment in the project area.[31] Protection from erosion that could be caused by slip between rock natural to the area and construction, or scour protection, will be installed around the turbine foundations as needed. Postconstruction monitoring will continue to periodically assess scouring and cable exposure. Preconstruction surveys and monitoring will also be conducted to further archaeological resource assessment. From each turbine location, at least one core will be taken for geological and archaeological analysis. Buffer zones will be enforced around potential ship wreck or cultural resource sites, and likely archaeological resources will be avoided. If survey results indicate the potential presence of a cultural resource, Cape Wind is required to avoid the potential resource by a buffer distance, or study it to determine it is not an actual cultural re-

28. Army Corps record of decision at 8, *available at* http://www.nae.usace.army.mil/projects/ma/CapeWind/ROD.pdf.

29. *Id.* at 9.

30. Sigend Cape Wind lease at 5, *available at* http://www.boemre.gov/offshore/renewableenergy/PDFs/CapeWind_signed_lease.pdf.

31. Army Corps record of decision at 8, *available at* http://www.nae.usace.army.mil/projects/ma/CapeWind/ROD.pdf. Signed Cape Wind lease at C-5.

source.[32] In the event that a cultural resource or human remains are discovered, Cape Wind must stop work and report the find to BOEMRE. Cape Wind must allow nearby indigenous tribal authorities and a qualified archaeologist to monitor sea bottom disturbing activities.

Conclusion

The controversies regarding renewable energy are essentially political and should be resolved by federal and state legislators and regulators. However, for energy developers, the details of resource allocation and risk distribution will be hashed out in contractual clauses, and courts will ultimately decide who bears the costs of accidents. Cape Wind has benefited from recent legislative and regulatory changes that have made it easier for wind farm projects to set up shop on the OCS. In working through these new statutory and regulatory schemes, the Cape Wind project cleared the brush—or laid the buoys—for other future offshore OCS wind farm developments. Analysis of the Cape Wind lease provides a blueprint to inform future offshore wind developers about the risks and liabilities they will be required to bear.

32. Signed Cape Wind lease at C-7.

2012 Update

By John J. Reilly and Carine M. Williams

In the year since publishing our article on the potential risks and liabilities of offshore wind projects, we have observed three important trends.

First, the Obama Administration has taken significant steps to expedite the administrative approval process, thereby reducing regulatory uncertainty. BOEM continued to work with the Massachusetts Renewable Energy Task Force and in February, 2012, BOEM issued a Call for Information and Nominations for Commercial Leasing for Wind Power on the Outer Continental Shelf Offshore Massachusetts (the "Call"). BOEM has invited the submission of nominations for commercial leases, and the Call is another concrete step toward lease issuance.

Nearly simultaneously, BOEM issued a Notice of Intent to Prepare an Environmental Assessment for Commercial Wind Leasing and Site Assessment Activities on the Atlantic OCS Offshore Massachusetts.

The comment period for the Call closed March 22, 2012. A significant number of developers expressed strong interest. Many of these developers, or their affiliates, also expressed interest in developing projects elsewhere in federal waters (*e.g.* Virginia).

BOEM has also narrowed the Wind Energy Area ("WEA") available for leasing. On May 30, 2012, BOEM identified a WEA that was about 39% of the area it had originally identified and about 90% of the area identified in the Call. The WEA now excludes an "area of high sea duck concentration" and an area of "high value fisheries," according to BOEM.

In most cases, the excluded area represents only a fraction of the total area designated by each developer, and therefore may not play a significant role in whether proposed projects move forward. However, the exclusions could foreclose more marginal projects that relied on the assumption that the previously identified WEA would remain entirely available for development. BOEM's environmental analysis under the National Environmental Policy Act ("NEPA") may result in further exclusion of areas with known North Atlantic right whale use, or of areas within 15 or 21 nautical miles of the inhabited coastline of Massachusetts, where projects may be visible from shore.

Second, opposition to off-shore wind energy remains strong and determined. For example, in 2010 the Federal Aviation Administration approved the proposed Cape Wind Project and determined it would not present a risk to aircraft radar. Opponents of the project appealed and, after another protracted review, the FAA again approved the project. However, the opposition is now calling for a federal investigation into claims that the administrations of Massachusetts Governor Duval Patrick and the White House pressured the FAA into ignoring public safety risks.

Finally, commercial developments have moderated some of the strongest arguments in favor of offshore wind and increased the economic competition facing these projects. For example, a significant decline in the price of natural gas has undermined the case for renewable energy. It is not clear if, or for how long, the decline in natural gas prices will last; but new methods for extracting natural gas, including "fracking" have raised expectations of an overabundance of natural gas in the United States in the near future.

Part Six
OTHER ARTICLES

Introduction

This chapter contains four noteworthy articles from *Infrastructure* that do not easily fit into the other categories in this volume.

In an illuminating article, Section Chair Patty Dondanville and her former associate, Melody Cross, explain the provisions of the Dodd-Frank Act that subject energy company swaps to the jurisdiction of the Commodity Futures Trading Commission (CFTC). In the article, the authors note that the CFTC had, as of the Fall of 2010, undertaken a "rulemaking marathon." As Ms. Dondanville makes clear in her update, the marathon continues, with no end in sight. While the CFTC has finalized some of its rules, the clarifications and guidance requested by the energy industry have not been addressed.

David Hardy and Marty Pugh, members of the Section's Tax and Accounting Committee, discuss the possibility of corporate tax reform following the August 2011 congressional compromise on the increase in the debt ceiling. They also review the recommendations and possible implications of the Simpson-Bowles Commission report.

In their update, Mr. Hardy and Ms. Pugh address the "fiscal cliff" that the United States is facing at the end of 2012 as a result of automatic tax increases and reductions in government expenditures. They offer little hope that fundamental tax reform will occur in the late 2012 lame-duck Congress, although they offer some hope that temporary delays in the tax increases and expenditure cuts may provide an opportunity for the new Congress to deal with tax reform.

This chapter also includes several articles from *Infrastructure* written by the Honorable Richard D. Cudahy, senior judge of the U.S. Court of Appeals for the Seventh Circuit. These include a tribute to Dr. Alfred Kahn on his 90th birthday and a review of Daniel Yergin's book *The Quest*, which the judge characterizes as both "encyclopedic" and a "page turner." As noted in the Foreword, Judge Cudahy has been and continues to serve as editor of *Infrastructure*.

Peter V. Lacouture
September, 2012

Chapter 28

Alfred Kahn on His 90th Birthday: The Birth of Deregulation*

*By Hon. Richard D. Cudahy***

Several months ago I was invited to participate in a conference at the University of Colorado Law School, honoring Dr. Alfred Kahn on his 90th birthday. I had known "Fred" (as we call him) since he was chairman of the New York Public Service Commission in the early 1970s, and I served in a like capacity on the Wisconsin Commission. He was later chairman of the Civil Aeronautics Board (CAB), where he spearheaded the historic deregulation of the airlines (already suggested by the Ford administration and precursor steps taken by former chairman, John Robson.) Later still, Dr. Kahn became chief advisor on inflation to the White House. Before his career in regulation, Fred was an economics professor at Cornell University and dean of the university's College of Arts and Sciences; throughout he has been a prominent economist, author, and extraordinarily popular speaker and discussant on ground-breaking economic ideas.

The organizer of the Boulder conference was Philip Weiser, a law professor and executive director of the Silicon Flatirons Center, which is attached to the law school. Professor Weiser provided the various documents generated at the conference, including a copy of Dr. Kahn's remarks and personal reminiscences about the historic deregulation of the airlines, about antitrust policy, and about the application of these developments to current topics.

Excerpts adapted from *A Grateful Response and Supplement* By Alfred E. Kahn, September 5, 2008, University of Colorado

I am overwhelmed by this celebration, and cannot possibly convey the full measure of my gratitude to my friends and collaborators—all of them also mentors—who have

* Originally published in *Infrastructure*, vol. 48, no. 1 (Fall, 2008). Alfred Kahn died on December 27, 2010, mourned by the whole world, after a long and immensely productive life.

** *Richard D. Cudahy is a judge on the U.S. Court of Appeals, 7th Circuit, in Chicago and coeditor of* Infrastructure.

organized and participated in it. In responding to these honors, I jotted down a reminder of Groucho Marx's advice to young would-be entrepreneurs: "The secret to success in business is a reputation for honesty and fair dealing . . . and if you can fake that, you've got it made;" in this case, substituting "modesty" if not "humility" for "honesty and fair dealing."

I'm going to concentrate first and logically on Phil Weiser's "Case Study of a Political Entrepreneur," which comes closest after Tom McCraw's classic *Prophets of Regulation* to a eulogy. By concentrating on the most highly publicized of my professional experiences—my leadership in the gradual dissolution of the Civil Aeronautics Board (CAB)[1]—it necessarily slights the earlier portion of my career in which I attempted first to systematically expound on the economics of regulation in volume one of my 1971 *Economics of Regulation* and then apply it when I chaired the New York public utility regulatory commission.

* * *

As to the results [of "regulatory reform" at the CAB, culminating in deregulation], to be sure, the 25- to 30-point increase in airline load factors achieved by the unleashing of competitive discounting meant increased crowding and discomfort, often severe, sometimes intolerable. But—the misguided policies of the FAA apart—it was precisely the failure of the industry under regulation to provide travelers of modest means with a choice of economy over comfort that constituted both the need for deregulation and the essence of its success. The experience wonderfully illustrates the principle that cartelization of a structurally competitive industry—in particular, the prohibition of price competition—sets off all sorts of other forms of cost-inflating competition, substantive and non-substantive, the fatal flaw of which is that it denies customers the choice of low-priced service without those amenities.[2]

Returning to Phil Weiser's characterization of my "political entrepreneurship," I initially declined the CAB chairmanship in the spring of 1977 because it seemed to me that in a new age of renewed anxiety about our energy situation—recall that the OPEC export embargo in 1973-74 had trebled the price of oil from about \$3.50 to almost \$12 a barrel—"I [did] not regard it as my highest aspiration to make it easier for people to jet all over the world." (And that was before I became aware of the disproportionate contribution of jet engine exhaust to global warming.) Indeed, recognizing that in the new world, telecommuting and teleconferencing would have to substantially displace physical transport, I timidly inquired about the possibility of switching with whoever might be offered the chairmanship of the FCC—"He can't possibly know less than I about the airline industry"—and I had been involved over the preceding two decades with the telephone business in various capacities.

It was only when I received a call from Senator Ted Kennedy (at whose hearings I had testified) saying, "Dr. Kahn? I want you to take that [CAB] job" followed by the message, "the President wants to see you," that I realized this was where genuine

1. This was anticipated, in a limited degree, in the second volume of my ECONOMICS OF REGULATION (1971).

2. Alfred E. Kahn, *The Threat of Latter-Day Progressives to an Authentically Liberal Economic Policy*, REG-MARKETS CENTER, 20-21 (2008).

regulatory reform was going to start and embraced the opportunity to "play the Walter Mitty role of a mouse driving that elephant," as I put it. The benefits to the flying public, authoritatively documented by Clifford Winston and Steven Morrison,[3] have been enormous.

I do not suggest that the world should acquaint itself with every nuance of my evolving views, but any implication that I came to the CAB with a fixed commitment to flat-out deregulation does an injustice to the complexities of the issue. For example, I continue to be ambivalent about such common regulatory policies as the subjection of various franchised utilities, such as municipal bus, cable TV, and telephone providers to the obligation to serve ubiquitously and on a 24-hour basis, or the similar imposition of common carriage obligations on telecommunication carriers.[4] It does an injustice also to the gradualness of my own evolving conviction that, so far as airlines were concerned, there was no acceptable halfway house of "regulatory reform" on the road to flat-out economic deregulation.

In his recent memoir, Alan Greenspan summarizes my list of the absurdities forced upon me by the regulation of price competition that fairly soon led to that conviction:

My favorite description of this was by Alfred Kahn, a wisecracking economist [*moi*?] from Cornell University whom Jimmy Carter made head of the Civil Aeronautics Board and who became known as the Father of Airline Deregulation. Speaking in 1978 on the need for change, Fred couldn't resist riffling on the thousands of picayune decisions he and the board were called upon to make: "May an air taxi acquire a fifty-seat plane? May a supplemental carrier carry horses from Florida to somewhere in the Northeast? Should we let a scheduled carrier pick up stranded charter customers and carry them on seats that would otherwise be empty, at charter rates? . . . May a carrier introduce a special fare for skiers but refund the cost of their ticket if there is no snow? May the employees of two financially affiliated airlines wear similar-looking uniforms?" Then he looked at the congressmen and said, "Is it any wonder that I ask myself every day: Is this action necessary? Is this what my mother raised me to do?"[5]

To that same list, I add two other favorites:

- How many facilities on what is purported to be an organized tour might the tour operator *neglect* to inspect on the premises, while still qualifying for free passage?
- Then there was the early evening telephone call, well after office hours, from someone whose name I didn't recognize, asking me what had happened to his petition for approval of an arrangement he had made (once again, with an unlicensed or supplemental carrier) to transport a cargo of his sheep from some place in Virginia to England. His need for prompt approval, he averred, was urgent because the sheep (I should be more specific, the *ewes*) were in heat and being transported for breeding purposes.

---

3. Clifford Winston and Steven Morrison, THE EVOLUTION OF THE AIRLINE INDUSTRY (Brookings Institution Press, 1995).

4. See exchange with my colleague, William Taylor, *supra* note 2, pp. 39-30.

5. ALAN GREENSPAN, THE AGE OF TURBULENCE—ADVENTURES IN A NEW WORLD, New York, 2007, pp 71-71.

Hardly the view of a preconverted deregulator, it reflects six months of experience of trying to "reform" regulation, gradually and partially. It was only over that time that I came to realize there was indeed no acceptable halfway house; only a few months later, industry leaders themselves either came to the same conclusion or recognized the necessity of adjusting to *mine*.

In correcting the historical record, I cannot refrain from observing also that while graciously giving me this credit, Alan Greenspan characterizes deregulation consistently and ungraciously as "the Ford Administration's great unsung achievement": [the italics are mine] President Carter, Senators Ted Kennedy, Howard Cannon, and Bob Packwood, (then-Professor) Stephen Breyer, and at the White House, Mary Schuman—later Boies—receive none at all.

The irony of those omissions was further exemplified by an uneasy meeting that I had a few months later with Frank Fitzsimmons, the powerful boss of the Teamster's Union, in which, speaking in my new and not-very-congenial role of advisor on inflation to a president he probably held in contempt, I tried to persuade him to comply with our wage guidelines—fully recognizing that the only effective recompense I could offer was the one neither President Carter nor I was willing to consider: a promise to relent in our efforts to deregulate trucking. In that sense, we clearly had the last laugh—at the predictable price, however, of having eventually to leave the curing of inflation to Fed Chairman Paul Volcker (also a Carter appointee), whose successful restraints were steadfastly continued by Mr. Greenspan.

There are other parts of my history as regulator, some clearly compatible, others really inconsistent with the picture of me that Phil [Weiser] has drawn from my airline experience:

- My determined application to the regulation of electric and telephone services in New York State of the marginal cost pricing principles expounded in my first volume—regarded as sufficiently revolutionary at the time to inspire an unsuccessful effort to get me to recuse myself from electric rate proceedings for having "prejudged" that issue. It is singularly pertinent here to admit the envy I experienced upon discovering that these efforts of mine had been anticipated by another state commission, Wisconsin's, under the chairmanship of one Richard Cudahy—an envy mitigated by my assumption that one or another of the responsible parties had been aware of my first volume, published only a few years previously.
- My long opposition to AT&T's bundling its own customer premises equipment with its franchised monopoly telephone service and its refusal to permit the attachment of competitively provided equipment, as first expressed in a 1956 memo I sent to Arthur Burns, then chairman of the President's Council of Economic Advisors. As a member of his senior staff, I composed the memo in indignant reaction to an FCC decision sustaining AT&T's barring the clip-on attachment to the customer's phone of the Hushaphone device, prohibited by AT&T on the ground that it made voice messages unintelligible. ("All the party at the other end has to do," I observed, "is say, 'I can't understand you!' or, more helpfully, 'Take that damned muffling device off your phone!'") Two decades later, we generalized this policy at the New York Commission.

- My parting memorandum to AT&T in 1969, after several years' membership in its national Economic Advisory Council, urging it to abandon its exclusionary practices that ultimately led to dissolution, and instead adopt what I labeled "A Grand Competitive Strategy."
- My testimony in Congress in opposition to several "Bell bills" seeking to preserve or restore the Bell monopolies.

It has taken 30 years for my earlier prognostication about aviation to be vindicated: no industry has been more adversely affected than commercial aviation by $140 a barrel oil. [P.S. At least it appeared so at the time. More recently, the prices collapsed below $50 a barrel, as the OPEC member countries have as yet been unable to agree on allocating among themselves the reductions in output necessary to reverse that trend.] I admit to some rueful satisfaction in having been prematurely prescient, even though it will mean an equally dramatic reversal in the accomplishments of deregulation. It was a glorious ride, however bumpy for the drivers, but it is, alas, largely over. How "largely" I will not try to predict, but I have no doubt consumers will continue to be better served under deregulated competition than by restored governmental cartelization.

The Skunk at Our Picnic: My Views on Antitrust Policy

Taking your acceptance of the invitation to this conference as reflecting the agreement of most of you—eighteenth to twentieth century liberals alike—with what I did for or to the airlines, I hope you will find it interesting, and not merely provoking, if I confront the far wider spectrum of our opinions about the antitrust policy that takes over responsibility for protecting consumers when direct regulation is withdrawn.

To put it simply, my views in antitrust cases are more likely to be reflected in the (alas) dissenting opinions of Justices Stevens, Souter, Ginsburg, and Breyer than in the predominating opinions of Justice Scalia. There! To my regret, I've probably alienated enough of you to dissipate your collective (along with Milton Friedman's and Alan Greenspan's) approval of my role in airline and trucking deregulation.

As a self-proclaimed twentieth century liberal, I have long been an antitrust true believer of the pre-Chicago variety, emphasizing its role as a proscription of anticompetitive *conduct*—collusion and exclusion of rivals from a fair opportunity to compete—and (how old-fashioned can one get?) the *intent* that may be inferred from it. In my view, any doubts that this was the intention of the 1890 Sherman Act should have been put to rest by the 1914 Federal Trade Commission Act, with its flat prohibition of "unfair methods of competition." (*Period. Repeat: period.*)

The last half-century has, in contrast, witnessed the virtual triumph of the opposing view of latter-day conservatives, rationalized by University of Chicago economists, highly sophisticated liberals of the eighteenth century variety, that the prohibitions of antitrust and of discrimination in particular should apply only upon clear demonstration of a genuine threat of injury to the *competitive process* and hence *to consumers*.[6]

6. *But cf.* Fishman v. Estate of Wirtz, 807 F.2d 520, 525-563 (7th Cir. 1986) (Cudahy, J.) (Adopting the pre-Chicago view over Judge Easterbrook's dissent).

This issue is clearly exposed in the carefully articulated proposal of the ambitious Digital Age Communications Act (DACA) Project, sponsored by the Progress and Freedom Foundation, in which Phil Weiser was an active participant, explicitly recommending application of the Section 5 FTC Act unfair methods of competition model, which accords completely with my own position, but then recommending that the prohibition apply only to practices or behavior that demonstrably "pose a substantial and non-transitory risk to consumer welfare"—a clear victory for the University of Chicago, and probably also representing a consensus view of reputable economists.

At the cost of provoking many of you who applaud my eighteenth (but not my twentieth) century liberalism, I am compelled to repeat my long-expressed belief that there *is* such a phenomenon as predation, that it has occurred—in the airline industry among others—to the injury of consumers; that it can be inferred and sufficiently established from a pattern of *conduct* by incumbents before, during, and after the entry and exit of the provocateur-victim; and the simplest preventive and remedy, suggested many years ago by Professor William J. Baumol,[7] would be a legislative requirement that putative predators be placed on notice that they would be required to continue their competition-meeting/beating offering for some fixed period of time (say, a year) after exit of the competition-initiating supplier. As I have further explained elsewhere, such a rule would leave to the putative predator—*ex ante*—rather than the courts *ex post*—the now-critical determination of whether the successful, competition-beating response did or did not recover its marginal costs.[8]

It is only by a trick of rhetoric, however frequently repeated, that the incumbent is identified as a practitioner and advocate of 'hard,' the repulsed intruder of 'soft' competition. In the immortal words of John McEnroe, "You [Justices Kennedy and Scalia] *can't* be serious!"

The Skunk Has Its Uses—Resolving the Issue of "Network Neutrality"

By now the interested reader will surely have wondered when I was going to get around to the inevitable subject of network neutrality—and how long that was going to take. Be reassured— much too much has already been said on this subject, fuzzily and repeatedly. I challenge myself to reduce my equivocal views to a few bare propositions:

- To induce efficient behavior, the prices confronting buyers and sellers should reflect the marginal costs (causally) associated with current transactions.
- The rapidity of technological and commercial changes in telecommunications and the huge investments required to exploit them preclude anything even remotely approximating traditional cost-of-service regulation, whether of aggregate revenues or of the prices of individual services.

7. William J. Baumol, *Quasi-Permanence of Price Reductions: A Policy for Protection of Predatory Pricing*, YALE L. J., 89 (1979).

8. See Alfred Kahn, *Telecommunications: The Transition from Regulation to Antitrust*, 5 J. OF TELECOMM. & HIGH TECH. L., 159-188 (2006).

- Each of the principal providers of broadband Internet access—notably local telephone and cable companies—is subject to competitive pressure to offer the full range of services from its several platforms.
- When two multi-platform companies have come, arguably, to dominate these several markets, in very large measure by mergers of previous competitors, one cannot be fully satisfied that competition will sufficiently protect consumers or independent profferors of programming content. That "arguably" is a weasel word—the FCC has released large portions of the spectrum precisely to encourage wireless offerers, as a third, competitive option. It is not encouraging, however, that among the providers of wireless telephony only AT&T and Verizon actually bid in the recent large spectrum auction, emerging with the lion's share.[9]
- Concentration ratios in telecommunications are nevertheless moderate; the incursions of video companies such as Comcast and Time Warner into telephony and of telephone and satellite companies into television and the competition of both in the provision of Internet access are genuinely competitive.
- Recognizing that it is possible, consistently, to commend my work at the CAB while disagreeing with my antitrust philosophy (on the ground that governmental prohibitions of competition such as I helped abolish are more absolute than private restraints), I can only observe the congruity in principle with what I did there and recommend here.
- Contrary to the most emphatic advocates who would prohibit any and all differences in the charges for broadband Internet access, it is emphatically not discriminatory—or in itself undesirable—for providers to vary their charges depending on the demands that the several users impose on their networks for different guaranteed speeds of delivery. On the contrary, that is the result that would be produced by effective, consumer-serving and -protecting competition.
- Moreover, genuine price discrimination may be the only way of recovering the huge investments required to exploit the new technologies, and objectionable only if it is also anti-competitive.
- The only interventions clearly justified, therefore, would be antitrust-like in character—prohibiting discriminations *against providers of content competitive with the offerings of the carriers themselves* or their affiliates—and, similarly, refusals to interconnect with one another for the transmission of competitor-originating content.
- The version of antitrust that I urgently recommend—and have consistently for more than half century—would flatly condemn such discriminations against competitors, or refusals to deal with them, without the University of Chicago-mandated demonstration of injury to customers, such as the enduring 5 percent price differential required in the Department of Justice's merger guidelines.

9. Saul Hansell, *Verizon and AT&T Win Big in Auction of Spectrum*, N.Y. TIMES, March 21, 2008, at C3.

- I will have to save for a later day the formidable task of deciding where these last two propositions leave me in deciding the merits of denunciations such as Thomas Hazlett's of the FCC's recent condemnation of Comcast for assertedly discriminating against certain bandwidth-intensive applications competitive with its own.[10] I strongly suspect, however, that this case will have illustrated the likely differences in our views about the role and interpretation of antitrust that I have already labeled the first skunk at our picnic. I would be inclined to condemn any such discriminations per se, as my sole endorsement of a net-neutrality mandate.

~~~~~~~~~~

10. Thomas Hazlett, *FCC should leave net neutrality to anti-trust courts*, FINANCIAL TIMES, September 30, 2008 (see http://www.ft.com/cms/s/0/bac78ca4-8ee8-11dd-946c-0000779fd18c.html).
~~~~~~~~~~

Chapter 29

The Dodd-Frank Act: Why Utilities Need to Understand the CFTC

*By Patricia Dondanville and Melody R. Cross**

The dust has settled from the battles on Capitol Hill over financial reform. After President Obama signed the Dodd-Frank Wall Street Reform and Consumer Protection Act (the "Dodd-Frank Act") in July, the handshakes were exchanged and the Oval Office pictures were snapped. The ink is now dry on an historic piece of legislation. But the work to make financial reform a reality is far from complete. The Dodd-Frank Act has now been handed off to the "would-be regulators" and the "to-be-regulated" for translation into practical, clear, workable rules.

The initial reactions from American business leaders to the Dodd-Frank Act ranged across the spectrum. Some companies assumed it would not affect them, and so cheered its Wall Street reform headlines without analyzing the text. From the perspective of many of those who have delved into its provisions, a common reaction seems to be that the Dodd-Frank Act is scary. And it is. It probably scares the people the law was intended to scare, like speculators who make their money gambling recklessly in swaps markets and may be manipulating the markets or taking large risks that could threaten the financial system. But it also scares the companies, including energy companies, whose businesses depend on physical commodity transactions and related over-the-counter derivatives to manage the commercial risks of their day-to-day activities.

The over-the-counter or "OTC" (bilateral contract) markets for energy and energy-related commodities and derivatives have been developing rapidly over the past 20 years. These markets have become an essential risk management tool for an industry that the American public relies on year-round and around-the-clock for lights, heat, and computers in industrial plants, commercial businesses, and residences. In the wake of the 2008-2009 financial market meltdown, the federal government's reaction was to immediately and comprehensively regulate the "unregulated," "dark" derivatives markets. But in doing so, little distinction was made in the legislation between the finan-

---

* Originally published in *Infrastructure*, vol. 50, no. 2 (Winter, 2011).

** *Patricia Dondanville is a partner at Schiff Hardin LLP, and Melody R. Cross is an associate at Schiff Hardin LLP. This article represents the views of the authors, and does not necessarily reflect the views of Schiff Hardin LLP or any client of Schiff Hardin LLP. [Ms. Dondanville is now a partner at Reed Smith in Chicago.]*

cier on Wall Street and the electric company down the street. The sweeping nature of the Dodd-Frank Act will impose many new burdens on industries that were already comprehensively regulated and did nothing to cause the financial market meltdown. The discussion of the legislation's unintended consequences has reached a fevered pitch on blogs and editorial pages.[1]

Title VII of the Dodd-Frank Act is the section that deals with the OTC derivatives markets. Since the passage of the Commodity Futures Modernization Act of 2000, OTC derivatives based on energy and energy-related commodity transactions have been explicitly exempt from the Commodity Exchange Act (CEA). Energy commodities were "exempt" commodities, and swap agreements were exempt as well.[2] Title VII of the Dodd-Frank Act summarily eliminates the current exclusions and exemptions from the Commodity Exchange Act on which energy companies have relied for a decade to transact in the OTC derivatives markets. The Dodd-Frank Act instead brings all "swaps" under the jurisdiction of the Commodity Futures Trading Commission (CFTC) and all "securities-based swaps" under the jurisdiction of the Securities Exchange Commission. The law will require anyone considered a "swap dealer" or "major swap participant" to register and follow strict requirements for recordkeeping, reporting, business practices, capital, margin, and position limits. And the law requires any person or entity that enters into a "swap," to either clear that swap and transact on a CFTC-regulated exchange or other regulated entity, or to find an exception from the clearing and/or exchange-trading requirements.

The Dodd-Frank Act fundamentally altered the rules, the playing field, and the referees for transacting in energy and energy-related commodities and derivatives. Utilities will be affected and the cost of energy to the consumer will increase. The only question that remains is by how much. And the answer to that question will become clear over the next five months as the regulators convert hundreds of pages of law into dozens and dozens of rules that may or may not allow utilities to continue cost-effective hedging of the commercial risks inherent in their businesses.

Background: How Do Utilities Use "Swaps" Today?

Utilities use swaps to manage the commercial risks inherent in their public service business, risks like commodity price, and availability risk for the commodities they deliver to the consumers in their service territories. Those who pay attention to their monthly electric bill can understand the volatility of the price of power and gas. Price volatility in a commodity market derives principally from changes in market fundamentals—supply and demand in economic terms. In the energy industry, electric generation, natural gas production, and transmission or transportation events are economic supply issues. "Load" or "demand" for energy are utility terms for economic demand. As usual in the energy business, weather is the wild card (as is the inability to store power in commercial quantities). When a heat wave hits the entire Midwest in mid-July, the demand for electricity skyrockets. If the heat wave hits at the same time as a

1. *See i.e. The Hangover, Part II*, WALL ST. J. (NOV. 29, 2010).
2. *See* CEA §§ 2(h)(1) and 2(g) (pre-amendment).

generation outage in Michigan or Illinois, Midwest utilities have a problem. The same holds true for an unexpected and extended ice storm or blizzard during the long, cold Midwest winter.

To plan for both expected and unexpected, but always unpredictable, swings in supply and demand, utilities turn to the energy and energy-related commodities and derivatives markets. There, the companies are able to buy and sell natural gas, electric power or capacity, fuel for generation, or other energy-related products. The companies can also hedge commercial risks using financially-settled transactions. Utilities contract with each other or with other types of market participants, such as financial entities (banks, bank affiliates, or hedge funds), merchant generators, and natural gas producers, to obtain certainty and reduce the volatility of the prices they will pay and receive for energy. The utilities can then pass the hedging benefits on to the ultimate consumers of energy—American businesses and households.

Today, most energy hedging transactions are bilateral commercial contracts between "counterparties." Typically in each of these contract relationships, the legal and administrative terms are initially documented on a standard master or "umbrella" agreement form developed by an industry group (such as the ISDA Master Agreement or the EEI Master Agreement). The form documents are negotiated by attaching schedules and annexes to the form master agreement, and each such set of documents is tailored to meet the requirements and needs of each pair of counterparties.' Credit support/credit risk management terms for the trading relationship are carefully negotiated under an annex to the master agreement. In assessing relative credit risk, each party assesses the financial and operating strength of its potential counterparty and determines what sort of credit support, if any, would be required to transact once or many times with that counterparty. The counterparties may then decide to transact without credit support, collateral, or "margin," or they may then set up a protocol for measuring net (unsecured) credit exposure, and posting and exchanging credit support or collateral based on several factors, including the type of transactions that are contemplated between the parties.

Once a master agreement is in place, the two counterparties are then able to agree quickly and efficiently on individual transactions, without having to spend time and resources renegotiating the broader contractual and credit risk framework. Utilities seeking to hedge and mitigate their commercial risk typically have a number of these master agreement relationships in place so that they have many counterparty options for each hedge-taking into account the proposed size, duration, pricing, and other transaction-specific terms of the potential hedge and weighing that against the net credit risk exposure to and from the counterparty.

The Regulators
(And How the Dodd-Frank Act Changes the Landscape)

Natural gas and electric utilities are subject to comprehensive regulation on the federal, state, and sometimes local level. Moreover, the "markets" for natural gas and electricity transactions are also heavily regulated. The Federal Energy Regulatory Commission (FERC) is tasked with regulating the transportation and sale of electricity and natural gas in interstate commerce under the Federal Power Act (16 USC 791 et seq.) and the Natural Gas Act (15 USC 717 et seq.). FERC's mission is to assure that utilities provide reliable natural gas and electricity to American consumers and businesses, and to ensure that rates, terms, and conditions for such natural gas and electricity are "just and reasonable." Any rule that FERC promulgates, and any action FERC takes, is guided by that underlying mission.

In contrast, the mission of the CFTC under the CEA is to regulate commodity and derivatives trading markets. The CFTC's purpose is to promote price discovery and price transparency, so that commodity futures transactions can be conducted on liquid, fair, and financially-secure trading facilities. The public interest that drives the CFTC is to keep commodity trading markets transparent, liquid, and efficient. The CFTC has no statutory mandate to ensure the reliable, affordable delivery of energy.

The Dodd-Frank Act authorizes the CFTC to establish and define a new market structure for energy and energy-related commodity and derivatives transactions, and all other forms of OTC derivatives transactions. It empowers the CFTC to establish this new structure, and to exercise jurisdiction over all OTC derivatives, by regulating the derivatives transactions and by regulating the persons and entities that engage in such transactions.

The Dodd-Frank Act Authorizes the CFTC to Regulate Transactions and Persons

The CFTC's general directive from Congress under the Dodd-Frank Act is to have as many "swaps" as possible cleared by central clearing entities in order to reduce "systemic risk" to the financial markets, and to have as many "swaps" as possible traded on CFTC-regulated exchanges, or on or through other CFTC-regulated entities, in order to increase transparency in the markets. The CFTC has taken this directive to heart. As CFTC Chairman Gary Gensler noted in a speech: "We intend to comply fully with the statute's provisions and the Congressional intent to lower risk and bring transparency to the markets."[3] Commissioner Jill E. Sommers stated that "[g]enerally the headline is that swaps will now be subject to stringent regulatory oversight."[4] And, as Commissioner Bart Chilton commented:

> This new regulation is a game changer. Sometimes, as a regulator, I've felt they gave me a striped shirt and a whistle but not enough authority to really enforce the rules. Now the rulebook has been expanded. There will be more referees. The game will be a safer and sounder one.[5]

What seems to have been lost in the fervor of regulatory reform is that the CFTC, along with its sister regulators, is walking into a world of existing commercial transac-

---

3. Speech before the Futures Industry Association's Futures and Options Expo (Nov. 3, 2010) *at* http://www.cftc.gov/PressRoom/SpeechesTestimony/opagensler-57.html.

4. Speech delivered at Georgetown University (Oct. 26, 2010) *at* http://www.cftc.gov/PressRoom/SpeechesTestimony/opasommers-11.html.

5. Speech delivered at the University of Notre Dame (Nov. 1, 2010) *at* http://www.cftc.gov/PressRoom/SpeechesTestimony/opachilton-34.html.

tions and relationships. The Dodd-Frank Act has painted all "swaps" with a single brush—"requires regulation"—and handed everything over to the regulatory agencies to sort out. Congress has given expansive new authority to the CFTC, a financial markets regulator whose mission is focused on commodity transaction price transparency and that has historically not been involved in regulating the commodities and derivatives markets between commercial businesses. The CFTC must now regulate scores of commercial transactions between and among nonfinancial entities that utilize derivatives for a myriad of different reasons—some for commercial risk management reasons, some for speculative purposes, and everything in between.

Regulating Transactions: What is a "Swap"?

The Dodd-Frank Act makes it unlawful for a person to enter into a "swap" without complying with the CEA and the related rules to be published by the CFTC. If a company uses "swaps" in any part of its business, then the CEA will regulate those transactions beginning in July 2011.[6] The amended CEA contains a lengthy definition of the term "swap" that seems to encompass any transaction that transfers any financial risk from one contract party to the other contract party. The expansive nature of this definition is no accident.

The definition of a "swap" casts as wide a net as possible, rather than defining a closed universe list of transaction types. It then lists limited exclusions for transactions which Congress determined did not require new regulations, such as futures or options that are already traded on a CFTC-regulated exchange. For utilities, a key exclusion from the definition of "swap" is the exclusion for the sale of "a nonfinancial commodity . . . for deferred shipment or delivery . . . so long as the transaction is intended to be physically settled."[7] However, none of these underlined words is defined in or correlates directly to the wording in or interpretations under the pre-Dodd-Frank Act CEA, leaving little guidance for the future.

The imprecise wording of this and other provisions in the Dodd-Frank Act leaves much to the discretion of CFTC rulemaking in terms of how intrusive the new regulatory scheme will be for utilities. In the coming months, the CFTC must clarify what will and what will not considered a "swap," as well as clarify the exclusions and a host of related definitions. Hopefully, by doing so, the CFTC will give market participants certainty as to what transactions it intends to regulate. The CFTC has also been asked to clarify whether the certain existing regulatory exemptions, e.g., for commercial commodity options, are still applicable. In addition, the Dodd-Frank Act permits the

6. The Dodd-Frank Act was signed into law by President Obama on July 21, 2010 (the "Enactment Date"). It states that regulations "shall be issued in final form not later than 360 days after the date of enactment of [the Act]." The Dodd-Frank Act § 712(a)(3). The general effective date of Title VII, unless otherwise specified, is the later of 360 days after the Enactment Date or if a provision requires rulemaking, then 60 days after the rules are in final form. The CFTC shortens this definition to give its rulemakings focus, by identifying the generalized "Effective Date" as July 15, 2011. (*See, i.e.,* http://www.cftc.gov/PressRoom/SpeechesTestimony/genslerstatement112310.html).

7. CEA § 1a(47)(B) (as amended).

CFTC to exempt certain energy industry specific transactions (tariffed transactions) from this new regulatory regime. But it will be up to the utility industry (along with other interested parties and, perhaps, FERC or the RTOs) to request, and explain to the CFTC the need for, such broad conceptual exemptions.

Regulating Persons: Who Is Regulated?

The CFTC has also been given the power to regulate participants in the markets for swaps. The CFTC will register and regulate existing and new market infrastructure entities like central clearing organizations and "designated contract markets" (i.e., CFTC-regulated exchanges), as well as new entities labeled "swap execution facilities" and "swap data repositories" under the Dodd-Frank Act market structure. In addition, the CFTC will continue to register and regulate "futures commission merchants," "commodity trading advisors," and "introducing brokers," as it does now, even if those entities are engaged only in swaps, and not futures or exchange-traded options. Moreover, the CFTC will register and regulate two newly defined types of market participants—"swap dealers" and "major swap participants." These new types of market professionals will have reporting and record-keeping requirements, mandatory clearing and on-exchange trading, capital and margin, and other business conduct standards.

The Dodd-Frank Act provides an exception from clearing and exchange-trading requirements for "end users"—nonfinancial entities that use swaps to mitigate or hedge "commercial risk" so long as certain CFTC filings are made. However, the definition of "commercial risk," along with the details about applicability of the end-user exception, is left to the CFTC rulemaking process. Until the CFTC rules are finalized, utilities cannot be sure that they will be able to use the end-user exception or, if so, which risks they can hedge using swaps. Moreover, regardless of whether an entity is excepted from clearing and exchange-trading requirements, all market participants will still face new recordkeeping and reporting obligations under the Dodd-Frank Act.

The definitions of these new types of professional participants in the swap market—"swap dealers" and "major swap participants"—focus, among other criteria, on entities that make a market in swaps, have a substantial position in swaps, or whose positions create substantial swaps exposure for counterparties. It is unlikely that many natural gas or electric utilities will fall within either of these defined categories. But, once again, it bears noting that these terms are subject to CFTC rulemaking.

Important Questions for Which Utilities Need CFTC Answers

Once the definitions are clarified by the CFTC rulemakings, one of the two most important questions for utilities is whether they will be protected in their hedging activities by the "end user exception." End users of swaps will be able to opt out of clearing and, in most cases, will be concurrently exempt from a requirement to transact on an exchange.[8] In theory, the end-user exception *should* allow nonfinancial entities, such as utilities, which use swaps to hedge or mitigate "commercial risk," to continue to

8. Commodity Exchange Act § 2(h)(7) and 2(h)(8) (as amended).

hedge that risk as they have done historically in the OTC markets. However, end users are concerned that the exemption will be lost or made unusable during the CFTC rulemaking process—resulting in end users being inadvertently swept up in the Dodd-Frank Act regulations where Congress did not intend for them to be burdened.[9] That congressional "intent" is most clearly laid out in a letter written by Senators Dodd and Lincoln, as chairs of the responsible Senate committees, to Representatives Frank and Peterson, as chairs of the correlated House committees in Congress (the "Dodd-Lincoln Letter"). The Dodd-Lincoln Letter is cited numerous times in the congressional colloquies prior to voting on the Dodd-Frank Act. However, as the chair of the CFTC, Gary Gensler, has pointed out, it is not the Dodd-Lincoln Letter that guides the CFTC rulemaking, it is the Dodd-Frank Act itself.[10]

Even if an entity utilizes the "end user exception" from clearing and exchange-trading, end users who engage in swaps will still have to comply with CFTC registration, recordkeeping, and reporting regulations. And such regulatory compliance may be burdensome and costly. This, too, will be determined during the CFTC rulemaking process. The Dodd-Frank Act requires reporting of non-cleared swaps to one of the new registered entities or to the CFTC, and a swap to which no swap dealer or major swap participant is a party must be reported by one of the two parties to the transaction. Moreover, broad, internal recordkeeping policies are applicable in order for an end user to be in a position to comply with the CFTC reporting requirements. Finally, even if a utility presumes it will always be an end user and the nonreporting party, the end-user exception itself is predicated on the requirement that the end user notify the CFTC "how it generally meets its financial obligations associated with entering into non-cleared swaps."[11] The Dodd-Frank Act has authorized the CFTC to establish how detailed that notification needs to be (and how frequently it will need to be made.) These types of regulations will directly affect (increase) the costs borne by utilities to hedge their commercial risks using swaps.

In addition to these direct costs, the CFTC's regulation of other market participants will likely cause end-user utilities to incur indirect burdens and costs. After the definition of swap and the end-user exception, the third most important question for utilities is whether and how new CFTC margin rules for swap dealers and major swap participants will affect a utility's costs to engage in non-cleared swaps. The Dodd-Frank Act requires the CFTC to write margin rules that ensure the safety and soundness of swap dealers and major swap participants, and to avert systemic risk to the American financial system. However, if end users are (through broad or ambiguous rules) required to post margin for non-cleared hedging transactions, the economic benefit of the end-user clearing exception may be negated. The Dodd-Lincoln Letter made it clear this was not Congress's intent.

9. 156 Cong. Rec. H52248. Letter from the chairs of the U.S. Senate Committees on Financial Services and Agriculture (Sen. Christopher Dodd and Sen. Blanche Lincoln) to the chairs of the U.S. House Committees on Financial Services and Agriculture (Rep. Barney Frank and Rep. Colin Peterson) dated June 30, 2010.

10. Megawatt Daily, Sept. 17, 2010, at 1.

11. Commodity Exchange Act § 2(h)(7) (as amended).

The other, more subtle problem related to margin rules, is that if the end user's counterparty is required to maintain a certain amount of regulatory capital against an end user's transactions, it will pass those costs on to the end user. And, if the swap dealer is required for some reason to *post* margin to the end user, then the end user has to *hold and administer* that margin. In a bilateral, non-cleared world there is no central clearinghouse or exchange clearing member to hold and administer margin. There is only the other contract counterparty. And most utilities do not have sufficient back office staff to perform the necessary daily mark-to-market valuations on all outstanding transactions and hold, post, and exchange daily margin.

The whole concept of "margining" presumes a financial-intermediated world like the system that currently exists in the CFTC-regulated markets. And the costs of such financial-intermediation are one of the primary reasons why utilities today manage their commercial risks in the OTC markets.

The reforms Congress enacted under the Dodd-Frank Act were intended to bring "transactions and counterparties into a robust, conservative and transparent risk management framework." However Congress has acknowledged that not every transaction and counterparty needs to be regulated in this way.[12] Unfortunately, the text of the Dodd-Frank Act is broad and ambiguous, with additional confusion caused by missing cross-references and undefined or inconsistently referenced terms. The CFTC has been given the momentous task of creating regulatory order out of a sometimes chaotic and always complex tome of legislation. Although the CFTC has the ambition to bring order out of the chaos, the sweeping scope of change and the fragility of the various financial markets may require more time and study in order to impose such order without unintended and harmful consequences.

The Rulemaking Marathon (the CFTC Task Forces)

The CFTC rulemaking process began in September 2010, and the CFTC has, as of January 25, published two final rules, 33 proposed rules, and four of Advanced Notices of Proposed Rule-making for public comment.[13] As time marches forward, the overwhelming scope of this regulatory task is becoming clearer. The CFTC must promulgate and finalize rules under the Dodd-Frank Act that are effective to regulate a wide variety of markets, often in an environment of existing, specialized, and unique commodities and derivatives market structures.

The CFTC has established 30 "task forces," each comprised of CFTC staff members, and each focused on a specific topic under the Dodd-Frank Act. No one task force is dealing with all energy and energy-related (utility) issues. Some of the more impor-

---

12. The Dodd-Lincoln Letter.

13. CFTC Commissioner Scott D. O'Malia, Keynote Address by Commissioner Scott D. O'Malia, Title VII of the Dodd-Frank Act: 732 Pages and Counting, January 25, 2011, *available at* http://www.cftc.gov/PressRoom/SpeechesTestimony/opaomalia-3.html. Many more proposed rules were issued for comment by the CFTC in December 2010 and January 2011. For a current list see http://www.cftc.gov/LawRegulation/DoddFrankAct/Dodd-FrankProposedRules/index.htm.

tant task forces for utilities include: "Capital & Margin for Non-Banks" and "End User Exception." Each task force will recommend rules to the CFTC on its designated topics, and the public is invited to submit comments on those rules. Each task force has its own page on the CFTC website and its own e-mail address through which interested parties can submit comments. Utilities and utility trade associations are planning comments on 12 to 20 task force topics.

Although the CFTC has attempted to make the task forces an efficient division of labor, given the press of statutory deadlines, some in the industry have expressed concern that the task forces have evolved into separate "silos" of rulemaking—a structure that frequently requires commenters to repeat concepts and explanations to ensure that each individual task force is educated on the breadth of issues implicated by each discrete area of rulemaking. If each task force completes its marathon, and yet commercial business concepts and issues fall between the silos, the new Dodd-Frank Act market structure may yet prove unworkable.

Interim Deadlines

While all this rulemaking is proceeding, the CFTC has several interim statutory deadlines with which to contend. For example, in October the CFTC issued an "interim final rule" on swap reporting and record-keeping for noncleared "swaps." The interim final rule was supposed to tell entities transacting in noncleared swaps what CFTC reports they would need to file and, consequently, what records they should retain in order to be in a position to comply with CFTC reporting rules for "swaps" entered into prior to the enactment date of the Dodd-Frank Act. Unfortunately, the interim final rule was less than clear, partly because the definition of "swap" has yet to be finalized. Actual reporting has been deferred until new market infrastructure entities called "swap data repositories" are established (again through CFTC rulemaking). Most market participants are being advised that they should hold *all* information *related to* noncleared swaps entered into prior to the enactment date of the Dodd-Frank Act, freezing those records for and construing the term "swap" broadly until the CFTC gives further guidance. Some market participants have also asked the CFTC to implement a "safe harbor," so when the CFTC does begin requesting records, companies who have made a good-faith attempt to comply with the interim final rule will not be subject to penalties for inadvertently discarding information.

In late December, the CFTC issued a second "interim final rule" that purported to impose, without notice, recordkeeping obligations in respect of "transaction swaps"—those transactions entered into post-enactment date but prior to the effective date of final recordkeeping and reporting rules (which have not yet been proposed). The lack of notice, the accretive nature of the ongoing recordkeeping requirements, and the continuing ambiguities of undefined terms in the second interim final rule are troublesome.

The reporting requirements present an entire host of problems for energy utilities. Ultimately, the CFTC will have to identify precisely what will have to be reported, by whom, how it must be reported, to whom, in what format, and within what time periods. The Dodd-Frank Act calls for "real-time reporting." But, in the utility industry, the primary business focus is to deliver power and gas year-round and around-the-clock to

Main Street. Utilities are concerned that complying with such financial markets reporting rules will divert significant resources from utility operations while doing little to reduce systemic risk or bring "transparency" to the global financial markets.[14]

Another interim statutory deadline was for the CFTC to establish new regulatory position limits for futures, exchange-traded options, and "swaps" where the underlying asset is an "exempt commodity," which includes energy commodities. The position limits to be established are to be as appropriate to limit excessive speculation. According to the Dodd-Frank Act, the CFTC was to establish such position limits by January 17, 2011. But the CFTC has acknowledged that it does not have enough information about swaps markets (or the markets for individual underlying exempt commodities) to appropriately establish such limits.[15] Moreover the definitions and other rules that make up the foundation of the new market structure (including the definition of a "swap") were not finalized by the position limits deadline. Instead, on January 26, 2011, the CFTC issued for comment a proposed rule setting forth position limits for certain types of positions on certain exempt commodities.[16] Some CFTC commissioners have questioned whether position limits in energy swaps and commodities are appropriate at all, a matter that was debated by the CFTC even prior to the enactment of the Dodd-Frank Act.[17]

An additional statutory deadline of note was for a memorandum of understanding (MOU) establishing new jurisdictional lines between FERC and the CFTC, to be filed with relevant congressional committees by January 17, 2011.[18] The jurisdictional MOU was intended by Congress to encourage the agencies to work together to reduce overlapping and duplicative regulation of the energy markets, where in the past jurisdictional conflicts have been rife. The agencies were "to establish procedures to avoid any conflicting or overlapping regulation" so that the two agencies apply their respective authorities to ensure that the regulations created under the Dodd-Frank Act are effective and efficient. The utility industry was hopeful that the MOU would reflect agreement as to which regulator has primary (or secondary) jurisdiction over identified types

14. Commodity swaps overall (including energy, metals, agricultural, and other categories) represent less than one-half of 1% of the global OTC derivatives markets, *see* Table 19 of Bank for International Settlements semiannual OTC derivatives statistics *at* http://www.bis.org/statistics/derstats.htm (Dec. 31, 2009).

15. "In my view, no position limit is appropriate if it is imposed without the benefit of receiving and fully analyzing complete data concerning the open interest in each market." Concurring Statement Relating to the Commission's Proposal on Position Reports for Physical Commodity Swaps and Swaptions of Commissioner Jill Sommers dated October 19, 2010, *at* http://www.cftc.gov/PressRoom/SpeechesTestimony/CommissionerJillESommers/sommersstatement101910.html.

16. 76 Fed Reg. 4754 (Jan. 26, 2011) (Commissioner Bart Chilton concurring and Commissioner Jill Sommers dissenting).

17. "My grave concerns about moving forward with position limits have not been eased, and in fact, have only been heightened by certain provisions of Dodd-Frank. . . . I believe it is a mistake to interpret the arbitrary 180-day and 270-day deadlines as somehow trumping the requirement that the Commission make an appropriateness determination before imposing any position limits." Concurring Statement of Commissioner Jill Sommers, Oct. 19, 2010.

18. The Dodd Frank Act § 720(b).

of energy and energy-related physical or financial transactions, rather than continue the reciprocal "we have exclusive jurisdiction" standoff that has plagued the industry with unnecessary costs and compliance complexity. However, the statutory deadline passed and as of February 1, 2011, it seems no MOU has yet been agreed upon between the CFTC and FERC.

New "Cops" on the Energy Markets Beat

The Dodd-Frank Act gave the CFTC substantial new enforcement powers in the "swaps" markets—without guidance as to how the existing enforcement regimes in some markets should be coordinated. These new CFTC powers will likely result in more CFTC-FERC duplicative requirements and requests, and more compliance and enforcement complexity for utilities and other energy companies.

New Jurisdiction to Prohibit Market Manipulation and "Disruptive Trading Activity"

The CFTC is a financial market regulator focused on its mission to bring price transparency, liquidity and financial security to commodity and derivatives markets. The CFTC has a strong and effective enforcement staff to police the markets it regulates, and to punish violators of its market rules. The Dodd-Frank Act gave the CFTC new and expanded jurisdiction to prosecute "market manipulation" in the energy markets. The CFTC's enforcement jurisdiction is now concurrent with, if not broader than, FERC's jurisdiction and, in some cases, the jurisdiction of the antitrust regulators. But the CFTC is not governed by any of those regulators' enforcement precedents or agency interpretations. Again, utilities need to remember that the CFTC is not an energy market regulator. The activities of utilities as load serving entities will be analyzed not with their public service mission in mind, but with the same skeptical enforcement eye that analyzes the behaviors of any other market participant.

Be Aware—the Whistleblower Is Out There

Some commentators have called the Dodd-Frank Act whistleblower provisions the most dangerous and potentially costly provisions for energy companies. If a whistleblower provides to the CFTC "original information" that contributes to a CFTC enforcement action, and the CFTC "monetary sanctions" (including penalties, disgorgement, restitution, and interest to be paid) exceed, $1 million, new CEA § 23 *requires* payment to the whistleblower of a bounty between 10 percent and 30 percent of the amount of any such monetary sanctions.[19] Note that the whistleblower must be first in the door at the CFTC to be eligible for the bounty. But, if he or she qualifies, then there is a minimum reward of $100,000 and potentially much, much more.[20] The Dodd-Frank Act whistleblower provisions also provide job security for a whistleblower, with a private right of action to

19. CEA § 23(b)(1) (as amended).
20. CEA § 23(c)(2)(C) (as amended).

federal court for any claim that the company has retaliated against the whistleblower. This potential for both a bounty and job security might be especially attractive to a utility employee during a time period of regulatory uncertainty, employment insecurity, and economic hardship. In light of these new whistleblower provisions, utilities should review the effectiveness of their internal compliance programs.

Conclusion

The Dodd-Frank Act was enacted to increase transparency and stability in the financial markets. With such a broad and ambitious goal and with the political winds of change blowing in Washington, it may not be surprising that the law itself was written in sweeping and sometimes ambiguous language. The hope is that the CFTC, and other regulators, will clarify and synthesize the legislation into a workable regulatory framework, appropriately tailored for each different kind of transaction and each different market structure. A year may have seemed to Congress like plenty of time for the CFTC (and other regulators) to construct a safe and secure market structure for over-the-counter derivatives. But the Dodd-Frank Act does not just affect sophisticated financial market participants but also every day commercial businesses, and the myriad "markets" to be covered by such a new regulatory structure are dizzyingly complex.

Natural gas and electric utilities are a unique type of market participant—an end user with a commercial business to run *and* a public service responsibility to uphold. The energy swap transactions into which utilities enter are tailored to mitigate the unique commercial risks involved in generating, transmitting or transporting, and delivering natural gas and electricity to American consumers and businesses. No one on Wall Street has a similar public service responsibility. The reason utilities are challenged by the Dodd-Frank Act is the concern that their public service responsibility will get lost in the torrent of reform and the urge to meet unrealistic deadlines. And, if this concern is not addressed by careful, thoughtful, detailed rulemaking, the unintended adverse consequences for American energy consumers could be significant.

Be Aware. Utilities will be affected by this legislation and the rules that are being drafted. While end users will be likely be exempt from clearing and exchange-trading their swaps, there is no basis for assuming this will be a complete exemption from CFTC jurisdiction.

Be Prepared. Even the smallest natural gas and electric utilities should be educated about the potential changes the Dodd-Frank Act will require to energy and energy-related contracts, recordkeeping, and reporting requirements. Companies should begin to evaluate their energy contracting practices and current internal procedures, processes, and hedging with a view to the possible ways that the CFTC regulations will affect their businesses.

Get Involved. The CFTC is a financial markets regulator with little specialized knowledge of the energy industry. It is critical that the utility industry explain to the CFTC how it is different from the financial entities the CFTC is used to regulating. Utilities should consider joining in the public comment process to educate the CFTC on why the utilities have always been, and will always be, unique participants in the energy markets.

~~~~~~~~~~
~~~~~~~~~~

2012 Update

By Patricia Dondanville

The Regulatory Uncertainty Continues for Utilities

When our article was published in the *Infrastructure* Winter 2011 edition, we had no idea how long the regulatory uncertainty would continue under the Dodd-Frank Act and the Commodity Futures Trading Commission's (CFTC's) implementation rulemakings for energy companies, electric and natural gas utilities, and other commercial enterprises. The CFTC has now, on three different occasions, extended the deadline by which Congress expected the new regulatory regime for "swaps" to be in place when the Dodd-Frank Act was enacted in July of 2010. The first extension was granted on July 14, 2011, in a complicated exemption order intended to mitigate potential market disruptions if the "automatic" provisions of the Dodd-Frank Act had actually taken effect. That first extension was to have expired on December 31, 2011, the second extension was to have expired on July 16, 2012, and the current extension will expire on December 31, 2012, or such other compliance date as may be determined by the CFTC.

The CFTC has now proposed more than 50 rules for comment, held 18 public roundtables, received more than 35,000 comment letters on its proposed rules, and met more than 1,800 times with entities that anticipate being subject to the new regulatory regime. As of September 24, 2012, the CFTC has issued 39 final rules and 8 final orders. More than 15 of the final rules are designated as "major" rules under the Congressional Review Act, meaning that the Office of Management and Budget has determined, based on submissions by the Commission, that *each* of these major rules will result in or is likely to result in (1) an annual impact on the economy of $100 million or more; (2) a major increase in costs or prices for consumers; individual industries; federal, state, or local government agencies; or geographic regions; or (3) significant adverse effects on competition, employment, investment, productivity, innovation, or the ability of U.S.-based enterprises to compete with foreign-based enterprises in domestic and export markets.

In May of 2011, the CFTC (in conjunction with the SEC) issued a proposed rule and an extensive regulatory interpretation with respect to Section 721(a)(21) of the Dodd-Frank Act—the new Commodity Exchange Act definition of "swap" and the exclusions therefrom. Earlier, in late February of 2011, the CFTC also issued a proposed rule on commodity options, interpreting the Dodd-Frank Act to have eliminated the trade option exemption for nonfinancial (or "physical") commodity options between commercial entities, even where the parties intend physical settlement (or delivery and receipt) of the commodity. The public submitted more than 200 comment letters on those two proposed rulemakings. The energy industry sought clear guidance in particular on which energy industry transactions would fall within the definition of "swap" in new Clean Energy Act (CEA) 1a(47), and which would be excluded by new CEA Section 1a(47)(B)(ii). That provision, new CEA 1a(47)(B)(ii), provides a statutory exclusion from the defined term "swap" for "any sale of a nonfinancial commodity . . . for deferred shipment or delivery so long as the transaction is intended to be physically settled[.]" (See Section 721(a)(21) of the Dodd-Frank Act.)

Congress indicated in the "Dodd-Lincoln letter" (discussed in the original article and cited in footnote 9 thereof) that the CFTC should clarify through rulemaking that the exclusion is intended to be "consistent with the forward contract exclusion that is currently in the Commodity Exchange Act and the CFTC's established policy and orders on this subject. (See the Dodd-Lincoln letter at page 3.)

In mid-August 2012, the CFTC and the SEC published in the *Federal Register* a joint release embodying their "final" rulemakings and regulatory guidance on Section 721(a)(21) of the Dodd-Frank Act, interpreting the definition of "swap" and the exclusions therefrom. Separately, in late April of 2012, the CFTC published in the *Federal Register* its final "Commodity Option" rules, along with an "interim final" rule announcing a new exemption for nonfinancial commodity trade options between commercial entities, with several new conditions. In both of these purportedly final rulemakings, the CFTC requested more public comments on a number of aspects of the rules, conditions, interpretations, and guidance provided. Many of these requests relate directly to the regulatory treatment of contracts, agreements, and transactions common in the energy industry. Comments are now due in mid-October 2012.

Notwithstanding the continuing regulatory uncertainty surrounding the defined term "swap" and the nonfinancial commodity transaction exclusion therefrom, the commodity trade option exemption, and the conditions and regulatory guidance on which the public has not yet commented (as well as the CFTC's as-yet unanswered questions), these rulemakings have effective dates concurrent with the mid-October 2012 deadline for public comments. In mid-August 2012, the CFTC issued a "no action" letter in respect of the trade option exemption interim final rule—until December 31, 2012. As of September 24, 2012, no such relief has been issued in respect of the regulatory interpretations of the Dodd-Frank Act's definition of "swap" and the all-important exclusion for nonfinancial commodity transactions.

In addition to the regulatory uncertainty caused by these two incomplete rulemakings, the CFTC has yet to file with Congress the two memoranda of understanding with FERC that the original article discusses. (See footnote 18 and the accompanying text.) Such interagency memoranda were to have provided the energy industry with protection from overlapping and duplicative rules and enforcement proceedings. Moreover, the CFTC has pending before it numerous requests for rule amendments, interpretations, determinations authorized under its regulations, and for "no action" relief of various types and relevant to various of its Dodd-Frank Act rulemakings—many of which will affect the energy industry. Several of the regional transmission organizations and independent system operators, as well as trade associations for government-owned electric utilities and electric cooperatives, have filed petitions for "public interest waivers" of CFTC jurisdiction under Section 722(f) of the Dodd-Frank Act. Although the CFTC has proposed exemptions for these entities, those exemptions are not yet final and are, in certain respects, conditional. Moreover, a number of other important CFTC rulemakings have been proposed but not finalized (such as the CFTC's margin and capital regulations for "swap dealers" and exemptions from affiliated entities) or have not yet been proposed at all (such as the CFTC's promised guidance on guarantees of "swaps."

In late September 2012, several energy trade associations requested the CFTC to provide energy market participants with comprehensive relief to avoid serious disruption to the markets for both energy commodities and energy derivatives until such time as the CFTC completes its rulemakings implementing the Dodd-Frank Act's new regulatory regime applicable to nonfinancial energy and energy-related commodity "swaps." Since the original article was published in *Infrastructure* in February of 2011, there has been lots of rulemaking activity at the CFTC and elsewhere in global financial regulatory agencies. However, the regulatory uncertainty continues for energy companies, including electric and natural utilities, that rely on energy and energy-related commodities and derivatives to hedge the commercial risks arising from their operations.

Chapter 30

Debt Ceiling Debate Portends Corporate Tax Reform*

*By David R. Hardy and Martha Groves Pugh***

Amidst the intense partisan bickering of the summer months over the increase in the national debt ceiling, few areas of consensus or even compromise emerged. However, some of the announced possibilities for a compromise included increased tax revenues generally relying upon the recommendations of the Simpson Bowles-Bipartisan National Commission on Fiscal Responsibility and Reform, The Moment of Truth Report (hereinafter, the "Simpson-Bowles Report or report") released in December 2010.[1] The top Republican leadership expressed at various times its willingness to consider corporate tax reforms based upon the Simpson-Bowles Report recommendations: corporate tax simplification through a reduction of spending hidden in the tax code, which the report refers to as a reduction in tax expenditures, and the a reduction in corporate tax rates.[2] The final debt ceiling compromise signed into law on August 2, 2011, left many of the specifics of debt reduction for determination by a future congressional panel. It is by no means certain that corporate tax reform could be enacted prior to the upcoming national elections in 2012. Nonetheless, regulated industries such as those represented by the membership of the Public Utility, Communication and Transportation Law section would do well to consider the recommendation of the Simpson-Bowles Report and the effect that such enactment might have on their business, revenues, and financial statements.

---

* Originally published in *Infrastructure*, vol. 51, no. 1 (Fall, 2011).

** *David R. Hardy is a partner with Osler, Hoskin & Harcourt LLP in its New York office where his focus is corporate and international tax law. Martha Groves Pugh is counsel in McDermott Will & Emery LLP's Washington office with an emphasis on federal income tax issues.*

1. THE MOMENT OF TRUTH: REPORT OF THE NATIONAL COMMISSION ON FISCAL RESPONSIBILITY AND REFORM *available at* http://www.fiscalcommission.gov/sites/fiscalcommission.gov/files/documents/TheMomentofTruth12_1_2010.pdf (or go to www.fiscalcommission.gov/news and click on the title).

2. *Id.* at 15.

Deficit Debate

In the deliberations regarding the increase in the national debt limit, considerable attention was given to the importance of balance in the reduction of entitlement programs coupled with new revenue sources. While the far right members of the Tea Party movement were adverse to any deficit reduction funded by a source other than reduction in government spending, the more moderate elements of the Republican Party, including its principal leadership, Speaker John Boehner (R-OH), and Senate Minority Leader Mitch McConnell (R-KY), expressed openness to the consideration of tax reform as an element in the overall plan to reduce the federal deficit by $4 to $5 trillion dollars over the next 10 years. This message found some support in the statements of Eric Cantor (R-VA), House majority leader for the Republican Party and Paul Ryan (R-WI), the chairman of the House Budget Committee. In their comments, they appeared to echo the statements of the Simpson-Bowles Report panel that corporate competitiveness required major restructuring and rate reduction that would include closing of tax expenditures (also sometimes referred to loosely as "loop holes").

The enacted compromise contained no required revenue increases. To be sure, the discussion of corporate tax reform is complicated by itself and more complex when coupled with individual tax reform, which raise the "fairness" issues about the relative apportionment of the income tax burden among individual US individuals. In the deficit increase compromise, an initial $900 billion dollar increase in the debt ceiling is specified. The next $1.2 to $1.5 trillion in debt ceiling increase to be enacted before the end of 2011 would require reductions in spending or revenue increases proposed by a congressional panel. While revenue increases are not required in such a process, the failure to reach bipartisan congressional agreement on further deficit reductions will result in mandatory reductions to the defense budget and payments to Medicare service providers—priorities designed to induce both parties to compromise. Thus, while it is impossible to describe US corporate tax reform as imminent, it has certainly been identified in the mix of policy choices.

Simpson-Bowles Report Recommendations

During 2009, the Obama administration commissioned a bipartisan panel ("Fiscal Responsibility Commission") lead by very two credible senior citizens of our government—Alan Simpson, former Republican senator from Wyoming, and Erskine Bowles, former White House chief of staff under the Clinton administration, to consider options for revising the projected increases in our national debt. While the Simpson-Bowles Report did not obtain the level of consensus required to force the administration to formally propose their recommendations, its broad recognition of the fiscal crisis and the brave recommendations received much applause throughout the media and the economic and business communities.

The report broadly described how the national debt calculated even at the federal level only (excluding state and local debt) was on a course to exceed 100 percent of the gross domestic product, levels at which interest on the debt becomes crippling. The report proceeded to describe a mixture of reductions to entitlement programs, most notably Social Security cost-of-living adjustments, and defense budget and discretionary spending. While not specifically mentioned in the Simpson-Bowles Report, it has been frequently observed that the failure of the United States to enact credible budgetary corrections will undermine the United States credit rating and invariably lead the markets to demand higher interest rates for the US debt, further increasing the interest cost of the national debt. Such interest rate increases obviously make more difficult the reversal of long-term structural deficits. With these expenditure recommendations came a broad group of significant tax reforms. Both for individuals and for corporate taxpayers, the reforms called for a sharp reduction in tax expenditures and a commensurate reduction in tax rates designed to generate higher levels of compliance. Among the individual changes would be to convert mortgage interest deductions and charitable donation deductions to 12 percent tax credit, to tax interest on newly issued municipal bonds, to phase out itemized deductions, to cap tax-free employer-provided health insurance, to tax capital gains and dividends at ordinary rates, and to reduce individual tax rates from the current 35 percent (reverting in 2013 to 39.6 percent) to between 23 percent and 24 percent.[3] While the reader will quickly see the constituencies forming against each and every such proposal, one can also observe the coverage, the broad participation, and the logic of the structure.

The Fiscal Responsibility Commission's recommendations for corporate tax reform were even more striking than the individual changes. The commission specifically recognized that American corporations have now faced the highest nominal rates of income tax of all of our trading partners. While effective rates of particular corporate taxpayers vary depending upon losses, debt structure, and foreign income, the commission saw distinct economic benefits to American corporations and American employment from the elimination of incentives for the tax planning that American-based corporations have utilized. Thus, in its proposal, the Fiscal Responsibility Commission would eliminate the domestic manufacturing deduction, LIFO inventory, general business credits, and most other current tax expenditures.[4]

In addition, it would convert the United States to a territorial income tax system like that employed by nearly all of our trading partners under which US corporations would not pay US income tax on active business income earned outside the United States or received from affiliates operating outside the United States.[5] Under this structure, corporate tax rates would be reduced from the current 35 percent to 28 percent roughly equivalent to the rate being imposed now, or soon to be imposed, by Canada, the UK, the Netherlands, and others. Notwithstanding, the courageous and farsighted approach of the Simpson-Bowles Report and the universal praise it received, the report was dropped into the budgetary debate in Washington making barely a ripple. The administration has not yet proposed legislation to take into account the report's recommendations. However, the report has established a significant and universally recognized base line for the serious discussion of budgetary reform in the future.

3. *Id.* at 29–32.
4. *Id.* at 32–35.
5. *Id.*

Corporate Tax Reform Uncertainties

All observers of the American political process will quickly recognize that tax reform is among the most challenging areas in which to generate consensus. Politicians have become increasingly unwilling to consider tax changes in years prior to national elections because the consequence of improperly assessing the public's attitudes can be political death. For this reason, among others, it is often assumed that it is only in the congressional term immediately following a national election, where one party or the other appears to have some form of national mandate, that tax reform can emerge. One resounding difference between the Republican position and the Democratic position on tax reform is the Republicans' unwillingness to consider corporate tax reform separate and apart from individual tax reform.

In addition to the timing uncertainties, the regulated industries have a somewhat unique relationship to income tax that also makes the impact of the corporate tax reform recommendation of the Simpson-Bowles Report even more uncertain. The Fiscal Responsibility Commission's recommendation for corporate tax reform was in no small part based upon its assertion that US multinational corporations competed in an international marketplace where their foreign competitors were generally not taxed on their international income. This competitive disadvantage to US corporations could result either in the loss of US employment or progressively in the acquisition of US corporations by foreign multinational conglomerates that were operating with a competitive advantage.

In the context of regulated companies, however, governments have imposed economic rate regulation on companies because they are perceived to be natural monopolies that do not face competition. Thus, in order to provide a regulated rate of return on equity to electric distribution and transmission utilities, gas and oil pipelines, and other industries subject to rate regulations, such companies are permitted to include their income tax expense as a cost of service and add it to the rates charged to their customers. In this respect, regulated companies act much like what many economists have asserted a corporation actually does, which is to pass its income tax costs through to customers as an increased cost of the goods and services they sell. Regulated companies are in a sense operating similarly to a withholding agent for sales tax or a valued added tax that many have asserted are much more efficient tax mechanisms, and less apt to disrupt and disturb efficient economic decision making. It is conceivable then that if corporate income tax reform were to occur, regulated industries would not be beneficiaries of the rate reductions being broadly offered. However, the authors perceive a greater likelihood that fundamental corporate income tax reform with reduction in rates coupled with reduction in tax expenditure would be applied uniformly to all corporate taxpayers including regulated companies.

Targeted Tax Expenditures

The Simpson-Bowles Report recommendations on corporate tax reform states that our current system "is a patchwork of overly complex and inefficient provisions that creates perverse incentives for investment."[6] The report also states that a reduction in complexity and rates should lead to better economic decision making and reduce the incentives for complex and improper avoidance schemes.[7] The view of the report is that if tax expenditures are eliminated, rates can be reduced. Moreover, it is possible that corporate rate reduction coupled with elimination of tax expenditures and the other competitive benefits to US-based corporations might actually be scored as a revenue generator by the Congressional Budget Office whose determinations are critical to the success of particular budget proposals.

Certain of the primary identified corporate tax expenditures have relatively little application to regulated industries. Thus, the repeal of the last in, first out (LIFO) inventory method of accounting, which may be extremely important to the natural resource industry and other manufacturing businesses, is relatively unimportant to regulated industries that generate revenue from service. So also, the elimination of tax on foreign source active business income would have relatively little application to the domestic activities of US-regulated businesses. Some corporations in regulated industries, of course, have acquired affiliates outside the United States and will be more sensitive to such a change. The Simpson-Bowles Report also identifies the domestic production deduction for elimination.[8] That 9 percent deduction for qualified production activities was extended to all US manufacturing companies as a replacement to the prior US export incentive (e.g., DISC, FSC, and Extraterritorial Income Exclusion).[9] US-regulated companies in the electric generation area have utilized such deductions but may well favor an exchange of those deductions for a reduction in rates generally.

Perhaps of greater significance to regulated corporations would be the proposal to eliminate general business credits and all other tax expenditures.[10] For some years, the development of alternative and environmentally preferable types of energy generation has been specifically induced by tax credits.[11] Credits have been used to support geothermal energy production, wind energy, solar energy, and bio-fuel development. Certainly, tax professionals have seen many instances where these credits have been utilized in a manner having little to do with the actual generation of the relevant product or technology, and some of the underlying businesses have no independent viability absent the tax credit. It appears relatively clear that the elimination of credits would result in a more effective tax policy, more efficient collection, and the reduction in incentives for abuse. On the other hand, certain energy policy goals for development of alternative generation of electricity would be underfunded in the absence of the existing credits. It will remain for Congress to determine whether the repeal of these credits needs to be offset by other specific economic subsidies to continue the encouragement of the growth of such businesses.

---

6. *Id.* at 32.
7. *Id.*
8. *Id.* at 33.
9. I.R.C. § 199 (1986).
10. Moment of Truth Report at 33.
11. I.RC. §§ 45, 48 (1986).

Financial Statement Impacts—Normalization

Whenever corporate income tax rates or structure are changed, corporate financial statements will be affected. If a corporation has net operating loss carry forward or alternative minimum tax credit carry forward, as many regulated companies do, such tax attributes would normally be carried on their balance sheet as a deferred tax asset. The value of these assets reflects the projected income tax rates that will be incurred. If tax rates drop, the value of deferred tax assets is reduced and this may result in a reduction of earnings potentially characterized as an extraordinary item.

Corporations subject to rate regulation have a different relationship to income tax than nonregulated businesses. These differences can cause unexpected balance sheet impacts when tax rates or methods change. In general, regulated companies treat their income tax expense as a cost of service that flows through to rates charged to customers. That simple statement obscures the incredible complexity of the calculation of tax expense particularly as it relates to long-lived assets that may be subject to different depreciation lives for accounting purposes and tax purposes.

For example, if a US electric company acquires new transmission lines with an economic life of 30 years, the rate regulators would generally expect that the cost of such new plant and equipment to be passed through as a cost of services ratably over the 30-year economic life of such equipment. Similarly, for rate regulation purposes the income tax benefit of such depreciation would also be applied to reduce the company's income tax over the same economic life. For income tax purposes, however, the acquisition of new plant and equipment may be subject to accelerated depreciation designed to create incentives for new plant and equipment acquisition to stimulate the economy. Currently, the US tax code includes a bonus depreciation policy that permits 50 percent (or 100 percent in certain instances) of the cost of new plant and equipment to written off in the year the equipment is first placed in service.[12]

These policy differences between the tax policy incentives designed to stimulate equipment purchases and the rate regulators objective of having rates reflect the true economic cost of service result in substantial timing differences between tax accounting and regulatory accounting. Thus, if a regulated industry acquires new plant and equipment and writes it off as a bonus depreciation item in the year it is placed in service against income subject to tax at the rate of 35 percent, regulators are generally required by the normalization rules to treat only the actual first year economic depreciation as having been incurred and to give effect only to that portion of the depreciation expense for tax purposes. The additional tax benefit caused by the federal income tax incentives create deferred tax benefits that the regulators will amortize over the economic life of the equipment. If the nominal tax rates drop from 35 percent to 25 percent during the time period between the plant acquisition and the amortization of such cost for regulated rate purposes, the regulated company in this example would end up actually paying substantially less income tax than it charged for rate making purposes. In some states, rate regulators have been aggressive in limiting tax expense

12. I.R.C. § 168 (1986).

to "taxes actually paid." If the normalization rules are not enforced to prevent this, corporate tax reform could cause unwelcome surprises for regulated corporations and their stock analysts.

Conclusion

While this summer's deficit debate was an unpleasant drama for the country, it clearly portends further installments devoted to revenue increases. Corporate tax reform is a very likely candidate as an avenue to raise revenue. Regulated corporations should consider carefully their unique objectives in this debate.

2012 Update

By David R. Hardy and Martha Groves Pugh

Since the publication of the original article on the debt ceiling in the Fall 2011 issue of *Infrastructure*, the U.S. debate regarding the important fiscal changes has sharpened in intensity without meaningfully advancing toward consensus. The U.S. economy remains sluggish despite some recovery from the recession. The imminence of the "fiscal cliff" posed by the combination of scheduled individual tax increases and governmental expenditure reductions threatens to push the U.S. economy back into recession in 2013. While this increases the probability of corporate tax reform aimed at increasing revenues, the nature of those reforms may not be clear until the seating of the new Congress in 2013.

As we previously reported, the debt ceiling compromise of August 2011 provided for fixed reductions in governmental spending, primarily on the defense budget and certain health-care service provider reimbursement amounts, if a bipartisan panel of congressional leaders were unable to enact alternative budget savings. During the Fall of 2011, that bipartisan panel was unable to reach any agreement. Accordingly, the specified $900 billion reductions for calendar 2011 were implemented as prescribed and an additional $1.2 trillion is scheduled to occur at the end of 2012. Yet the current Congress is in a legislative paralysis, predictable in a presidential election year.

Stories in the financial press predict that even without contagion from Europe's sovereign debt crisis, the United States faces a fiscal cliff at the beginning of 2013. The fiscal cliff refers to the combination of the expiration of the agreed-upon extension of the Bush tax cuts coupled with the scheduled implementation of the reduction in federal spending. Together the tax increases and the reductions in governmental expenditures would pull 4 percent of the U.S. gross domestic product out of the economy, pushing the country back into recession.

A fundamental reform of the corporate and individual income tax that includes base broadening and reduction in tax expenditures will likely not occur this year, even in the post-election lame-duck Congress. An additional tax extension for the Bush cuts and other adjustments to the mandated governmental expenditure reduction, however, might give the new Congress sufficient time to address these very significant changes in 2013 after the presidential and congressional elections.

Chapter 31

A Book Review: Daniel Yergin's "The Quest"*

*By Hon. Richard D. Cudahy***

Daniel Yergin has presented us again with a fascinating (and potentially best-selling) book about energy—a fitting sequel to *The Prize*, his Pulitzer-prized historical account of the oil business. *The Quest* is a unique combination: It joins an encyclopedic critique of practically every aspect of energy with the qualities of the page-turner—you can't put it down. Its 700+ pages seem to go by as if they were only 100.

Of course, it has its controversial aspects. One of these is Yergin's vociferous and extensive rejection of "peak oil" theories—the view of many working and academic geologists that peak oil production is an event now current or at least imminent, and production will henceforth decline like the right-hand side of a bell-shaped curve. This idea found its origins in the statistical work of Dr. M. King Hubbert, whom Yergin characterizes as an "eminent earth scientist of his time," but he subjects the theory to a withering critique on the merits, not to mention an unflattering portrait of Hubbert as something of a political crackpot and a nasty personality. Hubbert successfully predicted the peak of oil production in the United States (1970), and this is apparently the solid basis of his reputation as a seer.

Yergin's critique may be subject to some question in detail as in his claim that Saudi Arabia's long-standing oil production is still expanding—a conclusion in marked contrast with the work of the knowledgeable Matthew R. Simmons (recognized but without comment in a Yergin footnote), who sees Saudi reserves as heavily tapped and Saudi oil's prospects for growth as seriously impaired.[1] In general, "peak oil" is rejected by economists whose emphasis on technological innovation is a response to every note of doom and gloom. And Yergin is not to be outdone in his unqualified commitment to the potential of developing technologies to squeeze oil out of unyielding surroundings or to transform it from inhospitable forms (or otherwise to make oil

---

* Originally published in *Infrastructure*, vol. 51, no. 2 (Winter, 2012).

* *Richard D. Cudahy, a judge with the US Court of Appeals, Seventh Circuit, is editor-in-chief of* Infrastructure *newsletter.*

1. Matthew R. Simmons, Twilight in the Desert, The Coming Saudi Oil Shock and the World Economy (2005).

out of non-oil). Perhaps it would help to moderate slightly the bitter clash over "peak oil" to recognize that this theory purports to focus its forecast on "conventional" oil production, not just any stuff that can be made to emulate oil. Perhaps also, these differing views of the future merely reflect differing philosophies of history. The progressive view (Yergin's) with its faith that the human intellect can almost continuously make things better contrasts with the cyclical expectation that things inevitably get worse (perhaps for a long time) before they may eventually get better.*The Quest* begins with a thorough discussion of modern developments in oil and other hydrocarbons, evolved from the absorption of solar energy by organic matter under pressure. The exploitation of hydrocarbons laid the basis for the Industrial Revolution. There is extensive treatment of oil development in Russia and in former Soviet areas to its south. These latter areas (foremost, the Caspian) are where the earliest discoveries took place in the nineteenth century, and they are still significant with contention now centering on the building of pipelines, where the United States has sought to avoid transit through Russia. The biggest new fields are in Kazakhstan, where US companies have sought to be big players and pipeline routes (including routes to China) and financing continue to be issues. As a sidelight, a Dutch oil trader, John Deuss, provided the oil know-how in Kazakhstan, which was headed, as were most of the former Soviet Muslim states, by a former Soviet apparchnik.

Of particular interest in the oil discussion is the history and analysis of mergers to produce "supermajor" companies. Interestingly, the biggest of these was between Exxon and Mobil. In their former guise as Standard Oil of New Jersey and Standard Oil of New York, these were the two biggest pieces of Rockefeller's Standard Oil Company, broken apart by federal antitrust decree in 1911. But the Federal Trade Commission ruled, "that this was not 1911 but rather a very different world."

With interesting insights into developments in Iraq, Nigeria, China, and other venues, *The Quest* turns extensive attention to Venezuela and specifically to the career and misdeeds of Hugo Chavez, who emerges as its leading villain. This certainly accords with US foreign policy and media treatment, and I suppose it is no surprise for it to be a matter of such emphasis.

In any event, the book turns from such foreign musings to a very challenging analysis of the "unconventional" aspects of hydrocarbon recovery, including deep-water drilling—sometimes gone horribly wrong, as with the Deepwater Horizon in the Gulf of Mexico. Also, unconventional (to say the least) are the oil sands (also known as the tar sands) of Alberta, which are rated a "mega-resource" with, apparently, a major future in the North American energy picture. Yergin notes many of the potentially crippling cost and environmental difficulties of developing the sands, a process hugely consumptive of water and natural gas, blatantly disruptive of land, and prodigiously productive of carbon dioxide emissions.[2] There are questions (though not Yergin's) whether, considering the inputs (including natural gas), this process is a net yielder of energy. But Canada has relied on this process to claim 175 billion barrels of proven (oil sands) reserves, making Canada number two, just behind Saudi Arabia, in proven oil reserves. Yergin counts the

2. Kenneth S. Deffeye, Beyond Oil, The View from Hubbert's Peak,102-5, 107-8 (2005).

proven reserves as an enormous recoverable resource and, in accordance with his general outlook, looks to "further technological progress" to release a trillion or more additional barrels. Here Yergin's steadfast optimism contrasts starkly with much cold water that has been dowsed on these projects over the years.

Although also a hydrocarbon with a touch of the same carbon problems as its chemical cousins, natural gas looms as the growth fuel of the future. And its astonishing domestic availability in the form of shale gas is undoubtedly the foremost current cause for rejoicing in energy circles—and particularly for its promise in the generation of electricity. This prospect has been proclaimed by no less an authority than John W. Rowe, CEO of the electric (and nuclear-electric) giant, Exelon, recently in the pages of this periodical. Rowe sees the vast volumes of shale gas available from the fracturing of rock in US fields as a stabilizer of gas prices and hence of the resulting prices of electricity.Yergin totally agrees with this glowing estimate of shale gas, obtained by the "fracking" (hydraulic fracturing) of rock by water under high pressure, a process developed through the lonely persistence of Houstonian George P. Mitchell and improved by horizontal drilling. Yergin, I think, understands the clamorous objections to these developments as polluting the drinking water supply, but believes the problems manageable through careful attention and the application of an evolving technology. Shale gas, globally proliferating liquefied natural gas, pipeline gas all over Europe, and other developments comprise what Yergin sees as the "natural gas revolution." Presumably, this is an interim development on the way to a nonhydrocarbon future, but in his view there is no need to rush to this paradise. He sees it off in the distance but not without a lengthy prologue devoted to natural gas and other more or less familiar fuels.

But Yergin's exploration of energy is, of course, by no means limited to hydrocarbons. He devotes a generous treatment to the mysterious phenomenon of electricity, citing two great capitalists, J. P. Morgan, who helped to finance Edison's pioneering power plant at Pearl Street in New York City, and Samuel Insull, who developed the modern electric utility by exploiting immense economics of scale to drive prices down and usage correspondingly up, and furthered important metering and other technology. Unfortunately, Insull's final lurch into gigantism—the proliferating utility holding company—foundered on the rocks of over-leverage amid the storms of the Great Depression, leaving tens of thousands of stockholders stripped of assets and clamoring for his blood. After seeking refuge in Greece, he was tried for mail fraud before a jury in Chicago in 1934 and acquitted (after telling the story of his necessitous youth in England and assistantship to Thomas Edison in Menlo Park). Thereafter, he departed, almost penniless, to Paris, were he died in 1938. Insull also was one of the earliest to advocate state regulation of electric power.

Balancing the pioneering of capitalists in electricity was the government's role in the creation of the Rural Electrification Administration, bringing power to farms and transforming rural life. Also in the public sector were the Tennessee Valley Authority; the Hoover, Bonneville, and Grand Coulee Dams; and much else. Ronald Reagan prepared for his forthcoming political career by promoting electricity and its mushrooming uses on television for General Electric. The striking growth in need for power met the astounding release of energy by nuclear fission first in the promotion of Atoms for Peace and later in the nuclear Navy, through the engineering genius of Yergin's and

Jimmy Carter's favorite hero, Hyman Rickover. The partial meltdown of a nuclear reactor core at Three Mile Island in the Susquehanna River in 1979 signaled the end of nuclear power plant building in the United States, although there has been recent talk of revival that was muffled again by the Japanese earthquake and tsunami disaster at the Fukushima Daiichi nuclear station in 2011. Here, Yergin makes no effort to pronounce a final verdict but reports a smattering of cautious comments around the world, continued apparent support of nuclear power by the US administration, and John Rowe's continued preference for natural gas (on economic rather than safety grounds).

Another development of the 1990s was the arrival of restructuring or deregulation at the door of electricity. Because competition was an essential ingredient of this development and capital-intensive electric power was the least amenable of the infrastructure industries to effective competition and probably the most inherently fitted to monopoly, attempts to deregulate electricity seemed fraught with more problems and imperfect results than most similar efforts elsewhere. One pervasive problem was the practice of selling deregulatory efforts to the public as the royal road to lower rates, and then frequently not delivering them (or delivering just the opposite). Yergin describes and analyzes the efforts of California to lead the nation in adopting a comprehensive electric deregulation law, which led to a spectacular fiasco of rolling blackouts, bankrupt utilities, accusations of piracy against out-of-state generators, and, finally, the recall of a sitting governor. *The Quest*, I think, attempts a fair and balanced evaluation of these surprising developments, noting major contradictions in the law itself, unexpected electric demand conditions, irregular and fraudulent practices by out-of-state generators, and a variety of other causes of failure. The book, perhaps wisely, attempts to pass no final judgment on whether, in general, deregulation was a good idea—a proposition generally assumed but categorically rejected before he died by Joseph Swidler, former chairman of the Federal Power Commission and of the New York Public Service Commission.[3]

Not surprisingly, *The Quest* devotes a whole part to climate change, the origins of the theory and the global and domestic developments that have marked its impact on the world of energy. In what struck me as a perceptive introduction to the subject of climate change, Yergin recounts the doings of a British scientist, John Tyndall (described as "one of the great British scientists of the nineteenth century") in the 1850s in studying every aspect of glaciers in Switzerland, from which grew knowledge of an Ice Age and from that, knowledge of atmospheric conditions affecting the coming and going of the Ice Age—subjects that others before Tyndall had also explored. This seems a persuasive aspect of the climate change issue since it shows that the theory did not appear full-blown recently out of nothing as a response to some political need but has evolved naturally by degrees over many decades. Yergin's treatment of this belief, increasingly a political football, seems to me an eminently fair (and persuasive) statement of the science, its history, and the policy efforts resulting from it, unburdened with the econo-political baggage that can accompany it (e.g., international control, heavy requirements for planning and regulation, substantial economic burdens, etc.). Yergin effectively stands

3. Joseph C. Swidler, *An Unthinkably Horrible Situation*, 128 PUB. UTIL. FORT. 14 (Sept. 15, 1991) at 14.

behind climate-change-from-human-activity doctrine but equally supports cap-and-trade and other market remedies for environmental problems.

Moving from the problem—global warming—to the remedy—renewables—*The Quest* discusses the most promising of these at length. Wind is probably the most widely implemented and may be the most viable from a cost perspective. One of Yergin's fascinating historical notes involves the development of stand-alone wind machines on farms in the United States where the machines traditionally pumped water but came to generate electricity to light lights and power appliances. Much of this would pass into history when the New Deal's REA began to deliver cheaper power over grids to rural America, thus displacing the windmills. California became the site of what Yergin calls a "wind rush" and was for a time "the Saudi Arabia of wind." "Developers found out how truly violent and turbulent and unpredictable those [California] winds could be . . . ." The California wind business was heavily dependent on federal and state tax credits. Later, as energy prices dropped, the wind business declined with them. A persistent problem with wind is, of course, intermittency: wind doesn't blow consistently and may blow mostly at night when there is little need for power. To meet this problem, wind farms must generally be paired with a parallel gas-fired system at, of course, added cost. Also, wind farms in remote but windy prairies require a lot of transmission to reach the load—a cost element sought to be cured in part at least by locating wind machines in maritime sites, also windy, but closer to the load. Of course, placement on the water in itself is more expensive.Another renewable of promise is, of course, solar energy—first proposed by Einstein as described by Yergin in another of his many interesting historical asides. *The Quest* follows in detail the leading research developments involving solar energy over the years (and featuring photovoltaics) as well as the fluctuations in interest in this research and its applications as the price of oil rose and fell. This is, of course, an aspect of the phenomenon of interest in energy generally—only intense when oil prices rise to uncomfortable levels. And the other side of this coin in the solar and related fields is the importance of cost as a crucial condition of utility. Solar energy is also affected by the limitation of intermittency: it isn't much available on cloudy days or at all at night. Intermittency, of course, impairs dispatchability. Yergin attempts to explore solar's achievement of "grid parity" (a measure of comparative cost involving only direct costs to the consumer, not including investment in backup power and transmission) and believes that, where electricity may be expensive, grid parity may be near but not here yet. He quotes one authority that "All grid-connected markets are subsidized" and if there is a subsidy the market is not yet real.

Looking to the future and promising fuels, this book covers in detail the history and prospects of American ethanol (once denounced during Prohibition as pumped from a "potential speakeasy") as well as the Brazilian sugar-based variety. He notes the questions about the energy balance in using ethanol and pursues the prospects of cellulosic ethanol and its possible plant sources. In another vein, Yergin pursues the electric car, hybrids, and battery research. He even dips for a paragraph or two into fuel cells and the pros and cons of hydrogen. This book is encyclopedic. But thank God it does not read like an encyclopedia.

~~~~~~~~~~
~~~~~~~~~~

Appendix A

Chair's Column

Infrastructure, vol. 47, no.4, Summer, 2008

By T. Michael Payne

It is with pride and some trepidation that I begin my duties as chair of the Section. Pride, because this section is the third oldest in the ABA (1917) and its work involves industries that are vital to the welfare of American consumers, businesses, and every level of government. Trepidation, because I follow a long line of distinguished lawyers who have served as chairs. Bill Torgerson, the outgoing chair, did an outstanding job this past year. On behalf of all Section members, I thank him for his work.

I intend to continue to make this Section a valuable resource for its members, increasing diversity in leadership positions and working to increase members' involvement. In addition, I want to increase the number of "brown bag" lunch conferences on topics of importance to our practice areas.

As the primary corporate sponsor of this Section, LexisNexis has invited our committees and members to write articles that would be of interest to members and nonmembers. I ask that you work with your committee chairs and vice chairs to provide LexisNexis with six to 12 articles this year. This is also a good time to remind you that through our sponsorship agreement with LexisNexis, the Section's *Annual Report* and *Infrastructure* is searchable for free by Section members at http://www.abanet.org/pubutil.

In closing, I invite you to e-mail comments, suggestions, or criticisms that will increase the value of the Section to your practice to pubutil@abanet.org.

Chair's Column

Infrastructure, vol. 48, no.1, Fall, 2008

By T. Michael Payne

I hope everyone had a joyful, safe, and peaceful holiday and New Year. As we begin 2009, the economy, both in the United States and worldwide, continues to worsen. Consumers and businesses alike feel the pressure of what we now know is a recession. All eyes are turning to Washington, D.C., to see what the incoming administration is planning to do to address the situation. There has been a great deal of discussion surrounding a proposed economic stimulus plan that would be introduced to jump-start the economy.

What is of interest to our Section members is the discussion surrounding infrastructure investment. A recurring theme at our Council meetings is that this country's infrastructure is old and in need of repair or replacement.

While details remain to be worked out, and legislation enacted, the stimulus plan may include money to invest in improving roads and bridges, water lines and sewer lines, extended broadband to reach into rural areas, as well as an investment for renewable energy sources. There has also been talk about making money available to update the FAA systems that govern air traffic control. Although a recession is never good news, it could lead to some important work being done in areas everyone agrees are vital to our country and its citizens.

The economy and infrastructure issues will also be addressed at the Section's Annual Spring Meeting in Washington, D.C., on March 23, 2009. While the program continues to evolve, Rob Brubaker, program chair, plans to have panels discuss infrastructure as well as post-9/08 liquidity and finance challenges for capital-intensive industries. More details about the program will be forthcoming. I urge you to attend. You will be able to obtain CLE credits as well as catch up on what is happening in the industries where our Section is very active.

Chair's Column

Infrastructure, vol. 48, no.2, Winter, 2009

By T. Michael Payne

This issue of *Infrastructure* highlights one of the most valuable resources our Section has to offer its members—our committee reports. This edition showcases summaries of several Antitrust and Water Committees' reports. These two committees are important parts of our Section. I recommend that those Section members who are interested in joining these committees contact the current chairs.

As the Obama administration continues to make appointments to the Department of Justice's Antitrust Division and outlines its view of antitrust policy, the Antitrust Committee reports will offer timely information and insights into what is going on within the Beltway.

The Water Committee reports also offer very useful information. While most members have probably read about carbon footprints being discussed in terms of global climate warming, very few may be aware of the fact there is also a water footprint. Simply put, it takes a certain amount of water to produce food, goods, materials, and energy. When a company is deciding whether or not to build a nuclear power plant in Georgia, they must study the water footprint. Is there an adequate supply of water in Georgia to cool the reactor during the hot summer months? The failure to ask the question, or reaching an incorrect answer, could cost a company millions of dollars in excess expenses.

For details on these and all Section committees, go online to www.abanet.org/pubutil/home.html and click on "Committees" in the left-hand navigation bar.

Chair's Column

Infrastructure, vol. 48, no.4, Summer, 2009

By Linda L. Randell

I am honored to become chair of the Section of Public Utility, Communications and Transportation Law as of the ABA Annual Meeting at the beginning of August. I want to extend thanks and gratitude on behalf of the entire Section to Michael Payne for his service as chair this past year. Mike has emphasized accountability and responsibility, two attributes that have never been more important than they are in today's economy.

I hope to continue this emphasis on core values, and to focus on collaboration and the interdependence of the industries and practice areas represented in this Section. I encourage all of our members to join Section committees to assist you in keeping up with developments, and also to participate in the work of the committee.

I will be encouraging Section committees to work together on cross-industry matters. For example, energy policy and the future of energy development can touch on most Section committees—not just the Electricity, Gas, Nuclear Energy, and Oil Pipelines Committees, but also the Communications, Cable and Internet Committee (communications applications for the Smart Grid), Water Committee (water is a high energy use industry, and a necessary resource for energy), Environmental Committee (impacts of energy choices), Finance, Mergers and Acquisitions Committee (how to finance the infrastructure?), and Infrastructure Security Committee (cybersecurity concerns for the grid).

In addition, we have established a Renewable Energy Committee whose key areas of focus will include renewable energy financing, state and federal subsidies and incentives, environmental and zoning issues unique to the renewable energy industry, including renewable portfolio standards, legislation, public policy, and regulatory issues that affect the renewable energy industry. This committee is a great example of collaboration opportunities.

I look forward to serving the members of this Section. Please let me know what subjects are of interest to you and how the Section can provide information. For example, would you be interested in attending committee-sponsored webinars on specific topics? I would like to hear from you. E-mail me at linda.randell@uinet.com or pubutil@abanet.org.

Chair's Column

Infrastructure, vol. 49, no.1, Fall, 2009

By Linda L. Randell

Members of the Section of Public Utility, Communications and Transportation Law are both fortunate and challenged today. The areas in which we practice are at the heart of policy and technology discussions critical to the country's future. As a result, our need to keep up with developments in and affecting the infrastructure industries has never been greater. At the same time, however, the importance of cost and efficiency in gaining knowledge has probably also never been greater.

I am working with members of the Section's Council group, and in particular with the Section's officers and committee chairs, to make your job of keeping up with industry developments easier. Your membership in the Section includes the right to sign up for an unlimited number of Section committees to enable you to track your areas of work and interest. The committees' fall 2009 reports have recently been completed. In addition to having these reports posted on the Section's Web site, www.abanet.org/pubutul/home/html. I am asking each committee chair to e-mail his/her committee report directly to each member of the committee. (If you have not yet provided us your e-mail address, you can do so by e-mailing Monica Herrera at herreram@staff.abanet.org).

I am also encouraging each industry committee to provide short e-mail updates to committee members when significant events occur, such as case decisions with widespread application.

We are in the planning stages for a series of telephonic or Web-based programs on significant topic areas (renewable energy, for example) to be offered to Section members at little or no cost, as a benefit of Section membership. By the time I write my next chair's column for *Infrastructure*, I expect to be able to provide you with information on future programs.

Finally, please save March 15, 2010, on your calendar. This is the date of the Section's annual continuing legal education program in Washington, D.C. The program's working title is Climate Change—Understanding the Legal Issues. It will address climate change legislation and regulation, together with associated implementation and effects.

Please let me know what areas you would like the Section's programs to focus on. Even better, please consider committee participation so you can be a part of the process.

Chair's Column

Infrastructure, vol. 49, no.2, Winter, 2010

By Linda L. Randell

Two of my major goals as chair of the Section of Public Utility, Communications and Transportation Law are to make information on infrastructure industry developments readily available to members, and to encourage discussion of issues relating to how the future may address today's challenges. Both of these goals are met in our upcoming two-part continuing legal education teleconference on renewable energy development, experience, and potential future to serve a large portion of the country's energy needs. The two-part program—Renewable Energy in 2010—will be presented on February 18 (Part 1: Federal Initiatives that Target Renewable Energy) and February 25 (Part 2: Smart Grid Plus Lessons from the States).

We want to make practical information available to Section members conveniently and at a reasonable price. To facilitate government access to the information presented in the program, including the written materials prepared by the faculty members, we have established a reduced price for government lawyers. Section members will have received registration information and more specific program agenda via e-mail. . . .

If you are interested in working on future Section committee teleconference presentations or reports, I encourage you to speak with your committee chair.

I look forward to seeing you at the Section's March 15, 2010, CLE program in Washington, D.C., on Climate Change—Understanding the Legal Issues.

Chair's Column

Infrastructure, vol. 49, no.3, Spring, 2010

By Linda L. Randell

I am pleased to report that Climate Change—understanding the Legal Issues, this year's spring continuing legal education program of the Section of Public Utility, Communications and Transportation Law, was informative, thought-provoking and well attended.

The infrastructure industries that form the foundation of the Section's areas of interest are also fundamentally important in the consideration of many issues of national and international importance. I believe this is both a challenge and an opportunity for the Section. Our members work in these areas, have expertise, and have the ability to contribute to the dialogue. The Section can serve to educate and provide a forum for discussion.

In recent months, in addition to presenting panels on government, regulatory, investment, and litigation aspects of climate change, the Section has sponsored teleconferences on renewable energy. We are continuing to track developments promoting renewable energy and have a teleconference at the beginning of May on states' incentives to development. Please let me know if you have ideas for other teleconference topics.

The Section is presenting a program on the Smart Grid on August 7, 2010, at the ABA annual meeting. Everyone talks about smart meters, and the federal government has made billions of dollars of grants, but do you know what any of this means for you and your clients? I hope you will attend the program, and that you will be able to join us for the Section's business meeting, luncheon, and reception if you are attending the ABA meeting.

Chair's Column

Infrastructure, vol. 49, no.4, Summer, 2010

By Linda L. Randell

This is my last column as chair of the Section of Public Utility, Communications and Transportation Law. It seems appropriate, and perhaps inevitable, to look back at our accomplishments this year (August 2009–July 2010).

We have taken a leadership role in providing information and a forum for discussion of prominent, developing issues such as climate change, renewable energy, security and safety in transport and infrastructure industries, and the SmartGrid. In 2009, the Section formed a Renewable Energy Committee. The Renewable Energy Committee now has more than 100 members. The Section this year offered an increasing number of continuing legal education programs and teleconferences. *Infrastructure*, our quarterly publication, highlights topics in the infrastructure industries and practice areas included within the Section. We have recently published our 2010 compendium of recent developments. The Section's leadership is emphasizing the role of committees in communicating with, and benefiting from the efforts of, our members.

I want to thank the many people who have helped me in my work as Section chair this year, including the Section's officers and Council, committee chairs and vice chairs, and the Section members who have participated in the Section's activities and made suggestions of how we can improve. A special thanks to Tom Gadsden, who has been chair-elect this year; to Rob Brubaker, who has served as vice chair this year; and to Sam Porter, who chairs our Long-Range Planning Committee. And an extra thanks to Sue Koz, our Section director, and to Monica Herrera, the Section's administrative assistant, who are critical to the functioning of the Section.

I have had a wonderful time as Section chair. Thanks again.

Chair's Column

Infrastructure, vol. 50, no.1, Fall, 2010

By Thomas P. Gadsden

> "The role of the public utility lawyer is changing and becoming more important. He must continue to be an effective advocate before regulatory commissions on rate matters, which are themselves changing to reflect sociopolitical as well as economic factors. But, as deregulation of formerly all-regulated industries sweeps the country, as antitrust, labor and tax laws reach out to utilities, as financing difficulties increase, and as energy supply becomes our most vital national domestic issue, the public utility lawyer must advance persuasive legal arguments and lead political/public opinion in these areas as well."

So wrote Chair David R. Toll in his 1980 report to this Section's membership. Although some of us might resist the moniker "public utility lawyer" (and the gender-specific pronoun), perhaps thinking it a bit restrictive in the 21st century, the challenges described by David Toll are no less real 30 years later.

The Section of Public Utility, Communications and Transportation Law is unique in several respects. Unlike other groups, our principal focus is on a particular industry or, more accurately, group of industries, rather than a specific discipline (e.g., taxation). That said, our work cuts across multiple practice areas. Thus, we are transactional lawyers, regulatory attorneys, and litigators, bound together by our common interest in companies whose product historically has been deemed a public service.

Moreover, we are blessed to work with entities whose operations broadly define the quality of life that we enjoy. Reliable electric and natural gas service; a safe and continuous supply of potable drinking water; the instantaneous communication of voice and electronic data; the availability of multiple modes of transporting passengers and goods—these are all things that we tend to take for granted, but whose very existence requires constant investment and technological innovation.

I am deeply honored to lead, for the next year, a group of diverse and extraordinarily talented lawyers. Our committee chairs and vice chairs are busy at work developing programs on a wide variety of cutting-edge issues, ranging from pipeline safety to hydraulic fracturing to net neutrality to the Dodd-Frank Act to renewable energy incentives and so on. However, they need your help. If you are interested in publishing an article or assisting with a podcast or webinar or just becoming more actively involved in the work of the Section, please let me know at tgadsden@morganlewis.com. All comers are welcome and I promise I will get back to you.

Chair's Column

Infrastructure, vol. 50, no.2, Winter, 2010

By Thomas P. Gadsden

In January 1978, 1 accepted an offer from my current employer to work in what was then known as the "Government Regulation Section." In Morgan Lewis parlance, this, for the most part, meant representing public utilities before state and federal regulatory agencies. Because this was an area of practice I knew nothing about, my mentors, Bob Young and Alan Reed (both former PUCAT chairs), encouraged me to pick up a copy of *Public Utility Economics* by Paul J. Garfield and Wallace P. Lovejoy. In thumbing through that treatise, I quickly learned that public utilities were very different than other forms of businesses (pp. 16-17):

> Early in the development of the modern public utilities, it became apparent that competition as a form of market organization was both undesirable and incapable of enduring. At the same time, it also became apparent that it was desirable and, indeed, inevitable to have a single seller supply one or more utility services in a city or area. In short, monopoly was recognized as "natural" on the supply side of the market for public utility services.

Public Utility Economics was first published in 1964 and much has changed in the intervening 47 years. In the case of some former "public utilities," the conventional wisdom was overtaken by technology and the "natural monopoly" model largely abandoned. In other instances, a hybrid model, combining elements of both traditional public utility regulation and competition, has emerged. Indeed, it was primarily in recognition of the increased deregulation and diversification of certain of the industries we represent that we changed our name in 1991 from the Public Utility Law Section to the Section of Public Utility, Communications, and Transportation Law.

So much for history. On March 7, 2011, the Section will hold its Annual Spring Meeting in Washington, D.C. Our topic this year is "An Update on Competition Analysis in Regulated Industries." Our program chair, Ken Driver, has put together four outstanding panels of regulators and practitioners to explore developments in antitrust enforcement and mounting competitive pressures affecting the markets for electricity, communications, and transportation service. I strongly urge those who are able to attend.

Chair's Column

Infrastructure, vol. 50, no.3, Spring, 2011

By Thomas P. Gadsden

Shortly after I began the practice of public utility law, there was a partial meltdown at General Public Utilities Three Mile Island (Unit 2) nuclear generating plant. In commenting on that incident only a few months later, Francis X. Welch, who for several years served as editor of the Public Utility Law Section's *Annual Report*, wrote as follows:

> Three Mile Island was a good example of Murphy's Law in operation [footnote omitted]. It could be a blessing very much in disguise. Murphy's Law is simply common-sense recognition that no human activity can ever be made 100 per cent foolproof. This was never a valid excuse for giving up a worthy goal in frustration and doing nothing more about it. The Harrisburg accident does pose a serious regulatory challenge and responsibility to close the gap of human and technical error as tightly as possible by constant effort. it will probably result in great pressure on the Nuclear Regulatory Commission to embark on an ongoing program of vigilant inspection controls. If a previous series of sequential safety procedures were not enough to avoid mishap, that only means there must be more and better alternatives.

The earthquake, tsunami, and ensuing sequence of events that rocked northeast Japan in mid-March of this year has reignited the debate over the long-term viability of commercial atomic energy. Indeed, as of this writing, at least one country, Germany, has announced plans to exit the nuclear energy business.

Without purporting to speak for anyone other than myself, I am confident that the nuclear power industry once again will be equal to the challenge. However, those who make their way to Toronto for the ABA's Annual Meeting can decide for themselves. On Saturday, August 6, 2011, the Section will sponsor a special panel presentation entitled "Nuclear Regulation in North America After Fukushima Daiichi." We encourage all who can to attend.

Chair's Column

Infrastructure, vol. 50, no.4, Summer, 2011

By Robert Brubaker

I want to begin my first column as chair of the Section by saying how thankful I am for the opportunities to interact with the role models and esteemed lawyers I would never have known or learned from had I not been a member of the Section.

Our Section is just six years shy of its 100th anniversary. Over the past century, infrastructure industries have been at the forefront of economic and technological progress. The National Academy of Engineering included the following infrastructure-related innovations in their list of the 20 greatest engineering achievements of the twentieth century: electrification (no. 1); airplanes (no. 3); water supply and distribution (no. 4); radio and television (no. 6); computers (no. 8); telephones (no. 9); highways (no. 11); Internet (no. 13); and nuclear technologies (no. 19). See www.greatachievements.org. What could be more interesting and important than the infrastructure that undergirds our entire economy and that is intertwined with so many of our greatest inventions?

The regulated or once-regulated public utility–type industries that are the Section's focus have in common some form of similar legal duty to serve the public interest. These industries place heavy demands on the legal system, commensurate with the public's heavy demand for adequate, safe, reliable, affordable, and sustainable infrastructure goods and services. Lawyers working in this field are inherently preoccupied with understanding and advancing the public interest.

Article 1.2 of our Section's bylaws reminds us of the high purpose to which members are called:

> An especial purpose of the Section is declared to be to further the public interest as the prime factor in the development of public utility, communications and transportation law. . . .

The public utility, communications, and transportation law bar has their work cut out for them to help usher in the optimum twenty-first century infrastructure. The prime factor in this crucial time of major transition in infrastructure must continue to be furtherance of the public interest. The Section has never been more relevant, and I am confident it is up to the task.

Chair's Column

Infrastructure, vol. 51, no.1, Fall, 2011

By Robert Brubaker

The economy—jobs and debt especially—is uppermost on the minds of policy makers and the public. The "great recession" and global financial weakness are spurring everyone to think and care more about economics. A distinct strength of the PUCAT Section is its deep, sophisticated expertise in the economics of capital-intensive industries.

The Section has 10 industry committees and eight practice committees. These 18 committees focus on infrastructure providers that have in common, among other things, the economics of rates regulated (now or in the past) by one or more government agencies. Three of the practice committees—Antitrust; Finance, Mergers and Acquisitions; and Taxation & Accounting—deal almost exclusively with economic matters. All of the other 19 committees are substantially engaged in profound economic issues.

A central role of the Section is to identify and explain significant developments in infrastructure law and policy, as they occur, year after year. To do this well, the infrastructure law practitioner must have proficiency not only in the relevant law, but also in the intertwined economic, technological, and political fundamentals that shape infrastructure law and policy.

The early experiences of one infrastructure industry sector with respect to deregulation, consolidation, convergence, bankruptcy, disruptive technology, other economic issues are illuminating to other sectors that are likely to later confront some of the same issues. The times we are in give us every reason to continue enhancing our understanding of infrastructure economics, and the Section is the ideal forum for doing so.

Chair's Column

Infrastructure, vol. 51, no.2, Winter, 2012

By Robert Brubaker

The Section has a rich history of writing excellence and substantive expertise. The comprehensive annual *Recent Developments* publication, the *Infrastructure* quarterly, and the Spring and Fall reports produced by the each of our 18 industry and practice committees provide timely and objective content written by distinguished leaders in their fields.

At the 2011 Fall Council Group meeting, the Section established a new Book Board, adding to the breadth and depth of the Section's writing opportunities and offerings. The Book Board consists of a prominent and highly-qualified lineup of Section leaders. The board is chaired by Linda Randell, the 2009-2010 Section chair and former editor-in-chief of *Infrastructure* (and who was recently appointed by ABA President Bill Robinson to the Association's Standing Committee on Publishing Oversight). The Board members are Judge Richard Cudahy (current editor-in-chief of *Infrastructure*), Ken Driver, Sheila Slocum Hollis, Ernie Ierardi, Pete Lacouture (editor of *Recent Developments*), Mike McGrail, and Rene Ruiz.

The new Book Board will help potential authors with developing proposals, and will shepherd worthy book proposals through the process to publication. The board will have support from Rick Paszkiet, the talented director of ABA entity book content.

The Book Board will focus initially on practical, practice-oriented books that will be useful to Section members in their day-to-day work. Our Section is blessed with members who know their subject, and who can provide correct, objective, and balanced practice aides and reference materials.

Al Section members are invited and encouraged to let the Book Board know of their ideas for publications, and of their interest in writing. It is indeed exciting to anticipate the Section's upcoming contributions to the literature in our field, at a time when infrastructure issues are very much at the forefront of public and political consciousness.

Appendix B

Editor's Note

Infrastructure, vol. 47, no.4, Summer, 2008

By Linda L. Randell

Wow. This is my last note as the editor of *Infrastructure*. To all the chairs of the Section with whom I have been privileged to work in my two "tours" as editor: Thanks for your unfailing support and, of course, for writing the Chair's Column each issue. I want to extend a special thanks to Ray Bolze, who had the wonderful idea of establishing a chair's column in the first place. To those at the ABA who take our text and turn it into a finished publication: I appreciate your dedication and cheerfulness in the face of changing schedules. To Sue Koz, our Section director, who has been here throughout, and whose advice has been so valuable: You have my utmost gratitude and admiration.

This issue will not reach you until after the ABA Annual Meeting. The timing, therefore, is perfect for our publishing a list of the Section's leadership for 2008-2009. In addition, this issue includes an article featuring some of the topics addressed at the Section's spring program, "Innovations in Regulated Industries," along with part two of the article on developments in ERISA law.

Good luck to Judge Richard Cudahy of the Court of Appeals for the Seventh Circuit and to Dynda Thomas, a partner at Squire, Sanders & Dempsey, who will be cochairs of the Section's Newsletter Committee and coeditors of *Infrastructure*. I look forward to reading the upcoming issues.

Editor's Note

Infrastructure, vol. 48, no.1, Fall, 2008

By Dynda A. Thomas

The year 2008 started with a credit crunch and financial defaults and graduated to full market meltdown and financial crisis. Throughout 2008, an historic campaign and election spurred national debate on the challenges facing the U.S. economy and potential solutions to those challenges. All the while, wars continued on several fronts and hot spots throughout the world continued to have their impact on financial markets and world economies.

"May you live in interesting times." Whether the expression is a curse or a blessing is debatable. But we would all have to agree that we are, indeed, living in "interesting times." For those of us who work in regulated industries, this is especially true.

As 2009 begins and the new Obama administration works to usher in the "change" that is so highly anticipated, one topic often debated is the costs and benefits of regulation in certain industries. Regulation defines how many industries operate, how capital deployed in those industries is raised, and how technology developed in those industries is accessed by consumers. Industries as varied as communications, public utilities, cable television, and aviation work within the confines of regulation, and regulations direct and limit their operations.

In this issue of *Infrastructure*, we take a look at regulation and regulatory reform in the article by Judge Richard Cudahy on "Alfred Kahn on His 90th Birthday: The Birth of Deregulation," discussing regulation and deregulation in the public utility and aviation industries. This issue also includes a discussion of two approaches to pricing of commercial aviation take-off and landing rights at U.S. airports. Within each of the industries that are the focus of our Section, there are those who argue for minimal regulation and others who argue for more regulation. Our perspectives are as varied as the industries in which we practice, and so the regulation debate continues. As new coeditors of this newsletter, Judge Richard Cudahy and I want to take this opportunity to thank Linda Randell for her years of tireless service and dedication to the Section as the outgoing editor of *Infrastructure*. As a Section, we will continue to use *Infrastructure* to examine and debate issues and to share ideas on the direction and nature of regulation in our industries in these "interesting times."

Editor's Note

Infrastructure, vol. 48, no.3, Spring, 2009

By Dynda A. Thomas

A lot has happened in the short time since the swearing in of President Obama. All of the industries served by our Section have felt the impact of the economic downturn. Several of those industries have been focal points of policy discussion and debate. Indeed, many policies proposed and promoted by the Obama administration, positions taken by the executive branch and legislative policy makers, and opinions expressed in the polls have revolved around potential actions by the U.S. government and the private sector in the area of energy and energy infrastructure. Many of those actions will impact our readers. This issue of the Section newsletter addresses two issues relating to the energy industry: whether and how to develop new nuclear power facilities in the United States; and whether and how to make government investments in energy assets in the United States in a way that protects our existing infrastructure and promotes the country's energy policy.

Nuclear power units supply about 20 percent of the electricity produced in the United States. That percentage is likely to increase over time despite the challenges in the development and financing of nuclear plants and despite the debate surrounding various aspects of nuclear power. Our article on "New Nuclear Power" discusses the improvements to the process for development and the challenges for the finance of new nuclear power plants in the United States. The discussion highlights the significant changes in the licensing process from the last era of nuclear power construction in this country. The authors of this article walk through several important developments that are impacting the prospects for nuclear power in the United States. Specifically, the article covers: new federal and state regulation relating to licensing and financial incentives; the availability of credit and the complications caused by the long lead-time negotiations of engineering, procurement, and construction obligations; and potential and current legislation relating to renewables, fossil fuels, and greenhouse gases, both of which could increase the comparative attraction of nuclear power.

Like TARP, ARRA is now a term that we see and hear every day. Our article entitled "The Stimulus Bill and the Electric Industry" focuses on the potential funding in the energy sector that could come from the American Recovery and Reinvestment Act (ARRA). However, the potential consequences of such extraordinary government funding as well as the restrictions and limitations that arise under the ARRA legislation should not be overlooked and will help determine the degree to which such extraordinary funding is embraced by the industry. The four parts of this article discuss investment in energy infrastructure, investment in energy efficiency, significant rules and conditions that accompany funding from ARRA, and, finally, certain impacts of ARRA funding that are specific to electric utilities.

Editor's Note

Infrastructure, vol. 48, no.4, Summer, 2009

By Judge Richard D. Cudahy

This issue features railroads but in widely diverse contexts and with contrasting impacts on other important factors. One article is essentially news about the immediate prospects for high-speed passenger rail in the United States as favored for stimulus spending and as a high priority of President Obama. This is really news because high-speed rail, á la Japan or France, has been a glint in the American eye for many years and now it seems destined for realization in real time. The article explores this important subject, and its ramifications for such matters as energy and the environment, in some detail.

The other railroad piece discusses recent regulatory decisions about the obligation of railroads to transport hazardous materials (such as toxic chlorine) in circumstances where there are alternate sources of the materials nearer the destination and populous areas could be avoided by the shorter route. The article also discusses regulatory proceedings addressing railroad liability for accidents occurring in the transportation of hazardous materials.

These two articles cover some of the most important recent developments in both passenger and freight rail, which implicate key questions of energy and the environment.

Editor's Note

Infrastructure, vol. 49, no.1, Fall, 2009

By Dynda A. Thomas

For the industries included in our Section, the regulatory landscape continues to change as a result both of proposed legislation and increasing scrutiny by various federal agencies. In 2009, proposed federal legislation came from Capitol Hill in a variety of areas, regulation that would have wide-ranging impact on individuals and businesses.

In this edition of *Infrastructure*, we have included one article on the climate change regulation embodied in the Waxman-Markey bill. This article offers a strong commentary on the impact of this proposed legislation on electric and natural gas utilities, natural gas distribution companies, and their customers. In it, one company shares its own perspective on allowances for generators and customers, renewable energy requirements, the EPA's authority to regulate greenhouse gases, and the importance of the development of clean coal technology.

This edition also includes a review of the Obama administration's initial approach to antitrust review. This article focuses on the telecommunications industry and includes a historical review of the development of that industry and its treatment under antitrust regulation. Over the last decade, at the same time as these industries enjoyed game-changing technological advancements, they also enjoyed (at least arguably) a less rigorous approach to antitrust enforcement by the federal government. But during 2009, the Department of Justice and the Federal Communications Commission have indicated that they would change their approaches to antitrust enforcement relating to the telecommunications industry.

Certainly, these developments could have a significant impact on the economic performance of telecommunication businesses. As the economy rebounds, we will continue to watch further legislative and regulatory enforcement developments as they relate to industries of our Section.

Editor's Note

Infrastructure, vol. 49, no.2, Winter, 2010

By Dynda A. Thomas

This issue of *Infrastructure* is devoted to various aspects of the generation of renewable energy in the United States—specifically incentives, challenges, and the real world question, "who pays?"

In Part 1 of a two-part series, we explore two factors promoting renewable energy and one important hurdle to development. First, you will see a description of certain tax incentives directed to the development of energy generation facilities. Second, we review legislation, regulation, and several environmental decisions whose effect is to promote renewable energy technologies over fossil fuel technologies. Finally, you are introduced to *Illinois Commerce Commission v. FERG*, a Seventh Circuit case that wrestles with how the costs of the expansion of the nation's transmission grid will be allocated. The two-part series will conclude in the next issue of *Infrastructure* and will provide more insights into the challenges and opportunities of renewable energy.

A more detailed discussion of *Illinois Commerce Commission v. FERC* is included in this issue as well. The discussion details the court's conclusions, and notes that the question of how to allocate the cost of expensive, and critical, new transmission facilities remains unanswered.

Certainly, the country will continue to need additional new transmission facilities, and the cost of their development will grow over time. Uncertainty as to the allocation of costs will slow the development of new transmission facilities and will, therefore, impact the development of generation from renewable sources.

Editor's Note

Infrastructure, vol. 49, no.3, Spring, 2010

By Judge Richard D. Cudahy

This issue includes the second installment of the article based on the panel discussion of renewables held at the fall meeting of the Council Group. This Part 2 of the article will cover, first, a discussion of the smart grid having capabilities for advanced electricity transmission and distribution to get renewable energy to market. Next, there is coverage of portfolio standards for renewables. And, finally, we have a description of wind power development in Texas. We feel that this second installment of the article will complete a diverse survey of the field of renewable energy sources and related issues, which deserves relatively extensive treatment. However viewed, renewables are going to be an important part of the future.

The other emphasis in this issue is on the EPA's authority to regulate greenhouse gases, which the agency received under *Massachusetts, et al. v Environmental Protection Agency, et al.,* 549 U.S. 497 (2007). This is an extremely important regulatory development, and we have thought it worthy of discussion by lawyers representing industry as well as by the EPA itself. Obviously, these comments represent to some extent contrasting points of view, but we think they shed important light on what is a crucial legal development The Massachusetts case itself was a close call in the Supreme Court, being decided by a 5-4 vote, and it arms the agency with powers whose practical reach has yet to be fully defined.

We hope that all this important information will be helpful.

Editor's Note

Infrastructure, vol. 49, no.4, Summer, 2010

By Dynda A. Thomas

The energy industry operates in the face of continual change in market conditions and regulatory environment.

This edition of *Infrastructure* gives us the opportunity to continue to explore issues relating to two specific types of energy resources that we have addressed previously. While *Infrastructure* has previously provided an introduction to the NRC licensing process, this issue provides an updated perspective on how the licensing process has been working in practice. The wind power article focuses on several of the serious practical and political challenges that wind power projects are facing even as there is continuing momentum favoring renewable energy in the United States.

The benefit of diverse energy resources is clear. But, notwithstanding the clear benefit to the U.S. economy of a more diverse menu of energy resources, significant practical challenges and difficulties remain. Difficult policy decisions must be made so that we can move from potential power sources to actual power.

Editor's Note

Infrastructure, vol. 50, no.1, Fall, 2010

By Judge Richard D. Cudahy

This issue contains articles on subjects about as diverse (and important) as could be imagined. One is on the crucial development of shale gas as a decisive addition to the United States supply of natural gas and the implications of this event for electric generation. The latter aspect is emphasized by the authorship of the article, which features John W. Rowe, CEO of Exelon Corporation, one of the world's largest electricity generators (and a major nuclear force), and Ed Fortunato, a leading manager of that company. Obviously, huge supplies of domestic shale gas will have an impact on the authors' generation plans if the environmental problems of rock fracturing are successfully dealt with.

The companion article concerns a critical issue "fracturing" the Internet world—"net neutrality." As the article states, "'Net neutrality' is shorthand for both the historically open nature of the Internet and the principles necessary to preserve and promote that openness." The FCC is the scene of a battle over proposed "net neutrality" rules, and all the various Internet players and observers are locked in controversy over the subject. The presentation in this issue takes the fitting form of a pro and con discussion, which manages to be both very lively and very enlightening. This is a technology that is revolutionizing the world, and the current debate will determine its direction.

Editor's Note

Infrastructure, vol. 50, no.2, Winter, 2011

By Dynda A. Thomas

> Sometimes, [federal regulation] ha[s] gotten out of balance, placing unreasonable burdens on business—burdens that have stifled innovation and have had a chilling effect on growth and jobs. At other times, we have failed to meet our basic responsibility to protect the public interest, leading to disastrous consequences. . . . [T]oday, I am signing an executive order that makes clear that this is the operating principle of our government.
>
> This order requires that federal agencies ensure that regulations protect our safety, health and environment while promoting economic growth. And it orders a government-wide review of the rules already on the books to remove outdated regulations that stifle job creation and make our economy less competitive. It's a review that will help bring order to regulations that have become a patchwork of overlapping rules, the result of tinkering by administrations and legislators of both parties and the influence of special interests in Washington over decades.
>
> — "Toward a 21st-Century Regulatory System," President Barack Obama, *Wall Street Journal*, January 18, 2011

No, President Obama did not address those words specifically to us as members of the Public Utility, Communications and Transportation Law Section. No, he did not provide the text specifically for use in this column. But his statements have special relevance to us as lawyers working in regulated industries.

As lawyers, we see the impact that federal regulation has on the clients we serve. As consumers, we feel the consequences of federal regulation on prices and competition. As students of the Constitution, we can argue about the merits or constitutionality of the actions of federal regulatory agencies.

I urge you to review the articles contained in this issue of *Infrastructure* against the backdrop of President Obama's statements quoted above. The article relating to antitrust developments in the aviation industry highlights the impact of the FAA's determination on the Delta/US Airways transaction. The article on the Dodd-Frank Act discusses the expansive regulatory authority recently given to the Commodity Futures Trading Commission. Are existing regulations out of balance? Will new regulations bring balance? Perhaps this issue of *Infrastructure* will provide you with new insights as you consider these important questions.

Editor's Note

Infrastructure, vol. 50, no.3, Spring, 2011

By Judge Richard D. Cudahy

This issue features carefully researched and insightful analyses of key legal issues affecting most if not all of the infrastructure industries. The Peirce-Darrell piece explores the efforts of the United States Supreme Court to broaden and strengthen the coverage of contracts invoking the Federal Arbitration Act and requiring recourse to arbitration in the face of state legislation authorizing or requiring class actions, which are generally unavailable in arbitration. Alleged unconscionability of arbitration agreements or waivers of class actions has been another basis for resistance to arbitration. And some state courts have been creative and relatively successful in rescuing anti-arbitration legislation from easy preemption by raising the flag of consumer rights. But this article particularly explores the effects of the recent *Concepcion* decision of the Supreme Court and notes proposed federal legislation designed to rescue class actions.

The McDonald article examines the complex jurisdictional thicket defining the responsibilities of federal and state agencies for enforcement of antitrust laws and policies in merger cases involving the energy and transportation industries. In some cases, the enforcement bodies have a broad jurisdiction cutting across various industries but focusing on issues of competition. In other instances, their purview is limited to a particular industry or process, but their concerns cover the range of regulation and may approach competition under a public interest standard. The article is especially useful in describing overlapping or alternative sources of competition law.

Editor's Note

Infrastructure, vol. 50, no.4, Summer, 2011

By Dynda A. Thomas

In previous editions of *Infrastructure*, we have discussed the opportunities and challenges relating to nuclear power in the United States: financing, licensing, state regulation. Recently, although the debate over the disposal of nuclear waste continued, revised regulations relating to the licensing of commercial nuclear power plants seemed to herald an increasing prominence of nuclear power in this country.

But the events of March 11, 2011, set off a wave of reexamination and reconsideration of nuclear power. The accident at the Fukushima Daiichi nuclear power plant that followed the Japanese earthquake and the resulting tsunami has been the subject of much debate. Richard Meserve, the author of our article and former chairman of the United States Nuclear Regulatory Commission, provides some insights on some of the ramifications of the accident.

While the government of Japan has announced that it will turn away from nuclear power toward renewables, the US secretary of energy has stated that nuclear power remains a cornerstone of the US energy system. For its part, Germany decided to shut down its nuclear plants within 11 years, and Switzerland is following Germany's lead. But many other countries, especially those outside of Europe, continue to plan for increased reliance on nuclear power.

The Fukushima Daiichi nuclear power plant had been planned and developed after consideration of many possible areas of concern. However, the accident resulted when several worst-case scenarios occurred in combination or rapid succession. Experts are studying those factors and scenarios and may propose US regulatory changes to address them. As a result of that learning process, it is possible that nuclear power may actually become safer than before the accident. Certainly, we hope that those countries where nuclear power increases in prominence will take advantage of what's learned from the accident.

As described on the back cover, in the next edition of *Infrastructure* you will see a discussion of the development of the Cape Wind Energy Project—an off shore wind energy project being developed on the Outer Continental Shelf of the United States. Is it possible that the events at Fukushima could further accelerate projects like Cape Wind?

This is my last note as coeditor of *Infrastructure*. I have enjoyed the opportunity to work with Judge Cudahy, who will continue as the editor. I would like to give a special thanks to the chairs of the Section for providing their insights in the Chair's Column included in each issue, to the various committees of the Section for their ideas and support, and (of course) to the many authors who have made such important contributions to the Section.

Editor's Note

Infrastructure, vol. 51, no.1, Fall, 2011

By Judge Richard D. Cudahy

This is my first issue as sole editor-in-chief of *Infrastructure*, having lost the strong right arm of coeditor Dynda Thomas to higher Section responsibilities. I am eternally grateful to Dynda for her powerful input (especially in expanding the breadth of our coverage) over our years of association and hope her loss does not become too painfully evident in *Infrastructure*'s content to come.

In the current issue we are exploring two contrasting subjects: One, the rather exotic story of an ocean-based set of windmills—a maritime wind farm that is closer to load centers than equivalent energy sources in the equally windy prairies. And, two, a searching (if not exactly thrilling) probe of what's to be foreseen in the insatiable demands of the tax collector. Taxes may not excite, but they are inescapable forces shaping prospects and dictating developments. Taxes may even outdistance pledges and forecasts. So, we hope you find significance in both the promise of the sea-borne wind and the prosaic burden of tax threats perceived on the horizon.

And we continue to search for some balance between the accomplishments of infrastructure enterprises as such, with their particular problems—legal and otherwise—and more general business issues that are bound to affect efforts in the infrastructure. We thrive on and continually need your suggestions for helpful subject matter. E-mail topics to pubutil@americanbar.org.

Editor's Note

Infrastructure, vol. 51, no.2, Winter, 2012

By Judge Richard D. Cudahy

This issue is entirely a product of my judicial chambers—a fact I am a bit reluctant to disclose, since it might he erroneously thought to establish a trend. I am, as the title reveals, the author of the review of Daniel Yergin's epochal book, which in its very publication is a major event in the history of energy. This was a task I am perhaps only marginally qualified to attempt, but it was something I very much wanted to do. So, I did it. Andrew Moshirnia suggested the subject for the other article, "Whither White Spaces." He is my law clerk, has a doctor's degree in educational technology, and is expert beyond expert in the technology of the Internet. And, although a Californian, he's also a Green Bay Packers fan. So I asked him whether he would like to write on the subject that he had suggested (about which I knew nothing at the time of the suggestion). He consented, and the result is a superb article that explains in miraculously understandable English a bitter battle between determined claimants adhering to conflicting philosophies of regulation, crucial to the future of communications, with their respective viewpoints steeped in rather obscure technological lingo. For those who may be concerned, I assure readers that this "inbreeding" of authorship is not a harbinger of the future for this publication.

Table of Cases

Index

B

C

D

E

M

N

T

U

V

W

Y